Road to Pakistan

Road to Pakistan

The Life and Times of Mohammad Ali Jinnah

B.R. Nanda

Routledge
Taylor & Francis Group
LONDON NEW YORK NEW DELHI

First published 2010 in India
by Routledge
912 Tolstoy House, 15–17 Tolstoy Marg, Connaught Place
New Delhi 110 001

Simultaneously published in the UK
by Routledge
2 Park Square, Milton Park, Abingdon, OX14 4RN

Routledge is an imprint of the Taylor & Francis Group, an informa business

© 2010 B.R. Nanda

Paperback edition published 2014

Typeset by
Star Compugraphics Private Limited
D-156, Second Floor
Sector 7, Noida 201 301

All rights reserved. No part of this book may be reproduced or utilized in any form or by any electronic, mechanical or other means, now known or hereafter invented, including photocopying and recording, or in any information storage and retrieval system without permission in writing from the publishers.

British Library Cataloguing-in-Publication Data
A catalogue record of this book is available from the British Library

ISBN 978-0-415-72882-9

TO BABA

Contents

Preface   ix

1. Early Years   1
2. Politics Calling   11
3. The Rising Star   26
4. The Making of a Muslim Gokhale   38
5. The Advent of Gandhi   48
6. Eclipsed   62
7. Down But Not Out   73
8. In the Council Chamber   83
9. The Communal Tangle   94
10. On Centre-Stage   100
11. Dead End   108
12. Leader in Search of a Role   124
13. First Round Table Conference   135
14. Second Round Table Conference   147
15. Self-Exile   158
16. The Raj at Bay   167
17. Image of a Nationalist   176
18. Electoral Arena   191
19. The Moment of Truth   201
20. On the Offensive   212
21. The Congress Response   219

22.	British Response	234
23.	Inching Towards Partition	253
24.	Declaration of War	263
25.	The Die is Cast	277
26.	Phantom to Reality	294
27.	Towards Transfer of Power	313
28.	Post Partition	325
29.	Epilogue	329

Notes   334
Select Bibliography   351
About the Author   361
Index   363

Preface

I was 30 years old when the partition of India took place in 1947 and when, just five months later, Mahatma Gandhi was assassinated in January 1948. I recall the tidal wave of emotion I felt at the time. Understanding the events of the three-quarter century leading up to the creation of India and Pakistan as two sovereign nations at the end of British rule has been a passion and quest for me ever since. There were three protagonists in the struggle — the British, the Congress and the Muslim League. In my previous books, while I have dealt with the history of the period, the biographical focus has been on Congress leaders — Gokhale, Gandhi, Nehrus (Jawaharlal and Motilal). I felt it important to look at the events of the period through the biographical lens of the Muslim League leadership and that is how this book on Jinnah was conceived. Apart from published material, it is based on records held at the India Office Library in the UK, the National Archives of India and the Quaid-i-Azam Academy in Pakistan.

I would like to thank the eminent historian, Shri S.R. Mehrotra and the eminent sociologist, Prof T.N. Madan, both of whom have been kind in their encouragement through the years this book was under preparation and in their critical comments and suggestions which have been extremely valuable.

I would like to thank my wife, Janak. She has been very encouraging. She has also shown great forbearance not just during the writing of this book but with a lifetime of research and writing that has often kept me preoccupied and away, even if I was present. Her love and support have made my work possible. My son Naren has been of tremendous help to me, encouraging me and helping me with suggestions on the manuscript.

Chapter 1

Early Years

Mohammad Ali Jinnah, the founder of Pakistan, was born on 25 December 1876 at Karachi. He was the eldest of seven children of Jinnahbhai Poonja, a Khoja merchant whose father had emigrated from Gondal State of Kathiawar to Karachi, and Mithibai, who also belonged to a Khoja family of Gondal. There was hardly anything in his family background to indicate that young Mohammad Ali was cut out for a great role in the history of his country. Jinnahbhai Poonja had little formal education, but had a smattering of English. He built a thriving business in import and export trade by collaborating with Grahams Shipping and Trading Company, a British concern, which had an office in Karachi. Though a port and a trading centre for northwestern India, Karachi, with its population of 50,000 in the last quarter of the nineteenth century, was socially and politically a backwater. Mohammad Ali's education began in an infant vernacular school from where he went on to a Gujarati-medium madrasa. A bright, handsome and self-willed child, he seemed more interested in playing marbles with children of his own age than in books. This may have been due to indifferent teaching; perhaps the curriculum was unexciting and could not sufficiently awaken the interest of an intelligent child. He developed such an aversion to studies that he told his father he would rather work in the family shop than go to school. Jinnahbhai may have been surprised, but the child had already learnt the three R's and the prospect of his eldest son joining him in business may not have been unwelcome. A few weeks of slogging in the shop from early morning till late in the evening, however, chastened the boy and he went back to school. He could not, however, bring himself to take his studies seriously; his teachers despaired of his making any progress; he was pronounced 'horribly poor' in mathematics. It was decided to send him to Bombay where a loving aunt sent him to a school there. However, his mother missed him badly and he was recalled to Karachi.

The six-month stint in Bombay gave Mohammad Ali his first exposure to the world beyond his hometown. On returning to Karachi he rejoined the Sind Madressah-tul-Islam in Karachi, where he learnt both Gujarati and English. In March 1892, he was admitted to the Christian Mission School. This was his first opportunity to meet non-Muslim teachers and students. He remained a mediocre student, who shone neither in the classroom nor on the sports ground. He had been in the Mission School for hardly seven months when Sir Frederick Graham, head of the Karachi branch of Grahams Shipping and Trading Company, with which Jinnahbhai was collaborating, offered to arrange for Mohammad Ali to get training in business at the Company's headoffice in London. Mohammad Ali, who had never been too happy in the various schools he had attended, jumped at the idea of going abroad. His father was pleased at the new vistas opening for his son, but his mother was distraught. She could not bear the thought of parting with her son for two years. In addition, she dreaded the ultimate disaster of having on her hands an English daughter-in-law, and relented only when Mohammad Ali agreed to marry before he left India. Emibai, a 14-year old girl, was chosen from the ancestral village of Paneli in Gondal State. The marriage was celebrated in October 1982. Soon after, 16-year-old Mohammad Ali sailed for England.

II

Mohammad Ali arrived in London in early December 1882. Like most Indian students who came to England, he felt lonely. He was particularly ill-equipped for his new life. His schooling in Karachi's Gujarati-medium madrasa had been somewhat indifferent; he had not even passed the matriculation examination of Bombay University. His knowledge of English needed brushing up. But he quickly adapted himself to his new surroundings. He discarded his long Kathiawari coat and turban and switched over to western-style suits. He began his apprenticeship with Grahams Company in Threadneedle Street in right earnest. But as he pored over the files and ledgers of the company day in and day out, he became bored. He began to wonder whether a business career would suit him at all. We do not know which options he considered and why, but after ruling out commerce, he settled upon the legal profession. He may have been impressed, while he was a child, by the prestige commanded by English-trained barristers in Karachi and Bombay. At the turn of the century every ambitious Indian boy aspired to join the Indian Civil Service or, if that was not possible, to qualify as a barrister. Jinnahbhai was furious when he learnt that his son was giving up the coveted business apprenticeship for a career with an uncertain future. He ordered him to return home. Mohammad Ali was, however, adamant; he argued that there were better prospects in the legal profession; he assured his father that he would not ask him for more money but stretch the allowance he had been given for two years for another year, the time needed for a law degree. He decided to take the entrance examination, known at that time as 'Little Go', to secure admission to one of the Inns of Court. His petition for exemption from the Latin portion of the preliminary examination was granted, and in June 1893 he joined the Lincoln's Inn.

Having made up his mind to become a lawyer, Mohammad Ali, for the first time in life, took his studies seriously. It was an uphill task. He made three attempts to pass the Bar examination in 1894, but failed. This may have been due to his indifferent schooling in Karachi and weak grounding in the English language. But he persevered and in April 1895 qualified in all the papers, and was declared successful — the youngest among the fifty-three students who had qualified. In April 1896, on completing twelve terms, he was formally called to the Bar. He had put the intervening period to good use. He studied the English system of justice at work. He went to the courts and heard lawyers argue their cases. At dinners in the 'Great Hall' in the Lincoln's Inn, he took part in discussions between the students and the 'benchers', the senior members of the Inns of Court. Above all, he had the opportunity of serving his apprenticeship in an English barrister's chamber. All these experiences made an indelible impression on him.

Of one thing there seems no doubt. Young Mohammad Ali made the transition from rural Karachi to cosmopolitan London with remarkable speed and aplomb. He took to the English language, western dress and western mode of living, and felt perfectly at home. Five years earlier, young M.K. Gandhi had tried to ape 'the English gentleman', but, as we learn from his autobiography, he was too much of an introvert to continue the experiment for more than a few months. Jinnah's anglicism was uninhibited and permanent. He aspired to the lifestyle of an upper-class Englishman, achieved it and revelled in it.

III

Legal studies did not wholly absorb young Jinnah's student days. He developed an interest in politics, and especially the politics which concerned his country in England. It is doubtful if in his home or school in Karachi there was anything to awaken interest in politics. Indeed, it is doubtful if he ever read an English newspaper before he arrived in England. It was not unusual for Indian students coming to England to suddenly become aware of the fact that they were citizens of a subject country. This had happened to Aurobindo Ghose, Jawaharlal Nehru and Subhas Chandra Bose; it may have happened to Jinnah too. All his life he spoke with great reverence of Dadabhai Naoroji, one of the founding fathers of the Indian National Congress, who was residing in England. Jinnah's sister, Fatima Jinnah, tells us in her brief memoirs that her brother was deeply stirred by the controversies surrounding the election of Dadabhai to the House of Commons, and 'threw himself heart and soul into his election campaign and thereby caught the eye and won the esteem of Dadabhai Naoroji, the Grand Old Man of India.' She also tells us that her brother went to the House of Commons to hear Dadabhai Naoroji's maiden speech. This story has one snag. The polling for the Central Finsbury constituency, from which Dadabhai was elected as a Liberal MP (Member of Parliament), took place on 6 July 1892, and he delivered his maiden speech in the House of Commons on 9 August. However, Jinnah did not arrive in England until December 1892. Even if he had been there it is doubtful that 67-year-old Dadabhai Naoroji would have enlisted the services of a 16-year-old Indian boy, freshly arrived from India, for his electioneering.

Another myth about Jinnah's nationalist sympathies which has gained currency is that he was elected a member of the British Committee of the Indian National Congress. The records of the Committee do not show that Jinnah was considered for its membership while he was a student in England. Indeed, he was not eligible for its membership. The British Committee in London had Sir William Wedderburn as its chairman and its members were British politicians and retired civil servants who were sympathetic to Indian political aspirations, such as A.O. Hume, Alfred Webb, Henry Cotton and C.J. O'Donnell. Leading Congressmen from India during their visits to England were elected temporary members of the Committee: these included Pherozeshah Mehta, R.C. Dutt, Surendranath Banerjea, B.C. Pal, Lajpat Rai and Gokhale. Jinnah was elected a member of the Committee for the first time in 1906 for the period of his stay in England, and then again during his subsequent visits in 1913 and 1914.

One may discount the exaggerated claim for Jinnah's political activism in England during his student days, but there is evidence to indicate that he had developed a keen interest in politics. He became an avid reader of newspapers; he watched the British parliamentary system at work; he followed the controversies in the press between the protagonists of the two parties; and he occasionally sampled political oratory in Hyde Park, as well as from the visitors' gallery of the House of Commons. He took time off to attend lectures in London on subjects pertaining to India, and participated in discussions which followed. In 1896, when he was not yet 20, his comments reveal his ardent patriotism and the courage of his convictions. On 17 February 1896, five months before he returned to India, he was present at a meeting held under the auspices of the East India Association. The speaker was an Indian journalist, Alfred Nundy, and his subject was 'The Indian National Congress: Its Origin, Aims and Objects'. The *Journal of East India Association* (Vol. XXVIII) recorded the comments by young Mohammad Ali Jinnah at some length:

> Mr. Jinnah was glad the paper had been read before a society which badly needed its information. He had the greatest respect for the English nation, but this was a time for truth, not adulation. The Congress was not revolutionary. It did not mean to take up arms against the English. It only wanted to be heard, and it must be heard. If this were constantly refused, statesmen would understand what would be the consequences. The people of India wanted the same rights and privileges that Englishmen had. Mr. Nundy had referred to the simultaneous examinations [for the ICS] and the salt duty. The latter was an iniquitous tax, unheard of in any other country.

A fortnight after the East India Association meeting, Jinnah was present at a lecture delivered on 4 March 1896 by Mr Turkhud, the former Principal of a college at Rajkot, under the auspices of the National Indian Association in London. Lord Reay, the former Governor of Bombay, was in the chair. Jinnah took part in the discussion and criticized the speaker for omitting to speak 'of the better qualities of the people of Kathiawar, of their social system, and of the ethical principles which they hold. Lucidly as he had dealt with the subject, he had shown the darker side only, and he had given, mainly, accounts of the chiefs and princes of Kathiawar, while what the speaker [Jinnah] had expected to hear was about the people.'[1]

IV

During his three-and-a-half years in London, to law and politics were added another passion: the theatre. His secret youthful ambition, he told his sister, was to play the role of Romeo at the Old Vic. He was attracted by the idea of taking to the stage. The temptation was so strong that even after having been called to the Bar in 1896, he accepted a job in a theatrical company, which performed Shakespeare's plays. When he wrote to his father that he was abandoning law and taking to the theatre in England, he received a sharp reprimand: 'Do not be a traitor to the family'. Jinnah's mother and young wife had already died when he was in England. He did not want to break his father's heart, and decided to return to India immediately. His employers waived the three months' notice stipulated in the agreement, and let him go. One wonders what would have happened if he had defied his father again and returned to the stage. He may have made a name as an actor and settled in England for the rest of his life. There was, in his adolescent years, a strange restlessness in him. It seems in these early years Jinnah had an 'identity crisis'; he was groping towards something which he himself did not quite know. However, after returning to India in July 1896, he quickly settled down in the profession of law. His time in England had transformed him. His perfect attire and manners secured him access to the best European society in Bombay. He had acquired a good command of the English language. Despite his incipient patriotism, the stirrings of which he had left in England, he developed great admiration for the English way of life, for the English judicial system, and for the liberal and democratic political institutions of England. He even anglicized his name. In April 1896, three months before he left to India, the Lincoln's Inn accepted his application to change his name from 'Mohammad Ali Jinnabhai' to 'Mohammad Ali Jinnah', and he later started signing simply as M.A. Jinnah.

V

On 24 August 1896, M.A. Jinnah, Esq., Bar-at-Law, was registered as an Advocate of the Bombay High Court. He was nearly 20 years old at the time. He rented a room in a hotel on Charni Road and walked to and from his office in the Fort near the High Court every day, but hardly any brief came his way. The Bombay Bar was crowded, and Jinnah, as a new entrant, found himself in the ranks of briefless lawyers. Five years earlier, another young barrister, M.K. Gandhi, had the same experience after returning from England; despairing of making a decent living in Bombay, he reconciled himself to a modest practice in Rajkot, his hometown, in the interior of Gujarat, where he remained until he received a year's contract for a civil suit in South Africa. For Jinnah, his briefless interlude in Bombay was very trying; he could hardly make ends meet. Luckily he caught the eye of J.M. MacPherson, the Advocate-General of Bombay, who took a liking to the young, smart Khoja barrister, who behaved and even looked like a young Englishman. Thanks to MacPherson's recommendation, Jinnah was posted in leave vacancies as a Third Presidency Magistrate in Bombay. He heard petty criminal cases, but made an excellent impression. According to Jinnah's own account, Sir Charles Olivant, Law Member of the Governor's Council, offered him a permanent place in the judicial service on a salary of Rs 1,500 a month, a princely salary in those days, but he declined, saying he hoped to earn that much in a single day.

This stint as Presidency Magistrate in Bombay proved a watershed in Jinnah's career. He attracted the notice of judges, fellow lawyers and potential clients. By 1903, there was no dearth of briefs; his reputation grew and he rapidly climbed to the top of his profession. According to his nephew, Akbar Peerbhoy, Jinnah's income rose to Rs 20,000 a month during the war years, an estimate which was confirmed by Mohammad Ali Chaiwalla, Jinnah's onetime solicitor.

Formal, fastidious, discreet and sharp-tongued, Jinnah was a formidable advocate in the courtroom. He laboured hard at his briefs. When he stood up in the court and adjusted his monocle and looked at the judge, he made his presence felt as few of his contemporaries could. A number of anecdotes narrated by his contemporaries testify to his keen wit, great ability and high integrity as a lawyer. There was a client who was so pleased with Jinnah's services that he sent him an additional fee, which he declined with a note that he could not accept more than what had been originally agreed upon between them. Then, there was a judge who sought to reprimand Jinnah with the remark: 'Remember, you are not addressing a Third Class Magistrate'. 'Allow me to warn you', retorted Jinnah, 'that you are not addressing a Third Class Pleader'.

Jinnah's forte was not the knowledge of law, but the ability to advocate the case of his client. M.C. Chagla, who worked as Jinnah's junior for nearly six years and later rose to be Chief Justice of the Bombay High Court, has left a perceptive profile of Jinnah. He describes him as 'a poor lawyer but a superb advocate', who had 'a very striking personality', and whose 'presentation of a case ... was a piece of art.'[2]

Chagla read Jinnah's briefs, went with him to the court and listened to his arguments. What impressed him most was Jinnah's lucidity of thought and expression: 'There were no obscure spots or ambiguity about what Jinnah had to tell the court. He was straight and forthright and always left a strong impression, whether his case was intrinsically good or bad.' Jinnah believed that, however bad the case might be, it was the professional obligation of the lawyer to do his best for the client.[3] This was quite unlike M.K. Gandhi who, during his practice in South

Africa, refused to take up cases which were false, and who insisted on his clients making a clean breast of any violation of the law they might have committed and then appealing to the judge to take a lenient view.

Chagla pays high tribute to Jinnah's legal ability. But he also tells us that when he was struggling at the Bar and was in 'dire circumstances', he had received no sympathy from Jinnah.[4]

> I do not remember [Chagla writes] in all those years, Jinnah ever enquiring of me how I managed my finances or how I fared at the Bar. I have never come across any man who had less humanity in his character than Jinnah. He was cold and unemotional and, apart from law and politics, he had no other interests. I do not think he ever read a serious book in his life. His staple food was newspapers, briefs and law books. He did not even once raise his little finger to assist me at the Bar. But I owe a great deal to him because I learnt in his chamber not only the art of advocacy, but how to maintain the standard of traditions of the legal profession.[5]

Chapter 2

POLITICS CALLING

Jinnah returned to India in July 1896, and was enrolled as an Advocate of the Bombay High Court in the following month. As we have seen, as a law student in England he was shaping into an ardent nationalist and was in full sympathy with the ideals of the Indian National Congress. Since Bombay was the unofficial headquarters of the Congress, one would imagine that on returning to India he would immediately seek in it an outlet for his nationalist fervour. But this did not happen. Evidently, he restrained his enthusiasm for politics for nearly eight years while he was struggling to establish himself at the Bombay Bar. Not until 1904 did he seek election to the Bombay Corporation. As an up-and-coming lawyer, he had caught the eye of Sir Pherozeshah Mehta, whose domination of the Bombay Corporation, the Bombay Presidency Association and the All India Congress Committee was unquestioned. In the same year, Jinnah attended the meetings of the Reception Committee which elected Sir Henry Cotton, a British Liberal MP, to preside over the annual Congress session which was to be held in Bombay. Jinnah got himself elected as a delegate for this session. In April 1905, he was present at a public meeting chaired by Pherozeshah Mehta, held to protest against Lord Curzon's rejection of Gokhale's amendment to the Universities Validating Bill in the Imperial Legislative Council. In May 1905 he was nominated by the Congress to present India's grievances in Britain where a general election was imminent. The visit did not come through, but his selection, along with such a senior leader as Gokhale, to represent the Congress case was an index of his rising political stature.

In March 1906, Jinnah resigned from the Bombay Corporation; apparently it was too small a forum for the talents and ambitions of the budding politician. The same year witnessed his real debut on the stage of national politics. What brought him into the limelight was his bold criticism of the deputation of thirty-five Muslim leaders, headed by His Highness the Aga Khan, who waited upon Lord Minto, the Viceroy of India, on 1 October 1906. On that very day, Jinnah addressed a letter to the editor of the British-owned *Times of India,* questioning the representative character of the members of the deputation. 'May I know', he asked, 'whoever elected the gentlemen who are supposed to represent Bombay? It is such a pity that some people are always assuming the role of representatives without the smallest shadow of ground or foundation for it.' He also criticised the 'hush-hush policy' of the deputation. 'Nobody up to now knows', he wrote, 'what the deputation proposes to do. Is this the way to speak in the name of millions without informing them what is going to be done for them?' Not surprisingly, the *Times of India* did not publish this letter, but *Gujarati,* a local paper in Bombay, was more obliging. Soon afterwards, Jinnah readily signed a memorandum, which the Bombay Presidency Association sent to the Viceroy, opposing separate electorates for Muslims.

Three months later, in the last week of December 1906, Jinnah reverted to this subject at the Calcutta session of the Indian National Congress. He had the distinction of acting as Secretary to Dadabhai Naoroji, the 'Grand Old Man of India', who had come from England to preside over the session. Jinnah moved an amendment to a resolution on self-government moved by a Muslim delegate which demanded reservations for the 'educationally backward classes'. He objected to the application of this clause to Muslims and insisted that the Muhammedans in India should be treated like the Hindu community. 'The foundation upon which the Indian National Congress is based', he declared, 'is that we are all equal, that there should be no reservation for any class or any community.' Jinnah's amendment was approved unanimously, and the reference to 'reservations' in the resolution was deleted. Knowing as they did the conservative and reactionary state of Muslim politics, Dadabhai Naoroji, Pherozeshah Mehta and other senior Congress leaders could not but have been pleased to find, in the young Muslim barrister, a doughty champion of unalloyed nationalism. A few days later, while Jinnah was still in Calcutta, he attended a meeting which criticized the formation of the All India Muslim League as a separate political body for Indian Muslims, and was elected Vice-President of the newly formed rival organisation, the Indian Mussalman Association.

II

The significance of Jinnah's stance at Calcutta in December 1906 can be best understood in the light of the turn which Muslim politics was taking at the time. For nearly twenty years, the Muslim intelligentsia had followed the advice of Sir Syed Ahmad Khan, Secretary of Aligarh College, and by and large kept away from the Indian National Congress. Sir Syed regarded the principle of election with deep misgivings. Since Muslims constituted a quarter of the population, he argued that an elected democracy would be 'a game of dice in which one man had four dice and the other only one'. Even if legislatures were to be composed of Hindus and Muslims in equal number, separately elected by their own communities, Sir Syed wondered whether Muslim representatives could ever be a match for the Hindus.[1] Elections to legislatures and appointments to the Indian Civil Service through open competition were two of the main planks in the Congress programme, both of which, in Sir Syed's view, were calculated to strengthen the Hindus and to pose a threat to the Muslims, no less than to the British. He described the Congress programme as a 'race with persons [Hindus] with whom we have no chance of success'.[2]

Loyalty to the British Raj was one of the basic tenets of Sir Syed's philosophy. At a public meeting in 1884 he raised the issue to the religious plane. He was loyal, he said, because he was a sincere Muslim. 'The Koran is present for our guidance, which has ordained them [the Christians] and us to be friends. Now God has made them rulers over us. Therefore, we should cultivate friendship with them and should adopt that method by which their rule may remain permanent and firm in India.'[3] He ruled out any form of representative democratic government in which Hindus with their numerical superiority could get the upper hand. 'We do not want', he said, 'to become the subjects of the Hindus instead of the people of Book [Christians]. If our Hindu brothers of these provinces (UP) and the Bengalis of Bengal and the Brahmans of Bombay and the Hindu Madrasis of Madras wish to separate themselves from us, let them go, and trouble yourself about it not one whit. We can mix with the English in a social way. We eat with them; they can eat with us. Whatever hope we have of progress is from them.'[4]

Sir Syed argued that however admirable democracy might be for a homogeneous country like Britain, it could not work in India. 'India being the least homogeneous was the least fitted'. Was it not absurd, he asked, to expect an imperial power like Britain to consult the natives of India on such matters of high policy as peace and war? 'Can you tell me of any case in the world's history', he asked, 'in which any foreign nation, after conquering another and establishing its empire over it, has given representative government to the conquered people?'[5]

One of the basic premises of Sir Syed's political philosophy was loyalty to the British Raj. In an address to the Governor of UP in 1896 he declared that, should the necessity arise, 'the stout hearts and strong arms of the students bred in the [MAO] College, trained in the cricket and football fields, would be ready for facing the common enemy to prove that the Muhammadans of India, with their martial spirit burning, are ready to face bullets and bayonets in the defence of the glorious Empire to which it is our privilege to belong.' Sir Syed flatly rejected the concept of an Indian nationality, and questioned the wisdom of curtailing British monopoly of power and patronage in India. He became president of the Indian Patriotic Association established in 1880 to carry on propaganda against the Indian National Congress in Great Britain, and to strive to preserve peace in India and to strengthen the British rule.[6]

The head-on clash between the Indian National Congress led by A.O. Hume, Dadabhai Naoroji and W.C. Bonnerjee, and the Muslim intelligentsia in northern India led by Sir Syed came in the late 1880s, just when the Congress had incurred the bitter hostility of the British authorities in India. The next decade was a lean period for the Congress organisation. The Partition of Bengal once again galvanized it into frantic activity in 1905, but it created a situation in which the fears of the Muslim middle class and the interests of the British Raj converged. In the eyes of the Congress the partition of Bengal was a sinister British plot to weaken a politically conscious province, but to the Muslim middle class it was a welcome gift of a Muslim-majority province opening new vistas of education, employment and prosperity. Later the same year the victory of the Liberal Party in the general election in Britain, which thrilled nationalist India, aroused deep misgivings in the minds of the Muslim elite and the British bureaucracy to whom elective institutions were anathema.

The Viceroy, Lord Minto, and his colleagues distrusted and feared John Morley, the new Secretary of State, while nationalist India waited with bated breath for an announcement from Morley on a constitutional advance for India. Morley's statement, when it came, was far too cautious to gladden the hearts of the Congress leaders, but even its guarded reference to the reform of the Legislative Councils alarmed Muslim leaders who had followed Sir Syed's advice to completely shun nationalist politics. They knew that even Sir Syed had not been able to prevent the passage of the Indian Councils Bill of 1892. What was there to prevent Morley from sponsoring another instalment of constitutional reforms? The announcement that the Viceroy was about to constitute a committee of his Executive Council to frame a reforms scheme struck them as ominous. There may have been a good case for Muslims eschewing politics in the late 1880s, but its validity in 1906 seemed questionable.

These Muslim leaders did not want to remain passive spectators of events. Nawab Mehdi Ali Khan — better known as Mohsin-ul-Mulk — who had succeeded Sir Syed Ahmad Khan, sounded out Archbold, the British Principal who was spending his summer vacation at Simla, on the possibility of presenting a memorial to Lord Minto to draw his attention to the 'consideration of Muslim rights'. Never in the twenty-one-year history of the Indian National Congress had the Viceroy ever received a deputation from the college. However, in 1906 there were good reasons for the Viceroy to oblige Mohsin-ul-Mulk and his friends. It was evident that Secretary of State Morley was inclined to conciliate India's educated classes and to concede some of the demands of the Indian National Congress. The Viceroy and his advisers were already planning to use the Princely order and the landed aristocracy as a counterpoise to the Congress. They could not but welcome any indication from the Muslim leaders of north India to challenge the claims of the Hindu educated classes which formed the backbone of the Congress. It is difficult to say how far the Muslim youth was really exposed in 1906 to the nationalist virus emanating from the adherents of the Congress, but this possibility was shrewdly played up by Principal Archbold to win the sympathy of the Viceroy's advisers.

On 1 October 1906 a Muslim deputation headed by the Aga Khan waited upon Lord Minto at Simla and presented a memorial. Most of the thirty-five signatories belonged to the titled and landed — gentry the Nawabs, the Khan Bahadurs and the CIEs. The memorial included almost every demand that could possibly be made in 1906 on the British Government on behalf of the Muslim community vis-a-vis the Hindus. However, its primary object was to prevent the extension of elective principle to the legislatures, and, if that was not possible, to find some means of offsetting the numerical inferiority of the Muslim community. Lord Minto, whose comments on complicated matters were usually ambiguous, did not hesitate to tread the tricky constitutional ground and to pronounce on fundamental issues. He began by appreciating the 'representative character' of the deputation and hailed his guests as 'the descendants of a conquering and ruling race'. He readily endorsed the thesis of the deputation that representative institutions of the European type were entirely new to India, and that their introduction required great care, foresight and caution. Above all, with unusual alacrity, he conceded the major demands of the memorialists. 'The pith of your address', he said, 'as I understand it, is a claim that any system of representation ...' whether it affects a Municipality, a District Board or a Legislative Council, 'in which it is proposed to introduce or increase an electoral organization, the Mohamedan community should be represented as a community .... You justly claim that your position should be estimated not merely on your numerical strength, but in respect to the political importance of your community, and the service it has rendered to the Empire. I am entirely in accord with you.'[7]

Lord Minto knew what he was doing. His object was to win over the Muslim community and prevent it from going the Congress way. The full implication of his reply to the Muslim deputation were to unfold gradually. Besides the promise of separate electorates and inflated representation, the Muslim community was encouraged to form a separate political party. Within two months, the All India Muslim League was born at Dacca. Among its professed objectives were the promotion of loyalty to the

British Government, and the protection and advancement of Muslim interests. The Aga Khan promised the Viceroy that every important step by the League would be taken in consultation with the government. The British-owned *Englishman* of Calcutta wrote: 'The League will provide an effective answer to the Congress'. The *Times of India* welcomed the formation of the All India Muslim League on 'the safe and sure rock of loyalty to the British Raj'. To keen observers of the political scene, the events of 1906 seemed like an Anglo–Muslim plot to thwart Indian nationalism.

Two years later, in December 1908, in his Reforms Scheme published in London, John Morley made provision for 'electoral colleges' to which a fixed number of Hindus and Muslims were to be returned 'in the ratio of populations'; these colleges were later to elect members of the Provincial Councils in like proportion. The combination of joint electorates and proportional representation served the two-fold purpose of securing equitable Muslim representation and preserving harmonious relations between the two communities. However, a fierce agitation against this provision was launched simultaneously in India and England. At its Amritsar session in December 1908, the All India Muslim League denounced the electoral college scheme as a betrayal of the Muslim community. On 31 December 1908 the London *Times* published a cable from its Bombay correspondent stating that the protest of the Muslim League against the electoral colleges was 'echoed by all Indian Muslims'. Two weeks later, it dwelt on Muslim discontent in India: 'The approaching *Muharrum* is awaited with anxiety in Calcutta'. Such insinuations by Muslim leaders and the Anglo-Indian press surprised and even unnerved Secretary of State Morley as this new development could endanger the passage of his Reforms Scheme through the House of Lords which had a Conservative majority. To William Lee Warner, a member of his Council, whose ultra-conservative views in recent months had begun to jar on him, Morley now turned for help to make 'peace with the Muhammedans'. Morley was unprepared for this storm. The electoral scheme was one of the twelve issues on which he had sought the advice of his departmental committee in the India Office and accepted its recommendations. On 27 January 1909, Morley received a Muslim League deputation, headed by Ameer Ali, the president of the League's London branch, and gave in to the pressures operating on him and executed a complete volte-face. From the joint electorate with proportional representation for the two communities, Morley swung to separate electorates and weighted representation for the Muslims. The amended Reforms Bill which was passed by British Parliament in 1909 was a signal triumph not only for the two-year-old Muslim League, but also for the Anglo-Indian lobby in India and Britain.

A British historian who had made a close study of Muslim politics in modern India, picturesquely described the Simla Deputation of October 1906 as 'an outcome of a marriage of convenience between British political necessity and upper-class Muslim interests.'[8] The electoral arrangements in the Minto–Morley reforms were the offspring of this marriage. In July 1909, Lovat Fraser, editor of the *Times of India,* confided to the Private Secretary to the Viceroy: 'Men like the Aga Khan plainly feel that in pressing for separate treatment for Muhammedans, they are fighting our battle much more than their own. We have far more to lose than the Muslims by an entente between Islam and Hinduism.'

III

The Simla Deputation and the incorporation of separate electorates in the Minto–Morley reforms were to seriously affect the course of Indian politics. They were also to remould the political career of Mohammad Ali Jinnah. From what little evidence we have about his three-and-a-half years as a student in England, it seems he had at an early stage learnt to identify himself completely with the ideas and policies of the Indian National Congress. Such an attitude was unusual for Muslim students from India studying in England as most of them came from northern India, and had imbibed the pro-British and anti-Congress prejudices of the Aligarh school of politics since the days of Sir Syed Ahmad Khan. Jinnah had been insulated from these prejudices because he grew up in Karachi and was a Khoja Shia, thus belonging to 'a minority within a minority'. The Khojas in western India had prospered in trade and banking and came into close contact with the Hindus and the Parsis. Unlike the Muslim middle class and the feudal gentry in northern India, the Khojas had little interest in securing jobs in government and so did not view educated Hindus as competitors and rivals. That the Khojas, as a community, had a good rapport with the Hindus and Parsis seems to have worried some British administrators. 'I am told', Lord Lamington, the Governor of Bombay, wrote to the Viceroy, Lord Minto, on 1 April 1907, 'that the Khojas, a sect of the Shias, a small community and comparatively recent converts to Muhammedanism and looked on with suspicions by their co-religionists, ... [have] a tendency to consort with the Hindus, and as being unreliable in their political conduct.'[9]

Eight years later, in January 1916, when Jinnah was one of the front-ranking politicians, the British Commissioner of Police of Bombay wrote: 'Mr. Jinnah is not regarded by the Sunnis of Bombay as a Muhammedan, and his avowed object in the [Muslim] League [session] is to form a political coalition with the Hindu National Congress in order to present a united Hindu–Muslim demand to the British Government for concessions and self-government, [which] did not commend itself to the Sunni Muslims of Bombay, who believe that if such a scheme fructifies, they will be left in the lurch, all the advantages being swallowed by the Hindus and minor Muslim sects suchlike the Khojas who are attached to the Hindus ....'[10]

At the Calcutta Congress (1906), at which he had shot into prominence as a young and intrepid Muslim nationalist, Jinnah had acquired greater access to the inner counsels of the Congress. In November 1907 he was present at the meeting of the Congress leaders held at Pherozeshah Mehta's residence, which changed the venue of the Congress session from Nagpur to Surat. During the Chritsmas week Jinnah attended the Congress session at Surat and witnessed the tumultuous scenes which led to the split between the 'Moderates' and 'Extremists'. It is a curious fact that, though Jinnah was Pherozeshah Mehta's blue-eyed boy an admirer of Gokhale, and aligned with the Moderate party, he also developed great respect for Bal Gangadhar Tilak. In July 1908 he filed a bail application in the court of Justice Davar of the Bombay High Court on behalf of Tilak, who had been charged with sedition for writings in his weekly paper, *Kesari*. Eventually, Tilak chose to argue his case himself, and Justice Davar sentenced Tilak to six years' rigorous imprisonment. Jinnah expressed his sense of outrage by boycotting the dinner given by the Bombay Bar Association for Davar on his receiving a knighthood.

In December 1908 Jinnah was at Madras to attend the annual Congress session and was called upon to support a resolution moved by Surendranath Banerjea, the veteran Congress leader of Bengal, on the scheme for constitutional reforms which was being piloted through the British Parliament by Secretary of State Morley.

Jinnah had stepped on to the political stage in 1906. In two years he had made a mark in Congress circles as an able and fearless advocate of unalloyed nationalism. The fact that this young, articulate Muslim barrister could rise above the narrow separatist politics being promoted by the influential feudal Muslim leadership with the backing of British rulers delighted the ageing Congress leaders. Little did they know that Jinnah's wings were soon going to be clipped by the very forces against which he had so valiantly pitted himself.

IV

Sir Harcourt Butler, who was one of the major British players in the drama which culminated in the historic Simla Muslim Deputation in October 1906, wrote at the time, 'I do not believe that any scheme for it [the Muslim memorial] would ever get through the Secretary of State, even if it got so far, which I gather is unlikely.'[11] Butler was right: two years later Morley decided in favour of joint electoral colleges to which a fixed number of Muslims and Hindus were to be returned in the ratio of their populations. The combination of the joint electorate and proportional representation could secure equitable Muslim representation, and also preserve harmonious relations between the two communities. The Muslim intelligentsia in northern India was, however, in no mood to accept joint electorates. The Anglo-Indian press in India and the Tory press in England conjured up a spectre of Muslim revolt.

That separate electorates were the thin end of the wedge between the two communities was seen at once by shrewd observers of the political scene. In March 1909, Motilal Nehru wrote to his son that 'Hindu–Muslim antagonism has grown, and our Anglo-Indian friends have distinctly scored in the matter, and no amount of Council reforms will repair the mischief.'[12] Equally prophetic was the verdict of the veteran Bengali civilian, economist and nationalist, R.C. Dutt: 'The *Times* had endeavoured ... to separate the Northern States from the Southern [States] during the Civil War in America. There, the *Times* failed — the Americans knew better than to be divided. But our simple Muslim compatriots have been easily gulled and separation has been decreed.'[13]

The Congress leaders, both in India and Britain, were taken aback by the strident opposition to Morley's scheme of electoral colleges by the Muslim League. If they expected young Jinnah to commend to his co-religionists the merits of Morley's original scheme and point out the divisive aspect of separate electorates, they were in for disappointment. Jinnah did not raise his voice in favour of Morley's scheme as might have been expected from the stout champion of joint electorates who had won accolades from the Calcutta session of the Indian National Congress in 1906. On the contrary, he wrote a letter to the *Times of India* (20 February 1909): Morley's scheme as it stood did not 'secure to the Muhammedans the reasonable certainty of returning their real representatives'. He suggested modifications such as the increase of Muslim representation from 25 to 33 per cent, and if this was not feasible, he called for separate electorates for his co-religionists. This was a moment of truth for Jinnah. He could have adhered to his principled stand of opposition to separate electorates, which had singled him out as an uncompromising nationalist. But he quickly realized that the Muslim leadership was overwhelmingly in favour of separate electorates and had the backing of British officials. He knew that the surest path to eminence in politics lay in the membership of a legislature. It was election to British Parliament which had made Dadabhai Naoroji the 'Grand Old Man of India'. It was in the Bombay Legislative Council and the Imperial Legislative Council that Sir Pherozeshah Mehta and Gopal Krishna Gokhale had made their mark. Jinnah saw the writing on the wall. Once separate electorates were introduced for the Muslim community, he would have to depend exclusively on the votes of his co-religionists. In December 1906, he had condemned both separate electorates and a separate political organization for Muslims. He could no longer afford to take this stand in 1909.

Jinnah's compulsions soon became visible. In February 1909, he readily responded to an invitation to attend a meeting of the Council of the Muslim League. He was elected to the Imperial Legislative Council by the non-official Muslim members of the Bombay Legislative Council by five to three votes; eight Muslim gentlemen had decided his fate. This was to be his constituency whose support he would need in future for his political survival. There was no point in reading to these provincial politicians homilies on undiluted nationalism; he had to take into account their fears and prejudices. Henceforth he must underscore his Muslim identity. One of the first things he did after entering the Imperial Legislative Council early in 1910 was to seek the redress of a long-standing Muslim grievance on the validation of Muslim Waqfs.

The change in Jinnah's political posture became clear at the Allahabad Congress in December 1910 when he was asked to move a resolution opposing the extension of the principle of separate electorates to local bodies. He said he was moving the resolution only in deference to the wishes of senior Congress leaders, but while doing so, he did not represent the views of his community, nor had he any mandate from it on this issue. No longer did he expound the virtues of the joint electorate; indeed, he was almost apologetic about it. Two years later, at a meeting of the Muslim League Council in December 1912, he publicly took a stand which flatly contradicted the cherished goal of Indian nationalists. Since the foundation of the Indian National Congress in 1885, its leaders had set their hearts on the goal of self-government on 'colonial lines' so that India could achieve the status of Canada, Australia and other British Dominions. Jinnah was present at the meeting of the Council of the All India Muslim League in December 1912 when the aims of the Muslim League were amplified to include 'the attainment of a system of self-government suitable to India'. One of the members objected to the words 'suitable to India', and said that it was a meaningless sentence and that 'people ought to be told that India wanted self-government on colonial lines'. At this point Jinnah made an intervention which was obviously intended to placate the conservative, pro-British and anti-Congress majority in the League Council. According to the record of the proceedings:

> Mr. M.A. Jinnah pointed out that a system of self-government on Colonial lines was not feasible for India .... Though he was

a Congressman, yet he knew that it was wrong in this matter .... Replying to Nawab Viqar-ul-Mulk, who mentioned that the time had not come for the attainment of self-government, the speaker said that nobody asked for it to be given tomorrow or the day after. It was the goal and ideal of the nation, and might be attained a century hence.[14]

This was the time when Jinnah, while continuing his link with the Congress, thought it politic to play to the gallery in the meetings of the League. He had little in common with the feudal gentry who enjoyed British patronage and dominated the League. Of Ameer Ali, who controlled the London branch of the League, Secretary of State Morley wrote that he was 'a vain creature with a certain gift of length, and I believe that I could convert him from the Crescent to the Cross if I could make him only a KCSI.' As for the Aga Khan, his loyalty to the British Raj was absolute: in the First World War, he acted as an Imperial agent. Jinnah was unlikely to be comfortable in this motley group, but its support was important to him if he was to project his Muslim identity. During these years he was obliged to walk a tightrope — while claiming to be a Congressman, he had to make a place for himself in the Muslim League. He was in fact slowly drifting away from the Congress. He attended the Congress session at Madras in December 1908, but absented himself from the 1909 session at Lahore, the 1911 session at Calcutta, the 1912 session at Bankipur and the 1914 session at Madras. In 1913 he formally enrolled as a member of the Muslim League, even though he had been attending its meetings informally. He hated to sever his connection with the Congress, but such was the divergence between the composition, ideas and policies of the two parties that it was getting more and more difficult for him to continue to profess allegiance to both. Luckily for him, events in India and Europe in 1913–14 brought about a rapid reorientation of Muslim politics in India, which resolved Jinnah's dilemmas and created opportunities for him for a pivotal role in Indian politics.

Chapter 3

THE RISING STAR

In his *Studies of Indian Life and Sentiment* published in 1910, Sir Bampfylde, a retired civilian and the first Lieutenant-Governor of East Bengal and Assam, described Indian Muslims as the natural allies of the British Raj. 'By their religion and political ideas', he wrote, 'they are less disposed than the Hindus to dissent from the assumptions which lie at the root of imperial authority.'[1] This verdict made good sense, especially in 1910, when the Minto–Morley reforms had put a seal on the Anglo–Muslim alliance. This alliance, which rested on a perception of common interests by Muslim leaders and British officials, was soon to be shaken by events beyond the frontiers of India. The misfortunes of Turkey were to make a strong impact on the Muslim community in India and to estrange it from the government.

In September 1911 came the news of the Italian invasion of Turkey. The secret alliance of the Balkan powers against Turkey, Russian support to this alliance, and the neutrality of western powers seemed a sinister development by Indian Muslims who tended to see in it a concerted effort to expel Turkey from Europe, and a clash not only between Asiatics and Europeans, but between the Cross and the Crescent. What incensed Muslim opinion was the indifference of Great Britain to the fate of Turkey, once her traditional ally. Indian Muslims' sympathy for Turkey and the Ottoman Caliphate was based more on sentiment than on rational arguments, but it was sincere, deep and widespread. Two brilliant editors, Mahomed Ali of the *Comrade* and Abul Kalam Azad of *Al Hilal,* took up the cause of Turkey. The resentment over the Balkan Wars rose to fever pitch; it took an anti-British and even an anti-Christian turn. Muslim alienation was aggravated by the revocation of the partition of Bengal, which was announced by King George V at the Coronation Durbar held at Delhi in December 1911. The announcement was welcomed by the Congress leaders who had looked upon the partition as a festering sore on the Indian body politic. The Muslim intelligentsia, however, saw the announcement as a victory of Hindus over Muslims, of political agitation over unquestioning loyalty to the government. The diametrically opposite readings of the leaders of the two communities revealed the wide chasm which divided them. Yet, by a curious twist of political logic, the annulment of the partition of Bengal worked towards a Hindu–Muslim rapprochement. Some Muslim politicians began to wonder whether it was safe for their community to rely wholly on the patronage and goodwill of the government, which itself was subject to pressures from nationalist agitation in India and from policy-makers in London. Would it not be prudent for Muslims to mend fences with the majority community? These doubts grew as Muslim discontent was fanned during these years by other controversies, such as the establishment of a Muslim university and the Kanpur mosque affair. The loyalist League leaders began to lose their influence in their community; they were finding it difficult to rein in the younger men. From among the graduates of Aligarh emerged a group of young politicians who were vocal, defiant and not easily amenable to the guidance of the traditional leadership of the community or to the advice of British officials. They reacted sharply to the events in Turkey, to the annulment of the partition of Bengal and to the harsh terms imposed by the government for the establishment of a Muslim university. They treated the older Muslim leaders as the young Hindu extremists of Bengal and Maharashtra had treated the Congress veterans before the Surat split. Men like Mahomed Ali, Abul Kalam Azad and Mazhar-ul-Haq refused to be muzzled.

The change in mood of the Muslim community, while it lasted, affected the orientation of Muslim politics, partially substituting anti-British for the earlier anti-Hindu feeling. The Hindu leaders, who had been outraged by the final shape of the Minto–Morley reforms, were also beginning to realize that the tension between the two major communities of India was an unhealthy development. The bone of contention was separate electorates. As the prospects of Hindu–Muslim cooperation brightened, the Hindu leaders swallowed their objections to separate electorates. They readily responded to the overtures of the group of young Muslim politicians, who, having wrested control of the Muslim League from its traditional leadership, were willing to bring it into alignment with the Congress. The process of reconciliation between the two parties was hastened by the outbreak of the World War in 1914. With rising hopes of constitutional reforms after the war, Indian nationalists had an incentive to close their ranks. In December 1915, the Bombay Congress amended its 1908 constitution to end the feud between the Moderates and the Extremists. It also authorized negotiations with the representatives of the Muslim League, which was also holding its session at Bombay during the same week.

II

The proposal to hold the annual session of the Muslim League in Bombay in the Christmas week of 1915, so as to synchronize it with that of the Congress, had met with fierce opposition in and outside the Muslim League Council, but it was pushed through by the Raja of Mahmudabad, Wazir Hasan of Lucknow and Jinnah. Among the most bitter opponents of the proposal was Maulvi Rafi-ud-din, a staunch loyalist and president of the Bombay branch of the Muslim League. The Governor of Bombay, Lord Willingdon, was called to intervene. He chaired a meeting of the Muslim leaders of Bombay at which a compromise was reached: the annual session of the League was to be held at Bombay, but it would pass a resolution declaring loyalty to the government. The truce between the rival factions did not last long. When the League session actually commenced in Bombay in December 1915, with Mazhar-ul-Haq in the chair, the nationalist tone of the proceedings jarred on the pro-British and anti-Congress leaders of the League, who hired a group of hooligans and broke up the meeting. The 'young group', headed by Mazhar-ul-Haq, Jinnah, Mahmudabad and Wazir Hasan, found a safer venue in the Taj Mahal Hotel for the rest of the proceedings. They elected Mahmudabad as president of the All India Muslim League in place of the Aga Khan, and appointed a committee to confer with other communities and organizations for framing a joint scheme of constitutional reforms.

The Bombay session of the All India Muslim League was made possible by the efforts of the Raja of Mahmudabad and his protégé, Wazir Hasan. The 'Lucknow clique', as the British officials called it, the coterie of Muslim politicians of UP patronized by the Raja of Mahmudabad, had joined hands with Jinnah from Bombay, Mazhar-ul-Haq from Bihar and Fazl-ul-Haq from Bengal. It pursued its plans with great alacrity and skill. Mahmudabad and Wazir Hasan joined the reception committee of the Congress session which was to be held at Lucknow in December 1916. They manoeuvred the League Council into a decision to hold the 1916 session of the All India Muslim League at Lucknow at the same time, and they elected Jinnah to preside over it. The choice was significant. Jinnah had joined the League only three years earlier, but he was reputed to be a disciple of Dadabhai Naoroji and Gokhale, and was held in high esteem in Congress circles. His election to the League presidency was designed to facilitate negotiations with the Congress, whose leaders geared themselves to make generous concessions to Muslim demands. A Hindu–Muslim accord was in sight. The All India Congress Committee drew up a scheme of constitutional reforms in April 1916 and immediately sent a copy to the headquarters of the All India Muslim League at Lucknow. The main features of this scheme were elected majorities in the central and provincial legislatures, election of half of the central and provincial executives by members of the respective legislatures, jurisdiction of the legislatures over all legislation, except those pertaining to foreign, military and political affairs which were subject to the veto of the Viceroy and provincial governors. In July 1916, Wazir Hasan, secretary of the Muslim League, circulated a scheme to the members of the League Council which was similar to the Congress scheme, except that it also prescribed separate electorates for Muslims. In October 1916 came an impressive demonstration of political unity, when nineteen out of twenty-five elected members of the Imperial Legislative Council signed a memorandum demanding constitutional reforms on the lines of the Congress–League scheme.

The joint reforms scheme was ratified a year later at Lucknow at a joint meeting of the committees appointed by the two parties. Much as it went against the grain, the Congress leaders conceded separate electorates and agreed to the principle of minorities being represented in excess of their population. In Bihar, where Muslims were 13 per cent of the total population, they were given 25 per cent of the seats in the provincial legislature; in Bombay where their population was 20 per cent, they received one-third of the seats; in the Central Provinces, where Muslims constituted 4 per cent, they got 10 per cent representation; and in Madras, with a population of 7 per cent, they got 15 per cent representation. As a quid pro quo, the League representatives agreed to reduce Muslim representation in the Punjab (which had a Muslim population of 55 per cent) to 50 per cent. In Bengal, where Muslims had a population of 52 per cent and only 10 per cent seats in the provincial legislature, in 1916 they were allotted 40 per cent seats.

III

The Lucknow Pact was a feather in Jinnah's cap. It was a virtual coup. He and his friends had been able to talk the

Congress leaders into jettisoning their fundamental tenet of a joint electorate. In 1909, while the Minto–Morley reforms were on the parliamentary anvil in Britain, no front-ranking Congress leader had favoured electorates based on religion. They were all agreed that separate electorates and would be a wedge in Hindu–Muslim relations and would prevent the growth of Indian nationality. Even Gokhale's acquiescence was no more than the acceptance of a *fait accompli;* he had an uncomfortable feeling that the alliance of Tory politicians and Muslim Leaguers in London had outsmarted him and his Congress colleagues at the final stages of the passage of the Reforms Bill through the British Parliament. Seven years later, the Congress leaders accepted at Lucknow separate electorates and weighted representation on the basis of religion. Tilak, who in the 1890s had berated Ranade and Gokhale for not standing up to Muslim communalism, lent his powerful support to separate electorates in 1916. At the plenary session of the Congress he dealt with the charge that the Muslim League had succeeded in driving a hard bargain: 'It has been said, gentlemen, by some brethren, that we Hindus have yielded too much to Mohammedan brethren. I am sure I represent the sense of the Hindu community all over India that we could not have yielded too much. I would not care if the rights of self-government were granted to the Mohammedan community only.' Tilak and his colleagues believed that with one great gesture they had put an end to Muslim fears and suspicions. They seem to have been swept off their feet by their own optimism. The notion that a joint manifesto by two major political parties, representing the two major communities of India, would immediately bring the imperial power to heel was naive in the extreme, but widely current in nationalist circles. In the event, the next instalment of constitutional reforms took three years to be enacted. Ironically, while the Reforms Act of 1919 embodied a diluted version of the political part of the Lucknow Pact, it adopted its communal provisions in entirety. Minto and Morley, the architects of the reforms of 1909, had a guilty feeling even as they yielded to the demands of the Muslim League for separate electorates. The dangers of a separate register for a religious community were recognized by the authors of the Montagu–Chelmsford Reforms in their report nine years later:

> Division by creeds and classes means the creation of political camps organized against each other, and teaches men to think as partisans and not as citizens; it is difficult to see how the change from this system to national representation is ever to occur. The British Government is often accused of dividing men to govern them. But if it necessarily divided them at the very moment when it proposes to start them on the road to governing themselves, it will find it difficult to meet the charge of being hypocritical or short-sighted.[2]

Nevertheless, separate electorates for the Muslim community came to stay; indeed they were extended to other communities, Sikhs, Christians, Europeans and Anglo-Indians. In 1916 they were embodied in the Lucknow Pact made between the Indian National Congress and the Muslim League, which set the seal on Hindu–Muslim cooperation. Jinnah asserted that with the satisfactory solution 'of the most formidable problem that stood in the path of Indian progress, our constitutional battle may be said to have been half won already.' He added that the Congress–League scheme was the united demand of educated India; all that remained to be done was to get a bill drafted by constitutional experts and to send it with a Congress–League deputation to London for enactment by the British Parliament. He rejoiced that the 'vigorous spirit of patriotism and national self-consciousness' had brought Hindus and Mussalmans together in 'loving and brotherly service for the common cause'. In his Presidential Address to the League session, he called upon his co-religionists to join Hindus in the struggle for the attainment of political freedom:

> The whole country is awakening to the call of its destiny and is scanning the new horizon with eager hope. The Mussalmans

of India would be false to themselves and the traditions of their past if they do not share to the full the new hope that is moving India's patriotic sons today or had they failed to respond to the call of their country. Their gaze, like that of their Hindu fellow countrymen, is fixed on the future.[3]

Never had such stirring words been spoken from the platform of the Muslim League during the ten years of its existence. Loyalty to the British Raj, antipathy to the Congress and distrust of the Hindu majority had characterized much of the political discourse at the League's meetings. Its leaders consciously and demonstratively distanced themselves from the demands of the Indian National Congress for constitutional reforms because they did not want to alienate the British Government and were obsessed with safeguards for the Muslim community. In his address,[4] Jinnah frankly acknowledged that the All India Muslim League had been founded as an organization with the main object of safeguarding Muslim communal individuality, and keeping it strong and unimpaired in any constitutional adjustment. The creed of the League had, however, broadened with the growth of political life in the country. It was, he said, 'a matter of infinite gratification' to him that the Muslim communal position had been met 'in an ungrudging spirit by the leaders of the great Hindu community.' He rejoiced to think that 'a final settlement had at last been reached which set the seal on Hindu–Muslim cooperation and opened a new era' in the history of India.

IV

The Christmas week of 1916 was the high watermark of Jinnah's career. He was conscious and proud of his role in the achievement of the Congress–League accord. The Lucknow Pact had brightened the prospects for post-war constitutional reforms. It had also brightened Jinnah's own prospects on the national stage. He was the only leader who wielded influence in both the communities. The Lucknow Pact had resolved the dilemma which had tormented him since the incorporation of separate electorates in the Minto–Morley reforms. His Muslim identity no longer clashed with his national identity. The controversy on separate electorates was over. The Muslim demands for safeguards had been conceded by the Congress. Henceforth there was no need for him to walk a tightrope in Indian politics; he did not have to temper his patriotism with prudence. An opportunity came in June 1917 when Annie Besant, one of the most popular politicians and a foremost leader of the day and the founder of the Home Rule League, was interned under the orders of the Madras government. For nine months Jinnah had kept out of her movement, but in the summer of 1917 he plunged into it. It was an index of his rising stature that he was elected president of the Bombay Home Rule League. He organized branches of the Home Rule League in different parts of the city. On 30 July he presided over a public meeting at Bombay which was addressed by, among others, Tilak, Motilal Nehru and Sarojini Naidu. In the course of an impassioned indictment of the Government of India and the Madras government, Jinnah declared that Indian acquiescence in the policy of the government would mean the end of all constitutional and lawful agitation. He questioned the right of the government to decide what was lawful and constitutional without reference to courts of justice.

The crisis over Mrs Besant's arrest did not last long. On 20 August 1917, Edwin Montagu, Secretary of State for India, declared in the House of Commons that the policy of the British Government was that of 'the increasing association of Indians in every branch of the administration, and the gradual development of self-governing institutions with a view to the progressive realisation of Responsible Government in India as an integral part of the British Empire.' This declaration was widely acclaimed in India. Mrs Besant was released on 17 September and there was immediate relaxation in the political atmosphere.

Addendum

The Pinnacle of Happiness

In April 1918 Jinnah married Ruttenbai or Ruttie as she was known, the daughter of Sir Dinshaw Petit of Bombay. M.C. Chagla, who was at that time assisting Jinnah in his chambers, related a very interesting dialogue between Jinnah and Sir Dinshaw after their return from Darjeeling where Jinnah had met Ruttie and fallen in love with her. Chagla wrote: The story about Jinnah's marriage is extremely interesting, and I do believe it is authentic. Sir Dinshaw Petit (of Bombay) and Jinnah were great friends, and the former was very fond of the latter and admired his stout-hearted nationalism and also his impressive personality. Once Sir Dinshaw, while he was in Darjeeling, invited Jinnah to spend his holidays with him. Sir Dinshaw's 16-year-old daughter, Ruttie, was also with her father in Darjeeling. Jinnah and she came into close contact and decided to get married. Jinnah then went to Sir Dinshaw and asked him what his views were about intercommunal marriages. The question caught Sir Dinshaw off guard. At length, he expressed his emphatic opinion that it would considerably help national integration and might ultimately prove to be the final solution to inter-communal antagonism. Thereupon Jinnah calmly told him that he wanted to marry his daughter. Sir Dinshaw was taken aback. He had not realized that his remarks might have serious personal repercussions. He was most indignant, and refused to countenance any such idea which appeared to him absurd and fantastic.[5]

After this acrimonious discourse between Jinnah and Sir Dinshaw, according to Kanji Dwarkadas whom Sir Dinshaw knew, he took a High Court injunction against Jinnah marrying or having any contacts with his minor daughter. Ruttie decided to defy her father. As she reached eighteen (20 February 1918), she walked out of the parental house (18 April 1918). To Mohammad Ali

Jinnah, who was not only a lawyer but by nature a law-abiding person, Ruttie's action was somewhat confusing, but he acted as a lawyer. He at once consulted his friends and took Ruttie to the Jama Mosque where Ruttie's conversion to Islam took place in front of a great religious scholar, Maulana Nazir Ahmad Khujandi. According to the details of the *Nikahnamma*, the dowry was settled at one thousand one rupees. However, Jinnah presented Ruttie one hundred and twenty-five thousand rupees as a gift. The marriage with Ruttie was actually the opening of the second phase of his marital life after a gap of some twenty-one years.[6] But Sir Dinshaw was furious; he never saw his daughter again.

Lady Reading says about Ruttie that her attire was a liberty scarf, a jewelled bandeau and an emerald necklace. She is extremely pretty, fascinating, terribly made up. All the men raved about her, the women sniffed.

Hector Bolitho writes: 'Soon after Jinnah's marriage ... he was invited, with his wife, to dine at Government House. The story is that Mrs. Jinnah wore a low-cut dress that did not please her hostess. While they were seated at the dining table, Lady Willingdon asked an ADC to bring a wrap for Mrs. Jinnah, in case she felt cold. Jinnah is said to have risen and said, "when Mrs. Jinnah feels cold, she will say so, and ask for a wrap herself". Then he led his wife from the dining room, and from that time, refused to go to Government House again.'[7] It is said that this was the beginning of differences between Jinnah and Lord Willingdon.

From 1918 to 1920 she also attended the annual sessions of All India Muslim League and the Indian National Congress. In 1918 these annual sessions were held at Delhi under the presidentship of A.K. Fazlul Haq and Pandit Madan Mohan Malaviya respectively. Nawab Yameen Khan writes that to attend this session Mohammad Ali Jinnah came to Delhi. His wife also accompanied him and they stayed at Maiden's Hotel.[8]

In 1919, Jinnah went to London with Ruttie who was in an advanced stage of pregnancy at the time. Jinnah took on rent a flat near Regent Park. Close friends, such as Dewan Chaman Lal, a young barrister, and Sarojini Naidu, who had come to London to present the Indian National Congress's point of view, paid occasional visits and discussed matters of mutual interest. One evening, in mid-August, Jinnah took Ruttie to the theatre, but they had to leave in a hurry as Ruttie was not feeling well. Dina, their only child, was born in August 1919. She was extremely good-looking.[9]

Until the end of 1927 the relationship between Jinnah and his wife was smooth and pleasant. In August 1927 she was in Simla where Jinnah had gone to attend the Legislative Assembly session. She accompanied him to Calcutta for the annual session of the All India Muslim League. However, in January 1928, after their return from Calcutta, Ruttie and Jinnah drew apart, primarily because of the differences in age and habits. She left the house on Mount Pleasant Road and went to the Taj Mahal Hotel.[10]

Chapter 4

THE MAKING OF A MUSLIM GOKHALE

The agitation provoked by the internment of Annie Besant at Coimbtore in June 1917 lasted just three months, but it had for the first time sucked Jinnah into the whirlpool of nationalist politics. He broke out of the cocoon of the studied moderation of the pre-war era. When he joined the Home Rule League, he took with him the whole legal profession of Bombay. He collected around him a band of admirers, such as Shankarlal Banker, Omar Sobhani and Kanji Dwarkadas. He addressed public meetings in middle and lower middle class localities. He was delighted by the popular applause. Public adulation boosted his morale; he was becoming less and less tolerant of the high-handedness of the bureaucracy and was ready to confront it whenever an occasion arose. And there were to be quite a few such occasions in the next eighteen months.

In the winter of 1917, Edwin Montagu, Secretary of State for India, arrived with a small team of advisers. 'My visit to India', he wrote in his diary soon after setting foot on Indian soil, 'means that we are going to do something big ... it must be epoch-making or it is a failure.'[1] For this self-imposed mission he had unusual qualifications. He was singularly free from the pride of race or office. Invited to a luncheon party in Calcutta at the house of B.N. Basu, a member of the India Council in London and a former president of the Indian National Congress, Montagu cheerfully stood up with the others during the singing of *Bande Mataram*, the song of Indian nationalism and the symbol of sedition in the eyes of the British in India. During the next five months Montagu applied himself to the problem

The Making of a Muslim Gokhale ॐ **39**

of devising a new constitution which would set India on the road to self-government. On 26 November 1917, along with the Viceroy, Lord Chelmsford, he received a joint deputation of the Congress and the Muslim League. There were, Montagu noted in his diary, 'the real giants of the Indian political world, including Jinnah, Annie Besant, Hasan Imam, Mazhar-ul-Haq and Gandhi'. He drew a pen portrait of Jinnah in his diary:

> Young, perfectly mannered, impressive-looking, armed to the teeth with dialectics, and insistent upon the whole of his scheme ... Chelmsford tried to argue with him, and was tied up into knots. Jinnah is a very clever man, and it is, of course, an outrage that such a man should have no chance of running the affairs of his own country.[2]

Three months later, in February 1918, when Montagu had another interview with Jinnah, he noted Jinnah's radical stance on constitutional reforms and emphasis on advance in the central rather than provincial administration. Jinnah impressed the Liberal Secretary of State, but the Viceroy and high British officials in Simla and Bombay were not too happy with his utterances and activities.

II

Jinnah's speeches inside and outside the Imperial Legislative Council acquired a new pungency. In September 1917, while speaking in the Imperial Legislative Council, he refuted the statement of a European member that Muslims would not get their proper share if the competition for entrance examination to the Indian Civil Service was simultaneously held in India and England: 'Mohammedans are today in a better position than perhaps the Hon'ble member knows', Jinnah said, 'and are quite prepared to compete with their Hindu brethren and, therefore, there need be no anxiety of any kind whatsoever on the part of the Government or the Mohammedans .... Let it be open competition to anyone — Europeans, Hindus, Mohammedans and Parsis, etc. — and the fittest get in; the survival of the fittest should be the rule for recruiting to the highest service.' He expressed his disappointment at the refusal of the Royal Commission on Public Services to increase opportunities for recruitment of Indians to higher services. At a public meeting in Allahabad, he said there were powerful vested interests blocking the path of the Indian people towards self-government. The first was the British bureaucracy, which had enjoyed a monopoly of power and was unwilling to part with it. The second was the European commercial community, who enjoyed a monopolistic control over Indian commerce and had fully exploited it for more than two centuries. What did the European businessmen mean, Jinnah asked, when they spoke of their 'stake' in India? There was, of course, British investment of some 300 million pounds in India out of the total British investment of 1,700 million pounds all over the world. Most of this investment was in countries like Russia, Japan, Persia and Argentina, in the governments of which Britain had no voice. Was it not ridiculous for British businessmen to argue that, so long as these 300 million pounds were invested in India, the people of India must remain under British rule? The third opponent of Indian self-government was the military establishment which also had a monopoly because Indians had been denied commissioned ranks.

Commenting on Annie Besant's internment in June 1917, Jinnah described the government's policy as one of 'repression with one hand and concessions with the other'. 'No self-respecting people', he said, 'could accept it'. In an interview to the *Bombay Chronicle* he went so far as to pronounce the administration of Lord Chelmsford a failure, and to call for his recall. Such trenchant criticism could hardly endear Jinnah to the British rulers in India. It seemed to them that he was on the warpath. Small wonder that Jinnah had a number of clashes with them. The first serious clash came at the War Conference convened by Lord Chelmsford at Simla in May 1918. In a personal letter to the editor of the *Times of India*, Sir John Maffey, Private Secretary to the Viceroy, wrote: 'Jinnah's performance at the close [of the Conference] left a nasty taste in the mouth of the Bombay delegates ... but to the people unprejudiced, who knew of Jinnah, his performance seemed merely clumsy and ungentlemanly. His audience was cold and reception chilly. It was not a star performance ....' Maffey added that the Viceroy had deliberately turned down Jinnah's request for an interview because he had been infuriated by a telegram from Jinnah which said: 'We cannot ask our young men to fight for principles, the application of which is denied to their own country. A subject race cannot fight for others with the heart and energy with which a free race can for the freedom of itself and others.'

Nearly a month later, Jinnah had another head-on collision with Lord Willingdon, the Governor of Bombay, who was presiding over a provincial War Conference to mobilize public opinion at a time when the war was not going too well for the Allies. The Governor called upon Bal Gangadhar Tilak to speak, but did not allow him to move any amendment, nor to reply to his highly critical comments on the Home Rule movement. After Tilak walked out of the conference hall in protest, Jinnah rose to speak and regretted that the Governor had cast doubts on the sincerity and loyalty of the Home Rule party. As regards the German menace, which was right at their door, Jinnah declared, 'The Indian people wanted a citizens' army and not a purely mercenary army'. The British officialdom was scandalized by Jinnah's audacity. Willingdon wrote to Secretary of State Montagu, clubbing Jinnah with 'extremist' Congress leaders like Tilak and Annie Besant, 'who have no feeling of what is their duty to the Empire in its hour of crisis'.

The mutual antipathy between Jinnah and Willingdon had a dramatic climax when a meeting was called in Bombay's town hall by the pro-government elements in Bombay to approve a proposal for a memorial to Willingdon who was about to retire. The Home Rule party in Bombay decided to frustrate the attempt to honour a Governor whom it detested. An appeal was issued by Jinnah, B.G. Horniman, Jamnadas Dwarkadas and other local leaders inviting the public to attend the meeting to express their disapproval of the proposal. On 11 December, the Home Rulers, most of whom were students, assembled in strength and queued up outside the town hall from the early hours of the morning and, when the door was opened at 10 am, occupied most of the seats. When there was no more room in the hall, they sat on the steps of the town hall. The police were called to clear the hall, but could not do much. Inside the hall there was so much noise and confusion that the proceedings could not begin till late afternoon. A resolution proposing the memorial was moved by the organizers of the meeting and declared as carried, but nobody could hear anything. The meeting ended in pandemonium. Jinnah led the crowd to Apollo Street and addressed them:

> Gentlemen, you are the citizens of Bombay. You have today scored a great triumph for democracy. Your triumph today has made it clear that even the combined forces of bureaucracy and autocracy could not overawe you. December the 11th is a Red-Letter Day in the history of Bombay. Gentlemen, go and rejoice over the day that has secured us the triumph of democracy.[3]

Jinnah's admirers, in recognition of his leading role in the anti-Willingdon demonstration, raised within one month a large sum — Rs 65,000 in one-rupee subscriptions — to build the 'Jinnah People's Memorial Hall' in the compound of the headquarters of the Indian National Congress. Annie Besant came down from Adyar to open the hall. This incident deepened the British distrust of Jinnah. He became the *bete noire* of high officials at all levels. Lord Chelmsford detected in him 'a root of bitterness ... which cannot be eradicated'. His successor, Lord Reading, said that Jinnah and Sarojini Naidu were 'both fair of speech and black of heart — real irreconcilables'. What really baffled and exasperated the British officials was that a Muslim politician spoke the same language as the most radical Congress leaders. This exasperation was evident a few months later in August 1919, when Jinnah appeared before the Joint Select Committee of Parliament on the Reforms Bill in London.

Jinnah told the Committee that the All India Muslim League, on whose behalf he was speaking, had adopted a programme — the attainment of self-government under the aegis of the British Crown — and 'thereby came into line with the Indian National Congress'. He demanded, in accordance with the joint Congress–League scheme, 'a transfer of power from top to bottom', in the provincial as well as the central government. The members of the Committee, who took antagonism between Hindus and Muslims for granted, shot question after question to embarrass and trip up Jinnah. But he was more than a match for them. Out of nearly 300 questions put to him it is interesting to sample the handling of a few of the trickier ones.

Question: In the course of your [written] evidence you have several times mentioned a problem of unimaginable magnitude — the uplifting of the masses. Did I rightly understand that you think British administration has done nothing or too little in that respect?

Answer: If you ask me, the British administration has done very little.

Question: You feel you and your friends in power could do more?

Answer: I am certain of it.

Question: Mr. Jinnah, you are the first Mohammedan witness who has appeared before this Committee.

Answer: I believe so, so far as I have read the evidence before the Committee.

Question: You appeared before [the Committee] on behalf of the Muslim League, that is on behalf of the only widely extended Mohammedan organization in India.

Answer: Yes.

Question: You said you spoke from the viewpoint of India. You speak really as an Indian nationalist.

Answer: I do.

Question: Holding that view do you contemplate early disappearance of the separate communal representation of the Mohammedan community?

Answer: I think so.

Question: That is to say, at the earliest possible moment you wish to do away in political life with any distinction between Mohammedans and Hindus?

Answer: Yes, nothing will please me more than when that day comes.

Question: You do not think it is true to say that the Mohammedans of India have very special political interest ... ?

Answer: In India the Mohammedans have very few things really which you can call matters of special interest for them — I mean secular things.

Question: Would it not be an advantage in the case of occurrence [of Hindu-Muslim riots] if the maintenance of law and order were left with the executive side of the government?

Answer: I do not think so .... If you ask me, very often these riots are based on some misunderstanding, and it is because the police has taken one side or the other that has enraged one side or the other. I know very well that in the Indian [Princely] states you hardly ever hear of any Hindu-Mohammedan riots ...

Question: The fact remains that these riots have been interracial, Hindus on one side and Mohammedans on the other. Would it be an advantage that the minister, the representative of one community or the other, should be in charge of the maintenance of the law and order?

Answer: Certainly ... recently in the whole district of Thane, Bombay, every officer was an Indian, from top to bottom, and I do not think there was a single Mohammedan — they were all Hindus — and I never heard any complaint ...[4]

The courage, the conviction and the clarity of Jinnah's exposition of the nationalist case was reminiscent of the performance of his hero and mentor, G.K. Gokhale, before the Welby Commission in 1897.

III

In retrospect, it seems that the Lucknow Pact was a turning point in Jinnah's political evolution. Very early in his career — precisely in 1908–9 — his wings had been clipped by the incorporation of separate electorates for Muslims in the Minto–Morley reforms. He knew that he needed a legislative career essential for his political survival, and henceforth he would have to seek his evolution from an exclusively Muslim constituency. The small, politically conscious and vocal Muslim electorate was traditionally pro-British, anti-Hindu and anti-Congress. It was no longer possible for him to give vent to his unalloyed nationalism; he had to be especially careful in Muslim gatherings. As we have already seen, for five years, from 1908 to 1913, he had practised a tightrope walk on the political stage between his Muslim and national identities. He could not have prolonged it indefinitely. By 1913, he was drifting towards the Muslim League. Luckily for him, events outside

India — the travails of Turkey and the outbreak of the First World War — brought about a drastic transformation in the Indian political scene. The Anglo-Muslim alliance came under great strain, and a small radical group, which included Jinnah, managed to acquire control over the All India Muslim League and was able to steer it in line with the Congress. Jinnah was one of the main architects of the Lucknow Pact. He succeeded in securing the consent of the Congress to the main demands of the Muslim community, namely separate electorates and weighted representation. A joint scheme of reforms was framed and presented to the government. Jinnah appreciated the generosity of the Congress and believed that the Lucknow Pact would lead to a permanent accord between the two political parties and the two major communities. It was this belief which produced the radical slant and the sharp pungency of his speeches, writings and activities, and which incurred the hostility of the British authorities.

The demonstration in Bombay against Lord Willingdon in December 1918 has been described as Jinnah's finest hour. There is no doubt that it enhanced his reputation as an intrepid Indian nationalist. M.C. Chagla, who was a student leader in those days, recalled in his memoirs that Jinnah was 'the idol of the youth'. He 'was the uncrowned King of Bombay'.[5] Jinnah's reputation was built on solid foundations. He was one of the leading lights of the Bombay Bar. He was a member of the Imperial Legislative Council. He was the President of the Home Rule League in Bombay and the Chairman of the Board of Directors of the *Bombay News Chronicle*, the main nationalist newspaper in Bombay. He was the only political leader in the higher echelons of both the Indian National Congress and the All India Muslim League. At the age of 42, he was in the front rank of India's leaders.

Mr Walker, a British journalist who accompanied Montagu during his visit to India in 1917–18, told him: 'In Bombay there is only one man — Jinnah. At the root of Jinnah's activities is ambition. He believes that when Annie Besant and Tilak have disappeared, he will be the leader.' We do not know whether Walker based this assessment on conversations with Jinnah or with other politicians and journalists, but what he said would have made sense to knowledgeable observers of the political scene at the time. It seems impossible that such an idea had not crossed Jinnah's mind. He had no doubt about his own talents in law and politics; he felt second to none. As a young man he had aspired to be a 'Muslim Gokhale'. This noble ambition was now within the realm of practical politics. There was no doubt that in the reformed Legislative Councils, with their wider franchise, increase in the number of elected members and wider powers, he would have a pivotal role to play. He had no doubt about a bright future for himself and for his country. Little did he know, as 1919 dawned, that all his calculations and daydreams were going to be shattered by the emergence on the political stage of an ascetic-turned politician, of whom he had so far taken hardly any notice.

Chapter 5

THE ADVENT OF GANDHI

When Jinnah was a law student in England, another Gujarati man, seven years older than he and a barrister of the Lincoln's Inn, arrived in South Africa on a year's contract to help an Indian merchant in a civil suit pending in a Pretoria court. Jinnah returned to India in 1896, but Gandhi stayed on in South Africa for nearly twenty years, not so much to practise law as to organize the small, beleaguered minority of Indian immigrants against racial discrimination at the hands of the dominant European community and the colonial government. In the first decade of the twentieth century, while Jinnah was forging ahead in law and politics in Bombay, Gandhi was locked in a seemingly unequal struggle with the colonial regime in South Africa.

Jinnah and Gandhi were not to meet until Gandhi's return to India in 1915, but they were not ignorant of each other's activities. Gopal Krishna Gokhale, who was Jinnah's hero and mentor in politics, had boundless admiration for Gandhi. At the Lahore Congress in December 1909, he described Gandhi 'as a man among men, the hero among heroes, the patriot among patriots and one may well say that in him Indian humanity has reached its high watermark.'[1] Gokhale repeatedly brought up the issue of Gandhi's struggle in South Africa in the Imperial Legi-slative Council. Jinnah had strongly supported him and flayed the South African government for its un-abashed racialism.

During these years Gandhi was closely following the events in India and especially in Bombay. In 1908 he wrote in his journal, *Indian Opinion,* that there was a suggestion that 'Mr. Jinnah should be invited to the satyagraha struggle in South Africa'. Earlier in the same journal, he had written that he had 'great respect for Mr. Jinnah.' In March 1908, when Jinnah was in England, he showed Mr Ritch, one of Gandhi's South African associates, a telegram from a Muslim merchant of the Transvaal, complaining against Gandhi's compromise with General Smuts, and alleging that Gandhi's movement was ruining Muslim merchants in South Africa. Jinnah does not seem to have taken any notice of this complaint; apparently he knew that Gandhi had done much to unite the Indian immigrants hailing from different regions and provinces in their struggle against the South African government. Indeed, this was one feature of Gandhi's struggle which Jinnah lauded in his speech at a reception held in January 1915 at Bombay by the Gurjar Sabha, an association of Gujaratis, to welcome Gandhi. Jinnah, who was in the chair, paid a glowing tribute to Gandhi and his wife, Kasturba. 'Such a son of India and such a daughter of India', he said, 'not only raised the reputation of India but had vindicated the honour of the great and ancient land ... and the whole world admired the trials and tribulations and sacrifices Mr and Mrs Gandhi underwent for the cause of their country and their countrymen.' Under Gandhi's leadership, Hindus and Muslims 'showed themselves unanimous, absolutely one, on the South African question ....' This 'was the first occasion on which the two sister communities stood together in absolute union and it had its moral and political effect on the settlement of the question.'[2]

Gandhi thanked Jinnah for his warm words of welcome, and then, according to the report in the *Bombay Chronicle* (15 January 1915), said, 'While he [Gandhi] was in South Africa, and anything was said about the Gujaratis, it was understood to have a reference to the Hindu community only and Parsis and Mohamedans were not thought of'. He added he was pleased 'to find a Mohamedan member of the Gurjar Sabha as the chairman of this function'.[3]

According to Stanley Wolpert, Jinnah's American biographer, if Gandhi had 'meant to be malicious rather than his usual ingenuous self, he could not have contrived a more cleverly patronizing barb, for he was not actually insulting Jinnah, after all, just informing everyone of his minority religious identity.'[4] It is arguable that Gandhi's remark was a tactless and gratuitous comment on a Muslim leader who was proud of his secular credentials. Wolpert is, however, wide off the mark in his inference that this first comment by Gandhi on Jinnah 'set the tone of their relationship, always at odds with deep tensions and mistrust ... never friendly, never cordial'. As we have already seen, there had been no ill feeling between the two men while Gandhi was in South Africa and, as we shall see, there was to be none in the years immediately after his return to India. The fact is that during these early years their public lives followed parallel paths; paths which did not meet, but they did not cross either. Their meetings were few and far between and usually on formal occasions. Their personalities had taken distinct forms and their world views differed, but as yet there was no hint of any competition between them.

Gandhi received a hero's welcome on his return to the homeland, but, in his Kathiawari turban and cloak and with his strange views, he seemed to most English-educated Indians a queer and quixotic figure — in the words of young J.B. Kripalani — 'an eccentric specimen of an England-returned-educated-Indian'.[5] At the very first public reception accorded to him he rebuked a Parsi press correspondent, who addressed him in English. 'I have not forgotten', he said, 'my native tongue during my stay in South Africa'.[6] One of the first things he did was to set up a small ashram at Ahmedabad to lodge his co-workers, so that they could resume the life of simplicity and service in which they had been nurtured in South Africa.

In November 1917 Jinnah was present at a Provincial Political Conference at Godhra in Gujarat. At the instance of Gandhi, who was presiding, Jinnah moved a resolution welcoming Secretary of State Edwin Montagu's forthcoming visit and pleading for the acceptance of the Congress–League scheme. After Tilak had spoken in Marathi, his mother tongue, Gandhi requested Jinnah to speak in Gujarati. Jinnah agreed, but after speaking in Gujarati for a couple of minutes switched to English amidst roars of laughter in which Gandhi joined. In the eyes of the

Indian political elite of the day Gandhi's insistence on the mother tongue in preference to English was one of the several bees in his bonnet.

II

There was not much interaction between Jinnah and Gandhi from 1915 to 1918, but it was not due to any estrangement or latent antagonism. Jinnah's involvement in nationalist politics had grown during the war years. He had joined hands with a group of young Muslim nationalists of north India — the Raja of Mahmudabad, Mazhar-ul-Haq and Wazir Hasan — to steer the All India Muslim League into alignment with the Indian National Congress. He was one of the principal architects of the Lucknow Accord of 1916, and the Congress–League scheme for constitutional reforms, presented to the British Government. During the next two years he vigorously campaigned for the acceptance of this scheme as the united demand of the people of India. If Gandhi was only a spectator of this high drama on the Indian political stage, it was by choice. It had long been Gokhale's wish that Gandhi return to India from South Africa and enrich its public life, but he feared that because of his long sojourn in a foreign country Gandhi was out of touch with the conditions in his own country. Gokhale had great admiration for Gandhi, but he also laughed at some of his ideas and told him, 'After you have stayed a year in India your views will correct themselves'.[7] Even before Gandhi set foot on Indian soil, he had promised Gokhale, whom he called his 'political guru', that he would travel round the country for a year and see things for himself before committing himself to any course of action. Gokhale passed away within six weeks of Gandhi's return, but Gandhi kept his promise to the deceased leader. In those early months of Gandhi's return to India, police reporters often found his speeches colourless. So did the Indian intelligentsia who found politics missing from much of what he said and wrote. He dwelt on the iniquities of the system of indentured labour and the grievances of Indians overseas.

He pleaded for 'swadeshism' — the use of articles made in India. He deplored the inconveniences and insults and the downright degradation to which millions of the common people were subjected while travelling third class in railway trains. He denounced the evil of untouchability. He called for raising the status of Indian womanhood and said, 'They can no longer be treated as dolls or slaves.'[8] He pointed out the absurdity of educated Indians speaking in a foreign language to express their innermost thoughts. He expatiated on the superiority of the Indian civilization over the 'materialist civilization' of the west.

Besides his pledge to Gokhale, Gandhi had another reason for opting out of politics: this was because of his attitude to the First World War. He was on his way to India from South Africa when war clouds burst over Europe in the summer of 1914. He arrived in London on 4 August, the day on which Britain declared war on Germany. He lost no time in declaring his unconditional support to Great Britain. 'I knew', he later recalled in his autobiography, 'the difference of status between an Indian and an Englishman .... I felt then that it was more the fault of the individual officials than of the British system, and that we could convert them by love. If we would improve our status through the help and co-operation of the British, it was our duty to win their help by standing by them in their hour of need.'[9] Though not in the best of health, he raised an Indian Volunteer Corps for ambulance work in the European theatres of war. By September 1914 nearly sixty Indians residing in England, mostly students, headed by Gandhi, were being trained in first aid. Were it not for a severe attack of pleurisy, Gandhi may well have continued to serve in the ambulance unit he had raised and his return to India may have been indefinitely delayed.

When Gandhi returned to India early in 1915, he sensed that nationalist opinion was almost unanimously opposed to unconditional support to Britain. Gandhi declared that he did not favour a bargain with the British Government. He told the Gujarat Political Conference in November 1917: 'That we have been loyal at a time of stress is no test of fitness for swaraj. Loyalty is no merit. It is a necessity of national existence all the world over.'[10] Most political leaders considered Gandhi's views naive, and agreed with Tilak that Britain's need was India's opportunity, that it was the duty of Indian patriots to strike when the iron was hot, and extort from the government concessions in constitutional reforms and admission of Indians to higher ranks in the army. This is exactly what Jinnah told the War Conference convened by the Governor of Bombay in June 1918:

> If you wish to enable to help you ... you must make the educated people feel that they are citizens of the Empire and the King's equal subjects .... 'We want action and immediate deeds. I will give one instance. At the Delhi War Conference (held in April 1918) we passed a resolution recommending that a substantial number of King's commissions should be granted to the people of India', but nothing has been done.[11]

Gandhi's attitude to the war differed not only from that of Jinnah, but from almost all nationalist leaders. At the Delhi War Conference, convened by Lord Chelmsford, Gandhi supported the official resolution on recruitment with a single sentence in Hindi: 'With a full sense of my responsibility, I beg to support the resolution.'[12] He took his solemn one-sentence speech at the War Conference so seriously that after the Conference he embarked on a recruiting campaign in his home province Gujarat and wrote to other Indian leaders to follow his example. 'What a proud thing it would be', he wrote to Jinnah on 9 July 1918, 'if we recruited and at the same time insisted on amendments in the Reforms Schedule!'[13]

III

The Viceroy's War Conference had underscored the fact that Gandhi was ploughing a lonely furrow in Indian politics. Since his return from South Africa, he had made it a point to attend the annual meetings of the Indian National Congress. He was usually accorded a seat of honour on the dais, and was called upon to speak on the grievances of Indians in South Africa, but he did not figure among the front-rank national leaders. The political stage was dominated by Tilak, Annie Besant and Jinnah. Gandhi was at Lucknow in December 1916, but he had no part in the making of the accord between the Congress and the League. He deliberately kept out of the Home Rule movement. He was not directly associated with the major developments in nationalist politics during the war years. He was included in the Congress–League deputation, which waited on Secretary of State Montagu and Viceroy Lord Chelmsford in November 1917, but he was not one of its spokesmen. To the visiting Secretary of State, he seemed 'a political lightweight ... a social reformer with a real desire to find grievances and to cure them, not for any reasons of self-advertisement, but to improve the condition of his fellowmen ...' In an introduction to the collection of Gandhi's writings and speeches published in 1917, Sarojini Naidu, the young poetess, compared him with the Buddha and the great saints of Bengal—Chaitanya and Ramakrishna.

This image of a social reformer did less than justice to Gandhi, but it was fostered by his habit of dwelling on moral principles and political techniques rather than on constitutional issues. What really separated him from political parties and politicians was his South African experience. Among the discoveries he had made in those twenty-odd years was that constitutional agitation had definite limits for a subject people. He found that a political contest was not merely between conflicting arguments, but between clashing interests, and that a stage could be reached when something more than reasoning was required. Since 1885, and indeed since the beginning of the nineteenth century, Indian politics had been organized on the British model of constitutional agitation— of prayer, petition and protest. True, in the wake of the partition of Bengal there was some talk of 'passive resistance', but nothing much came of it. The Moderates had a horror of 'passive resistance', but for the Extremists also it had remained no more than a slogan. It soon became clear to Gandhi that no prominent politician in

India shared his enthusiasm for 'passive resistance' or satyagraha, as he called it. Most Indian leaders professed to respect him for his South African record, but much of what he said on currrent political issues struck them as highly impracticable, if not irrelevant. It became quite a fashion to acknowledge his idealism, but to dismiss it as irrelevant to the workaday world. In February 1916 one of the founders of the Home Rule movement, Annie Besant, wrote in her journal, *New India,* that Gandhi's views were 'suited better for a far-off posterity than for today'. In December 1917, when Gandhi was invited to chair the All India Humanitarian Conference in Calcutta, the choice must have seemed most appropriate to his contemporaries.

What dismayed Gandhi was the insulation of Indian politicians from rural India where more than 90 per cent of the population lived. The belief that the game of politics was best played by the educated, and especially the western-educated elite, in town halls or council chambers was common to both the Moderates and Extremists. The Moderates had a particular horror of the 'mob'. Gandhi considered the barriers between the intelligentsia and the masses a fatal handicap to national evolution. 'Without penetration into the villages', he wrote to the editor of *The Hindu,* 'our Home Rule schemes are of little value'.

The representatives of the British Raj in India judged Gandhi better than most Indian politicians; they were not so dismissive of him. They did not accept his professions of loyalty at face value. They knew he had been a thorn in the side of the colonial government in South Africa. The fact is that during these years Gandhi himself was torn between his resolve not to embarrass the government during the war and his instinct to stand up for the victims of injustice or oppression. He believed that in satyagraha he possessed an efficient instrument for rectifying injustice, righting wrongs and resolving conflicts. Having wielded it with a measure of success in South Africa, he felt he could not deny it to those of his countrymen who came to him for help. The fact that he was committed to abstention from political agitation during the war did not prevent him from championing the just grievances which could not brook delay.

In 1917 he was invited to Champaran in Bihar to look into the grievances of indigo cultivators against European planters. The magical effect of his presence on the peasantry flabbergasted the local authorities. They ordered his externment from the district and his prosecution if he did not comply. This gave Gandhi the ideal opportunity to stage passive resistance on the South African model. The Viceroy and his advisers did not relish the prospect of such a campaign led by Gandhi, and that too in wartime. They did not want to alienate him if they could help it. They resorted to the face-saving device of appointing an inquiry committee, of which Gandhi was made a member, to investigate the facts about indigo plantations and propose remedies. The crisis was tided over, but the government was left with an uncomfortable feeling that Gandhi had scored in the battle of wits. So it was less willing to conciliate him a few months later, when he took up the question of remission of land revenue in Kaira district in Gujarat, where the crops had been damaged by heavy rains. After exhausting all constitutional channels to secure redress, Gandhi announced a passive resistance struggle. The agrarian campaign deepened British suspicions of Gandhi's motives. Lord Willingdon, the Governor of Bombay, described him as 'honest but a Bolshevik and for that reason very dangerous'.[14] The impression grew in official circles that Gandhi tended to exaggerate, if not to invent, grievances and to meddle in matters which were none of his concern. He had bombarded the Viceroy with letters urging the release of the Ali brothers (Mahomed Ali and Shaukat Ali) who had been interned during the war without trial. He joined the chorus of protests against Annie Besant's arrest and in-carceration in the summer of 1917; he questioned the wisdom of imposing restrictions on Tilak's movements within the country. And he did all this, while professing to be a sincere friend and a well-wisher of the English nation! In May 1918, C.F. Andrews related to Gandhi a conversation he had in Simla with the Private Secretary to the Viceroy: 'Then he said that you were a very difficult man to get on with, and he was afraid that some point would crop up and there would be a split up.'[15]

In April 1918, the Viceroy warned Gandhi that with all his peculiar views and fads he would be alone in India some day: 'There will be none to agree with you or follow you'.[16] Curiously enough, Gandhi was himself aware of his isolation. 'I am supposed', he said, 'to live in the clouds. I am so marked out as a man apart that everyone thinks that nobody can put into practice what I say.'[17] In the summer of 1918 Gandhi frankly acknowledged his political isolation in a letter to Tilak, the prominent leader of the Congress, who had invited him to attend the special session of the Congress on the differences between the Moderate and Extremist factions of the party:

Gandhi to Tilak, 18 August 1918

I do not propose to attend the Congress or the Moderates' conference either. I see that my views are different from those of either. You and Mrs. Besant do not agree with me [on the attitude towards the war]. Then there is another difficulty. I think we must accept the Montagu–Chelmsford Scheme in principle, but quite clearly state what improvements we want in it and fight unto death to get them accepted by the Government. It is clear that the Moderate party will reject the principle of fighting altogether. If you and Mrs. Besant agree in principle, you will certainly not fight in the same spirit as I. Mrs. Besant has clearly told me she is not a Satyagrahi. You look upon Satyagraha as a matter of necessity, a weapon of the weak, not as I view it. I do not wish, therefore, to appear to agree with you and create confusion. Nor do I wish to form a new faction and start an agitation in the Congress against you.[18]

As we have seen, Jinnah's influence and prestige reached their zenith in the latter half of 1918. In contrast, Gandhi's political fortunes were touching their nadir. Ironically, the creed of satyagraha, which had separated Gandhi from both the government and the political parties of the day and kept him on the periphery of nationalist politics, was soon to catapult him into the centre of the political stage.

IV

On 19 January 1919, the Government of India published drafts of two Bills, which came to be known as Rowlatt Bills. The first Bill was meant to so amend the criminal laws as to curb activities dangerous to the state. The second Bill which was more stringent was designed to retain emergency powers of the Defence of India Act in peacetime. It could be retrospectively applied to offences committed before it was passed; it permitted detention of suspects without trial; it abridged court procedures and restricted the right of appeal. Jinnah condemned these Bills when they were introduced in the Imperial Legislative Council and warned the government: 'You would create in the country from one end to the other a discontent and an agitation, the like of which you have not witnessed'. There was, he said, 'no precedent or parallel in the legal history of any civilised country to the enactment of such laws'.[19]

There was a rare unanimity among the Indian leaders on opposition to the Rowlatt Bills. Tej Bahadur Sapru described them as 'wrong in principle, unsound in operation and too sweeping'. 'We think', V.J. Patel said, 'that all our constitutional agitation for any reforms whatever would die if these Bills are passed'. Gandhi urged the non-official Indian members of the Imperial Legislative Council to put up a united front against the Bills. 'Though I have not left my bed still', he wrote to Srinivasa Sastri on 9 February 1919, 'I can no longer watch the progress of the Bills lying in the bed'.[20] In the third week of February, a group of Bombay politicians led by B.G. Horniman, editor of the *Bombay Chronicle*, and included Shankarlal Banker, Umar Sobhani, Sarojini Naidu and Jamnadas Dwarkadas, arrived at the Sabarmati Ashram in Ahmedabad to see Gandhi. They were all activists of the Home Rule League of Bombay and members of what the British officials dubbed 'the Jinnah clique'. They begged Gandhi to lead a campaign against the Rowlatt Bills. They were joined by Vallabhbhai Patel, Indulal Yajnik and others who had worked with Gandhi in the Kaira no-tax satyagraha a few months earlier. The diary of Gandhi's secretary, Mahadev Desai, mentions a 'war conference' on 23 and 24 February 1919; this was a picturesque description of the twenty-odd men and women who congregated round Gandhi's sickbed to discuss the Rowlatt Bills. Gandhi told them that a satyagraha struggle was no picnic, and that they would have to incur great risks. On their insistence he agreed to initiate a campaign against the hated Bills and drafted a 'satyagraha pledge'. Each participant was to promise that, in the event of these Bills becoming laws, he 'shall refuse civilly to obey these laws and such other laws as a committee to be hereafter appointed may think fit, and ... follow truth and refrain from violence to life, person or property.'

The satyagraha pledge was signed by fifty people before it was published; in three weeks the number of signatories rose to six hundred. These figures were not such as would alarm the government. Intelligence reports even from Gandhi's native province Gujarat doubted whether there was any great body of popular support behind him. After seeing him in Delhi in March 1919, Chelmsford assured the Secretary of State that Gandhi had 'not chosen his ground well for a thorough-going passive resistance'. 'It was time', the Viceroy wrote, 'to call Gandhi's bluff'.[21] In retrospect, it may appear that the Viceroy was underrating the potentialities of satyagraha, but most observers of the Indian scene at the time would have agreed with him that Gandhi was on a weak wicket. He had no political party behind him. The Satyagraha Sabha, which he founded for this campaign, was hurriedly set up, and lacked proper organization. Prominent political leaders were unanimous in denouncing the Rowlett Bills, but hardly anyone was prepared to carry his opposition to the extreme step of resorting to civil disobedience. On 2 March several prominent members of the Imperial Legislative Council issued a joint manifesto assailing the Rowlatt Bills, but at the same time disapproving of civil disobedience.

Gandhi was undeterred by this widespread scepticism. He had not yet fully recovered from his recent illness, but he decided to tour the country and educate the people on the implications of the satyagraha pledge. While Gandhi was in Madras he awoke one morning and told his host, C. Rajagopalachari, that 'in the twilight condition between sleep and consciousness'[22] it had occurred to him that the country should be called upon to observe a day of *hartal*, when all business should be suspended and people should fast and pray as a protest against the hated legislation. 'When I suggested the Sunday demonstrations and fast', Gandhi confessed later, 'I thought I would be laughed at by most people as a lunatic. But the idea struck the imagination of an angry people.' If the enthusiastic response of the people to his appeal surprised Gandhi, it alarmed the government, which passed the first Bill on 18 March and postponed further consideration of the second Bill. At Delhi, where owing to a misunderstanding the *hartal* was observed on 30 March, the police opened fire to disperse a crowd. The countrywide demonstrations on 6 April were on the whole peaceful but they unhinged the authorities. The mighty imperial edifice was shaken by a political earthquake, the tremors of which pervaded the secret telegrams exchanged between the Government of India and the provincial governments. Sir George Lloyd, Governor of Bombay, telegraphed on 7–8 April 1919: 'Yesterday's demonstrations were large. Owing, however, to the knowledge of the presence of a military force they passed off quietly .... It will almost certainly be necessary for me to proceed against Gandhi and others ....'[23] Lloyd asked for the deportation to Burma of Horniman, Jamnadas Dwarkadas, Umar Sobhani, Sarojini Naidu, Shankarlal Banker, Jinnah and Gandhi. The Government of India cabled its consent on 12 April, but doubted the expediency of including Jinnah in the list, and added that Gandhi should not be deported unless some further occurrences took place.

Jinnah tendered his resignation from the Imperial Legislative Council on 18 March, writing to the Viceroy that the 'passing of the Rowlatt Bill ... has severely shaken the trust reposed by them in British justice'.[24]

Gandhi was arrested on the night of 9 April while he was on his way to Delhi, taken back by train to Bombay and set free. He would again have courted arrest by leaving for Delhi were it not for the fact that the news of his arrest had provoked serious disturbances in Bombay, Ahmedabad, Nadiad and other places in his own province which was the least expected to forget his fundamental principle of non-violence. He observed a three-day fast to expiate his 'Himalayan miscalculation' in launching a mass movement without making sure that the people were ready for it. He was as unsparing in his denunciation of mob violence as of official excesses. He intervened effectively to stop the violence in Bombay and Ahmedabad. But unknown to him, a great tragedy was being enacted in the Punjab. On 10 April, there was a riot at Amritsar, and three days later, Brigadier-General Dyer ordered firing on an unarmed crowd in Jallianwala Bagh, which left at least 379 dead and 1,270 injured. The Punjab Government, headed by Sir Michael O'Dwyer, convinced itself that there was a conspiracy to overthrow British rule, and imposed martial law in several districts. The mutiny phobia, to which the British officials and non-officials in India were periodically prone, precipitated the tragedy of the Punjab in that fateful spring of 1919, when panicky magistrates and trigger-happy majors heaped nameless indignities on the people.

Gandhi confessed that the violence which had occurred in the wake of the satyagraha against the Rowlatt Bills was for him a matter of the deepest 'regret and humiliation'. Those who joined satyagraha demonstrations, he said, were 'bound at all hazards to refrain from violence ... The time may come for me to offer satyagraha against ourselves'.[25] He suspended satyagraha on 18 April. It had lasted barely two weeks, but it marked the beginning of the process that was to convert him from a spectator to an arbiter of events in nationalist politics.

Chapter 6

Eclipsed

Jinnah heaved a sigh of relief when Gandhi suspended satyagraha on 18th April. As we have seen, he had denounced the Rowlatt Bills in the strongest terms when they were introduced in the Imperial Legislative Council. His warnings had gone unheeded, but immediately after the passage of the first Bill, he wrote to the Viceroy, tendering his resignation from the Imperial Legislative Council. He felt he could be 'of no use to my people in the Council nor consistently with one's self-respect is cooperation possible with a Government that shows such utter disregard for the opinion of the representatives of the people in the Council chamber .... In my opinion a Government that passes or sanctions such a law in times of peace forfeits its claim to be called a civilised Government ...'[1]

Jinnah himself did not sign the satyagraha pledge, but several Bombay politicians, who had closely worked with him in the Home Rule League and had been instrumental in pulling Gandhi from his sick bed, did so. On 6 April, the day chosen by Gandhi for a *hartal* to protest against the hated law, Jinnah presided over a public meeting at Bombay. And a month later, along with C.R. Das, he tried to enter the Punjab to provide legal aid to the accused in the martial law cases, but was not allowed to do so.

Gandhi's satyagraha had lasted barely a fortnight, but the popular response to it shook the government as well as the political leadership of the day. It became clear that Gandhi was going to be a force to reckon with in Indian politics. Jinnah left for England on 7 June to give evidence before the Joint Select Committee of Parliament on the

Reforms Bill. A week later, in the course of the voyage, he penned a long friendly letter to Gandhi:
Jinnah to Gandhi, 14 June 1919

> I wanted to see you before I left, but I had to rush things and hence I could not manage to look you up. I should like to know direct from you as to how things are moving in India. So if you would care to write to me I shall feel extremely grateful to you for it. Of course any information which you may be pleased to give me will be treated as confidential and therefore I trust you will not hesitate to keep me in touch with what is going on India.
>
> I hope that I may be able to help the cause of our motherland by my efforts in England for I fear that at present the Government in India, individually and collectively, lost their heads ... My last talk with the Governor of Bombay disappointed me very much.
>
> I hope you are well and that you will write to let me know what you think of the situation from time to time. I am longing to see the text of the reforms bill. You will also let me know what you think of it.[2]

Gandhi's response to Jinnah's letter was prompt, candid and cordial.

Gandhi to Jinnah, 28 June 1919

> I was delighted to receive your letter. I shall certainly keep you informed of the doings here. I cannot say anything about the Reforms Bill. I have hardly studied it. My preoccupation is Rowlatt legislation; add to that the Punjab .... Transvaal and swadeshi, and I have more hay on my work than I can carry. Our Reforms will be practically worthless, if we cannot repeal Rowlatt legislation, if a strong committee of enquiry is not appointed to investigate the Punjab affairs and to revise what appear to be excessive sentences, if ... the Transvaal Indians [are] not protected from further encroachments on their liberty, and if India does not take up and appreciate the work of swadeshi. The first four are needed as much to test our strength as to test the measure of the goodwill of the Englishmen, and the last, swadeshi, is an earnest of our love for our country ...[3]

Gandhi went on to tell Jinnah that he was thinking of resuming civil disobedience, but assured him that he would take all precautions, that were humanly possible to take, against recrudescence of violence. He ended his letter on a personal note: 'Pray tell Mrs. Jinnah that I shall expect her on her return to join the hand-spinning class that Mrs. Banker Senior and Mrs. Ramabai, a Punjabi lady, are conducting. And, of course, I have your promise that you would take up Gujarati and Hindi as quickly as possible ....'[4]

One can well imagine Jinnah and Ruttie roaring with laughter at these homilies by Gandhi when momentous issues like the future of the Indian constitution were on the parliamentary anvil. It was difficult for them, as indeed it was for most other Indian politicians, to grasp the hidden message in Gandhi's emphasis on the use of the spinning wheel and the mother tongue as instruments of identification of the political elite with the teeming millions of India.

II

When Jinnah arrived in England, Tilak was there in connection with his suit against Valentine Chirol of *The Times*. Other eminent leaders who had gravitated to London included Surendranath Banerjea, Srinivasa Sastri and Annie Besant. They appeared before the Joint Select Committee of Parliament and did what a decade earlier Gokhale and his associates had done when the fate of the Minto–Morley reforms was in the balance. They paced the corridors of Westminster; they sought out sympathetic members of parliament; they briefed newspaper editors and addressed public meetings. Their object was to mobilize enlightened opinion in Britain to prevent the Anglo-Indian lobby and the Tory politicians from checkmating Edwin Montagu's efforts to launch the Indian people on the road to self-government. Jinnah had two additional and important assignments — appearance before the Joint Select Committee of Parliament, and the presentation of a memorial to the British Prime Minister on the Turkish question.

This was not the first time that Jinnah had come to England to ventilate popular grievances or lobby for constitutional reforms, but this was his longest and happiest visit. Ruttie, his wife, was with him and he was in high spirits. They made a charming couple, the cynosure of all eyes in any gathering. Despite his busy political agenda, Jinnah found time to be present on a few social occasions. Dewan Chaman Lal, an Oxford graduate and a young barrister, who knew the young couple, recalled that Jinnah had come to London with his beautiful wife and won the heart of everyone. He had tremendous vanity. He was immaculately dressed but there was nothing apart and aloof about him .... There was a touch of the histrionics about him; nevertheless ... he refused to take [others] seriously just as much as he refused to take himself seriously.'

On 17 November 1919, after five months' stay in England, Jinnah returned to India. In an interview to the *Bombay Chronicle,* he confessed that the results of his visit were modest and undramatic. But he was hopeful that if India sent her 'real representatives' to London for sustained propaganda, a great deal could be achieved. He was confident that more could be accomplished in London than 'anywhere under the iron heels of Indian Rowlatt Act rule.' Six weeks later, at the Amritsar session of the Indian National Congress, Jinnah admitted that the reforms as finally enacted were not entirely satisfactory, but he felt there was no alternative to making the best of them. 'I am', he said, 'no friend of Mr. Montagu. I characterized his proposals before the Joint [Select] Committee as proposals based upon timidity and prejudice'.[5] He had no doubt, however, that Montagu had laboured for Indian reforms as no other Englishman had. This was the line which Motilal Nehru took in his Presidential Address to the Amritsar Congress. Interestingly enough, Gandhi's major intervention in the deliberations at Amritsar came in favour of working the reforms; it led him into collision with Tilak, C.R. Das, B.C. Pal and other 'Nationalist' leaders. Gandhi had been deeply touched by a Royal Proclamation by George V issued on Christmas eve in which he had appealed that 'so far as possible any trace of bitterness between my people and those who are responsible for my Government should be obliterated'. This 'is a document', declared Gandhi, 'of which the British people have every reason to be proud, and with which every Indian ought to be satisfied', but 'it remains to be seen whether the trust will filter down to the Civil Service.'[6] He insisted that the Congress resolution on the reforms strike a positive note and include an expression of gratitude to Secretary of State Montagu, the chief architect of the reforms. Supported by Jinnah and Malaviya, Gandhi gave the impression of being a Moderate and a constitutionalist.

As the New Year dawned, it seemed as if the trail of bloodshed and bitterness left by the tragic events of 1919 would at last be obliterated. After the Reforms Bill had been approved by the British Parliament it was natural that the eyes of Indian politicians should be riveted on the first elections to be held under the new constitution. Every party was watching the moves of its rivals and planning its own strategy. Tilak and Annie Besant, who had been allies in the Home Rule movement, were at loggerheads. Tilak was, however, riding high; he was launching his Congress Democratic Party to fight the elections, and was discussing with his friends the selection of candidates from Maharashtra. There was hardly a politician in the country who did not aspire to a seat in a provincial or the central legislature. In 1920, when Motilal Nehru learnt that his son, young Jawaharlal, had made his first impressive foray into agrarian politics in the district of Pratapgarh in the United Provinces, he at once saw the possibility of putting him up as a Congress candidate against the local Raj.

In 1910, and again in 1916, Jinnah had been elected by a Muslim constituency to the Imperial Legislative Council; he went back to it in 1920 for election to the new central legislature. He had no party of his own, but he had a high standing in the Muslim League as well as in the Congress. He was in touch with Tilak and their views seemed to converge on national problems; there could be little doubt that he would have a pivotal role in any nationalist group which would emerge in the legislature.

III

Indian politics thus seemed to be moving in traditional grooves in the first half of 1920. An outcry was being kept up against the Punjab atrocities and the British betrayal of Turkey; deputations were being led to the Viceroy in Delhi and the Prime Minister in London. At the same time, the political parties were preparing to contest the elections to the new councils. Gandhi gave little inkling that he was about to strike out in a new direction. He spent many laborious weeks in drafting the Congress report on the martial law regime in the Punjab; he patiently corresponded with the authorities in the province to secure relief in individual cases; he joined the Khilafat deputation to the Viceroy in January 1920, and three months later, he thought of visiting England to plead the Khilafat case before the British ministers. As late as May 1920, he wrote an article entitled, 'What Should the Voters Do?'[7] in which he exhorted the people to send only men of character to the new legislature. There is no doubt, however, that unknown to the public, and even to some of his closest colleagues, Gandhi's views on the political situation were in a state of flux during these months. His feelings of relief and gratitude on reading the Royal Proclamation in December 1919 did not last long. The harshness of the Treaty of Sevres towards Turkey shocked him, and the majority report of the Hunter Committee seemed to him 'thinly disguised whitewash'.

On the Khilafat issue, he felt the British Government said one thing and did another. From the letters written by Mahomed Ali, who headed the Khilafat delegation to Europe, it became clear to Gandhi that the policy of the British Government was much more devious than he had suspected.

Gandhi's faith in British sincerity had already been shaken in the spring of 1919; in the summer of 1920 it was shattered. He was deeply human, almost sentimental, even in politics. In the closing months of 1919 and early in 1920 he was scanning the horizon for a gesture which would restore his faith in the fairness of British justice. He was clutching at every straw. The Royal Proclamation of December 1919, which he had hailed as a harbinger of a new era, turned out to be no more than the felicitous phraseology usual on such occasions. At the Amritsar Congress he had thrown his weight in favour of cooperation with the government; five months later he veered to the opposite extreme. When the All India Congress Committee met at Benares at the end of May 1920, the members were startled by Gandhi's proposal for non-cooperation with the government as a mark of sympathy with Indian Muslims on the Khilafat issue. Most of them felt that Gandhi had lost his sense of proportion. The Punjab and the Khilafat affairs were after all just two of the twenty-nine items on the agenda for this meeting of the All India Congress Committee, and in any case the really urgent and important issue was that of the impending elections to the reformed councils. However, in the prevailing political climate in the country, Gandhi's critics thought it politic not to dismiss his proposal out of hand, but to head him off by referring it to a special plenary session of the Congress in September. It is significant that when the All India Congress Committee called for the views of the provincial Congress committees on non-cooperation, only one, that of Sind, came out in full support of Gandhi's programme.

As the special Congress session commenced on 4 September 1920, the dice seemed to be heavily loaded against Gandhi. It was customary for the president of the session to give a lead to the party on crucial issues, but Lajpat Rai, who presided over the special session, was equivocal on non-cooperation; he did not want, he said, to anticipate the decision on a question on which the country was sharply divided. The programme presented by Gandhi included the surrender of titles and honorary offices, withdrawal of students from schools and colleges, aided or controlled by the government, boycott of courts by litigants and lawyers, refusal by 'clerical, labouring and military classes' to serve in Mesopotamia, and boycott of British goods and of the new legislatures.

Gandhi's resolution met with bitter and determined opposition in the Subjects Committee. The strategy of Gandhi's opponents was to express their approval of his programme in theory, but to whittle it down in practice. Among those ranged against him, besides Jinnah, were C.R. Das, B.C. Pal, G.S. Khaparde, B.S. Moonje, N.C. Kelkar and the Maharashtrian politicians who considered themselves heirs of great Tilak who had died only a month before the Congress met. Gandhi's critics were in a quandary; even as they opposed non-cooperation, they could not afford to appear less radical than Gandhi. They took their stand on an amendment moved by B.C. Pal, which endorsed the principle of non-cooperation, but proposed a deputation of Congress leaders to visit England to demand 'complete swaraj', and meanwhile recommended the adoption of a highly diluted form of Gandhi's programme. Gandhi's resolution was under fire in the Subjects Committee for three days. His critics felt that they had reason, commonsense and experience on their side. 'There was not a single argument of any value advanced against my proposition', C.R. Das told the Subjects Committee, 'except one, namely— Mr. Gandhi — Mahatma Gandhi — said this and said that'.[8] Das was heckled. So was Gandhi, but he stood like a rock, unmoved by hostile criticism. Despite Gandhi's impassioned eloquence, the only important leader who cast his lot with him was Motilal Nehru. Nevertheless, the Subjects Committee rejected B.C. Pal's amendment and passed

Gandhi's resolution by a narrow majority — 148 members voting for and 133 against it. In the plenary session, Gandhi secured 1,855 votes as against 873 secured by B.C. Pal. Since the total number of delegates registered at the Congress was 5,814, it seems a large number of delegates either absented themselves or refrained from voting.

IV

Gandhi was able to get his programme through the Congress, but the Calcutta special Congress was by no means a great triumph for him. All that he had managed to do was to escape being defeated. His opponents remained sullen and unreconciled to the verdict of the Congress. Lajpat Rai, the president of the session, in his concluding remarks said he was sorry that Mr. Gandhi 'in his wisdom' should have tacked the Indian National Congress on to the Central Khilafat Committee.

When the All India Congress Committee met at Bombay early in October, Jinnah and V.J. Patel clashed with Gandhi. The three months, which spanned the special Congress, session at Calcutta and the annual session at Nagpur, witnessed a tug-of-war between the advocates and the opponents of non-cooperation. Lajpat Rai and V.J. Patel cast doubts on the feasibility of Gandhi's methods. C.R. Das, who had led the opposition to Gandhi at the Calcutta special Congress, convened a conference in Benares to unite the opponents of non-cooperation. Among those who were sceptical of non-cooperation at the Nagpur session was its president, C. Vijiaraghavachariar, the veteran Congress leader from Madras. He lamented the atmosphere of 'dismay, grief and fierce passions and animosities' all around.

When Gandhi moved his resolution for the change of the creed of the Congress, proposing 'the attainment of Swaraj by the people of India by all legitimate and peaceful means', Jinnah objected that it was impractical and dangerous to sever the British connection without greater preparation for independence. He did not dispute the fact that 'the Government has done us repeated wrongs of an enormous character which made our blood boil, but that is not the issue before the people'. He said the weapon of non-cooperation could not destroy the British Empire; 'it is neither logical nor is it politically sound or wise, nor practically capable of being put in execution'. He admitted that Gandhi commanded the majority in that gathering, but pleaded to him to pause, to cry halt before it was too late.[9]

Jinnah was repeatedly heckled during his speech. At one point, when he referred to Gandhi as 'Mister', the crowd cried, 'Mahatma'. When he called the Khilafat leader, Mahomed Ali, 'Mister', he evoked shouts of 'Maulana'. This time Jinnah remonstrated: 'If you will not allow me the liberty to address you and speak of a man in the language in which I think it is right, I say you are denying me the liberty which you are asking for.'[10] After saying this he left the meeting in protest.[11]

Gandhi had to reckon with opposition on all sides, but he carried the day. The Nagpur session was a turning point in the history of the Congress as well as in Gandhi's political career. Nagpur was the capital of the Central Provinces; its Chief Commissioner, Sir Frank Sly, was quick to realize the significance of the dramatic events which had taken place right under his nose.

Sir Frank Sly to Lord Chelmsford, 1 January 1921

The outstanding feature of the Congress has been the personal domination of Gandhi over all political leaders and followers alike. He has carried through the policy that he had decided for this Congress without any material modification. All opposition to his views has been overcome, without difficulty, owing to his strong hold over the bulk of the delegates and visitors, with whom his word is law. C.R. Das and his Bengal party failed even to put forward the Machiavellian scheme, evolved by them for wrecking non-cooperation, by proposing that all forms of non-cooperation, including the most extreme, should be simultaneously introduced at once, which they knew would not be accepted by Gandhi .... The Moderates of Nagpur were not heard; the Extremist opponents under Khaparde and Dr. Moonje were brushed aside. Pandit Madan Mohan Malaviya's effort was nugatory. Jinnah carried no influence. Lajpat Rai wobbled and then became silent. I understand their view to be that it was hopeless to attempt any real opposition in the temper of the meeting, and that they must wait for a more favourable opportunity.[12]

Nagpur confirmed Gandhi's ascendancy over the Congress beyond any doubt. C.R. Das, Lajpat Rai, V.J. Patel and Kasturi Ranga Iyengar, who had earlier opposed Gandhi's leadership and programme, decided to swallow their dissent, rather than commit political harakiri. Those who continued to oppose Gandhi, such as Annie Besant, Khaparde, Hasan Imam, B.C. Pal, Harkishen Lal and Jinnah, ceased to count in nationalist politics.

Chapter 7

DOWN BUT NOT OUT

Jinnah had his say in the midst of persistent heckling, but he was so angry and disgusted at the end of it all that he walked out of the Congress session in Nagpur with his wife and caught the first train to Bombay. He did not stay on even to attend the annual session of the Muslim League, which was about to be held at Nagpur. Perhaps he realized that the Muslim League had also been swept away by the Gandhian tide and that he was likely to get no better hearing from it than he had from the Congress. On his way to Bombay, he was jeered at by some of the non-cooperators travelling by the same train. His experience of the annual Congress at Nagpur was thus even more shocking than that of the special session at Calcutta three months earlier. He had literally been hounded out of nationalist politics. His labours of a decade had been destroyed in one day. He had worked for a concord between the Congress and the Muslim League and for a united front on the constitutional issue against the British bureaucracy in India and the Tory politicians in England. He had been looking forward to the working of the Reforms Act of 1919, in the spirit of Tilak, 'to accept what was offered and to fight for more'. Suddenly, he found himself irrelevant in the two main political parties, with the making of whose policies he had been associated during the preceding five years. Even the modest political base he had built for himself in Bombay city during the war years had been undermined when Gandhi, after taking over the presidency of the Home Rule League, changed its constitution. Gandhi's intention may have been simply to bring the Home Rule League into alignment with the Congress, but to Jinnah, Gandhi's action seemed high-handed and even vindictive. The incident rankled even eleven years later when he narrated it to Srinivasa Sastri in London during the Round Table Conference. Whatever Jinnah's resentment against Gandhi may have been he saw that, in 1921, it was no use pitting himself against him; the people were with him. It was open to Jinnah to do what some other stalwarts, such as Motilal Nehru, Lajpat Rai and C.R. Das, did when the choice seemed to be between political extinction and surrender to Gandhi. Jinnah could also jump on to the Gandhi bandwagon, but this went against the grain. He had always been proud of his independence; he could not bring himself to play second fiddle to anyone, not even to Gandhi. He was repelled by the religious overtones of Gandhi's campaign, and even by his asceticism. He did not relish the idea of discarding his Savile Row suits, putting on khadi shirts and *dhotis*, squatting on the floor and haranguing mobs of illiterate peasants and the urban proletariat on the iniquities of foreign rule. Nor could he accept Gandhi's programme of non-cooperation with the government, which included the boycott of councils and courts and renunciation of the two spheres, law and politics, in which he had won his laurels.

Jinnah's biographers have represented the Nagpur session of the Congress in December 1920 as the venue of a straight fight between Jinnah and Gandhi. It was nothing of the kind. Jinnah was not the major figure in that historic drama which changed the course of Indian history. After the Nagpur session, Jinnah had literally become a political orphan. Most of the Indian politicians, who Edwin Montagu had described as the 'giants of Indian politics'[1] in his diary in 1917, had three years later suddenly shrunk to pygmies. Annie Besant, Tej Bahadur Sapru, Srinivasa Sastri, Ramaswami Aiyar, B.N. Basu, Hasan Imam and others found themselves in the position of generals whose troops had deserted them. Most of them were victims of the Gandhian deluge, and had resigned themselves to their fate. Jinnah was not, however, the man to accept defeat so easily. This was partly because of his grit and partly because unlike most Moderate leaders he had an option. For seven years he had nurtured the All India Muslim League. As recently as September 1920, he had presided over its special session at Calcutta. Since 1913, when he formally joined it, he had been able to build a commanding position for himself in the League in alliance with a small radical group headed by the Raja of Mahmudabad, Wazir Hasan and Mazhar-ul-Haq. They had succeeded in pulling the League out of its conservative, pro-British and anti-Hindu grooves and made its 1916 accord with the Congress possible. It was this accord which had given Jinnah his high standing in both the Congress and the Muslim League. What Jinnah could not foresee was that the dominance of his north Indian friends in the Muslim League would be shortlived. The Raja of Mahmudabad, the leader of this group, was one of the biggest landowners in UP and therefore highly vulnerable to official pressure. This became clear when the government put the screws on him to wean him from having any truck with agitational politics. The Raja decided to save his estate, and both he and his henchman, Wazir Hasan, beat a retreat from active politics. In any case they had no place in the Muslim League when it embraced the Khilafat cause and non-cooperation which were the main political issues in 1920.

This was not the first time that Jinnah had to fight for his political survival. In 1908 Morley's announcement in parliament on separate electorates had confronted him with a dilemma: he had to choose between the Congress and the League, between his principles and political expediency on the vexed issue of separate electorates. As we have already seen, he adopted Fabian tactics and played his cards skilfully. During the next five years, from 1914 to 1919, he carved a place for himself in the highest echelons of both the Congress and the League.

II

Deeply embittered as he was by his humiliation at Nagpur and his utter isolation in nationalist politics in the beginning of 1921, Jinnah decided to put on a brave face. Many years later he compared politics to a game of chess. Grim as the situation was in 1921, he acted with cool calculation. He saw that Gandhi had captured the imagination of the people for the time being and it was no use denouncing him publicly. He rejected overtures from the government and some of his friends in Bombay who were forming an 'Anti-Non-Cooperation Society'. Six weeks after the Nagpur Congress, while speaking at Bombay on the death anniversary of Gokhale, he described Gandhi as a 'great man' and said that he had 'more regard for him than for anyone else', but considered his programme impractical. 'If they were going to regulate everything in their country by the doctrine of non-violent non-cooperation, he was afraid they were forgetting human nature ... Gandhi's programme was based on the doctrine of soul force and it was an essentially spiritual movement .... It was not a political programme though it had for its object the political goal of the country .... Not one in a million can carry out Mr Gandhi's doctrine which has its sole arbiter ...'[2]

Eased out of both the main political parties, Jinnah had to find a new role for himself on the sidelines of Indian politics. He was no longer one of the arbiters of events, but he could play the role of a mediator between Gandhi and the government. For this he needed a reorientation of his political stance and to establish new channels of communication. He needed to renew contacts with his Moderate friends whom he had been neglecting. In the heyday of his popularity in 1918 he had clashed head-on with Lord Chelmsford and with Lord Willingdon, the Governor of Bombay, and incurred their bitter hostility. Never again was he to commit such an indiscretion. In the summer of 1921, while he was in London, he sought an interview with Montagu, urged him to defuse the political crisis and offered his own services for this purpose. Montagu immediately relayed Jinnah's views at some length to Lord Reading who had recently succeeded Lord Chelmsford as Viceroy. Montagu wrote to Reading that Jinnah wanted 'to throw himself into a peace movement.... Though rather small for such colossal boots, the role of a Botha is to him attractive'.[3] He advised the Viceroy to grant an interview to Jinnah when he returned to India. The interview took place on 1 November 1921. Within six weeks came the opportunity for mediation which Jinnah was seeking. He became one of the three secretaries of a conference of 300-odd political leaders, mostly Moderate politicians, who assembled in Bombay in the last week of December 1921 and called upon the government to give up its repressive policy, and at the same time urged the Congress to abandon non-cooperation to pave the way for a Round Table Conference. A few days earlier, Jinnah had visited Ahmedabad to meet Gandhi who, after his initial favourable reaction, demanded fuller information about the date and composition of the proposed conference and insisted on the presence of the Ali brothers. It seemed to Jinnah and his fellow mediators at the time that Gandhi's intransigence had wrecked the conference. Little did they know that nearly a month before, when they had met in Bombay, the proposal for a truce and a Round Table Con-ference had been scotched in London. Originally mooted by Madan Mohan Malaviya, it had struck an answering chord in Lord Reading who was anxious to avoid a *hartal* and hostile demonstration when the Prince of Wales visit-ed Calcutta in the third week of December. The Viceroy felt that if the British cabinet gave him a free hand quickly enough, he could transform the political scene in India. It was a race against time, but late on the evening of 18 December, in a long cable to Montagu, he unfolded his plan.

Reading to Montagu, 18 December, 9.40 pm

The situation is now developing very rapidly. Time is very short. As the Prince of Wales arrives on 24th, I leave Calcutta on the 22nd and if anything is to be arranged it must be by the 22nd .... Immediate objective is to prevent trouble or demonstration ... when His Royal Highness arrives ....The proclamation of volunteers ... and the consequent demonstrations and arrests have created a state of tension which although non-violent at present is nevertheless causing great excitement throughout the country .... The policy of merely enforcing the law is of course negative.

At this moment I am not myself prepared to go further than to say that I can conceive proposals for the amendment of the present Act [of 1919] with the objectives of improving the constitutional machinery and advancing on the road to ultimate goal of Dominion Status. But yet I do see that the pace is quickening ...[4]

Prime Minister Lloyd George was not in England when the Viceroy's cable arrived, but Montagu was able to arrange a meeting of senior members of the coalition government, including Curzon and Churchill. Their reaction to the Viceroy's proposal was one of total disbelief and dismay. They rejected the idea of a conference with Gandhi and other political leaders; they would not compromise the whole policy of the government and endanger British rule in India in order to ensure a good reception for the Prince of Wales.

The Viceroy's plea for a truce with Gandhi and the Congress at this time indicates that as 1921 drew to a close, a sense of impending crisis was pervading the highest echelons of British administration in India. Sir George Lloyd warned Montagu: 'I feel the position is really grave .... I have never until now felt that the situation was fundamentally so dangerous'.[5] A few days later he warned the Viceroy that it would soon be no longer possible to keep the army and the police from political infection. The fortnightly reports from the chief secretaries to the Home Department at Delhi in January and February 1922 were suffused with anxiety. Sir Harcourt Butler, Governor of UP, was worried about the possibility of a Muslim rising.

The British sensed a new hostility towards themselves in legislatures, towns, even in the countryside. A British historian has described 1920–21 as 'probably the worst moment for Britain's imperial rulers ... between the Mutiny and 1942'.[6] We learn from the British cabinet papers that, in February 1922, Prime Minister Lloyd George considered it necessary to draw the attention of his cabinet colleagues to 'the demoralization of opinion among civil servants and members of the European community in India'. These reactions in official circles at the highest levels confirm the impression gleaned from contemporary nationalist sources that, early in 1922, the non-cooperation movement was on the crest of a rising wave.

All this was to change suddenly. On 7 February a clash occurred between a procession of Congress and Khilafat volunteers and the police at Chauri Chaura, a small village in Gorakhpur district in the United Provinces, in which the police station was burnt down; among the twenty-two victims of the mob fury was the young son of the police sub-inspector. The news of the outrage was a bolt from the blue for Gandhi. He came to the conclusion that the atmosphere in the country was too explosive for a mass movement and decided to revoke his plans for launching civil disobedience. The fact is that even before the tragedy at Chauri Chaura he had been disturbed by the news of sporadic violence at several places and the spirit of violence permeating the non-cooperation movement. He regarded non-violence as a fundamental principle on which there could be no compromise. He consulted such members of the Congress Working Committee as were not imprisoned and convened a meeting of the All India Congress Committee and obtained their approval for the suspension of civil disobedience. His colleagues and followers in the Congress and Khilafat organizations were stunned. By unilaterally abandoning civil disobedience he had thrown away the strongest weapon in the armoury of satyagraha. The British authorities heaved a sigh of relief. They did what they had not dared to do for three years: arrested Gandhi, tried him and sentenced him to six years' imprisonment.

III

Suspension of civil disobedience by Gandhi in the wake of the Chauri Chaura incident in February 1922 was a bitter pill for his followers, but it was manna from heaven for Jinnah. He saw it as a vindication of the stand he had taken at the Nagpur Congress in December 1920. Had he not warned that it was impossible to keep a mass movement non-violent? When Gandhi came down to Bombay from Bardoli for discussions with Moderate leaders after his decision to withdraw civil disobedience, Jinnah, who had so far been deferential to Gandhi in public, for once forgot his good manners. Jayakar recorded in his diary on 9 February 1922: 'Gandhi in Bombay on invitation from us. Spent nearly whole day in conference with him .... Jinnah's and Wadia's treatment of Gandhi was most discourteous, but he [Gandhi] replied with great veneration especially to Wadia'.[7] A week later, Jayakar recorded: 'Jinnah came out strongly against Gandhi and desired to form a new party. Natarajan and I declined to join'.[8]

While the country was yet to recover from the shock of the revocation of civil disobedience, Gandhi's arrest and trial, Jinnah was trying to form a new political party. Any hope he had of filling the political vacuum caused by Gandhi's absence from the scene was not to be realized. Jinnah's Moderate friends in Bombay did not share his calculation that the collapse of non-cooperation would finish the Congress as a party and Gandhi as its leader.

Jinnah failed to form a new nationalist party, but he had a second string to his bow; he could revive the Muslim League which he had been sedulously nurturing since 1913. Indeed, he had presided at Calcutta in September 1920 at its special session which accepted Gandhi's non-cooperation programme. Three months later, in December 1920, the decision was confirmed at the Nagpur session of the League. Jinnah did not attend the Nagpur session of the League; he knew that his voice would be a voice in the wilderness. The Muslim League had also fallen in line with Gandhi's programme and indeed had become a virtual adjunct to it. No session of the League was held in 1922. In March 1923 Jinnah made a valiant effort to convene a session at Lucknow and had his friend, G.M. Bhurgri, elected president. The meeting was marred by a clash between the old guard of the Muslim League and the Khilafatists led by Dr Ansari. The latter were averse to abandoning the programme of non-cooperation, while Jinnah and his supporters wanted to steer the League back to its traditional grooves of constitutional politics.

Jinnah's efforts to recover the ground he had lost three years earlier were thwarted, but luckily for him the political situation took a hopeful turn with imminent elections to the legislatures under the Act of 1919. A strong group in favour of ending the boycott of legislatures emerged in the Congress. It was headed by C.R. Das and Motilal Nehru. Born lawyers and orators, they had reluctantly concurred with the boycott of councils in 1920, but two years later, when mass civil disobedience was no longer on the Congress agenda, they argued that the only way to keep up the spirit of resistance to the government was to enter the legislatures set up under the constitution, not to work it, but to expose its limited and irresponsible character. Finding themselves in a minority in the Gaya Congress, Das and Nehru founded a new party, the Swaraj Party, within the Congress which accepted the Congress creed and the principle of non-cooperation but favoured entry into legislatures. They conceded that the legislatures, as they were constituted by the British government, did not give real power to the people, but they believed that the legislatures could be used as instruments of constitutional warfare. If they could muster sufficient strength to reject official bills and refuse supplies, the government would be compelled to use its special powers or to give in to the verdict of the legislature; thus through 'continuous, consistent obstruction' they could turn the councils from a tool in the hands of the Imperial government into a thorn in its side. The Swarajists had to face strong opposition in the Congress from those who did not favour any change in the programme prescribed by Gandhi, but as the general election drew near, there was a compromise and the Swarajists were allowed to contest the elections. Jinnah, who was closely observing the situation, also decided to contest. His friend Sir Purshotamdas wrote to Sir Sivaswami Aiyar: 'Jinnah is standing from the Mohammedans of Bombay city. His policies are the same as before, and I do not think he belongs either to the Swarajists or [to the] Khilafatists'.[9] Jinnah did not really need the support of any political party. He had been elected from the Muslim reserved constituency to the Imperial Legislative Council, and he could safely stand from it again, even though the franchise was much wider. He easily won the election; his two opponents withdrew before polling day. Little did he know that the focus of politics was about to shift to the legislatures, a political forum in which he was at home, and his victory would not only break his political isolation, but enable him to occupy a pivotal position on the national stage.

Chapter 8

IN THE COUNCIL CHAMBER

Gandhi was in jail, and his non-cooperation movement had been in abeyance for six months, but in the general election the Swarajists and Khilafatists, who fought it in his name, swept the polls. The Moderate leaders, some of them veterans of the pre-Gandhian era, were routed. Surendranath Banerjea, one of the founding fathers of the Congress and the hero of the partition of Bengal, was defeated by 'an amiable doctor [B.C. Roy] whose name was known chiefly to his numerous patients'.[1] Luckily for Jinnah, he had a safe constituency in Bombay city which was reserved for Muslims. The two Swarajist candidates, who had ventured to oppose him, beat a retreat before the election. Jinnah had considered it prudent not to defy the boycott of legislatures by the Congress in 1920. After three years in the wilderness he was back on the political stage. He was able to collect under his wing sixteen members who hailed from different provinces under the umbrella of a new political party, the 'Independent Party'. They included his friend, Sir Purshotamdas Thakurdas, Kasturbhai Lalji, the Ahmedabad mill-owner, B.C. Pal, a firebrand of the agitation against the partition of Bengal, who had since mellowed into a Moderate politician, K.C. Neogy, a young upcoming politician from Dacca, and venerable Madan Mohan Malaviya who did not join the Swaraj Party even though his sympathies were with it. But most of the other members of Jinnah's party were political nonentities, such as Harchandrai Vishindas, Sardar Mutalik, K.K. Nambiar, K. Rama Iyengar, Ramachandra Rao and Ranglal Jodia, until they were elected to the Central Legislative Assembly. They hailed from different walks of life.

They included landlords, merchants and moneyed men who commanded enough local influence to get elected as 'Independents'. Jinnah's party had only two Muslim members — Jinnah himself and G.M. Bhurgri who died soon afterwards. It was scarcely a political party as it is commonly understood. Its members had not fought the election on a common ticket; they owed their success to their personal influence and effort. They came together after the election to be able to pull some weight in the legislature, and accepted Jinnah as their leader because of his stature as an all-India figure and his reputation as an able and secular politician.

The Central Legislative Assembly in the 1920s was a very different body from the Imperial Legislative Council in which Jinnah had sat amidst an overwhelming majority of official and European members, with the Viceroy in the chair. In the 'reformed' Central Legislative Assembly, under the Act of 1919, the number of British officials and their Indian nominees had been reduced, but they still formed one-third of the strength of the House. It had wider powers of debate than those of the old Imperial Legislative Council, but no more than one-seventh of the budget was votable by it, and the Viceroy could veto resolutions passed by it, and certify as law a measure rejected by it. The provinces were governed under a hybrid system, known as dyarchy, which entrusted some departments to the control of popular ministers and left the others, such as law and order and finance, in the hands of officials directly responsible to the British Governor.

II

On 30 January, Sir Frederick Whyte, the President of the Central Legislative Assembly, swore in the members. On the following day the Viceroy, Lord Reading, addressed both the Houses of Legislature, and on 1 February the regular session commenced.

The election had returned a solid bloc of forty-one members of the Swaraj Party which was a wing of the Congress party. 'A notable victory', this is how Lord Reading described the Swarajists' electoral performance and predicted a constitutional deadlock. 'It is quite clear', he wrote to Montagu, 'Swarajists have done exceptionally well. They have completely routed the Liberals and the Moderates in most contests and will be a formidable opposition to the government both in the provincial councils and the central legislature'.[2] To Lord Olivier, the successor of Montagu, he wrote, 'upon the extension of the reforms, they [the Swarajists] will claim to have mandate and will presumably vote solidly and will doubtless have the support of most of the remaining non-officials, probably with the exception of the Europeans and some few Indians. They will be able to carry a resolution in support of the immediate extension of reforms .... It seems pretty certain that if we can give nothing better than the negative answer, there will be a persistent and systematic obstruction to the Budget.'[3] Motilal Nehru, the leader of the Swaraj Party, was indeed daring to challenge the government, but had to contend with a solid bloc of forty official and nominated members.

C.R. Das, the President of the Swaraj Party, and Motilal Nehru had failed to draw Jinnah into their party, but they persuaded him to agree to form the Nationalist Party, a joint front of the Swaraj Party and the Independent Party. With the backing of Madan Mohan Malaviya and the addition of Moderate members, the new party reached the strength of seventy-five members, enough to outvote the government. Thus, thanks to the cooperation of Jinnah and Malaviya, the Swaraj Party obtained the support of nearly thirty members. Jinnah's Independent Party, consisting of seventeen members, held the balance between the forty-one-member Swaraj Party and the official bloc of about the same number.

The second Central Legislative Assembly, under the Act of 1919, was a colourful body. It had some outstanding political leaders who would have made a mark in any parliamentary body in the world. Sir Frederick Whyte, the first full-time president of the Assembly, was noted for his dignity, impartiality and tenacious memory which enabled him to recognize every member by name and face almost on the opening day. The leader of the House was Sir Malcolm Hailey, the Home Member of the Government of India, who was noted for his great experience, astuteness and skill in debate. He was soon to be succeeded by the more genial Sir Alexander Muddiman. Motilal Nehru, Leader of the Opposition, had a towering personality. A renowned lawyer, he seemed to be in his element in the legislature. He kept a vigilant watch and a firm hand on his party, which came to be instantly recognized in and outside the House as a disciplined assault force. Madan Mohan Malaviya's immaculate dress, noble bearing and silvery eloquence won him the respect of all sections of the Assembly. However, his deeply religious outlook and strict orthodoxy, which gave him his unique hold on the Hindu masses, made his politics suspect to Muslims. Bepin Chandra Pal was one of the heroes of the partition of Bengal, but in 1924 he was an extinct volcano. V.J. Patel, the de facto deputy leader of the Swaraj Party, became a thorn in the flesh of the executive, first as an unrelenting critic, and then as the president of the Assembly. There was, however, no doubt that one of the most striking figures in this Assembly was Jinnah. We have a pen-portrait of Jinnah on his feet in the Central Legislative Assembly by British historian Percival Spear, as he saw him in 1924:

> He was then important because his group held the balance between the Swarajists and the government. Thin to leanness and icily handsome, he affected at that time an overpowering sartorial elegance in the western manner. His voice was quiet, his gestures, his manner Olympian and aloof, as if he was surveying a world of insects or distastefully prodding with a needle some lifeless exhibits. Perhaps his manner suited the occasion by repaying to the government benches the disdain with which they had until recently regarded the nationalists.[4]

On 8 February 1924, within ten days of the opening of the session of the second Central Legislative Assembly, a resolution was moved by Dewan Bahadur Rangachariar, a non-Swarajist member, demanding a Royal Commission for the revision of the Government of India Act so as to secure for India the status of a Dominion within the British Empire. More important than this resolution was an amendment to it moved by Motilal Nehru, proposing that a new constitution should be framed by 'a representative Round Table Conference' and approved by a newly elected Central Legislative Assembly before it was embodied in a statute by the British Parliament. Sir Malcolm Hailey opposed the resolution and catalogued the numerous interests which blocked India's progress, such as those of the Princely states, European commerce, the Secretary of State's services and religious minorities in the country. Hailey affirmed that the British Government was the sole judge of the manner and measure of constitutional advance to be made, and that the next step — the appointment of a Royal Commission — according to the preamble of the Act of 1919 under which the country was governed, was not due until 1929.

Motilal Nehru questioned Hailey's premises. 'Now, Sir', he said in his maiden speech, 'our answer, straight and clear, as unequivocal as the Preamble, is that the Preamble is bad, the whole Act [of 1919] is bad .... [and is] devised to postpone, to stifle and to suppress the natural desire [for freedom] in the country.' He said he had deliberately toned down his amendment to secure the cooperation of other parties in the Assembly. 'We have come here', he told the Treasury benches, 'to offer our cooperation, non-cooperators as we are, if you will care to cooperate with us. That is why we are here. If you agree to have it, we are your men, if you do not, we shall, like men, stand upon our rights and continue to be non-cooperators.'[5]

Jinnah supported Motilal's amendment, in the drafting of which he had a hand. Seventy-six members voted in favour of it and forty-eight against it. The latter included the compact bloc of officials, nominated non-officials, Europeans and a few Indian members who were always at the beck and call of the official whip. This was the first and most spectacular defeat inflicted by the Nationalist Party on the government and it was made possible by the cooperation of the Independents and Moderates with the Swaraj Party. Thanks to this cooperation, the first four budget demands were rejected in their entirety; the Finance Bill was thrown out on its introduction, and again on the following day, after it had been returned by the Viceroy for reconsideration. The Assembly despite official opposition passed a number of resolutions demanding the release of political prisoners, the repeal of repressive laws (especially the Bengal Regulation III of 1818) and the imposition of a countervailing duty on South African coal imported into India. Later in the year the government suffered a crushing defeat when the Assembly rejected the proposals of the Lee Commission on the superior Civil Services in India.

Jinnah was wholeheartedly cooperating with Motilal Nehru, and his speeches were infused with an ardent and defiant nationalism which was reminiscent of his utterances in 1918. When one of the official spokesmen, Sir Charles Innes, remarked that, thanks to British rule, India had not known chaos and anarchy for a century, Jinnah replied:

> I grant it that it is a good argument, as it goes ... We have not seen the horrors of chaos and anarchy, but what have we seen, I ask again? Sir, the horror of being a disarmed people; we have seen the horror of being kept out of that ring of monopoly in the administration and the government of our country. We have .... experienced the horror of helplessness in the defence of our own country .... We have seen the horror of keeping a large body of people in darkness, denying them even elementary education .... After a hundred years' rule, can you compare your education policy with any civilised country .... There is one way and one way alone for India to free herself from these horrors, and it is to replace that irresponsible bureaucracy by a Cabinet responsible to the Legislature of the representatives of the people .... India today is in a very critical condition. Believe me I do not say this as words of menace or threat. But let me tell you, India

is determined to win her freedom, and the measure and time, either you determine in a reasonable spirit and or else, she will determine for herself.[6]

In a speech on the Indianization of the officers' cadre in the army, Jinnah pointed out that the government was selecting annually ten young Indian men for training in the military academy in Sandhurst, and that at this rate it would take 200 years to complete the process of Indianizing the cadre of officers of two divisions of the Indian army. Denouncing the Bengal Criminal Law (Amendment) Ordinance, he asked the British officials to 'come down from your high pedestals and discuss with us what India wants and meet us reasonably.'[7]

Referring to the habit of official spokesmen putting forward the excuse of 'public opinion', and differences among Indians for all their acts of omission or commission, Jinnah said, 'I ask the Government — do they always do a thing or not do it because there is difference of opinion in the country? They only do it when it suits them. As a friend of mine once said, if out of 325 millions there should be one man in India who agreed with the Government of India, that was public opinion.'[8] Occasionally he sent the House into peals of laughter, as when he said, 'I am always afraid of Government when they agree with me. I have great regard for my friend, the Home Member, but when he agrees with me, I sometimes say to myself — "perhaps I am wrong."'

III

On 25 February 1925, when Motilal Nehru moved a resolution on behalf of the Swaraj Party rejecting the demand for the expenses of the Railway Board, Jinnah stood up to oppose it. He said he had made a mistake during the previous year and would no longer be a party to the 'Swarajist policy of obstruction and wrecking the constitution', and that he would determine his attitude to each measure that came before the Assembly on its merits.

With the secession of Jinnah's Independent Party, Motilal's resolution was rejected.

Three weeks later, when the Finance Member sought permission to introduce the Finance Bill, the Swaraj Party opposed it, but was again unsuccessful. The results of the divisions on the budget ceased to be predictable as they had been in 1924, when the Swaraj Party with the support of the Independents had carried everything before it. For example, on 6 March the motion on cotton excise was carried against the government. But on the following day, a motion moved by a member of the Independent Party on 'Taxes on Income' was defeated by forty-one to sixty votes, the Swarajists and four Independent members forming the minority, while the majority of the Independent members walked into the government lobby. On 12 March, on a 'cut' proposed by a Swarajist member under the head 'Salt', the Independents voted with the official bloc to defeat it, though Jinnah himself abstained from voting.

There were several occasions during this session on which the Swarajists and Independents voted together, such as the rejection of the travelling allowances of the members of the Governor-General's Executive Council, the abolition of the Bengal Ordinance, and the abolition of separate compartments in railway trains for Europeans. Nevertheless, the fact remained that the Nationalist Party, which had banded together most of the elected Indian members of the Legislative Assembly, had disintegrated.

The Swarajists were taken aback by Jinnah's sudden withdrawal of support. Their victories in the Central Legislative Assembly in 1924 had boosted their morale, and strengthened their position in the Congress and the country, and they had intended to continue the pressure on the government. They were not convinced by the arguments which Jinnah gave for his volte-face. As V.J. Patel pointed out, 'the Nationalist Party, by the very constitution under which it came into being, is bound to a policy of obstruction once it is found that the national demands are not conceded'.[9]

Motilal Nehru was furious at the turn of events. For a whole year he and Jinnah had worked together and the Nationalist Party had kept the government on the defensive. Now, suddenly, the secession of the Independent Party had left the Swaraj Party in the lurch. During the discussion on the Finance Bill, there were sharp exchanges between the erstwhile partners of the coalition on the floor of the House:

M.A. Jinnah:	That was my position. You reversed the policy.
Motilal Nehru:	Who reversed it?
M.A. Jinnah:	Your Party.
Motilal Nehru:	Was it reversed by the members of the Swaraj Party or of the Independent Party?
M.A. Jinnah:	I am not responsible for it.
Motilal Nehru:	You sent in your resignation.
M.A. Jinnah:	No. Therefore, Sir, it is no use our friends talking of what happened last year. Do you want to wash dirty linen on the floor of this House?
Motilal Nehru:	You are doing it.
M.A. Jinnah:	Because you misrepresent things you are forcing me. I refrained from doing it, but you repeatedly asked, 'What did you do last year?'
Motilal Nehru:	Go on, wash your dirty linen ....
M.A. Jinnah:	.... But I tell you that you are not going to get me to agree to pursue a policy of obstruction ... to pursue a policy of wrecking and recklessness by merely resorting to these tactics.
Motilal Nehru:	We do not depend on you.[10]

Clearly, Jinnah's critics did not make allowances for his political and personal compulsions. He was leading a heterogeneous party whose members had nothing in common except a nominal allegiance to his leadership. Some of them represented commercial and industrial interests and could not afford to oppose the government constantly; others were essentially apolitical individuals dependent on the patronage of local British officials in their provinces. Apart from the problem of keeping his flock together, Jinnah had to take into account the result of his association with the Swarajists on his own political future. The Swarajists formed the dominant group in the coalition. Jinnah feared that his own party might be reduced to an adjunct of the Swaraj Party and he himself as a junior partner of Motilal Nehru who had hogged all the publicity for the victories of the Nationalist Party. Whatever Jinnah's motives for his decision, there was no doubt that his break with the Swarajists was politically a masterstroke. It was perceived as such by Sir Alexander Muddiman, Leader of the House in the Legislative Assembly, who, in a note dated 31 March 1925 to the Viceroy, wrote that Jinnah's breach with the Swaraj Party had 'put him in a position of considerable importance and he came forward and grasped the position with firmness ....' He rated Jinnah as 'the best debater in the House and a far better tactician than his rival [Motilal Nehru]'.[11]

During the remaining years of the second Central Legislative Assembly, Jinnah held the balance between the Swarajists and the government. With a small heterogeneous party, only an astute politician could have achieved such a position. It was a tactical triumph for Jinnah but it concealed a strategic defeat. Ever since his appearance before the Joint Select Committee of Parliament in 1919, he had been making vigorous efforts for the liberalization of the Act of 1919 so as to secure more powers for popular representatives in the legislatures, both in the provinces and at the centre. He had made his plea to Secretary of State Montagu and Viceroy Lord Reading in 1921 and taken every opportunity to press it forward. He had joined in the formation of the Nationalist Party to press for the same demand in the Legislative Assembly. The cooperation of the Swarajists, Independents and Moderates had created a difficult situation for the Government of India throughout 1924, but in the following year it was rescued from it by Jinnah himself. Sir Frederick Whyte, President of the Legislative Assembly who in his report of 30 March 1925 to the Viceroy, put it

> The Independent Party under Mr. Jinnah's leadership gave the constitution a new lease of life .... The [constitutional] deadlock, which seemed inevitable after the General Elections of 1923, actually arrested constitutional progress in 1924, but has for the moment been removed in 1925. If the Independent Party can maintain its freedom of action and will consent to use its power in the Assembly in the spirit displayed in the past session, the constitution may continue to function not unsuccessfully till its term in 1929.[12]

The almost united action of the elected members under the umbrella of the Nationalist Party had inflicted a series of defeats on the government in 1924 and the Viceroy had been compelled to enact legislation by certification against the decision of the legislature. Even supplies had been refused and the Viceroy had to use his veto powers.

By pulling the rug from under Motilal Nehru's feet, Jinnah had been able to assert his independence and occupy his pivotal position in the legislature. 'The outstanding feature of the Delhi session was', to quote Sir Frederick Whyte, 'Mr. Jinnah's personal ascendancy over the Chamber .... As leader of the Independent Party, he was arbiter in many important decisions ...'[13] Whatever satisfaction Jinnah's enhanced status and prestige may have given him, it had consequences which he had not foreseen nor perhaps desired. By easing the pressure on the government he had destroyed whatever chances there were of an early constitutional advance in the provinces and at the centre before the stipulated review in 1929, a consummation which had been nearest to Jinnah's heart since 1919.

Chapter 9

THE COMMUNAL TANGLE

Gandhi's sudden cancellation of the civil disobedience campaign which he was about to launch in February 1922, and the decline of the non-cooperation movement which followed it, had an unexpected fallout: deterioration in Hindu–Muslim relations. The unity between the two communities in the heyday of the non-cooperation movement was now a mere memory. Indian politics acquired a new bitterness. Some Hindu leaders felt that there had been a dangerous awakening in the Muslim masses through the coalescence of the Khilafat and non-cooperation movements, while Muslim politicians wondered whether they had too readily followed the lead of the Indian National Congress in fighting for a new political order in which their interests might not be secure. In such an atmosphere of mutual suspicion and fear, every incident was twisted, and every move of one community became suspect to the other. The *Shuddhi* movement for the reconversion of those Hindus who had embraced Islam and the *Sangathan* movement for the unity of Hindus evoked counterblasts from Muslims in the form of *Tabligh* and *Tanzim* movements.

Gandhi said he did not regret his support to the Khilafat movement. He refuted the charge that he had played with the masses and roused them. 'The awakening of the masses', he wrote, 'was a necessary part of their training. I would do nothing to put the people to sleep again'. However, he felt it was essential to divert this awakening into constructive channels. He expressed his sorrow at the bitterness and bloodshed which he saw around him. He had two main aims in lending support to the Khilafat movement, which, of course, was an exclusively religious movement for the Muslims, to prevent it from turning violent and to draw the Muslim community into the orbit of the nationalist movement. He achieved a great measure of success in his first aim, but not in the second. The 'grand alliance' between the Congress and the Khilafat organizations did not mature into a permanent Hindu–Muslim accord. On the other hand, communal bitterness led to mob violence. The number of serious communal riots rose steeply — there were eleven riots in 1923, eighteen in 1924, six in 1925, and thirty-five in 1926. In a riot in Kohat in September 1924 in the North-West Frontier Province, 155 Hindus were killed and the entire Hindu population was driven out of town and took refuge in Rawalpindi in the Punjab. Anguished by these events, Gandhi undertook a three-week fast in Delhi in the house of Maulana Mahomed Ali, who had been his chief lieutenant in the Khilafat movement. A 'Unity Conference', which drew leaders of all parties, was convened at Delhi within a week of the commencement of the fast. It affirmed the freedom of conscience and religion, condemned the use of compulsion and violence, and passed resolutions to generate goodwill and to dissipate mutual suspicion and fear.

Gandhi's fast had only a momentary effect. But he continued his efforts to educate the people to draw them out of the mental morass into which they had slipped. He devoted a whole issue of his weekly journal, *Young India*, to the analysis of communal tension and violence. He argued that a civilized society which had given up violence as a means of settling individual disputes must also eschew violence for reconciling differences between groups and communities. Disagreements must be resolved by mutual tolerance and compromise, private arbitration, and, in the last resort, by appeals to courts. As he saw it, the points of friction between the two communities were a travesty of religion. Was it religion, he asked, that drove a group of Hindu worshippers to lead a procession noisily when Muslims were praying in a mosque? Was it a religious obligation laid on Muslims to lead cows to slaughter to wound the feelings of their Hindu neighbours? Gandhi believed that there was a desire in both the communities to live in peace, but it was the 'middle-class men' who engineered riots for their own ends, and made *badmashes* (hooligans) their henchmen. In a letter (12 November 1924) to Jawaharlal Nehru, he suggested the formation of 'a flying column' of Hindu and Mohammedan workers who could, at a moment's notice, be deputed to 'afflicted parts for investigation'. If the statements made in the press turned out to be true, 'the culprits should be exposed. If they are false, the newspaper reporters should be brought to book'.[1]

Gandhi's appeals for religious tolerance fell on deaf ears. In May 1925, he said: 'My wings have been clipped and I find myself entirely helpless in this matter. Once upon a time I considered myself a physician who knew the cure .... But I find I can do nothing.' Sometimes he was driven to despair by this issue. 'I see neither Hindus nor Muslims are prepared to try my prescription. If Hindus imagine Swaraj is possible by cutting off from Muslims, they are living in a fool's paradise, and if Muslims dream of the restoration of the Mughal Empire without the support of Hindus, I shall say the same thing for them.'[2]

There was no perceptible improvement in the communal situation. On 20 May 1926, Motilal Nehru wrote to his son:

> The Hindu–Muslim problem is now getting more and more acute. No sooner a riot is suppressed in one town than there is an outburst in another.
> The Ali brothers have completely lost their heads .... Almost all public men have now taken sides. Abul Kalam Azad spent three days with me .... We are trying to form a centre party of such [men] as are still unaffected by communal bias. It is to be non-political and non-party...

The manifesto of the new 'centre party' signed by the veteran Swarajist leader and the young Maulana (who retired from the Khilafat organization of which he was president for the year) propounded unexceptional principles, appeal to reason, just and fair play, but it could not put out the communal fire stoked by religious fanaticism, social tensions, economic rivalries and vested interests of all sorts, including those of the ruling power, which kept the communal cauldron on the boil. The 'centre party', known as the Indian National Union, was still-born and the 1926 elections to the central and provincial legislatures were fought less on issues of public importance than on trivial but emotive issues such as music outside mosques and cow slaughter. In January 1927 Gandhi told a public meeting in Bengal that the Hindu–Muslim problem had 'passed out of human hands into God's hands'.

II

Jinnah did not agree with Gandhi's approach to the communal problem. He advocated Hindu–Muslim unity and considered it a sine qua non for India's progress. In November 1924, three days after the All-Parties Conference was convened by Gandhi, in an interview to the cor-respondent of *The Hindu*, Jinnah said:

> What we want ... is ... mobilization of politically-minded people in India and it must be done purely on political lines and as far as possible religion should be separated from politics. Then alone is it possible for Hindus and Muslims and other communities to work together with one sole burning feeling of patriotism.[3]

Jinnah was jealous of his reputation for freedom from religious bias. In March 1925, when tempers were rising high in the Central Legislative Assembly after his defection from the Swaraj Party, a Swarajist member, Jamnadas Mehta, charged that Jinnah had ceased to be a nationalist leader and had become 'a leader of communal strife'. Jinnah's riposte was sharp. 'I stand here', he said, 'with a clear conscience and I say that I am a nationalist first, a nationalist second and a nationalist last .... I once more appeal to this House, whether you are a Mussalman or a Hindu, for God's sake, do not import the discussion of communal matters in this House and degrade this Assembly, which, we desire, should become a real national Parliament.' It must be said to the credit of the second Legislative Assembly that the leaders of most of the parties represented in it agreed to avoid contentious communal issues.

One wonders whether Jinnah realized that the insulation of the legislative chambers from the communal virus was no solution to the problem the country faced. Unlike Gandhi, Jinnah did not undertake fasts, send mediators to riot-afflicted areas, or write articles on how to combat communal antagonisms. He hardly ever referred to the immediate provocations for communal riots, such as music outside mosques and cow-slaughter, which made people cut each other's throats. He felt the communal problem had to be tackled by the political leaders at a political level. In his speeches he attributed tension between the religious communities to anxieties about their political future and their distrust of each other. He believed that the remedy was a communal pact on the composition of elective bodies in the provinces and at the centre.

At a meeting of a committee appointed by the All-Parties Conference in Delhi in January 1925, with Gandhi in the chair, Jinnah argued that the dispute between Hindus and Mussalmans, on the question of representation in elective bodies and share in government employment, was a dispute 'which had been a terrible monster in the way of the country's progress'. He avowed his own dislike of separate electorates, but stressed the strength of Muslim feeling in their favour. He said that the population basis for representation was not acceptable to the Mussalmans. In short, the solution lay in the sort of approach followed in the Lucknow Pact, of which he had been one of the main architects. In 1916 he had described the Pact as a 'final settlement' between the two communities, but nine years later, he was telling the Hindu leaders that it 'was never intended to be permanent'. He put forward additional demands on behalf of his community, such as ensuring one-third seats for Muslims in the central legislature, reservation for Muslims in government services and Muslim majorities in the Punjab and Bengal legislatures by reservation, and creation of new Muslim-majority provincial administrations in the NWFP and Baluchistan, and in Sind which was to be separated from Bombay.

Jinnah's flat repudiation of the Lucknow Pact astounded the Hindu leaders. They were not convinced by his arguments for his volte-face, but he went on to repeat these demands from the platform of the All India Muslim League at its annual sessions in 1925 and 1926, without evoking any response from the Hindu leaders. It was only in 1927 that circumstances arose in which he was able to produce a plausible constitutional package for rapprochement between the two communities.

Chapter 10

ON CENTRE-STAGE

The communal tension of the post-Khilafat period reached its peak in 1926 and was reflected in the results of the general election held at the end of the year. The Swaraj Party survived it, but it had to face strong opposition from the Hindu Mahasabha and its allied organizations in northern India; in the United Provinces, it lost all the seats it contested for the Central Legislative Assembly except that of Motilal Nehru. The assassination of Swami Shraddhanand by a Muslim fanatic created a sensation and raised the communal temperature. The top leadership of the Congress was deeply concerned, and when the party met for its annual session at Gauhati, it called upon the Working Committee to take immediate steps 'for the removal of the present deplorable differences between Hindus and Mussalmans' and to report to the All-India Congress Committee within three months.

By a strange coincidence, at this time Jinnah had his own reasons to work for a Hindu–Muslim accord. The strength of his party — Independent Party — in the Central Legislative Assembly had been depleted by the communal polarization in the country. In the previous Assembly (1923–26) it was a multi-religious party, consisting of seventeen members, of whom only two, including Jinnah, were Muslims. It held a balance between the main opposition, the Swaraj Party, and the Treasury benches. In the words of Sir Frederick Whyte, the then President of the Assembly, Jinnah occupied a 'commanding position'. All was changed by the 1926 general election; the strength of his party was reduced to ten members of whom only two were Hindus. He could no longer claim to be the leader of a national party, nor could he claim to represent his own community. The Swaraj Party, consisting of thirty-eight members, had six Muslims who, not elected on its ticket, had joined it after the election. Most of the other Muslim members of the Assembly were not attached to any party, and usually voted with the government.

In March 1927, Jinnah made a brilliant move which raised his stock overnight, not only in his own community but in the country. The British Government was expected to announce the appointment of a Royal Commission to undertake a constitutional review of the Reforms Act of 1919. It seemed to Jinnah just the right moment to evolve proposals for a Hindu–Muslim accord as he had done in 1916 when a joint Congress–League scheme had been hammered out for presentation to the British Government.

On 20 March 1927 he convened a conference of Muslim leaders in Delhi. Of the twenty-nine leaders who attended it, sixteen were members of the Legislative Assembly and two were members of the Council of State. Among those present were Dr M.A. Ansari, the eminent Congress leader, and Maulana Mahomed Ali, the Khilafat leader. Jinnah put forward a constitutional package for a Hindu–Muslim accord on the basis of joint electorates, if certain substantial reciprocal concessions were made by the Hindus. These concessions were: separation of Sind from Bombay, introduction of constitutional reforms in Baluchistan and the North-West Frontier Province to bring them on a par with other provinces, ensuring Muslim majorities in the Legislative Councils of the Punjab and Bengal, and ensuring at least one-third representation of Muslims in the Legislative Assembly.[1] When Jinnah had first spelt out these demands to the Congress leaders in January 1925, they had been rejected out of hand. However, in 1927, the Congress was in a more receptive mood because the bitter pill of the sectional Muslim demands, over and above the terms of the Lucknow Pact of 1916, had been sugar-coated by Jinnah with the provision for joint electorates. The Congress leaders considered separate electorates a curse and were prepared to pay almost any price to get rid of them. Separate electorates had been first incorporated by the British Government in the constitutional reforms of 1909 despite opposition from the Congress. Seven years later, the Congress, under the leadership of B.G. Tilak, had reluctantly assented to them in the Lucknow Pact, but the fear that separate electorates would be fatal for national integration remained. It was therefore not surprising that the inclusion of joint electorates in the Delhi Muslim Conference proposals elicited a positive response from Congress leaders and the nationalist press. *The Tribune* (23 March 1927) described it 'as the most important event that has taken place in this country. The Congress Working Committee hastened to welcome the restoration of joint electorates in legislatures in return for certain concessions to the Muslim community. The All-India Congress Committee met in Bombay on 15 May and endorsed the Delhi Muslim Conference proposals. Jinnah was delighted with the Congress response. All that remained now was ratification of his proposals by the annual plenary sessions of the Congress and the Muslim League due to be held at the end of the year. While he planned the strategy for securing the approval of the Muslim League, he felt that a strong and secular Congress leader was needed to preside over the next Congress session to get his proposals through it. He sounded Gandhi through Sarojini Naidu for the choice of Motilal Nehru. On 20 July 1927 Gandhi wrote to Jawaharlal Nehru who was in Europe: 'Sarojini Devi [Naidu] suggested under pressure from (the Maharaja of) Mahmudabad and Mr Jinnah that I should press [your] father to accept the presidential chair (of the Congress) for the coming year.'[2] Motilal Nehru, however, declined the honour on the ground that he was about to leave for Europe to join his son there. Both Gandhi and Motilal Nehru supported Dr Ansari's election to the presidency of the next Congress session.

II

The Hindu Mahasabha welcomed joint electorates. However, it was averse to conceding Muslim demands as a quid pro quo. The Hindu Mahasabha was the first to strike a discordant note, but a graver threat to Jinnah's scheme soon came from his own camp. The Mahasabha's stand gave some Muslim leaders, such as Sir Muhammad Shafi, the president of the Punjab Muslim League, an excuse to back out. He had participated in the Delhi Muslim Conference but was already having second thoughts about its decisions. On 1 May, Shafi declared that Muslims would never accept joint electorates. His example was followed by Sir Abdul Rahim, the president of the Bengal Muslim League, who also declared himself in favour of separate electorates.

The rebellion of the League leaders in two important provinces, the Punjab and Bengal, was a direct challenge to Jinnah's leadership. He took up the gauntlet and convened a meeting of the League Council at Delhi. The rebels, who came to be known as the Shafi faction, challenged the legality of the meeting and walked out. They declared that they would hold a separate session of the All India Muslim League at Lahore. Jinnah had been watching the moves of the rebels with mingled anxiety and contempt. In a letter (6 December 1927) to Saifuddin Kitchlew, the secretary of the All India Muslim League, he wrote that the Muslim League must not 'fall a prey to the reactionary forces of the Punjab which are worked up by interested persons'.[3]

A week later came two manifestos issued by the rebel groups, from the Punjab and Bengal, over the signatures of Muslim League leaders headed by Sir Abdul Qaiyum and A.H. Ghuznavi respectively. In a press statement, Jinnah ridiculed them as men 'who have spent a great part of their lives roundabout the Secretariat seeking official favours. These two manifestos are obviously a put-up job'. He exhorted his co-religionists not to 'lay themselves open to be auctioned to the highest bidder' as the signatories of these manifestos suggested, and not to 'tread the path leading to their perfidy'.[4] Evidently, Jinnah was hinting at the British inspiration behind the dissident groups. We now know from the cables exchanged between Delhi and London that the Government of India was an anxious but not a disinterested observer of the making and unmaking of Jinnah's proposals for a Hindu–Muslim accord.

Viceroy to Secretary of State for India, 26 March 1927

> The meeting of Muslims held on 20th in Delhi was only an informal conference. I understand no definite resolution was put and no vote was taken. The conclusions were communicated semi-officially to the Press by Jinnah.
>
> Jinnah finds his position as nominal leader of what is practically a Mahomedan party [in the Central Assembly] most precarious. Some form of compromise with the Hindus is not only demanded by his political beliefs, but is probably an essential condition of his retaining position as a political leader.
>
> A new phase of discussion has no doubt been initiated.... It would be premature to assume and certainly dangerous to say that the Muslims have accepted the principle of joint electorates.[5]

In another communication to Secretary of State Lord Birkenhead, Viceroy Irwin explained that the joint electorates were not so much 'dangerous' for Indian Muslims as for the British Raj. 'They [Muslims] are, after all, our best friends and, however impartial it may be our duty to be, we are not called upon, as I see it, to throw over our friends for new allies, [the Hindus], whose friendship has been a very uncertain quantity.'[6]

III

While Indian politics were in a flux, a new strand was added by the announcement in November 1927 of the appointment of a Royal Commission for a review of the constitution as stipulated in the Government of India

Act of 1919. The members of the Commission, with the exception of its chairman, Sir John Simon, were all second flight men; the junior member of the Commission, as Simon describes him in his book, *Retrospect*, was Clement Attlee, the future Prime Minister of Britain, but in 1927 a back-bencher in the House of Commons. What hurt the nationalist feeling was that no Indian had been included in the Commission, which thus came to be looked upon as an inquisition by foreigners into India's fitness for self-government. Jinnah had been urging the Viceroy to ensure that at least two Indians were included in the Commission, but his advice fell on deaf ears. His strong feelings on the implied insult to India were to come out later in one of his rare angry outbursts: 'Jallianwala was physical butchery. The Simon Commission is the butchery of our soul.'[7] Meanwhile, on 16 November, a joint manifesto was issued by the Indian National Congress, the All-India Muslim League, the Liberal Federation, the Hindu Mahasabha, the Chamber of Commerce and the Mill Owners' Association, declaring their resolve not to 'take any part or share in the work of the [Simon] Commission as at present constituted'.[8]

Jinnah's decision to boycott the Simon Commission was opposed in his own community by the Shafi group and other dissidents in the Muslim League who argued that it was in Muslims' interest to cooperate with the Simon Commission in order to get the best possible deal from it. They accused Jinnah and his adherents of sacrificing Muslim interests. They announced that they would not attend the annual League session at Calcutta, but would hold a separate session at Lahore at the same time.

The split in the All India Muslim League was now open. Undeterred, Jinnah went ahead to make the Calcutta session a success. He was able to draw a large and representative gathering of delegates from all parts of India, including the Punjab and Bengal. Mahomed Yakub, deputy speaker of the Central Assembly, presided and among those who attended it were Maulana Mahomed Ali, M.C. Chagla, Saifuddin Kitchlew, Sir Ali Imam, Maulana Shaukat Ali,

Yakub Hasan, Maulana Zafar Ali Khan and Abul Kalam Azad. Dr Ansari came to the Calcutta League meeting after presiding over the Congress session at Madras. Two important resolutions were passed by the plenary session. One was for the adoption of the Delhi Muslim Conference proposals which had just been ratified by the Indian National Congress at Madras; it also authorized the Council of the All India Muslim League to confer with other parties for a constitution in which the interests of the Muslim community were adequately safeguarded. The other resolution called for the boycott of the Simon Commission.

A significant feature of this session was the presence of Hindu Mahasabha leaders, especially Madan Mohan Malaviya. Invited to address the delegates by the president, Malaviya described the appointment of the Simon Commission as a 'God-given opportunity' to rouse the people of India to 'a sense of duty and responsibility'.

On the last day of the session, Jinnah delivered a fighting speech:

> A constitutional war has been declared on Great Britain. Negotiations for a settlement are not to come from our side. Let the Government sue for peace. We are denied equal partnership. We will resist the new doctrine to the best of our power .... I welcome Pandit Malaviya and I welcome the hand of fellowship extended to us by Hindu leaders from the platforms of the Congress and the Hindu Mahasabha. For, to me this offer is more valuable than any concession which the British Government can make. Let us grasp the hand of fellowship.[9]

IV

Not since 1918 had Jinnah spoken with such patriotic fervour from a public platform. He had good reasons to do so. In December 1927, his proposals for a Hindu–Muslim accord had been ratified by the Indian National

Congress as well as the All India Muslim League; both had also decided to boycott the Simon Commission. He had overcome the challenge of the pro-British factions of his party in the Punjab and Bengal. In particular, the Shafi group had been exposed as what it was, a splinter group, seemingly propped up by the authorities. However, the annual session of the League at Calcutta was a spectacular success; it confirmed Jinnah's leadership and his policies by re-electing him as working president for the next three years.

The year 1927 was a momentous one for Jinnah, a year of solid achievement. With his proposals for a Hindu–Muslim accord, he had bounced back on to the centre-stage of Indian politics in the role of a 'Muslim Gokhale'. His task was cut out for him — to keep up the pressure on the government through the boycott of the Simon Commission and to frame and formally present a joint Hindu–Muslim scheme for reforms to the British Government Little did he know that all his calculations were about to be upset by unexpected turns and twists of national politics.

Chapter 11

DEAD END

The Indian National Congress and the Muslim League both had called for the boycott of the Simon Commission at their annual meetings in December 1927, but the Congress had gone further and decided to respond to the challenge of the arrogant Secretary of State, Lord Birkenhead, in a speech in the House of Lords on 24 November, 1927:

> I have twice in the three years, during which I have been the Secretary of State, invited our critics in India to put forward their own suggestions for a constitution, to indicate to us the form which in their judgement any reform of the constitution should take. That offer is still open.[1]

A month later, at its Madras session, the Congress authorized its Working Committee to confer with other parties to draft a 'Swaraj constitution for India'. Invitations were issued to twenty-nine organizations, including the All India Muslim League, the Hindu Mahasabha and the Central Sikh League. An All-Parties Conference met at Delhi on 12 February 1928, with Dr Ansari, the Congress president, in the chair. It continued its deliberations on the outline of a constitution for ten days. Jinnah was present and found that the representatives of the Hindu Mahasabha opposed the Delhi Muslim Conference proposals of March 1927. They rejected the demand for the creation of more Muslim-majority provinces even with the quid pro quo of the joint electorates for the Hindus. Jinnah sensed that the attempt to draft a constitution with the consent of so many parties, which had hardly anything in common, had little chance of success. His scheme of

Dead End ❧ 109

Hindu–Muslim accord, which he had been protecting from Extremists of both the communities throughout 1927, was in jeopardy. He believed that he had produced a balanced constitutional package; if the Muslims had secured major concessions in the form of additional Muslim-majority provinces, the Hindus had also got joint electorates, which they had all along demanded. From the outset he had been saying that his constitutional package was to be accepted or rejected *in toto* as any tinkering would destroy it. Even in the Calcutta session of the All India Muslim League, in which an overwhelming majority of delegates had followed his lead and endorsed his proposals, Jinnah had not concealed his nervousness about the ultimate response from his own community, when he said:

> We have got a majority in this House, but still shall we be able to carry the majority in the country? Nothing will please me more, but, at the same time, it will be fair to say that I am not so sure that I am satisfied that the majority of Mussalmans throughout the country are in favour of it. That remains to be decided, and it will be our business to try our best to make the people understand and convince them that this proposal is the finest thing that can happen to Mussalmans and India.[2]

II

On 22 February 1928 the All-Parties Conference, faced with acute differences, especially on the communal issues, adjourned after appointing a committee of twenty senior leaders, including Ansari, Motilal Nehru, Madan Mohan Malaviya, Lajpat Rai, Annie Besant, Tej Bahadur Sapru, Jayakar, Maulana Mahomed Ali and Jawaharlal Nehru. The committee was asked to report to the Conference its recommendations on the constitution of a 'Swaraj Parliament' and on such matters as franchise, Declaration of Rights, rights of labour and peasantry, and problems of Indian states. Jinnah made it clear that he and other representatives of the Muslim League would consider other aspects of the constitution only after the Hindu–Muslim question had been settled.

Jinnah was in a quandary. On the one hand he had to cope with the intransigence of the Hindu Mahasabha, and on the other hand with the opposition by a section of his own party. He was unhappy to see the All-Parties Conference setting aside his proposal, which had received the imprimatur of the annual plenary conferences of the two main political parties, and throwing the whole constitutional issue into the melting pot. He saw Muslim leaders enthusiastically joining in the discussion of details of constitution-making. Though a veteran lawyer and parliamentarian himself, he deliberately kept clear of these digressions; for him the first priority was the share for Muslims in the future constitutional package. He wrote a note of dissent, disassociating himself from the proceedings of the All-Parties Conference until a decision was reached on Muslim demands. He resorted to a stratagem to which he would often resort in future — to buy time. He argued that he could not commit himself without consulting the Muslim League Council. The Council met on 8 March and decided, evidently at Jinnah's instance, that the Muslim League would take part in future meetings only if a Hindu–Muslim accord was reached to its satisfaction. He was invited to attend the next meeting of the All-Parties Conference at Bombay on 19 May, but a fortnight before the meeting he sailed for Europe, where his wife Ruttie had gone in the middle of April. Motilal Nehru sent a telegram requesting him to nominate someone to deputize for him during his absence from India but did not receive any reply.

III

Jinnah's visit to Europe in the summer of 1928 differed from his previous visits since his student days. For one thing, it was unplanned; its immediate provocation was Ruttie's decision to leave his roof and to sail for Paris with her mother on 10 April. It was an irony of fate that just when he was facing roadblocks in politics, he found his marriage on the rocks. All his previous visits overseas had been planned either as pleasure trips or political missions. But in 1928 there was very little for him to do in England; the Simon Commission had been appointed and official and public interest in that country was almost wholly focused on it.

The state of Ruttie's physical and mental state doubtless weighed on Jinnah's mind, but he was also extremely worried about the political situation in the homeland. One of his fellow passengers on the *S S Rajputana* was Dewan Chaman Lal, a Congress member of the Central Legislative Assembly and a favourite of Motilal Nehru. Chaman Lal recalled many years later that Motilal had told him that Jinnah's Hindu–Muslim accord had all but succeeded. 'Give me three leaders', Jinnah said, 'to join me over a unity programme ... and Swaraj will not be a mere dream, but a matter brought within the realm of real politics.'[3] The three Hindu leaders Jinnah named were Motilal Nehru, Lajpat Rai and Madan Mohan Malaviya. Implicit in this argument was the assumption that if the Congress and the Hindu Mahasabha played ball, he could get the Muslim League to agree. Unluckily for Jinnah, appointment of the Simon Commission and convening of the All-Parties Conference had set in motion forces which were going to turn Indian politics, including Muslim politics, upside down.

In May 1928 the Bombay meeting of the All-Parties Conference, which Jinnah could not attend, appointed a committee of ten members, with Motilal Nehru as chairman, 'to consider and determine the principles of constitution for India'.[4] It included Motilal Nehru, Sir Ali Imam, Tej Bahadur Sapru, M.S. Aney, Subhas Chandra Bose, G.R. Pradhan and Shuaib Qureshi, who signed the report of the committee. One member, M.R. Jayakar, resigned on grounds of health, and N.M. Joshi, a trade union leader, did not attend any meeting. Sir Ali Imam, because of ill health, could not attend most of the meetings. Shuaib Qureshi remained the only active Muslim member who agreed with the majority view on the recommendations of the report, except on reservation of seats for Muslims on a population basis in the legislatures of the Punjab and Bengal in which Muslims were in a majority. He was, however, brought round to the majority view.

The report of the committee, which came to be known as the Nehru Report, acknowledged that the communal problem in India was primarily a Hindu–Muslim problem. It pointed out that if religious and cultural autonomy was guaranteed in a 'Charter of Fundamental Rights', the communal problem would be solved. The committee accepted dominion status for India. The system of government was to be based on the rule of law, fundamental rights and parliamentary democracy, with universal adult franchise both at the centre and in the provinces. The Muslim demand for the separation of Sind from Bombay was accepted, and so was the demand for grant of the same constitutional status to the North-West Frontier Province which other provinces enjoyed. It listed subjects defining the jurisdiction of central and provincial governments. The residuary powers were vested in the centre. It did not concede the Muslim League's demand for one-third reservation of seats in the central legislature, nor for reservation of seats for the Muslims in the Punjab and Bengal in which they were in a majority. It provided for joint or mixed electorates throughout India. There was to be no reservation of seats for Muslims in the House of Representatives (lower house at the centre), except in the provinces where they were in a minority. Such reservation was, however, to be in direct proportion to the Muslim population in every province where they were in a minority. Reservation of seats, where provided, was to be for ten years.

IV

The Nehru Report was submitted to Dr Ansari, president of the All-Parties Conference, in August 1928. A plenary session of the Conference was convened at Lucknow at which the Maharaja of Mahmudabad, in his presidential address, recalled the halcyon days of the Lucknow Pact of 1916 and hoped that the same spirit would pervade their deliberations. Dr Ansari described the Nehru Report as the 'last hope of 300 millions of human beings'[5] struggle for freedom from foreign rule and internal dissensions'. A resolution appreciating the work of the committee was passed with one dissentient — the enigmatic Maulana Hasrat Mohani.

The Lucknow meeting of the All-Parties Conference discussed the report clause by clause. For the first three days it examined the form of government, the question of dominion status versus complete independence for India, the separation of Sind from Bombay, the upgrading of the constitutional status of the North-West Frontier Province and Baluchistan, and the issue of reservation of seats in legislatures. On the fourth day the Conference was thrilled to learn that the Hindu and Muslim delegates from the Punjab had come to an agreement on the acceptance of joint electorates without reservation of seats for any community in the Punjab, provided adult franchise was introduced. Among the nine Muslim leaders who expressed their agreement was Saifuddin Kitchlew, Secretary of the All India Muslim League, and among the Hindu leaders was Lala Lajpat Rai. A similar agreement was made in Bengal by Akram Khan and J.M. Sen Gupta.

The communal arrangements approved by the Lucknow meeting of the All-Parties Conference drastically modified the proposals of the Delhi Muslim Conference of March 1927. They did away with the reservation of seats for Muslims in the legislatures of Muslim-majority provinces of the Punjab and Bengal. They rejected the demand for one-third representation for Muslims in the central legislature and for a joint machinery in the form of a standing committee to determine what were inter-communal matters in respect of which three-fourths of the members of any community could veto the legislation. It was significant that these changes were made with the enthusiastic support of the vast number of Muslim delegates present, including some belonging to Jinnah's own section of the Muslim League. Before leaving for Europe, he had not left any instructions nor nominated a deputy to represent him at the meetings of the Conference. M.C. Chagla, who was known to be quite close to Jinnah at that time, tells us in his memoirs that Motilal Nehru was inclined to concede separate electorates to Muslims, but he argued that they were drafting a constitution not for the present, but for the future, and must not, therefore, incorporate into it any principle which on the face of it was anti-national.[6] Ultimately, Motilal agreed, and joint electorates were accepted as one of the basic principles of the Nehru Report.

It was not only Chagla who took an ultra-nationalist stand. On 25 October 1928, in a manifesto issued by Muslim leaders in support of the proposals in the Nehru Report they declared: 'We feel assured that the position of Muslims under the Nehru [Report] proposals, as modified by the All-Parties Conference, will be in no way worse and in some respects [would be] better than under the resolution adopted by the All India Muslim League at the Calcutta session [in December 1927]'.[7] They also expressed the hope that the All India Muslim League would ratify the proposals at its annual meeting at Calcutta at the end of the year. Among the fourteen signatories to the manifesto were the Maharaja of Mahmudabad, who was to be elected president of the annual session of the Muslim League at Calcutta, and such eminent figures as Seth Yakub Hasan, Saifuddin Kitchlew, Maulana Zafar Ali Khan, Maulana Abdul Bari, Syed Mahmud and M.C. Chagla. Evidently their undiluted nationalism had received a boost from the patriotic fervour generated by the boycott of the Simon Commission.

Motilal Nehru had gone to Lucknow with deep misgivings, but was gratified at the reception of his report at the Conference and its smooth passage. Annie Besant, the grand old lady of the Home Rule movement, was overjoyed to see 'Indian unity and Indian freedom' triumphing over 'communalism and sectarianism'. Chagla was sure 'the communal bogey has been at long last laid'.[8] Dr Ansari said his 'life's work, i.e. the bringing of the unity of all people has been achieved'.[9] The Maharaja of Mahmudabad doubted whether Sir John Simon would be able to reply to the united challenge posed by the All-Parties Conference.[10] Such was the optimism animating the delegates that they decided to re-appoint the Nehru Committee and authorize it to select a parliamentary draftsman to put the constitution approved by the Conference in the shape of a Bill, presumably for introduction in the British Parliament.

V

Jinnah returned to India on 26 October. He had been away for nearly six months. The long stay in Europe had not helped him in effecting reconciliation with his estranged wife. However, it had been useful in keeping him away from the Indian political scene, of which he had become a helpless spectator. His proposal for a Hindu–Muslim accord, which had brought him to the centre-stage of politics the previous year, had been virtually consigned to the wastepaper basket by the Lucknow Conference. The All-Parties Conference still dominated the political scene. He decided to distance himself from it while he was in Europe; he continued to do so even after his return.

Motilal Nehru had been very keen to secure Jinnah's attendance at the Lucknow meeting of the All-Parties Conference in August and had even postponed it for a few days to fit in with Jinnah's expected return, but Jinnah changed his programme because of his wife's illness. On 29 September Motilal wrote to a friend in Bombay to let him know the exact date of Jinnah's arrival as 'so much depends upon Jinnah that I have a mind to go to Bombay to receive him'.[11] He could not go to Bombay, but on 28 October, two days after Jinnah's return, he wrote him a very cordial letter urging him to give favourable consideration to the report of the committee headed by him:

The members of the Committee representing as they do all possible schools of thought in the country are not supposed to represent the organizations to which they belong but to act independently more as judges ... than as members or the advocates of the said organizations. The Report ... proceeded on this basis and it has not adopted *in toto* the view of any particular party. Speaking for myself, there are points in the Report on which I not only as a member of the Congress but also as a detached individual do not agree. The Report is nothing more than the maximum agreement between the parties. As you have rightly stated in your interview, there is still room for the parties concerned to have the recommendations altered at the convention to be held on the 17th December in Calcutta.[12]

VI

Motilal was hoping that Jinnah's presence would be a counterpoise in the proposed National Convention at Calcutta to 'Shaukat Ali and other reactionaries'. He was soon disillusioned. Jinnah spurned Motilal's invitation. He refused to express his views on the Nehru Report either on the plea that he had to consult the Council of the Muslim League or because he had to get a mandate from the annual meeting of the All India Muslim League. By the third week of November Motilal had lost all hope of securing Jinnah's cooperation at the National Convention and even made himself believe that he could do without it. On 24 November he wrote to Gandhi:

The Provincial Muslim Leagues of the Punjab and Bengal, the only two provinces that matter have adopted the Lucknow decisions by overwhelming majorities and given up their demand for reservation of seats for majorities .... Evidence is accumulating that the (Nehru) Report and the Lucknow discussions will be approved by a substantial majority at the open session of the League in Calcutta .... Practically, the whole of the Muslim Press with the exception of two papers of not much consequence is also supporting the Report. This has greatly perturbed the Muslim members of the Assembly belonging to Jinnah's party, who are one and all bitterly opposed to the Report and the Lucknow decisions. All told they number 8 or 9 .... In his anxiety to keep his hold on these people Jinnah is playing into their hands.[13]

The fact was that Jinnah had no intention of attending the National Convention. Chagla tells us that soon after landing in Bombay, Jinnah pulled him up for accepting the Nehru Report in his absence. Publicly, however, Jinnah did not commit himself on the merits of the report; he contented himself with such vague generalities as 'Muslims must organize themselves and stand united', and 'the road to Indian freedom is Hindu–Muslim unity'. He was sore at heart at having been let down not only by the Congress leaders, but by the members of his own party, which was sharply divided on the Nehru Report. How sharp the division was within the Council of the League soon became apparent to Jinnah. In the last week of November he presided over its meeting and found there was no agreement. He postponed its consideration till the end of December 1928 when the annual session of the League was due to be held at Calcutta. The same meeting elected the Maharaja of Muhamudabad, a strong supporter of the Nehru Report, as president of the Calcutta session by a majority of two votes. The supporters and opponents of the report were so evenly matched that a few days later the League Council rejected the Nehru Report. Because of these dissensions Jinnah decided to watch and wait before taking a final stand in public on the Nehru Report until the All India Muslim League met at Calcutta.

VII

The annual session of the Muslim League, to which Jinnah had been looking forward for resolving all his problems, commenced at Calcutta on 26 December 1928. According to M.C. Chagla, on the very first day, at the meeting of the Subjects Committee, Jinnah proposed outright rejection of the Nehru Report, but was persuaded to try for a compromise with the National Convention which was also in session at Calcutta at that very time. He agreed to lead a deputation from the League with a proposal for the minimum modifications in the report to make it acceptable to the Muslim League. On the following day, the proceedings of the National Convention were interrupted for the announcement that the Muslim League was going to be represented in the Convention for the first time. The announcement was greeted with cheers and a thirty-seven-member subcommittee of the Convention was instantly set up to confer with the Muslim League. The two delegations met the same evening in Motilal Nehru's tent in the premises of the National Convention. Jinnah proposed six modifications, of which three were really important: reservation of seats for Muslims in the legislatures of the Punjab and Bengal, vesting of residuary powers in the provinces instead of at the centre, and reservation of one-third seats in the central, legislature for Muslims. The League was offered some minor concessions, but its three major demands were turned down. The following day, on 28 December, Jinnah came to the plenary session of the National Convention and moved a resolution asking for the acceptance of his proposals in a reasoned and eloquent speech:

> I think it will be recognized that it is absolutely essential to our progress that Hindu–Muslim settlement should be reached and that all communities should live in a friendly and harmonious spirit in this vast country of ours. No country has succeeded in either wresting a democratic constitution from a domination of another nation or establishing representative institutions from within without giving guarantees for the securities of the minorities wherever such a problem has arisen. Majorities are apt to be oppressive and tyrannical and minorities always dread and fear that their interests and rights, unless clearly and definitely safeguarded by statutory provisions, would suffer and be prejudiced, and this apprehension is enhanced all the more when we have to deal with a communal majority .... It is essential that you must get not only the

Muslim League but the Musalmans of India, and here I am speaking not as a Musalman but as an Indian.[14]

A number of speeches were delivered at the Convention, but none in support of Jinnah's proposals. No Congress leader spoke. The Liberal leader, Tej Bahadur Sapru, said: 'The simple position is that for the sake of settlement you are invited by Mr. Jinnah, however illogically and unreasonably, to agree to this proposition, which I consider is not inconsistent with the Nehru Report.... Speaking for myself, I would like you to picture Mr. Jinnah, whom I have known intimately for fifteen years. If he is a spoilt child, a naughty child, I am prepared to say, give him what he wants and be finished with it.'[15] Rallia Ram, a Christian delegate, said '.... I am an Indian Christian for I feel that the time has come when people should leave their religion at home and enter this Convention as Indians and Indians alone.'[16] It became clear to Jinnah that he was addressing an unsympathetic audience. The National Convention was not in a mood to reopen the communal issue which had already been debated, in which seventy-odd parties were represented, at length and settled in previous meetings. If Jinnah had responded to Motilal's earnest pleas even in November, some of the modifications he was suggesting at the National Convention might have been accepted. Though the Convention had already been in session for four days and was to continue its deliberations for another three days, the communal problem was no longer on its agenda. There were other issues arising from the Nehru Report with which it was grappling, such as dominion status versus complete independence as a goal.

VIII

The most critical comments on Jinnah's resolution came from his fellow lawyer and one-time friend in Bombay, M.R. Jayakar, who questioned Jinnah's credentials. Mr Jinnah, he said, spoke for only a small minority of Mohammedans;

a large bulk of the community was with Sir Muhammad Shafi, and there was 'a considerable portion' who were opposed to Jinnah and were holding a conference over which the Aga Khan was to preside. In short, the demands put forth by Jinnah did not proceed on behalf of the entire Muslim community or even a large portion of it. These comments must have hurt Jinnah the more because there was more than a grain of truth in them. The Muslim League had split, and Jinnah's own faction was badly divided over the Nehru Report. This became manifest when the All India Muslim League resumed its session on 29 December. He decided not to press for the rejection of the Nehru Report even as the Maharaja of Mahmudabad did not agree with him. The session was marred by bitter differences on other questions too. On 30 December the session was postponed for want of a quorum. The Maharaja of Mahmudabad was not present. Jinnah took the chair; after disposing of some routine items on the agenda he abruptly adjourned the plenary session and announced that the Council of the League would summon it again before the end of May.

The adjourned session was held at Delhi on 30 March 1929. Jinnah found, to his dismay, that the contending factions were no nearer an agreement. He acknowledged that there were three groups in the party: one urging the adoption of the Nehru Report, the second calling for the rejection of the Nehru Report, and the third demanding a compromise. All his efforts at reconciling differences in the League Council failed. Supporters of the Nehru Report claimed to be in a majority; they held a meeting and adopted the report by a voice vote. A number of rowdies from the town invaded the hall and shouted slogans against the supporters of the Nehru Report. Jinnah arrived on the scene and addressed the meeting and adjourned the session *sine die* and declared that the League Council would meet to discuss the situation.[17] Records of the plenary session of the League and subsequent sessions show that no resolution on the Nehru Report was passed even in subsequent annual sessions.

IX

Jinnah's failure to get the Nehru Report rejected by the All India Muslim League in 1928 and 1929 showed that the nationalist Muslims were still a force to reckon with in the League Council and in the plenary annual sessions of the League. It also exposed his tenuous control over his party. His chief occupation as 'working president' of the All India Muslim League was to reconcile personal and factional differences and somehow to keep up a façade of Muslim unity. He himself could survive only by continually adjusting himself to the existing balance of forces in Muslim politics. After 1920, he had to take into account the clout of the emerging leadership in the Muslim-majority provinces of the Punjab and Bengal, who had their own regional and personal ambitions. He made his peace with them by supporting the demand for statutory Muslim majorities in the legislatures of the Punjab and Bengal. As David Page, a Canadian historian, puts it, Jinnah's main difficulty was that 'he had no solid political base. He was a consultative politician in an age of political responsibility.' He could survive only by acting as a broker between the Muslim politicians in the provinces and the Congress leaders.[18]

X

The rebuff to Jinnah at the National Convention has been described by a Pakistani historian as a 'watershed'[19] in the history of the Indian freedom movement. This verdict does not bear critical scrutiny. In retrospect, it seems that Birkenhead's challenge to Indian political parties to produce an agreed constitution was a trap for the nationalist opposition. The attempt to achieve unanimity on all issues, and especially on 'power sharing', in the constitution among thirty-odd parties representing diverse and conflicting interests was too ambitious. Gandhi had foreseen this; even as the All-Parties Conference began its work he had wisely advised Motilal Nehru to confine its scope to basic principles and not get involved in the details of constitution-making. On the communal issue he had advised him to adhere to joint electorates, but 'unless Muslims agree there is to be no going back by us on reservation of seats.'[20]

The belief that a Hindu–Muslim Pact would drive the British Government to hasten the devolution of power from British to Indian hands was inherited by Jinnah from his mentors in the Moderate era before the First World War. The Congress–League scheme of 1916, an off-shoot of the Lucknow Pact with the framing of which he had been associated, was duly presented to the British Government, but had little effect on the tenor of the Reforms Act of 1919, except for its communal provisions. Even if the Nehru Report with or without the modifications proposed by Jinnah had been approved by the Muslim League at its Calcutta session, it would have made no difference to the final result. There was no possibility of the British hailing the Nehru Report as the united voice of political India. In August 1928, just when Indian nationalists were celebrating the success of the All-Parties Conference in the unanimous adoption of the Nehru Report, Lord Irwin wrote to the Secretary of State, Birkenhead, on 28 August 1928:

> Most people seem to think that 90 per cent of Muslim opinion which is not represented on the All-Parties Conference will have nothing to do with joint electorates and even among 10 per cent which remains — made up as it is of Khilafatists and Jinnah's followers — there will be some dissentients. Already a move was afoot to summon the Aga Khan to India to marginalize the Jinnah faction of the Muslim League by mobilizing pro-British elements in the Muslim community under the banner of a new political organization 'All Muslim Parties Conference.'[21]

In his biography of Jinnah, Stanley Wolpert says that Jinnah's parting speech at the National Convention on

28 December 1928 was his 'swan song to Indian nationalists'. As we shall see, Jinnah did not break off with the Congress and Indian nationalism in 1928. He still talked of Hindu–Muslim unity, and tried to mediate between the Congress and the government in 1929. He took part in negotiations on the communal issue and on the political advance at the federal centre in the Round Table Conference in 1930–31. Four years later he held parleys with Rajendra Prasad, the Congress president, for a Hindu–Muslim accord. It was not until 1937 — eight years after the controversies on the Nehru Report — that Jinnah turned his back on Indian nationalism.

Chapter 12

LEADER IN SEARCH OF A ROLE

The Muslim League session and the National Convention at Calcutta were a frustrating experience for Jinnah, reminiscent of his experience at the Nagpur Congress eight years earlier. Indeed, 1928 was one of the unhappiest and loneliest years of his life. By the end of the year his proposals of March 1927 for a Hindu–Muslim accord, which had been hailed as a great achievement, had been consigned to the dustbin of history and his political fortunes were at their nadir. He had supported the renunciation of separate electorates, cherished by the bulk of the Muslim elite as a valuable asset, but it was in return for substantial constitutional safeguards for Muslims. The Indian National Congress and the Muslim League both had endorsed his scheme, but the All-Parties Conference and the Nehru Report rejected the 'safeguards', and let the joint electorates remain. In the eyes of the co-religionists (except nationalist Muslims) Jinnah was made to look politically naive and inept.

Jinnah's task for 1929 was cut out for him; he had to live down the events of 1928, to restore his credibility in the eyes of his supporters, and to rally the Muslim League which was in total disarray. By March 1929, he hit on a plan to solve both his personal and political problems. He compiled a comprehensive charter of Muslim demands for constitutional safeguards which incorporated every possible demand that could be made on the majority community and could satisfy every section of the Muslim community. His 'Fourteen Points' included a federal constitution with residuary powers vested in the provinces, one-third Muslim representation in the central legislature and central and provincial cabinets, separate electorates, separation of Sind from Bombay, reforms in the North-West Frontier Province and Baluchistan on the same footing as in other provinces, and an adequate Muslim share in all services of the state and local self-governing bodies. The British-owned *Statesman* seized on one of the demands — the need for the consent of three-fourths of the Mohammedan representatives to any measure affecting a religious community — and wrote that it would mean 'a denial of the power of legislation to the [Legislative] Councils, for there is in practice no Bill that could be framed that could not be held to apply to the Mohamedan community.'[1]

In December 1928 Jinnah had failed to persuade the National Convention at Calcutta to accept three of these demands. Three months later when he increased the number of demands to fourteen, Motilal Nehru described them as 'preposterous'. Jinnah's decision to raise stakes so steeply did not make any sense if his object was a Hindu–Muslim accord acceptable to both the communities. Evidently, his object at this time was not to convince the Hindus or even the British, but to rehabilitate his own reputation as the 'defender of the faith' in the Muslim community and to consolidate his fragmented party, the Muslim League. With his all-embracing charter of Fourteen Points, he had outbid all political rivals for all times and insured himself against any future aspersion on his devotion to Muslim communal interests, his nationalistic professions notwithstanding.

This was not the first time that Jinnah had abruptly changed his political posture for his survival. In 1908–9, he had abandoned his advocacy of joint electorates after the Minto–Morley Reforms introduced separate electorates for Muslims. In 1921, after his marginalization at the Nagpur Congress, he had toned down his nationalist rhetoric and mended his fences with the British authorities. From 1924 he began to call for a revision of the Lucknow Pact to which he had been party, and which he had described in 1916 as a 'final settlement of Hindu–Muslim differences', in order to placate powerful regional leaders such as Fazli Husain and Abdur Rahim, who wanted Muslim majorities in the legislatures of the Punjab and Bengal to be guaranteed in the future constitution.

Jinnah's deftness in changing political postures did not go unnoticed by his contemporaries. On 26 June 1927 Dr Ansari, in a letter to Sarojini Naidu, wrote: 'He [Jinnah] is a nationalist at heart, but turned into a communalist by the exigencies of time (like Jayakar), but I have little faith in anyone who can change his convictions so readily to suit the circumstances.'[2]

Motilal Nehru made the same point in a letter to Gandhi:

Motilal Nehru to Gandhi, 2 October 1928.

> But for one weakness, he (Jinnah) is thoroughly sound. He is always afraid of losing his leadership and avoids taking any risks in the matter. This weakness often drives him to support the most reactionary proposals. In reality he has no following at all and his so-called followers are men who fully understand his weakness and bend him to their own will. After he has played into their hands it pays them to boom him as a great leader of the Mussalmans. He cannot of course always defend his attitude when talking freely with me and other friends. His one explanation is: 'My dear fellow I have to take these fools with me'.[3]

While Jinnah was trying to retrieve his position in Muslim politics, he was also trying to mend his fences with the British authorities who had not been too happy with his Hindu–Muslim accord initiative and his part in the boycott of the Simon Commission. The accord was now dead, and the boycott was no longer a live issue. Chastened by the events of 1928, Jinnah was no longer in a mood to continue what he had described at the Calcutta session of the Muslim League as a 'constitutional war against Britain'. In 1921, after the severance of his

Leader in Search of a Role ~ 127

relations with the Congress, he had decided that the best role for him in politics would be that of a mediator between Muslims and Muslims, between Muslims and Hindus, and between the nationalist opposition and the government. He had momentarily departed from this role in 1927 and 1928 with disastrous results. Luckily, the developing political situation in 1929 gave him the opening for a mediatory role.

II

The Nehru Report produced by the All-Parties Conference had envisaged a parliamentary system of government; dominion status was to be the basis of its recommendations to secure the lowest common measure of agreement among the Congress, the Moderates and other groups. The younger leaders of the Congress were opposed to dominion status and did not like Indian freedom to be hedged in by any limitation. Jawaharlal Nehru and Subhas Chandra Bose threatened to resign from the Congress; they founded the Independence for India League to promote among Congressmen the ideology of complete independence.

The annual session of the Congress was due in December 1928 in Calcutta. A head-on collision between the old guard and the younger group in the Congress seemed inevitable. Motilal Nehru, who had been elected to preside over the session, anticipating the crisis in Calcutta, urged Gandhi to attend the session. Gandhi had taken little part in the All-Parties Conference or in the drafting of the Nehru Report. He had also taken little active interest in the Congress session at Gauhati in 1926 or at Madras in 1927. It is doubtful if he would have taken any more interest in the Calcutta session in December 1928, were it not for urgent summons from elder Nehru. In the Subjects Committee, which screened resolutions for the plenary session, the discussions on dominion status were long, heated and bitter. Gandhi suggested a via media: the Congress should adopt the whole of the Nehru Report, including the dominion status formula, but if it was not accepted by the government within two years, the Congress should opt for complete independence and fight for it, if necessary, by invoking the weapon of civil disobedience. On the insistence of younger members, Gandhi amended his resolution, giving London only one year to concede dominion status or else face a civil disobedience movement. The amended resolution was carried in the Subjects Committee as well as in the plenary session; the voting — 1,350 for and 97 against — gave a clear majority to Gandhi's resolution, but the issue hung in the balance till almost the last moment.

The Nehru Report and the All-Parties Conference were attempts on the part of the Congress leaders to achieve a consensus among Indian parties in order to present a united demand to the British Government. There is little evidence to show that the Nehru Report received a serious consideration in official circles. 'The British Parliament could never accept a position', declared the Viceroy on 28 January 1929, 'which would reduce it to being a mere registrar of the decisions of other persons'.[4] The controversy on dominion status versus complete independence had an unexpected but momentous result: it opened the way for Gandhi's return to politics. If the British Government did not agree with the demands of the Congress — and there was little prospect of their doing so — the Congress was committed to civil disobedience and it was obvious to all that Gandhi alone could conduct such a movement. In March 1929, Geoffrey Dawson, the Editor of *The Times*, after a three-month tour of India, noted that the situation in the country was 'one of comparative calm on the surface but expectancy beneath', that official circles acknowledged Irwin's sympathy and sincerity, but were not so sure of his being a man of 'active determination'.[5] Of the latter quality Irwin gave (in Dawson's words) evidence by giving his consent to the launching of the Meerut Conspiracy Case, and enacting the Public Safety

Bill and the Trade Disputes Bill. There were not a few in the Viceroy's entourage who would have liked him to nip in the bud the challenge of 'complete independence' by jailing Jawaharlal Nehru and Subhas Chandra Bose and giving India a salutary dose of a resolute government. But Irwin was a wiser and sadder man since he had concurred in the proposal for an 'all-white' commission and did not include any Indian in it. He also wanted to reverse the process of estrangement of Indian opinion, which had gone on unchecked since November 1927. The Simon Commission report was not to be published until May 1930, but Irwin was aware of the trend of these recommendations and knew that they were not likely to cut much ice with Indian public opinion. He had planned to visit England in the summer of 1929 for his mid-term holiday. He decided to take the opportunity of discussing Indian affairs with the Home government.

Irwin's mission was facilitated by a change of government in England. A Labour ministry headed by Ramsay MacDonald took office in June 1929. The new Secretary of State was Wedgwood Benn (later Lord Stansgate). Though Benn confessed to a Labour member that he knew little about India 'on the principle', as he put it, 'that cabinet ministers should be appointed to the posts about which they know least';[6] this testimony was borne to his sincerity by friends of the Indian National Congress in England. One of them, H.S.L. Polak, an associate of Gandhi in South Africa, urged Gandhi to seize 'every opportunity of contact that now presents itself owing to the change of Government and circumstances in this country'.[7] Graham Pole, a Labour MP, assured Sapru that 'Benn is entirely with us and working magnificently ... [and] regards himself as representing Indians not the British'.[8]

Irwin secured the endorsement of the British cabinet for his proposal for a Round Table Conference in London between the representatives of India and Britain to discuss the framing of a new Indian constitution. He was authorized to herald the announcement of the Conference by a declaration affirming that the goal of British policy of India was dominion status. Neither Lloyd George nor Lord Reading, the two stalwarts of the Liberal Party on whose support the Labour ministry's life depended, gave much encouragement to the Viceroy, nor did the idea of a new declaration evoke enthusiasm among his own friends in the Conservative Party.

Irwin returned to India on 25 October 1929. Six days later came his long-expected declaration:

> In view of the doubts which have been expressed both in Great Britain and India regarding the intentions of the British Government in enacting the Statute of 1919, I am authorized to state clearly that in their judgement it is implied in the declaration of 1917 that the natural issue of India's constitutional progress, as there contemplated, is the attainment of Dominion Status ....[9]

The Viceregal announcement was an ingeniously worded document which could mean much or little. The Moderate (Liberal) leaders, to quote Irwin's biographer, saw the Conference 'as their supreme opportunity for the full exercise of their intellectual powers and from henceforth they were Irwin's faithful allies'.[10] The Congress leaders, scanning the horizon for a gesture which could open the path to self-government and prevent a clash with the government, discerned the possibility of what Gandhi called a change of heart.

The Viceroy had done his public relations job so well that Sapru, V.J. Patel and Malaviya were able to arrange a Leaders' Conference on 1 November — the day after the declaration — and to issue a 'joint manifesto' welcoming the declaration, under the signatures of Gandhi, Motilal Nehru, Dr Ansari, Sapru, the Maharaja of Mahmudabad, V.J. Patel and even Jawaharlal Nehru.

The manifesto was well received in India but a storm broke over Irwin and the Labour government in England. The British press and Parliament subjected Irwin's words to a protracted post-mortem. Lord Reading, whose opinion as a former Viceroy carried much weight, declared that the announcement was calculated to undermine the prestige and authority of the Simon Commission. Lloyd George, the leader of the Liberal Party, poured scorn on Wedgwood Benn, whom he called 'the pocket-edition of Moses'. Baldwin, the leader of the Conservative Party, whose protege Irwin was believed to be, did not really rally to the support of the Viceroy's policy. Sir John Simon and his fellow Commissioners, who had not been consulted, felt that they had been shabbily treated by the Labour government; after the announcement of a Round Table Conference their report was likely to have only academic interest. Under such heavy fire, the Labour government was driven to be on the defensive. The Secretary of State explained away the declaration as a 'restatement', and an 'interpretation' of Montagu's declaration of August 1917. *The Times* (4 November 1929) compared Irwin's words with a speech delivered by Birkenhead in 1927 and saw no difference between them.

Circumstances had compelled the Labour government to belittle in Britain what the Viceroy was trying to boost in India. The real difficulty, as John Morley had bewailed twenty years earlier, lay in synchronizing clocks in different hemispheres: it was not easy to devise a formula 'that could pass for self-government in India, and for British Raj at Westminster'. The debate in the British Parliament damaged the emotional bridge which Irwin's declaration of 31 October had sought to build between India and Britain. During the succeeding six weeks, Irwin set out, with the willing cooperation of Sapru, V.J. Patel and Jinnah, to repair the damage. Sapru requested Motilal Nehru to convene a meeting of the signatories to the Delhi Manifesto at Allahabad where the Congress Working Committee was to meet on 16 November. Sapru succeeded in securing an endorsement of the Delhi Manifesto at this meeting and passed on the good news to the Viceroy. Sapru advised Irwin that he should see Gandhi to further ease the situation. Jinnah, who met the Viceroy in Bombay, also advised him to see Gandhi. Sarojini Naidu, at Jinnah's instance, readily commended the proposal to the Mahatma. V.J. Patel and Sapru remained in touch with Motilal Nehru. The interview with the Viceroy, on which such great hope had been built, took place in the Viceroy's House in New Delhi on 23 December. It proved a complete fiasco. The Viceroy felt almost personally betrayed; the edifice he had been constructing laboriously since the summer crumbled to pieces before his eyes. The intermediaries professed to be bewildered by Gandhi's attitude. He asked the Viceroy to guarantee that immediate dominion status would be granted. Motilal Nehru took the same line. The attitude of the Congress leaders struck Sapru and Jinnah as incomprehensible, inconsistent and inexcusable. In fact it was not the volte-face which it appeared to them. The Delhi 'Joint Manifesto', which Jawaharlal Nehru had been persuaded to sign against his better judgement and Subhas Chandra Bose had refused to sign, had interpreted the Viceregal declaration to mean that the Round Table Conference 'would meet not to discuss when Dominion Status should be established, but to frame a Dominion Constitution for India'. This interpretation, as Irwin complained to Sapru, was a 'strained' one. The sincerity of the peacemakers, who had no personal axe to grind, was patent enough; and so was that of Irwin, who was risking his political future by venturing on a policy which was anathema to his own party in England. But no amount of personal sincerity and goodwill could alter the basic facts of the Indian political situation in December 1929. The Congress was committed to a civil disobedience movement if dominion status was not granted by the end of the year. The Viceregal declaration of 31 October 1929 was an attempt to prevent that con-tingency. But the strength of this declaration was its vagueness, which was dissipated by the bluntness of Lloyd George, Reading, Simon, Churchill and Birkenhead. The debates in the British Parliament deflated the initial optimism of the Congress leaders. To Jawaharlal Nehru, who was repenting his signature to the Delhi Manifesto, which he described as a 'dangerous trap',[11]

Gandhi wrote on 7 November: 'I believe myself that there is a greater chance of the Congress coming over to your view than your having to resign from the presidentship.'[12] What Gandhi wanted, and needed, on the eve of the Lahore Congress was something definite, some proof of the British desire to part with power. Irwin, chastened by the recent criticism in England, was not in a position to make a precise commitment; on the contrary, he was deliberately playing for safety. When the news of the forthcoming interview of Gandhi and Motilal Nehru with the Viceroy appeared in the press early in December, Irwin sent frantic messages from his camp to Sapru and V.J. Patel urging them to emphasize that the interview had been arranged at their (the intermediaries') suggestion, 'otherwise those who wished to make mischief in England would at once say that the Viceroy was trying to buy off Congress Extremists.'[13]

As for Wedgwood Benn, despite the eulogies he had earned from his colleagues in the Labour Party, he was under no illusion as to his limitations. 'We cannot face an election on an Indian issue', Benn had frankly told Fenner Brockway soon after taking office.[14] The Labour ministry could not last a day without the support of the Liberals; a radical departure in India was sure to unite the Liberals and the Conservatives and to sweep the Labour Party out of office. There is no evidence that Benn and Irwin were convinced of the feasibility, or even of the justice, of conceding full dominion status in 1930, but even if they had been, they could not have carried the British Parliament and the public opinion in Britain with them. It needed a series of civil disobedience campaigns by Gandhi, the Second World War and a Labour government in power (not merely in office) to contemplate a real transfer of power from Britain to India. It is impossible to resist the conclusion that the chances of a political settlement in December 1929 were overrated by the 'peacemakers', who were victims of their own optimism. Jinnah and Sapru had a lingering regret that the game was spoilt by the unpredictable Mahatma; and that things might have turned out differently if Irwin and Motilal had been able to meet by themselves on 15 November.[15] Motilal, however, said that he 'lacked the stout optimism of an Indian Liberal who can read a definite "no" as a clear "yes"'. Motilal, who was a party to the Calcutta Congress compromise of the previous year, could hardly have taken a line in opposition to his own son and Gandhi.[16] A shrewd observer had predicted early in December 1929 that 'Motilal Nehru will in the end be overcome by his paternal affection'.[17] It was not only paternal affection, but the aftermath of the Parliamentary debates and the imminence of the Lahore Congress which had led Motilal to fall in line with his son. He told V.J. Patel, one of the mediators, a fortnight before the interview with the Viceroy, that he 'did not expect any results' from it. 'At present', he added, 'all roads lead to Lahore'.[18]

Chapter 13

First Round Table Conference

The Round Table Conference met in London in November 1930. Among the eight-nine delegates there were fifty-seven from British India, sixteen from India's Princely states, and sixteen from the three British political parties. All the Indian delegates were nominees of the Viceroy and were supposed to represent various interests in the country. The largest political party, the Indian National Congress, was, however, not only unrepresented, but had launched a civil disobedience campaign to end foreign rule. Prominent among the Muslim delegates were the Aga Khan, Sir Mohammad Shafi, Maulana Mahomed Ali and Jinnah. The Hindu delegates included some eminent Liberal leaders, such as Tej Bahadur Sapru, Srinivasa Sastri and M.R. Jayakar. The Hindu Mahasabha was represented by B.S. Moonje, the depressed classes were represented by B.R. Ambedkar, the Sikhs by Sampuran Singh and Ujjal Singh from the Punjab, the Indian Christians by K.T. Paul and the Anglo-Indians by Col Gidney. Three of the rulers of Indian states — those of Jammu and Kashmir, Bhopal and Patiala — were themselves attending the Conference, while the other states were represented by their ministers or special envoys.

For Jinnah the meeting of the Round Table Conference in London in November 1930 was the fulfilment of a long-cherished wish. From 1919, when he appeared before the Joint Parliamentary Committee on Montagu–Chelmsford reforms in London, he had been protesting against the inadequacy of the Reforms Act of 1919 which had conceded only partial popular control at the provincial level and none at all at the centre. In 1924 he had joined hands with Motilal Nehru in the Central Legislative Assembly for carrying through a resolution demanding a new constitution framed by a representative 'round table conference' for approval by a newly-elected Legislative Assembly before it was embodied into a statute by the British Parliament. Four years later, in 1928, Jinnah had called for a boycott of the Simon Commission, because he considered the dissociation of Indian representatives from the process of constitutional reforms as 'an insult to every self-respecting Indian'. In November 1929, when Lord Irwin announced that a Round Table Conference of both Indian and British representatives would be convened in London to hammer out the next instalment of reforms, Jinnah was delighted. In the closing months of 1929 he had readily joined Tej Bahadur Sapru in an attempt to mediate between the Congress and the government in order to stave off a civil disobedience campaign by the Congress and to persuade it to participate in the Round Table Conference. Even though the mediation failed and the Congress went ahead with its 'non-violent rebellion', Jinnah continued urging Lord Irwin to do his utmost to satisfy India's political aspirations and to prevent further alienation of the Indian people from the Raj. In the last week of April 1930, when the country was stirred by Gandhi's 241-mile march from Ahmedabad to Dandi on the western sea coast to break the Salt Laws, Jinnah wrote to Lord Irwin, underscoring the urgency of making the Round Table Conference a success. 'The question', he wrote, 'is not so much as to who goes to the Conference, but what will he bring [to India]'.[1] His fear was that the British bureaucracy in Delhi and the Anglo-Indian and Tory lobbies in London would frustrate the Viceroy's effort to open a new chapter in Indo-British relations. The crux of the matter, Jinnah told Irwin, was 'how far you would or the Government of India [would] support constitutional advance?'[2] He pleaded with Irwin to be in London when the Conference was in session. He suggested that the British opposition parties be excluded from the Conference; evidently he feared that they would act as a brake on the Labour Government. Jinnah did not realize that Irwin was in no position to keep the opposition parties in Britain out of the Round Table Conference, nor was he strong enough to stand up against the phalanx of the reactionary British bureaucrats in India. Despite Jinnah's hints, Irwin did not consult him on the selection of even Muslim delegates, though he gave him letters of introduction to Secretary of State Wedgwood Benn and some other senior politicians in Britain. 'I have seen a good deal of Jinnah from time to time', Irwin wrote to Benn, 'and have met very few Indians with a more acute intellect or a more independent outlook — not of course that he always sees eye to eye with the Government. But he is not lacking in moral courage, has been very outspoken against civil disobedience and is genuinely anxious to find the way to settlement.'[3]

II

Soon after his arrival in London, Jinnah called on Benn. 'Of all the delegates', Benn wrote to Irwin, 'I think the two who have impressed me most are Sapru and Jinnah. The marked difference between them and their class and the common run of [other Indian] delegates is a note of equality instead of the over-ingratiating tone which characterizes so many of them.'[4]

The Conference was inaugurated on 12 November with a brief ceremony by the King in the Royal Gallery of the House of Lords. The royal speech was heard by all the delegates standing and was broadcast by the BBC in its world service. The King departed as soon as he concluded his speech, and Prime Minister Ramsay MacDonald was voted to the chair. On behalf of the Indian delegation, Srinivasa Sastri gave an eloquent oration. It was a ceremonial function but Jinnah, however, decided to say something concrete about the Conference and the significance of the task before it. Addressing the Prime Minister, he said: 'The declarations made by British sovereigns and statesmen from time to time that Great Britain's work in India was to prepare her for self-government have been plain .... But I must emphasize that India now expects translation and fulfilment of these declarations into action.' He welcomed the Prime Ministers and representatives of the British Dominions to the Conference and said: 'I am glad that they are here to witness the birth of a new Dominion of India which would be ready to march along with the British Commonwealth of Nations.'[5] Jinnah's audacity in raising basic constitutional issues at the inaugural session did not go down well with the British delegates and officials. Even Wedgwood Benn who had formed a good opinion of him noted a certain 'demeanour of insolence' in his speech. Malcolm Hailey, the Governor of the United Provinces, who was the Viceroy's unofficial envoy to the Conference, reported to him that 'Jinnah is of course a good deal mistrusted .... He declined to give .... a copy of his speech in advance as all the others had done. But then Jinnah was always the perfect little bounder and as slippery as the eels which his forefathers purveyed in Bombay market.'[6]

The Conference resumed its plenary meetings in St. James Palace on 17 November. The first five days were devoted to important issues as to whether the Indian constitution should be federal or unitary. Jinnah clarified his stand in emphatic terms. 'India wants', he said, 'to be a mistress in her own house'. He could not conceive of any constitution for India which did not transfer responsibility in the central government to a cabinet responsible to the legislature.[7] Addressing the Prime Minister, he said, You, Sir, two years ago, presiding at the British Labour Conference in London in 1928, said, 'I hope that within a period of months, rather than years, there will be a new Dominion .... that will find self-respect as an equal within the Commonwealth — I refer to India.'[8]

In his speeches in the business sessions, Jinnah effectively rebutted the arguments of some British delegates and rulers of Princely states, and warned against 'watering down' or weakening the proposed federation for India to such an extent that it remained no federation at all. If the princes were reluctant to join an all-India federation, he was in favour of British India going ahead and forming a federation of its own. While expressing his disapproval of the launching of civil disobedience by the Indian National Congress, he told the Conference that the Congress did not consist of reckless or irresponsible men. 'Let me tell you', he said, 'you have got among them the stable and solid elements and the commercial classes.... Your (British) economic policy and your commercial policy have shattered the faith of the commercial class in India.' He asked the British Government 'whether it was its intention to build up an executive responsible to the legislature and the legislature to be based on the confidence of the people of India, or on the confidence of the people of England or the British Parliament?' The second approach, he said, would not succeed. As for the 'safeguards' in the proposed constitution to limit popular control by reserving powers with the Governor-General or with the Governors, he wanted them to be kept to the minimum. He asserted that the transfer of responsibility to Indian representatives at the centre in the government of India was imperative. 'I say, trust your Finance Member [minister] and give him real responsibility'.[9]

III

On 11 December 1930, Tej Bahadur Sapru wrote home that he did not want to be 'a party to the intrigues that are going on among us'. What Sapru did not know was that the most dangerous intrigue to wreck the Round Table Conference was being hatched back home in India. It was masterminded by Fazl-i-Husain, the Muslim member of the Viceroy's Executive Council. Sir Geoffrey de Montmorency, the Governor of the Punjab (under whom Fazl-i-Husain had served as a minister), while recommending him for promotion to the Viceroy's Council had described him as an 'extremely able and long-sighted man' who excelled in keeping together his party in support of the government. His faults are sometimes a too ardent communalism and sometimes a degree of cleverness in negotiations which higher standards than his own do not pass as within the legitimate sphere of action by a Government Member [minister].'[10]

According to Azim Husain, Fazl-i-Husain's son and biographer, it was under his pressure that the Viceroy selected only those Muslim delegates whose views were in accord with the All Parties Muslim Conference, a rival party floated in 1927–28 by Fazl-i-Husain and Mohammad Shafi to checkmate the All India Muslim League headed by Jinnah. Fazl-i-Husain had the last word in the choice of the Muslim delegates for the Round Table Conference. Left to himself he would have excluded even Jinnah, but Jinnah's political stature in and outside the central legislature, and Irwin's high opinion of him, made this impossible. However, if Jinnah could not be excluded, he could be neutralized. Fazl-i-Husain sought the help of Malcolm Hailey in securing the nomination of Professor Shafaat Ahmad Khan of Allahabad University. He told Hailey, 'Frankly, I do not like the idea of Jinnah doing all the talking and there being no one strong-minded enough to make a protest in case Jinnah starts expressing his views when those views are not acceptable to the Indian Muslims.'[11] Hailey knew that Shafaat Ahmad Khan was politically a cypher, but he could be 'useful to Shafi and also form a somewhat effective counterpoise to Jinnah'. Fazl-i-Husain took infinite pains 'to coach' the Muslim delegates, especially the Aga Khan, Zafarulla Khan and Shafaat Ahmad Khan, and gave them detailed instructions while they were in London and 'kept them well posted with weekly airmail letters'.[12]

It is well at this stage to examine the strategy and tactics of the man who, as a member of the Viceroy's Executive Council during the years 1929–35, was to exercise a crucial influence not only on the policy of the Government of India on communal issues, but on the whole course of Muslim politics in India. In a note to the Viceroy written on 18 August 1930, Fazl-i-Husain laid bare his views on the Hindu–Muslim problem and on constitutional reforms for India. He pointed out that while the Congress — and therefore the Hindus — had not cooperated with the reforms introduced in 1919, the Muslims had worked the reforms and the result was that 'Muslim India in most of the provinces got established in a position of authority and influence and thereby was in a position to remove such disabilities and handicaps from which the community was suffering for a long time.' He criticized the report of the Simon Commission which had recommended abolition of the official bloc in the legislatures, with which Muslim members were allying themselves to counterbalance the Hindu majority. In his view, Indian Muslims were happy enough with the existing constitutional position and did not feel that they were 'called upon to commit suicide with the object of promoting the good of India'.[13] He wanted nothing more than the raising of the North-West Frontier Province to the status of a full-fledged province, the separation of Sind from Bombay, a 'definite majority' for Muslims in the Punjab and Bengal, and an adequate share for Muslims in cabinets and at various levels of administration.

There was, Fazl-i-Husain wrote, a strong school of thought among Indian Muslims which held the view that 'inasmuch as the present position is to their advantage, their siding with the diehards in England, if it succeeds, cannot, politically speaking, be to their disadvantage.' He was frank in saying that the Muslim delegation should seek the support of the opposition parties, especially the Conservative Party in Britain, to restrain the Labour Government from taking any substantial step towards reforms or diluting the Muslims' exclusive 'safeguards' vis-a-vis the Hindus.[14]

It did not occur to Fazl-i-Husain that some members of the Muslim delegation, whom he had himself nominated, would, in the climate of a free country, get bitten by the patriotic bug and forget his 'coaching'. During the voyage and after arrival in England they began to show an inclination towards a compromise with the Hindus. On 8 November, Shafi assured Lord Irwin that the Muslim delegation was holding together, that he and the Aga Khan as its representatives proposed to meet the Hindu leaders, and were hopeful that an agreement would be reached which would improve the prospects of a successful conclusion of deliberations at the Conference. On 19 November, Wedgwood Benn noted in his diary that Shafi had delivered 'a very good speech', the keynote of which was the Muslim desire for advancement of responsibility at the centre. A week later, the Aga Khan told Benn that, within a very short time, there would be an agreement on communal matters.[15] On the same day, Benn recorded in his diary that Dr Moonje of the Hindu Mahasabha was hopeful about a Hindu–Muslim accord.[16]

Fazl-i-Husain got wind of the goings-on in London and wrote in his diary on 3 December: 'News from Round Table Conference indicates that Labour Government made attempts to make Muslims agree to some sort of joint electorates. Shafi, Bhopal, Sultan Ahmad, Fazlul Haq, Hidayatullah were ready for the game, but others were against it. Muhammad Ali was also helping, and no doubt Jinnah too, though himself remaining in the background. I had to take strong action, and the situation has just been saved.'[17]

Fazl-i-Husain's 'action' was to arrange for the despatch of scores of telegrams addressed to the British Prime Minister, the Secretary of State and the leaders of Conservative and Liberal parties in England from Muslim organizations in India, threatening to disown any agreement which abrogated separate electorates for Muslims and did not provide for statutory majorities in the Punjab and Bengal. Fazl-i-Husain's message was also a clear signal to the members of the Muslim delegation at the Round Table Conference to stand pat on the Delhi Muslim Conference demands and the Fourteen Points, including the separate electorates, and not to make the slightest concession to the Hindus for a Hindu–Muslim accord. Fazl-i-Husain's henchmen, Shafaat Ahmad and Zafarulla, personally alerted the Muslim delegates to the risk of their being repudiated by their co-religionists when they returned to India. Fazl-i-Husain explained the logic behind his strategy to Shafaat Ahmad on 20 December 1930:

> Now what is it that the Labour Government offer? We give you responsibility at the Centre if you settle your communal disputes. Now who will benefit more by responsibility being introduced at the Centre at this stage, Hindus or Muslims? Undoubtedly, the Hindus .... Then why should Muslims, who are politically, educationally and economically weaker in the country pretend that by ousting the British power from India and by introducing responsibility they stand to gain so much that, for it, they are prepared to sacrifice communal interests?[18]

The effect on the Muslim delegates of Fazl-i-Husain's reprimand was immediate; the patriotic impulse was curbed, and they were back on the traditional communal track. John Coatman, who was keeping the Viceroy informed, noticed the results of pressure from India upon Shafi; 'At the beginning of December he was urging Muslims to give up separate electorates, by Christmas he was an extreme communalist.[19] He, Ghuznavi and the Aga Khan saw other British politicians such as Lord Reading and Lord Peel, and sought the support of the Liberal and Conservative [parties] against the claims of Hindus, or otherwise, they warned, the Muslims might join in the attack on the British government.'[20] Coatman noted that the Hindus were prepared to concede all the Muslim demands in return for joint electorates, but this is what the Muslim delegates could not concede after Fazl-i-Husain had pulled them up. Wedgwood Benn noted a change in Jinnah's own posture. 'Jinnah is out and out for any agreement at all'. Benn noted that he made a point of having his dissent registered on nearly every question in the meetings of the committees of the Conference.' On 19 December, Sapru wrote home that the Muslim delegates' attitude had become 'extremely stiff and unreasonable ....

The Aga Khan, I am sorry to say, has completely changed and so has Shafi. The fact is that reactionaries among Mohammedans like Ghuznavi and Shafaat Ahmad have prevailed.'[21]

IV

For most Muslim delegates, the reversal of their stand on the communal problem and on the constitutional issue in general did not require much effort. Their patriotic stance at the Round Table Conference was in the nature of an aberration; they simply reverted to the position they were used to taking at home, where their constant preoccupation was with safeguards against possible Hindu domination in future rather than with freedom from foreign rule. Jinnah's position was different. He considered the Round Table Conference a great opportunity to secure effective substantial power from the British rulers to the people of India, and for this purpose he wanted a Hindu–Muslim accord. He was all for safeguards for Muslims; he had won for them separate electorates in the Lucknow Pact of 1916; in 1927, with his Delhi Muslim Conference proposals, he had tried to secure Hindus' consent to additional safeguards for the Muslim-minority provinces and statutory majorities in the Punjab and Bengal. He was the author of the Fourteen Points, but he knew well that it was difficult to get the consent of Hindus to such a huge package of safeguards without offering them some *quid pro quo*. So, at the Round Table Conference in 1930, as in 1927, Jinnah was inclined to agree to joint electorates for Muslims in return for substantial concessions in matters of reservations and other constitutional safeguards. Fazl-i-Husain's tight rein on the Muslim delegation made any compromise impossible. It was of course open to Jinnah to strike out an independent line and stick to his position both on the Hindu–Muslim accord and on the responsibility at the centre. But if he did so, he ran the risk of gross misrepresentation by his enemies in India. His real problem was that he had little in common with most of the Muslim delegates. It was a cruel dilemma for him; if he acted according to his judgement, he would not only be isolated in the delegation in London, but subjected to a tirade in the Muslim press in India. Since his exit from the Congress in 1920, his only constituency in Indian politics was the Muslim community. The price of defiance would, therefore, be political suicide. No wonder then that he swallowed the bitter pill and lined up with the rest of the Muslim delegation. On 12 January, he told a sub-committee of the Federal Structure Committee that a Hindu–Muslim settlement 'was a condition precedent for framing any future constitution'.[22] The following day he joined the Aga Khan and Shafi in a deputation to the Prime Minister whose diary reads: 'Busy day with interviews, most important being Mohammedans headed by Aga Khan with Shafi and Jinnah. They said there may be a civil war if their claims for security were not admitted. They could not trust the Hindus nor "co-operate with them in terms of confidence. They begged the Prime Minister to settle now in their favour, of course."'

The negotiations for a Hindu–Muslim accord continued almost till the end of the Conference, and at times it seemed that the only difficulty was Sikh opposition to statutory majority for Muslims in the Punjab. According to Wedgwood Benn (11 January 1931), in the Minorities Committee 'everybody appealed to Ujjal Singh to agree .... But he would not budge'. Even if the Sikhs had agreed, it is doubtful that the Muslim delegates would have agreed to surrender separate electorates in defiance of the fiat from Fazl-i-Husain. Such an agreement in any case would hardly have lasted after they returned to India. Benn, who had a ringside view of the Conference, wrote to the Viceroy on 18 February 1931 that the Muslims liked 'to put themselves in the position in which they would virtually exercise a veto on the constitution being discussed and advance both at the provincial and central levels of government with safeguards. Naturally, we are not anxious to go as far as this, and not out of any partiality for the Hindus, but because, frankly, it is very difficult to see a democratic system of government which is really run on a sectarian basis.'[23]

The First Round Table Conference ended on 19 January 1931 on an inconclusive note with a carefully phrased statement from the Prime Minister designed to please all. The Labour Government, even though it did not enjoy an absolute majority in the parliament, favoured advance on both at the provincial and central levels of government with safeguards, provided an all-India federation was established. But by the end of the Conference it became clear that it was difficult to devise a federal constitution that could reconcile the demands of Sapru and other Liberal leaders, the Princes, and the Muslims of India.

Chapter 14

SECOND ROUND TABLE CONFERENCE

In 1929, on the eve of the Lahore Congress, Jinnah had joined Sapru in parleys to prevent a conflict between the Indian National Congress and the government. He believed that a Round Table Conference in London was a wonderful opportunity to present India's case for self-government, and that the participation of the Congress would help to make it really representative of Indian political opinion. The Congress, however, went ahead and launched civil disobedience under Gandhi's leadership. The Mahatma announced that he would break the Salt Laws. He began his campaign on 12 March 1930 with a 241-mile march from Ahmedabad to Dandi, a village on the Arabian Sea coast. The tax on salt, though relatively light in incidence (amounting to just 3 annas per head), hit the poorest in the land. The first impulse of the government, as of the Congress intellectuals, was to ridicule 'the kindergarten stage of political revolution', and to laugh away the idea that 'the King-Emperor can be unseated by boiling sea water in a kettle'. The local officials tended to belittle the effects of Gandhi's march. If the salt earth collected by his party was confiscated after it reached the seashore, and no one was arrested, would he not look ridiculous? The government decided to watch the events and to take action only when the results of Gandhi's march became clearer.

Lord Irwin agonized for weeks over the pros and cons of Gandhi's arrest. C. Rajagopalachari, a shrewd observer, had, however, told Gandhi that his arrest was inevitable: 'They [the British] cannot let the conflagration grow on the ground that much salt cannot be made by you. It is not salt, but disobedience, you are manufacturing.'[1]

Far from proving a fiasco, as some British officials had hoped and Indian sceptics had feared, Gandhi's march electrified the entire country. The government at last did what it had been so long planning and at the same time dreading to do. It arrested Gandhi under an old law which empowered it to detain a person without trial in a court of law. Gandhi's imprisonment stimulated rather than slackened civil disobedience. The government retaliated with a number of 'ordinances' empowering it to ban the Congress organization, freeze its funds and choke its publicity channels. Over 60,000 civil resisters were arrested and clapped into prison. A striking testimony to the tremendous upsurge triggered by Gandhi's campaign is available not only in the reports of Indian and foreign journalists, but in government records of the time and in the private correspondence of the Viceroy and his advisers. For example, in June 1930 Sir Frederick Sykes, the Governor of Bombay, was lamenting that the whole population of Bombay had been 'carried away on a wave of semi-hysterical enthusiasm', and Sir Harry Haig, the Home Member of the Viceroy's Executive Council, ruefully acknowledged 'the power and success of the Congress movement'.

Lord Irwin was directing the sternest repression Indian nationalism had hitherto known, but he did not really relish this role. 'You know', he wrote to V.J. Patel, the President of the Central Legislative Assembly, 'that no one wishes more fervently than I that the affairs of India may speedily be again guided into smoother waters.' In a letter to Governor Sykes, he wrote: 'I believe it to be out of the question to expect to crush the whole movement in any dramatic fashion .... It seems to me that the right and the only policy is conciliation-cum-repression, i.e. to repress where necessary but losing no opportunity of emphasizing that a happier way is open.' Meanwhile, the official preparations for the First Round Table Conference had been on. It opened in London on 12 November 1930 and, as we have seen, it was deadlocked on the communal issue and ended on an inconclusive note on 19 January 1931. The Congress, the largest political party in the country, was not represented on it. Some of the Hindu Liberal delegates, who had left India in turmoil, wanted to return home with some tangible gains from the Conference and pleaded with Wedgwood Benn and Ramsay MacDonald for conciliatory gestures towards the Congress. In his farewell address to the Conference, MacDonald expressed the hope that the Congress would take part in the next session of the Conference. A little earlier, Lord Irwin's address to the Legislative Assembly included a surprisingly chivalrous reference to the 'spiritual force which impels Mr. Gandhi to count no sacrifice too great in the cause, as he believes, of the India he loves.'[2] About the same time, Benn wrote to Irwin about a dinner party in London to which he had invited Sapru, Jayakar, Sastri and some members of the British cabinet, and how these Liberal leaders had pleaded for some 'spectacular action'. Acknowledging that it was impossible to expect 'anything like submission or recantation' from the Congress, Benn wondered whether Lord Irwin could create a 'bilateral situation', which would lead to an amnesty and abandonment by the Congress of civil disobedience in favour of cooperation with the next session of the Round Table Conference. Irwin was thus encouraged by Benn to do what he was already wanting to do; he decided to release Gandhi and the members of the Congress Working Committee on 25 January 1931. The Working Committee assembled at Allahabad where Motilal Nehru was critically ill. It saw no justification to call off civil disobedience, but it withheld the decision from the press on receipt of a telegram from Sapru and Sastri who were on their way to India and were anxious to give the Congress leaders at Allahabad their first-hand impressions of the London Conference. Gandhi was not impressed by their accounts, nor did he profess to be very optimistic about the possibilities of an understanding with the government. Nevertheless, he wrote to Lord Irwin and asked for an interview. His argument was that the code of his non-violent struggle laid on him a moral obligation to respond to the Viceroy's gesture in releasing the members of the Congress Working Committee.

The Gandhi–Irwin parleys began on the afternoon of 17 February 1931. They lasted for a total of twenty-four hours, spread over eight meetings. There were long intervals during which hopes of a settlement alternately receded and revived, but finally, on the morning of 4 March, an agreement was reached. The Delhi Pact, or (to give it its popular name) the Gandhi–Irwin Pact, provided for the discontinuance of civil disobedience on the part of the Congress, and the revocation of the ordinances and the release of civil disobedience prisoners on the part of the government. The amnesty did not cover political prisoners detained without trial or convicted for covert or overt violence. The restitution of lands sold to third parties and the reinstatement of those who had lost their jobs during the civil disobedience were also not included in the agreement. There was a concession in a small way to poor people on the sea coast to manufacture salt, and the recognition of picketing of foreign cloth shops. There was to be no inquiry into the allegations of excesses by the police; this was a crucial point on which both the Congress and the government were very sensitive, and negotiations nearly broke down over it. Gandhi did not insist on the inquiry when Irwin told him that, though he (Gandhi) had the right to ask for an inquiry, it was wise to let bygones be bygones and to not rake up bitterness.

Alan Campbell-Johnson, one of the first biographers of Irwin, was not wrong in reaching the conclusion that in the Delhi Pact, Gandhi's gains were consolation prizes and Irwin's only surrender was in agreeing to enter into negotiations. Gandhi's reasons for signing the Pact should, however be sought not in its clauses, but in the logic of the creed of a non-violent struggle (satyagraha).

'I have often wondered myself', Gandhi told the annual session of the Congress at Karachi after the Pact, 'what we are going to do at the [Round Table] Conference when we know that there is such a gulf between what we want and what has been as yet offered at the Conference. But considerations of a *satyagrahi* decided me. There comes a stage when he may no longer refuse to negotiate with his opponent. His object is always to convert his opponent by love. The stage of negotiation arrived when members of the Working Committee [of the Congress] were released after the Premier's declaration. The Viceroy also made an appeal to us to lay down arms and to indicate what we want.'[3]

Lord Irwin, who had signed the agreement with Gandhi despite the misgivings of his official advisers, left India at the end of his five-year term in April 1931. Gandhi was in Bombay to bid him farewell. The new Viceroy, Lord Willingdon, was also in Bombay, but did not send for Gandhi. The hard-headed British bureaucrats in Delhi and in the provincial capitals, to whom the Delhi Pact had been a bitter pill, found a sympathetic chief. Friction between the government and the Congress began within a few days of the signing of the Pact. The Congress received complaints that all the prisoners had not been released, and that forfeited lands had not been restored, nor the village officials who had taken part in the civil disobedience been reinstated. Gandhi went up to Simla to meet the Viceroy and proposed a judicial enquiry into the complaints on the working of the Pact. The government accused the Congress of acting in a spirit contrary to the Delhi Pact, which verged on repudiation by both sides. However, further negotiations made it possible to patch up a last-minute compromise, and Gandhi, who was nominated by the Indian National Congress as its sole representative, reached Bombay just in time to sail in the *SS Rajputana*. He arrived in London on 12 September 1931, five days after the inauguration of the Second Round Table Conference.

II

If the Gandhi–Irwin Pact of March 1931 was a bitter pill for the British bureaucracy in India, it was a bolt from the blue for the Muslim politicians who had been consistently pro-British and anti-Congress. They wondered whether the British were about to jettison the traditional Anglo–Muslim alliance. Some of them had been bitter opponents of the Congress but thought it prudent to approach Dr Ansari and Abul Kalam Azad to secure the support of nationalist Muslim leaders for their charter of Muslim 'safeguards' under the new constitution in return for Muslim acceptance of joint electorates. The Aga Khan described the evolving political situation to Jinnah soon after the Gandhi–Irwin Pact: 'We cannot tell for a certainty what attitude the English will finally adopt about India .... It may be possible for us to get all our demands from the Congress, plus weightage, plus majority on proportion basis in Punjab and Bengal with, of course, joint electorates .... My own idea is that the Muslims should get in touch with the Congress but not close the negotiations.'[4] To Fazl-i-Husain, the Aga Khan's mentor, the Gandhi–Irwin Pact, however, was a real challenge. We have already seen how he had blocked a Hindu–Muslim accord and stalled progress in discussions on constitutional reforms in the First Round Table Conference. He wanted maximum autonomy at the provincial level and a virtual status quo at the centre where the Hindus would be in a majority.

After Gandhi agreed to attend the Second Round Table Conference, Fazl-i-Husain insisted that no Congress Muslim should be included in the Muslim delegation. Lord Willingdon readily accepted his advice which ensured the exclusion of Dr Ansari from the Conference despite Lord Irwin's assurance to Gandhi. Fazl-i-Husain also managed to keep a tighter rein on the Muslim delegation than he had done the previous year. He named the Aga Khan as head of the delegation, and two of his own henchmen, Shafaat Ahmad Khan and Zafarulla Khan, as its secretaries.

Fazl-i-Husain to the Aga Khan, 23 May 1931:

All the Muslim members who were there [in the First Round Table Conference] last year have had talks with me and I feel Indian Muslims cannot thank you sufficiently for all you did.... I feel happy that you will be there to look after the Indian Muslim interest. All local governments and the Government of India have been considerate of Muslim interest up to a point, and I know there are large sections of British public opinion which want to do all they can to help Indian Muslims. However, I entrust the whole matter, which is extremely important, to your care.[5]

Fazl-i-Husain specially warned the Muslim delegates against succumbing to Gandhi's charisma. 'Whatever lionizing may take place of Gandhi in London', he wrote to Shafaat Ahmad Khan on 28 July 1931, 'if you played your cards well, [you] would have a pull over other communities inasmuch as you have Aga Khan with you who stands pre-eminently in English public life[6].... So if you held together and acted under Aga Khan's guidance ... the programme that has been chalked out remains unaffected with Gandhi's appearance at the Round Table Conference. It is only foolishness on the part of some Muslims to indulge in talks and gestures [relating to Gandhi] which can do no credit to their self-respect or strengthen Islamic teachings and culture.'

Jinnah was the only Muslim delegate whom Fazl-i-Husain could not order about, but his position in the Second Round Table Conference was even weaker than it had been in the First Conference. In 1930 Fazl-i-Husain had exercised remote control over the Muslim delegates from Delhi. In 1931 his intervention was open. The Muslim delegates were told in no uncertain terms that the Aga Khan was their leader, that they were to remain united because Islam was in danger after the Gandhi–Irwin Pact, that they must stick to all the demands made by the All

India Muslim Conference (a puppet organization of Fazl-i-Husain and his Punjabi friends) in 1929, and that not the slightest concession was to be made to the Hindus. Further, it was not in the interest of Muslims to demand responsibility at the centre where the continuance of British control was in Muslim interest.

The new Secretary of State, Sir Samuel Hoare, who succeeded Wedgwood Benn after the general elections in November 1931, was in no hurry to speed up the process of constitutional reforms for India. He assured Lord Irwin that he was treating Gandhi just as he was 'treating any other delegate of the Conference and doing everything to prevent his getting undue advertisement in the [British] press.'[7] A year earlier, when Sir Samuel was in the Opposition, he had confided to a sub-committee of the Conservative Party that it was perfectly possible to devise a constitution for India which looked like self-government but which managed to keep 'the verities and realities of power' in British hands. He saw in the concept of an all-India federation, comprising both British India and the Princely states, an excellent opportunity to inject a permanent conservative element into the central legislature and executive to act as a counterpoise to the Indian National Congress.

As soon as the Conference began in October 1931, it became obvious that the Muslim delegation was in an uncompromising mood. Srinivasa Sastri had already noted: 'This time Muslims are more sullen and militant. They are well in with the Conservatives. They want India to have provincial autonomy and no responsibility at the centre. The Mohammedans do not care for the latter at all.'[8] As a British historian puts it: 'The Hindus sensed that the tide had turned. A Tory-bureaucratic-Muslim alli-ance was at hand. An era of reaction was opening.'[9]

Jinnah did not change his stand in the Second Round Table Conference. As in the First, he called for safeguards for Muslims under the new constitution, but at the same time he demanded a definite advance towards self-government at the centre as well as in the provinces. He presented his views vigorously, in the Federal Structure Committee, on the need for popular control of finance and defence, the establishment of a Federal Court and other issues, and differed on these issues with the Aga Khan and other Muslim delegates such as Sir Mohammad Shafi. However, Jinnah's views did not prevail against the reactionary group organized by Fazl-i-Husain, which was opposed to any settlement with the Hindus until all their demands were conceded, and opposed any responsibility at the centre. The result was a standstill in the Conference, which was not unwelcome to the British Tories and bureaucrats. The British cabinet after the general elections in November was still headed by MacDonald but dominated by the Conservatives.

The Muslim delegates advocated separate electorates not only for themselves, but for other minority groups such as depressed classes, Indian Christians, Anglo-Indians and Europeans, who had joined them in a 'Minorities Pact'. Gandhi volunteered to seek an agreement in a surprising climb-down, expressed his willingness to concede most of the Muslim demands which the Congress leaders in the All Parties Conference had dismissed out of hand only three years earlier, such as separate electorates for Muslims, statutory Muslim majorities in the Punjab and Bengal, weightage in the Muslim-minority provinces, residuary powers in the provinces, and one-third seats for Muslims in the central legislature. But there were two conditions in Gandhi's offer: that Muslims endorse the Congress demand for self-government, and that after the introduction of the new constitution, a referendum of Muslim voters be held on separate electorates versus joint electorates. On 17 October, negotiations broke down over the comparatively minor issue of whether the question of a statutory Muslim majority in the Punjab legislature should be referred for arbitration to a Minorities subcommittee or to an outside judicial body. On 18 October, at the meeting of the Minorities Committee, Gandhi, while reporting the failure of the informal negotiations, proposed that the new constitution should provide for a judicial tribunal to examine communal claims. The Muslim delegates, however, insisted that the communal question must be settled prior to the drafting of any new constitution. The depressed classes (the section represented by Ambedkar) lined up with the Muslims; like the Sikhs and the Muslims, they also demanded satisfaction of their claims as a condition precedent to any constitutional advance. The Minorities Committee was adjourned indefinitely without arriving at any decision.

Jinnah's stand on constitutional reforms at the Second Round Table Conference remained basically the same as at the First Conference. Unlike the Aga Khan and his group, who took their cue from Fazl-i-Husain in Delhi, Jinnah did not exclusively harp on the communal issue; he wanted provincial autonomy, but no less important for him was the relaxation of imperial control over the central government.

However, when it came to the crunch the Muslim delegation in the Conference closed its ranks, and as it ultimately did, it was difficult for Jinnah to stand aside. His restraint made it possible for the Muslim delegation to give a demonstration of Muslim solidarity at the Conference. It could not have been an agreeable experience for him to choose between his principles and his political survival.

Gandhi had argued at the Conference that since the British government did not spell out the measure of the advance it was prepared to make towards self-government, there was little incentive for the parties in the Round Table Conference to agree. That Jinnah really held the same opinion came out in an unguarded moment. In a letter sent from London, Mahadev Desai wrote to Jawaharlal Nehru on 23 October 1931:

Dr. S.K. Datta told us a story which is sure to amuse you. He was dining with Jinnah the other day at an English friend's — Campbell Rhodes' [house]. Jinnah had been through his third bottle of champagne when the minorities question was being discussed. And Mr. Rhodes said, 'Why don't you give an agreed solution and compel Government to yield?' Jinnah under the sobering effects [!] of champagne replied: 'It is exactly where you are mistaken. It is impossible to have an agreed solution until we know what we are going to get and Government are putting the cart before the horse.'

This by the way is an instance which would provide a strong argument for the anti-prohibitionists.[10]

Chapter 15

Self-Exile

On 2 February 1931, soon after the conclusion of the First Round Table Conference, Jinnah told a correspondent of Reuters news agency[1] that he intended to 'stay on in England indefinitely to practise in the Privy Council and to enter Parliament' because he believed that during the coming year India's constitutional battle would be fought in London. He gave the same reason for his decision when he briefly visited India six months later. Plausible as the explanation seemed, it was not convincing. If the next instalment of constitutional reforms for India was on the parliamentary anvil it was hardly necessary for him to wind up his establishment in Bombay, make out a passport 'with England as the place of residence' and say good-bye to his country. In the years preceding the Minto–Morley and Montagu–Chelmsford reforms, he had made prolonged visits to England; he could have done so again. It was certainly a drastic step to turn his back on a legal practice and a political career built over a quarter of a century. He knew full well that the change from the Bar of the Bombay High Court and the Legislative Assembly in Delhi to the Bar of the Privy Council and the British Parliament in London was not going to be easy. What he could not admit in public was that it was the turns and twists of Muslim politics in his homeland which had driven him to self-exile in England.

II

M.R.A. Baig, who served Jinnah as his secretary in the mid-1930s, refers to the 'traumas' which Jinnah suffered successively at the Nagpur Congress session in 1920 and at the All-Parties National Convention at Calcutta in 1928. But these were not the only traumas which Jinnah had suffered. Indeed his political career seemed star-crossed. He was conscious of his abilities, he was confident, he was ambitious and he had set his sights high. But it was a strange irony that whenever he was about to reach the top of the political ladder, events beyond his control brought him down. He had hardly turned 30 when he first forged his way to the forefront of national politics; at the Calcutta session of the Indian National Congress in December 1906 he had questioned the representative character of the Muslim delegation which had waited on Lord Minto and demanded separate electorates for Muslims. Three years later, when separate electorates became part of the Minto–Morley scheme, it was borne upon him that henceforth he would have to depend upon an exclusively Muslim electorate for election to any legislature in India. Reluctantly, almost apologetically, he endorsed separate electorates and gradually became their champion. In 1916 he even persuaded the Congress leadership to accept this mode of election for his co-religionists in the Lucknow Pact of 1916. This was the time when he was hailed as an 'ambassador of Hindu–Muslim unity'. With one firm foot in the Muslim League and the other in the Congress, he was about to achieve his ambition of becoming a 'Muslim Gokhale'. This ambition was foiled by the dramatic emergence of Gandhi in 1919 as the dominant figure in national politics, while several veteran Congress leaders were marginalized. By the beginning of 1921 he was a political orphan. He could not fit in with Gandhi's ideas and methods and had no place in the Congress; henceforth his only constituency was to be the Muslim community. With great persistence and skill he rescued the Muslim League from the inertia and oblivion of the Khilafat period. In 1927 he took a bold initiative by holding a conference of all Muslim leaders and devising a formula for Hindu–Muslim accord, which provided for acceptance of the major Muslim demands in return for Muslim acceptance of joint electorates. His proposals were readily welcomed by the Congress and were hailed as a real breakthrough in Indian politics, but only for a while. By the end of 1928 the tide had turned against Jinnah. The Muslim League had split down the middle and the Congress acceptance of his proposals came to naught by an All-Parties National Convention. Early in 1929, Jinnah was in a serious predicament with the loss of credibility among his own co-religionists. It took him a year to recover from this blow. He disarmed his opponents by producing a huge package as the safeguards — the Fourteen Points — for Muslims in the new constitution. Luckily for him, Lord Irwin's announcement on dominion status for India and a Round Table Conference in London opened new vistas for him. He believed he could play a mediatory role between the Indian political parties, as well as between India and Britain. He was in high spirits when he left India for London in August 1930 to attend the Round Table Conference. He did not foresee the extent to which he was to be disabled from playing a pivotal role by the drastic realignments in Muslim politics with the appointment of Sir Fazl-i-Husain as a member of the Viceroy's Executive Council. It was Fazl-i-Husain who henceforth had the last word in selection of delegates; he dictated the line which they had to take. After having been the working president of the Muslim League for so many years, Jinnah had good reason to expect that he would be the *de facto,* if not *de jure,* chief of the Muslim delegation. But thanks to Fazl-i-Husain, the Aga Khan led the delegation. Fazl-i-Husain, through his remote control of Muslim delegates, scotched efforts at a Hindu–Muslim accord as well as any substantial progress towards devolution of power from Britain to India. Jinnah felt ill at ease in the Conference. He had his own views and expressed them fearlessly. Unluckily for him, his nationalist rhetoric did not go down well with both the reactionaries in the Muslim delegation and the British politicians and the bureaucracy. Jinnah noted during the discussions that the British delegates were dragging their feet when it came to an issue involving real transfer of power to Indian hands. He attributed this to the inability of the Hindus and the Muslims to agree. Further, there was the impasse on the communal issue. Jinnah knew full well that while some Hindu and Sikh delegates from the Punjab were adamant, the extreme rigidity of the Muslim delegation was being dictated by Fazl-i-Husain's henchmen in the Conference. Jinnah felt that in the circumstances he had no option but to toe the line of the Aga Khan and company; any other course would have given a handle to his opponents at home to malign him behind his back.

By the end of the Round Table Conference, Jinnah realized that his wings had been clipped by the emergence in strategic positions of powerful men in India and Britain who were hostile to him. It was galling for him that it was left to men like Fazl-i-Husain and the Aga Khan to guide the destiny of Indian Muslims. Colonel Wedgwood, then a new Labour leader in Britain whom Jinnah knew well, refers in his memoirs to the irony that 'he was perpetually turned down and passed over by men with less than half his brains or standing'. This grievance applied especially to Jinnah's position in the Round Table Conference. It was his isolation and marginalization in Indian politics which drove Jinnah to self-exile in the early 1930s.

III

By the beginning of 1931 Jinnah had made up his mind to wind up his establishment in Bombay and settle in London. He was no stranger to London. The two years and three-and-a-half months he spent there were the most formative period of his life. He quickly acclimatized himself to his new surroundings and took to English food, English dress, English language and English etiquette with great alacrity. He learnt to admire the British legal system and British political institutions. After returning to India he settled down in Bombay, but he made annual trips to England for business or pleasure. London was thus almost a second home to him after Bombay, and in 1931 he moved into a fine house in Hampstead's West Heath Road. It was a three-storey villa in the midst of an eight-acre garden and grounds. With him were his 13-year-old daughter Dina and his unmarried sister, Fatima, who had come to live with him in Bombay after the death of his wife Ruttie in 1929. He put Dina in a boarding school, but he had her company during school vacations.

Jinnah was able to secure chambers in the King's Bench Walk for his legal practice. In India Jinnah had divided his time between law and politics. He planned to do the same in England. If he had reckoned that, as an eminent lawyer and a seasoned politician from India, he could easily get a ticket for a seat in Parliament, he was in for a disappointment. His first choice was the Labour Party with whose policies he had some affinity. He had known Ramsay MacDonald when he was in the Opposition. He made soundings but drew a blank. He did not know that MacDonald had not been too happy at his bold stance in the Round Table Conference. The Aga Khan then approached the Conservative Party's central office and advised Jinnah to contact Sir George Bourger of that office to select a constituency from which he would like to contest. The Aga Khan was being too optimistic; the Conservative seats were not going abegging. All we know is that the Conservatives did not give him a ticket.

IV

The Conservative Party was hardly likely to welcome a Muslim leader from India who had made no secret of his nationalist proclivities. Unluckily for Jinnah, Sir Samuel Hoare, who belonged to the Conservative Party, for some inexplicable reason had taken a strong dislike to Jinnah. Having drawn a blank from both the Labour and Conservative parties, Jinnah saw that there was no chance of his entering British Parliament. He had no option but to focus on his practice at the Privy Council. Every day his English chauffeur, Bradbury, drove him from his West Heath Road residence to his chambers in the King's Bench Walk. The day was taken up with briefs, mostly from India. Many years later, one of his contemporaries, Lord Spence, told Jinnah's British biographer that Jinnah was 'most successful' in his legal practice in London. However, we have a contrary assessment in the autobiography of M.C. Chagla who had worked with Jinnah closely in his chambers in Bombay and knew him well. Chagla writes that Jinnah's legal practice at the Privy Council did not prosper as he had expected because he was 'essentially more of an advocate than a lawyer'.[2] In the Privy Council something more than a strong personality and the wiles of persuasive advocacy was required. Durga Das, an Indian correspondent who met Jinnah in London, carried the impression that Jinnah would have preferred a seat on the Judicial Committee of the Privy Council to arguing cases before it but that, alas, was not possible. The two high British officials who could sponsor his name for the Judicial Committee, Lord Willingdon, the Viceroy, and Sir Samuel Hoare, the Secretary of State, were not well disposed towards Jinnah.

Not much has been recorded on Jinnah's activities during these years. He had of course greater leisure than he had in India. He was fond of the theatre and took his daughter with him to a good play when she came home in the school holidays. But since he had little aptitude for making friends he was rather lonely. His sister, Fatima, kept the house in London, just as she had done after Ruttie's death in Bombay, but she was not much company for her brother. The Indian journalists who met Jinnah during these years had the impression that he had been disappointed with the Round Table Conference and had begun to doubt the sincerity of the British Government. Iqbal Singh, the London correspondent of the *Free Press Journal* of Bombay, recalled that Jinnah expressed radical views on political and economic issues (such as the Ottawa Agreement) which granted preference to British imports into India. Agatha Harrison of the India Conciliation Group, which lobbied for the Indian National Congress in London, invited him to give a talk and she came to the conclusion that Jinnah was 'an Indian first and a Muslim second'. In December 1933 he refused to see Rahmat Ali, a Muslim student in Cambridge, who wanted to discuss his pet proposal to create a separate Muslim state.

Jinnah wrote to his young friend, Abdul Matin Choudhury, in March 1933: 'I do not see what I can do there [in India] at present. You very rightly suggest that I should enter the Assembly. But is there much hope of doing anything there? These are questions which still make me feel that there is no room for my services in India ....'[3] A month later he told Choudhury that he was 'being called back to India without having any solid base'.[4]

By the end of 1932, Jinnah had realized that his plan of settling down in England was not practicable. But he feared that the adverse circumstances which had driven him into voluntary exile had not changed. The All India Muslim League, the party which he had so diligently nurtured in the 1920s, was in a bad way. It had never been a mass party; in 1927 it had only 1,330 members. Jinnah had to adjourn the 1928 session because of factional disputes. The 1929 session of the party was also adjourned for lack of a quorum; the adjourned meeting convened four months later in Delhi ended in a fiasco. The 1930 session at Allahabad which Jinnah could not attend because of the Round Table Conference, and which was presided over by the eminent poet, Sir Mohammad Iqbal, could not muster the quorum of seventy-five members. The attendance at the 1931 session in Delhi was scarcely 120. In order to increase the membership of the League, the annual subscription was reduced from 6 rupees to 1 rupee, and the admission fee of Rs 5 was abolished and the quorum was reduced at the annual sessions from seventy-five to fifty; But this did not help much because the organizers of the 1933 session in Delhi — no sessions were held in 1932, 1934 and 1935 — had a busy time, filling the empty hall with students of the Anglo-Arabic College. According to Khalid bin Saiyeed, during the years 1931–33 the annual expenditure of the All India Muslim League did not exceed Rs 3,000.

Jinnah was dismayed by the factional and personal rivalries in the small political elite, of which the League leadership was composed; he had no hold over them. Indeed he acted as the chairman of a board of directors; indeed his value in these gatherings was that he could reconcile opposing points of view and in the last resort prevent the Muslim League from splitting into different factions!

The Muslim League had split when Sir Mohammad Shafi and the Fazl-i-Husain group from the Punjab had rebelled against Jinnah's proposals for a Hindu–Muslim accord in 1927 and formed a rival body — the All India Muslim Conference. It was this new organization (that existed only on paper) which came to be treated by the government as the representative body of Indian Muslims during the years 1929–34. Conditions in the Muslim League deteriorated quickly after Jinnah retired to England in 1931. Two years of squabbles and mutual recriminations and the danger of fragmentation of the party drove the warring groups to seek a compromise. Jinnah was seen as a political conciliator. It was in 1933, when there was a strong impulse in the warring rival Muslim groups for effecting conciliation, that Jinnah was seen as the best person to perform the role of a mediator. He was elected President of the Muslim League in 1933 but he informed the sponsors that he would not be available until January 1934 when he would visit India. Apparently, he knew that time was on his side and that the squabbling factions in sheer desperation had called him to give some semblance of order to the All India Muslim League and this is exactly what happened. Jinnah was never quite sure as to how long the truce between the rival groups would last.

Dewan Chaman Lal, a member of the Legislative Assembly, who knew Jinnah very well, has recorded, after Jinnah returned to India:

> I met him at the Willingdon Club in 1934. He said to me and to my wife, when we asked him to stand for the election, 'No. I am finished politically ....' A few days later he told me, 'It is Jinnah's luck, I have been elected President of the League again.'[5]

Chapter 16

THE RAJ AT BAY

In 1930, when Jinnah arrived in London to attend the Round Table Conference, he had good reasons for optimism. He had been encouraged by the sympathetic attitude of Viceroy Lord Irwin and the Labour Party which was in power in Britain. By the end of the year, the situation changed completely. The Labour Party was voted out of office and was succeeded by a 'National Government' dominated by the Conservative Party. Wedgwood Benn, with whom Jinnah had developed some rapport, had been succeeded by Sir Samuel Hoare who conceived a dislike for Jinnah for no obvious reason. Lord Irwin was succeeded by Lord Willingdon who had loathed Jinnah since their clash in Bombay in 1918 when he was Governor of that province.

For more than two years, from mid-September 1931 till the end of 1933, Jinnah had lived in England, practically cut off from active politics in his homeland. These were the years when his arch opponent, Lord Willingdon, was Viceroy, and his arch rival Fazl-i-Husain was the Muslim member in the Viceroy's Executive Council. Not until both Willingdon and Fazl-i-Husain completed their terms in office could Jinnah breathe freely. While he was in enforced exile in London, Indian politics had undergone dramatic changes which need to be recapitulated to understand the situation with which Jinnah was confronted when he decided to re-enter the Indian political stage.

II

The most important event of these years was the campaign of civil disobedience launched by Gandhi on return from the Round Table Conference. The Gandhi–Irwin Pact had gone to pieces and Gandhi had no option but to resume civil disobedience. The British policy towards him and the Congress had been hardening since Willingdon assumed the Viceroyalty of India in April 1931; he had the reputation of being a strong and hard-headed administrator, and had every in-tention of living up to it. The Indian problem struck him primarily as an administrative one, requiring timely and judicious use of coercion to crush the troublemakers. Most of the British Governors in the provinces shared Willingdon's views; many of them were ready, even itching, 'to teach a lesson' to the Congress which, they believed, had thrived on 'half-hearted' measures of the previous regimes. Sir Frederick Sykes, the Governor of Bombay, had complained to Willingdon, soon after the latter's arrival in India in March 1931, of the 'disabilities' under which his government had to fight the Congress campaign in 1930. In a letter to the Viceroy (12 November 1931), he urged 'a really rapid, organized and weighty handling' of civil disobedience when it was renewed. The Government of India and the provincial governments were thus determined to give short shrift to the Congress, when Gandhi returned to India at the end of December 1931 from the Round Table Conference. The plans for dealing with civil disobedience were pulled out of the 'top secret' pigeonholes of the Secretariat, and put into operation with lightning speed. Within a few hours of the arrest of Gandhi and the members of the Congress Working Committee on 4 January 1932, a series of 'ordinances' were promulgated. Not only the Congress Working Committee but the provincial committees and innumerable local committees were also declared illegal; a number of organizations allied with or sympathetic to the Congress, such as the Youth Leagues, National Schools, Congress libraries and hospitals, were also outlawed. Congress funds were confiscated, Congress buildings were occupied, and almost every possible measure was taken to prevent the Congress from functioning. By skimming off its leadership and freezing its funds, the government hoped to demoralize the Congress. The powers acquired through the ordinances included those which permitted the administration to control or forfeit any funds 'which were suspected of being held or used for the purposes of an unlawful association'; officials were authorized to examine account books, make inquiries or order searches.

A new prison policy was devised with the dual purpose of deterring Congressmen from courting imprisonment and easing the pressure on gaols. In a circular letter dated 21 January 1932, the provincial governments were advised by the Home Department of the Government of India to impose fines in lieu of imprisonment or, in addition to short terms of imprisonment, to prefer collective fines to prosecution of individuals. Gaol administration hardened perceptibly. The first Congress campaign in 1930–31 had received a great impetus with the participation of women. In the second campaign in 1932–33 the treatment in gaols seemed to have been almost designed to scare away women. Mirabehn, Gandhi's disciple and the daughter of a former Admiral of the British Fleet, gave an account of the conditions in the Arthur Road jail in Bombay, which was a severe indictment of conditions in women's prisons. She noticed that women political prisoners were allowed to interview their children only through iron bars. Her neighbours in this jail were three criminals, two thieves and a prostitute; they were not locked up for the night, while the political prisoners were.[1]

III

An intense severity guided the government in its dealings with the press. The initial success of the Salt Satyagraha campaign in 1930 was attributed in official circles to the publicity it had received. In 1932, by a series of drastic measures, the freedom of the press was drastically curtailed. Apart from the prosecution of press correspondents, the forfeitures of securities from newspapers were used as deterrents. On 4 July 1932, just six months after the resumption of civil disobedience, the House of Commons was informed that action had been taken under the Press Law against 109 journalists and ninety-eight printing presses. In Bengal even the proceedings of the Provincial Legislative Council could not be published if they contained any criticism of the government. A number of provincial governments made it an offence for a newspaper to publish photographs of Gandhi and other Congress leaders; the Madras Government went so far as to authorize magistrates to destroy the portraits of Congress leaders.

In spite of the initial handicaps, no less than 61,551 convictions for civil disobedience took place in the first nine months of the movement in 1932; this figure was a little higher than that during the campaign of 1930–31. Judged by convictions, the movement was the strongest in the United Provinces, Bombay, Bengal and Bihar (each of which contributed more than 10,000 prisoners), and the weakest in the Punjab. In the small NWFP there were 5,557 convictions, just half those in the Bombay presidency.

Under the hammer-blows of the government, civil disobedience wilted; the number of convictions in a single month had come down from the peak figure of 17,818 in February 1932 to 3,047 in August 1932. The movement was at a low ebb when it was further set back by its author. The announcement of a fast by Gandhi to protest against the grant of separate electorates to untouchables stirred public opinion powerfully, but it also diverted it into non-political channels.

The Viceroy and his advisers, elated by their apparent success in suppressing the civil disobedience movement, were now able to visualize the Indian political scene without Gandhi; the Congress seemed to them demoralized and divided; the more moderate section of the party might be expected to coalesce with other groups to work the new constitution; it would be a combination which might be strong but not overwhelmingly so in the legislatures, and thus would cause no serious inconvenience to the government.

On 13 March 1934 Willingdon wrote to Samuel Hoare:[2] 'the present political situation is very dead and the governments — provincial and central — seem to pass their measures without much difficulty.' On 12 August he wrote: 'I feel, as a political leader, Gandhi is very nearly finished.' Samuel Hoare congratulated the Viceroy on his 'remarkable achievement'. The Viceroy believed that the fortunes of the Congress were at their nadir and it was just the right time to hold elections to the Central Assembly which had been overdue by two years. He gave secret instructions to the provincial Governors to do everything possible to help the pro-government candidates. 'The struggle', he told them, 'as we all know, is between the Congress and the government'.

IV

While the government was trying to combat civil disobedience and crush the Congress, it was also engaged in the process of formulating constitutional changes to conciliate Indian opinion. It was the dual policy of repression and reforms it had been following since the beginning of the twentieth century and which had resulted in the Reforms Acts of 1909 and 1919. The object of doling out reforms in instalments was to appease the moderate elements in the country who had been agitating for greater popular control of administration. In 1924, Jinnah's Independent Party in the Central Assembly had teamed up with the Swaraj Party headed by Motilal Nehru in demanding a Round Table Conference for revision of the Act of 1919.

The reform process had started with the appointment of the Simon Commission in 1927 and Lord Irwin's declaration on dominion status in October 1929. In the negotiations between the government and the Congress which followed this declaration, Jinnah had taken part along with the other 'bridge-builders' — Liberal leaders T.B. Sapru and M.R. Jayakar. But by the time Jinnah left for England to attend the Round Table Conference in 1930, civil disobedience had been launched by Gandhi. The Congress and the government were locked in a mortal combat. To Jinnah's dismay, the proceedings at the Round Table Conference in London were protracted and little progress was made in 1930. The Labour Government had been voted out and succeeded by a National Government headed by Ramsay MacDonald, but dominated by the Conservative Party. The Conservatives themselves were divided between hardliners, led by Winston Churchill, who were totally opposed to any devolution of power to Indian hands, but the majority of the Party was prepared to follow its leader Baldwin, who wanted to make a cautious advance in India. The British Government's dilemma was aptly summed up at that time by the *Manchester Guardian:* 'Since the British could neither govern nor get out of India, it was necessary to devise a constitution that seemed like self-government in India and British Raj at Westminster.' Interestingly, Samuel Hoare, who was later to pilot the Reforms Bill through the Parliament, assured a committee of the Conservative Party in 1930 that it was possible for Britain to 'yield semblance of responsible government and yet retain in our hands the realities and verities of British control'.

Samuel Hoare was speaking in 1930. Five years later, the Act of 1935 was passed by the British Parliament, endorsing a constitution which was marked by a series of checks and balances. For example, provincial autonomy was conceded and ministers responsible to the legislature were given a wide field, but the Governors had 'special powers' over vital subjects such as law and order and finance.

At the centre, the new constitution envisaged a federal legislature with 375 members, 250 of whom were to represent British India and 125 Princely states. Out of the 250 seats fixed for British India, eighty-two were allotted to

Muslims, eighty-six were 'general seats', and eighty-two were special seats for women, labour, etc. The Muslims and the Princes were each guaranteed a third of the seats in the Lower House of the legislature. The Princes were to nominate their representatives as they had no elected representative legislatures, and the Muslims' representatives were to be elected by Muslim members of the provincial legislatures.

Perhaps the bluntest comment on the proposed constitution was made by Clement Attlee, the leader of the Opposition, who told the House of Commons that the constitutional scheme in the Act of 1935 was deliberately framed to exclude as far as possible the Congress from effective power by giving undue weightage to the Princes and the minority communities.[3]

The separate electorates and the allocation of seats to various religious minorities in the provincial legislatures were prescribed by the Communal Award announced by Prime Minister MacDonald in August 1932. MacDonald had at first been reluctant to make such an award. He felt it was a thankless task; it was hardly possible to reconcile the contending claims of various religious communities. However, the Muslim delegation at the Round Table Conference made it clear that it would not discuss other substantive issues on the agenda until the question of 'safeguards' for Muslims in the future constitution was settled to their satisfaction. Winston Churchill and his diehard followers argued that since there was no agreement, further discussions on the constitution should be postponed until the Indians could agree among themselves. The Viceroy and his advisers, however, urged that the 'constitution-making' process should continue. In the weeks preceding the announcement of the award, the Viceroy earnestly pleaded with his superiors in London for the acceptance of Muslim demands. The new constitution offered an opportunity for rewarding and retaining the loyalty of the Muslim community and for checkmating the Hindu majority represented by the Congress.

Lord Willingdon to Sir Samuel Hoare, 10 July, 1932

Do please visualize the political situation here. The Congress are against us, the Moderates are not cooperating, and remember these two bodies are nearly all Hindus, who, while there are many really good men amongst them, have as a community been the leaders of every subversive movement during the past twenty years. The Moslems, who on the whole have generally supported Government, are, with the Princes, at present on our side. But if you give them anything less than what de Montgomery [Governor of the Punjab] proposes for the Punjab, and I propose for Bengal, I am quite certain they will non-cooperate too.

Willingdon went on to threaten his resignation if he could not have his way: 'If owing to your decision, I lost their [Muslim] support as well, I would probably have to ask you to send out someone else.'[4]

The demands first put forward in 1929 by the Muslim Conference were conceded. The North-West Frontier Province became a Governor's province. The Muslim share in public services was fixed at 25 per cent of all imperial appointments. As regards residuary powers, the Muslim demand that they should be vested in the provinces was not accepted, but as desired by them they were to be exercised by the Governor-General in his discretion. Muslims in the Punjab were given a statutory majority. In Bengal, Muslim seats worked out at 48.4 per cent; if they did not get the statutory majority it was because of representation which was to be given to Europeans. The weightage given to Muslims under the Lucknow Pact in 1916 was to continue in the provinces where they were in a minority.

The pressure from the Government of India had the desired effect. The Communal Award approved by the British Government and announced by Prime Minister MacDonald virtually conceded all the demands of the Muslim delegation at the Round Table Conference. A week after the announcement, Private Secretary to the Viceroy telegraphed to the Secretary of State: 'Muslims, generally, privately well pleased in all provinces, though publicly offering some protest as offset to Hindu demands.'[5]

The Muslim leaders, who had worked for this package of safeguards, were delighted with the result. 'We have succeeded', the Aga Khan wrote to Fazl-i-Husain on 10 May 1933, 'in settling this problem after years of strenuous work and a campaign for our rights which is unparalleled in the history of modern Islam.'[6]

Chapter 17

IMAGE OF A NATIONALIST

Jinnah's return to India in January 1934 marked his re-entry into Indian politics after about two years of voluntary exile. In March the feud in the All India Muslim League ended when the two rival groups, headed by Abdul Aziz and Hidayat Husain, agreed to bury the hatchet and elect Jinnah as president of the party. On 1 April, the Muslim League Council met in Delhi with Jinnah in the chair. In his very first speech he condemned the constitutional reforms outlined in the 'White Paper' issued by the British Government. He declared that the proposed constitution was unacceptable except for the Communal Award, which had to remain until a substitute, acceptable to both Hindus and Muslims, was found. Meanwhile, he appealed for communal unity to put up a united front against the British imposition of a retrograde constitution on India.

During the first three months after his return from England, Jinnah earnestly engaged himself in the task of rehabilitating the All India Muslim League which had become almost defunct during his retirement in England. The Delhi winter did not suit him; his frail health was unable to stand the strain of a hectic schedule in and outside the Central Legislative Assembly. In March, he suffered a serious collapse at Bombay, which Kanji Dwarkadas, a family friend of the Jinnahs, has described in his memoirs: 'One evening in March 1934, Jinnah rang me up and asked me to see him. I went at the appointed time but Jinnah did not turn up. I rang up his house and his bearer told me that Jinnah had taken seriously ill the night before. For five days he was unconscious and hovered between life and death — it was just touch and go, as the attack he had was likely to affect the heart. On the very day he regained consciousness, I called at his house.'[1]

The nationalist tenor of Jinnah's speeches and statements during his short stay in India had disconcerted the pro-British and feudal group of regional politicians headed by the Aga Khan and Fazl-i-Husain who had been able to dominate Muslim politics under Willingdon's regime. They had pushed Jinnah to the wall at the Round Table Conference, and marginalized the All India Muslim League in India by setting up the All India Muslim Conference. Soon after Jinnah sailed for England in May 1934, his opponents got together and announced the formation of a new party, The League Conference Parliamentary Majlis, to fight elections to the Central Legislative Assembly which were due later in the year. They included, besides the Aga Khan and Fazl-i-Husain, well-known Muslim leaders Sir Feroze Khan Noon, Nawab Sir Mohammad Yusuf Shareef and Sir Syed Raza Ali. The Nawab of Chhatari became the convener of the new party and Hidayat Husain its hatchet man. Hidayat Husain summoned an emergency meeting of the Council of the Muslim League without the approval of the president (Jinnah) of the party who was on his way to England. The notice of the meeting was not sent to those members of the Council who were believed to be Jinnah's supporters. The Council met at Simla and approved the formation of the new party. Hidayat Husain started tampering with the list of the members of the Council; he deleted the names of members who were not in his clique, and tried to get the office of the League shifted to another premises. However, the intrigue was scotched by the presence of mind and resourcefulness of Shamsul Hasan, the office secretary of the League, who persuaded the owner of the building to file a suit against the tenant (the Muslim League) for removing the furniture of the building without his permission. Since the proceedings of civil suits in India were even then notoriously protracted, the conspiracy was nipped in the bud.

When Jinnah returned to India at the end of the year, he was not deterred by what his enemies attempted in his absence. He firmly adhered to the nationalist line and agreed to enter into talks with the Congress leaders for a Hindu–Muslim accord.

It so happened that the Congress party, which had a solid bloc of forty or so members in the Central Assembly, needed the support of Jinnah's Independent Party if it was to defeat the treasury benches in the Central Assembly. Jinnah, on his part, was glad to renew his contact with the Congress leaders for the success of his two-fold programme promoting Hindu–Muslim unity and agitating against the proposed constitution. He agreed to talk with the Congress President for the settlement of the controversies on the vexed issue of the Communal Award.

II

As already seen, the Communal Award conceded practically all Muslim demands for 'safeguards' in the new constitution. Not surprisingly, it had caused bitter resentment among the Hindus and Sikhs of the Punjab and Bengal. When the Communal Award was issued the Congress party was outlawed and its leaders were in prison. Two years later, after Gandhi suspended civil disobedience, the government revoked the ban on the Congress and released its leaders. The Congress Working Committee met in June 1934. It condemned the 'White Paper' issued by the government and called for a Constituent Assembly elected on the basis of adult franchise to frame a new constitution for India. On the Communal Award, the Committee took the position that, though it was unsatisfactory, the alternative to it was an agreed solution between the communities and not an appeal to the British Government. Meanwhile, the Committee resolved 'neither to accept nor reject the Communal Award' till the division of opinion in the country lasted. Incidentally, this decision (which virtually accepted the Communal Award) was taken under pressure from the nationalist

Muslim leaders in the Working Committee, who felt that the Muslim opinion on the Communal Award was so strong that its rejection would be impolitic. Soon after the publication of the Communal Award Jinnah himself had confided to a Muslim politician that since Muslims had secured almost all that they wanted in the way of safeguards, they may as well concede joint electorates in return for the Hindus' agreement.

The Congress leaders, especially Dr Ansari, the most respected nationalist and influential Muslim leader in 1934, felt that Jinnah could help them in resolving the differences on the Communal Award. He wrote a warm letter to Jinnah welcoming him back to India:

> Now that you have returned to the [Legislative] Assembly again at a very critical juncture in the history of constitutional changes, your usual patriotic outlook and political foresight would prove a great asset to the opposition .... It is more than obvious that a very great deal would depend on the attitude the Muslim members may adopt at this time, and it is equally clear that yours will be the greatest share in shaping their outlook and views.[2]

In January 1935 Rajendra Prasad, as Congress President, and Jinnah, as president of the Muslim League, began their talks at Dr Ansari's house in Delhi to explore the possibilities of an accord between the Congress and the Muslim League on the Communal Award. Jinnah suggested that the Congress and the Muslim League should come to an agreement on the communal issue, leaving alone the Hindu Mahasabha on the one hand and the Muslim Conference on the other, adopt a common stand on political issues and, if necessary, fight the communalists on both sides. The talks continued with some interruptions till the end of February. After several meetings at Delhi and Bombay, they were able to draft a five-point formula which made some adjustments in the franchise and constituencies of the provincial legislatures. In the federal legislature, the seats allotted to Muslims under the Communal Award were to remain unchanged. What was important from the point of view of the Congress was that separate electorates were to be replaced with joint electorates. The 'joint formula' on the Communal Award and Jinnah's unequivocal condemnation of the proposed constitutional scheme raised high hopes among the Congress leaders, but these hopes were soon to be belied by Jinnah's volte-face. Jinnah was not satisfied with an accord between the Congress and the League; he insisted that the Congress should secure the agreement of Malaviya and other Hindu Mahasabha leaders before he recommended the five-point formula to his co-religionists. Jinnah knew full well that it was impossible for the Congress to compel the Hindu Mahasabha to withdraw its opposition to the Communal Award. In 1916 and 1927, when he had sought and obtained the agreement of the Congress to his proposals for a Congress–League Pact, he had not insisted on the prior approval of the Hindu Mahasabha. In 1935, his insistence on this condition was evidently an afterthought. It seems he sounded out his own adherents and found that the 'joint formula', and especially the provision of joint electorates in it, would not be acceptable to influential sections in his own community. Interestingly enough, the possibility of Jinnah's backtracking had been foreseen by Dr Ansari even before the talks between Jinnah and Rajendra Prasad started. In a letter to the editor of *The Bombay Chronicle,* Dr Ansari wrote on 30 December 1934: 'You know he [Jinnah] is always led by his followers rather than leading them'.

The Congress leaders were baffled and disappointed by Jinnah's volte-face. However, they drew some comfort from his speeches and statements in and outside the Central Legislative Assembly where he was unsparing in his criticism of the government. He also took care not to break off with the Congress. Just before he sailed for England in April 1935, he said that the attitude of the Indian National Congress on the Communal Award was 'reasonable and sensible' and expressed optimism about the prospects for Hindu–Muslim unity.

III

Jinnah returned from England after six months in October 1935; in the previous year he had spent seven months in England. His long absence from India at a time when his presence was urgently needed for the revival of his party is not easy to explain. It may have been partly due to his indifferent health and the need to rest and recuperate in England, but it seems he was also biding his time and waiting for his two principal opponents —Viceroy Lord Willingdon, and Fazl-i-Husain — to retire. Meanwhile, in August 1935, the British Parliament had passed the Reforms Act and elections were expected to take place by the end of the year.

As 1936 dawned, Jinnah saw that he could no longer delay his plunge into the political arena. Luckily, an opportunity came his way when he was approached by his young colleague in the Central Legislative Assembly, Khalid Latif Gauba, to visit Lahore, where Muslims and Sikhs were locked in a bitter conflict over the possession of the Shahidganj mosque. The mosque was built in 1722 by a rich Pathan, Falak Khan, about a mile east of the city walls of Lahore. It was the scene of massacre of some Sikhs in the last decade of the Mughal Empire. In 1762, during Sikh rule in the Punjab, the Sikhs took possession of the mosque and named it Masjid Shahidganj (mosque of martyrs). Twice in the nineteenth century, efforts were made by local Muslims to recover possession of the mosque through legal action; but the Sikhs having been in indisputable possession of it for a long time, Muslim pleas were rejected by the court on grounds of 'limitation'. In 1925, when the Sikh Gurdwara Act was passed, the issue was again taken to the court, but the Muslim petition was once again rejected. In July 1935 a serious situation arose when the mosque was bombed and destroyed. Muslim–Sikh riots followed in its wake in Lahore, and the army was called to quell them. Maulana Zafar Ali, a fiery poet and journalist, enrolled thousands of volunteers and launched a 'civil disobedience movement' for restoration of the mosque. More than a hundred Muslims lost their lives in the riots. Negotiations between the Sikhs and the Muslims failed. Luckily, no political party in the Punjab involved itself in this agitation. Neither the Government of India nor the provincial government wanted to intervene and left the dispute to be decided by the court. A religious leader, Peer Jamal Ali Shah from north Punjab, appeared on the streets of Lahore with nearly 50,000 followers, mostly on horseback, who were armed with long swords held aloft. He declared himself the leader of the Shahidganj mosque agitation and addressed meetings attended by thousands of Muslims. The Sikhs brought in a large number of bellicose Nihangs.

It was at this critical juncture that, accompanied by Gauba, Jinnah arrived at Lahore. On 21 February 1936, when Jinnah arrived at the Lahore railway station, he was received by a huge Muslim crowd. Interviewed by the Associated Press, he said, 'My task is purely that of a conciliator and peacemaker. I have arrived in Lahore in the full hope that the leaders of the various communities will help me to bring about a settlement, because the general and greater interest of the Punjab, and particularly the city of Lahore, will be best served by the three important communities, Hindus, Sikhs and Muslims, working together and cooperating in a friendly spirit. There are much bigger issues which the Punjab will have to tackle than Shahidganj, and it is only by unity that we can tackle the various problems ....'[3] That afternoon he attended the Friday prayers in the Badshahi mosque. According to Gauba, Jinnah was reluctant to make a personal appearance at the mosque as he was accustomed to conducting his political campaigns from his armchair and from his palatial mansion on Bombay's Malabar Hill. 'But Gauba', he said, 'I have never been to a mosque. I would not know what to do .... I am not very good either at prayers.' Gauba replied, 'but you have only to follow me'.[4] Gauba has left a graphic account of Jinnah's visit to the mosque:

As usual, Jinnah went in his London-tailored suit, immaculately pressed, a tall, starched collar and a flashing tie. He removed his shoes but saw to it that they were never far from him when he sat down. I had given him a few lessons as to the postures he had to make. It was difficult to get him to go down on his knees as Mohammad Ali Jinnah had never bowed to anyone, not even to God. But he learnt the procedure with a smile. At the mosque, however, he seemed to forget everything. I was aghast to see him squatting like a Hindu Brahmin with his knees and hands folded. Anyhow, the crowd took him to their hearts ....[5]

There was a congregation of 50,000 in the Badshahi mosque for Friday prayers. Two addresses of welcome were presented to Jinnah. In his reply he said that ever since his return from England he had been concerned about the serious developments in the Punjab and felt that it was his duty to come to the Muslims of Lahore. However, he added, 'you cannot carry on war and negotiations for a settlement at the same time. I, therefore, of my own accord asked you to stop civil disobedience. By stopping this movement in deference to my wishes you have already proved yourself to be a disciplined community .... I have come to help you. I have no other interest. Success and failure are in the hands of God.'[6]

Jinnah's visit to the Badshahi mosque was to prove more significant in Jinnah's life than he or his escort, Gauba, could have imagined. Immediately, the charmed intelligentsia of Lahore was deeply impressed by his frankness and skill in securing the revocation of civil disobedience by Muslim firebrands, and lowering the communal temperature. He met with leaders of all communities and pleaded for communal harmony. On the Shahidganj mosque issue, he said he had not come to Lahore to champion the Muslim case. He had only one object — to find a fair and just solution.[7]

On 1 March he was welcomed by Hindus, Sikhs and Christians at a crowded meeting at the Town Hall in Lahore. Questioned on his role in the Round Table Conference, Jinnah recalled:

I was considered the most individualistic member of the Conference. I displeased the Muslims. I displeased my Hindu friends because of the famous 14 Points. I displeased the Princes because I was deadly against their underhand activities and I displeased the British Parliament because I felt right from the beginning .... that it was all a fraud. Within a few weeks I did not have a friend left there. But whatever I have done, let me assure you, there has been no change in me, not the slightest, since the day when I joined the Indian National Congress. It may be I have been wrong on some occasions. But it has never been done in a partisan spirit. My sole and only object has been the welfare of my country. I assure you that India's interest is and will be sacred to me and nothing will make me budge an inch from that position.[8]

One can well imagine the effect of such a confession of faith by Jinnah on the multi-religious elite of Lahore at a time when the town had just passed through a period of serious communal tension. His pleas to all communities to rise above petty issues and think solely of the interest of the country were well received. While speaking at the Dayal Singh College on 5 March, he told the students, 'The only difference between you and me is that I am older than you. Although I began my life as a dreamer and an idealist like you, now when I have gone through almost the whole of it I have begun to realize the realities.' He deplored the lack of scrupulous and principled leaders and said, 'Have we one single leader in India or even in one community who can command the whole-hearted loyalty and allegiance of the country, or of the community, or even of the intelligentsia?' He then recalled his idol in Indian politics, the late Mr Gokhale. 'Give me more Gokhales ....', he said. 'India has everything. God has given her everything but man has not served her well. Let man serve India and you have bright days ahead of you.'[9]

IV

In retrospect, it seems Jinnah's visit to Lahore marked the inauguration of his campaign for the general election, under the new constitution, which was due at the end of the year. This became clear in April 1936 at the annual session of the All India Muslim League held at Bombay. It was chaired by Sir Wazir Hasan, who had been Jinnah's comrade-in-arms in 1916 in steering the League towards the Congress through the Lucknow Pact. In his speech at the League session, Jinnah denounced the new constitution in no uncertain terms. He said, 'India got 2 per cent responsibility and 98 per cent safeguards and special powers to the Governor-General', which was the 'grossest breach of faith on the part of Great Britain'. However, he favoured the working of the new constitution 'under protest, just like the German nation under the Treaty of Versailles'. But at the first opportunity he would, he said, 'tear off as many pages of the Government of India Act as possible'. Towards this end, he proposed to carry on a 'constitutional agitation inside and outside the legislatures to create those forces, which would constitute sufficient pressure to bend the British Government to the will of the people of India.'[10]

Earlier, in a speech at Delhi, Jinnah had called upon the Muslims to organize themselves, but at the same time to stand firmly by national interests; in fact, he said, they had to prove that their patriotism was 'unsullied and that their love of India and her progress is no less than that of any other community in the country'.[11] Invited to preside over the All India Students' Conference at Lucknow in August, he expressed his happiness at finding the 'students of every community, caste and creed on the same platform'. He appealed to them not to think of the problems that were facing India in terms of religion, but to teach a lesson to their elders who were spoiling national life by their communalism.[12] A few days later, he visited Calcutta University and addressed the students. Syama Prasad Mookerjee, the Vice-Chancellor and the future Hindu Mahasabha leader, welcomed him as a 'brilliant lawyer, a keen debater, and, above all, a great nationalist'. Jinnah replied that he was very glad that the students recognized him as a nationalist. It was perfectly true and he was proud of it.[13]

So eager was Jinnah to project his nationalist credentials that he was almost apologetic about separate electorates for Muslims; they were there, he said, not because of his asking; they had long been part of the political system in India. But so long as separate electorates existed, a separate organization of Mussalmans was an inevitable corollary. That did not mean, however, that such a position was an ideal one, or that he was satisfied with it. He had, however, to deal with realities and would do his best in the circumstances.[14] At a meeting in Peshawar in October, Jinnah declared, 'If out of the 80 million Indian Muslims I can produce a patriotic and liberal-minded nationalist bloc, who will be able to march hand in hand with the progressive elements in other communities, I will have rendered a great service to my community.'[15] He wanted to organize Muslims under the banner of the Muslim League, not against other communities, but in national interest. He would, he said, be perfectly happy if the Hindus also organized themselves in a unified party; it would then be easier 'for the best brains of both communities to sit together and decide national issues'.

Some of Jinnah's speeches in 1936 were reminiscent of the halcyon days of the Home Rule movement during the First World War and the Lucknow Pact. Once again, since his return to India in 1934, the principal plank in his programme had been Hindu–Muslim unity and a joint front against the British bureaucracy. Implicit in this stand was a plea for an entente between the Congress and the Muslim League. As we have seen, negotiations between the two parties in 1935 had failed, but the relations between them had not soured.

Indeed, Bhulabhai Desai, the leader of the Congress party in the Central Assembly, had developed a rapport with Jinnah. Congress leaders could not forget that he was the author of the Fourteen Points, which had boosted Muslim separatism, but they also knew that he was the only Muslim leader in India who could oppose the pro-British feudals who were dominating Muslim politics. In the spring of 1936, while Jinnah was carrying on his election campaign, he had good reason to expect that the Congress would, in the larger interest of the country, appreciate his efforts to bring the Indian Muslim community close to the nationalist mainstream. Unluckily for him, his calculations were soon to be upset by the turmoil within the Congress organization after Jawaharlal Nehru's arrival on the Indian political scene.

V

Nehru had been released from jail in September 1935 to join his ailing wife who was in a Swiss sanatorium for treatment of tuberculosis. Reading and reflection during his long spells of imprisonment between 1930 and 1935 had brought about a leftward shift in his political and economic views. It so happened that at the same time some young Congress intellectuals who admired Nehru were thrown together in jail. Inspired by Marxist literature, they formed the Congress Socialist Party in 1934. Nehru did not join this party, yet he was doubtless its hero; its founders believed they were echoing his views. They were critical of Gandhi's leadership and frankly doubted the efficacy of non-violent methods for the solution of India's political and economic problems.

Gandhi was aware of Nehru's own discontent; he attributed it to the fact that he had been out of touch with the situation in the country because of long incarceration in jail, followed by his enforced absence in Europe. It was Gandhi's idea to invite Nehru to preside over the annual Congress session, which was to be held at Lucknow in April 1936. When Nehru returned to India in March 1936 after the death of his wife, there was an air of tense expectancy. The Congress Socialists expected him to give a new, bold lead to Congress politics, while Gandhi and the older Congress leaders hoped that, sobered by the responsibility of his position as the head of the party, Jawaharlal would avoid a polarization which could threaten the unity of the party.

In his Presidential Address to the Lucknow Congress session in April 1936, Nehru declared that the only effective solution of the world's problems and of India's problems lay in socialism. He made it clear that he was not using the word in a 'vague humanitarian way, but in the scientific, economic sense .... I see no way of ending the poverty, the vast unemployment .... except through socialism. That involves vast and revolutionary changes in our political and social structure, the ending of private property, except in a restricted sense, and the replacement of the present profit system by a higher ideal of cooperative service .... In short, it means a new civilization, radically different from the present capitalist order.'[16]

Gandhi's hope that the responsibility of holding the highest office in the Congress would 'sober' Nehru had not been fulfilled. During the Congress session, the Congress Socialists who subscribed to Nehru's radical ideology had their way. The older Congress leaders were unhappy with Nehru's stand. They argued that it was inopportune, and even suicidal, on the eve of a general election, for the Congress to raise fundamental socio-economic issues, while the main political issue, the freedom of India, had not been resolved. Under the new constitution, the size of the electorate had increased from 2 per cent to 10 per cent of the population, but it was still largely drawn from the propertied classes. Meanwhile, after three years of massive repression by the government, the Congress party was in disarray; on the one hand it was suffering from inertia and internal dissensions, and on the other hand it continued to be the object of British hostility. It was banned in the whole of the North-West Frontier Province and in parts of Bengal. The anti-Congress forces, such as landlords and feudal elements, were receiving encouragement from the government.

After the Lucknow Congress, the tension between Nehru and the older Congress leaders escalated and led to a head-on collision when seven senior members of the Congress Working Committee, including Vallabhbhai

Patel, Rajendra Prasad and C. Rajagopalachari, resigned. Nehru had a lurking suspicion that attempts were being made to destroy him politically. There was, however, no conspiracy in the Working Committee to oust him; the majority in the Working Committee — the Rightists as they came to be known — were working not for a coup but for a consensus. Their object was not to isolate Nehru, but to restrain him from encouraging a socialist rebellion. A split in the Congress was what the British wanted and hoped for, but Gandhi acted quickly and firmly to resolve the crisis. He played it down as a 'tragicomedy', ruled out all public discussion of differences within the party and insisted on withdrawal of all resignations. Thus the crisis was over before it could damage the chances of success of the Congress at the imminent election.

VI

Nehru's socialist rhetoric at Lucknow had jolted not only the Congress Old Guard but also Jinnah. In his long address running into more than 10,000 words, Nehru made only a passing and critical reference to Congress policy on the communal problem: 'I have not been enamoured of the past Congress policy in regard to the communal question and its attempts to make pacts and compromises .... in my opinion, a real solution of the problem will only come when economic issues, affecting all religious groups and cutting across communal boundaries, arise. Apart from the upper middle classes, who live in hopes of office and patronage, the masses and the lower middle classes have to face identical political and economic problems.' 'He could not', Nehru added, 'get excited over this communal issue'.[17]

Jinnah's reaction to Nehru's Presidential Address was uncharacteristically restrained. The urgent need in India, he said, was to create unity out of discussion and not to fight each other. He urged Nehru to 'come down to earth and study the existing conditions in India'. As for Nehru's claim that he had a large body of Muslim followers, he said, 'it cannot be accepted by any intelligent man'.[18] He questioned Nehru's premises as well as his conclusions. There were, he said, 'not two but four parties in India, sitting, as it were, at a chessboard'. There were the British people as a collective entity. There were the Indian Princes, the Hindus and the Muslims. The Muslims were a minority community; it was not a religious question; all they wanted were sufficient safeguards which would inspire confidence about their future so that 'they can wholeheartedly join with the sister communities in the march for freedom'. He regretted that the largest organization in the country, the Indian National Congress, was 'behaving like an ostrich', putting its head in the sand. The Congress claimed to represent the entire nation and did not care about individual communities. The Congress attitude, Jinnah said, was: 'If you like to come with us, you may, or stay away if you choose. We will remain neutral and we are marching towards our goal.' It was wrong, he said, to adopt such an attitude. 'I venture to say that the Congress will never reach the goal they desire and we desire unless they appeal to the Muslims'. So far as the Muslims were concerned they owe a duty not only to the community but to the country. Whether the Congress wants them to join that body or not, they should organize themselves and compel the Congress to approach them for cooperation. He believed that with such organization the Muslims could arrive at a settlement with the Hindus as two nations, if not as partners.[19]

It is doubtful whether Nehru and other Congress leaders were listening to Jinnah's earnest appeal mingled with an ominous warning from the platform of the annual session of the Muslim League. The Congress leaders were first distracted by the internal crisis in the party and later by preparations for the forthcoming election. Meanwhile, time was running out for Jinnah. Mending fences with the Congress was important, but much more important and urgent was the stupendous task of gearing his party for the general election due in the beginning of 1937.

Chapter 18

ELECTORAL ARENA

In 1936 Jinnah was perhaps the most experienced legislator in India. He had been elected to the Imperial Legislative Council in 1910 and later to the Central Legislative Assembly, but he had never led a political party at a general election. The Independent Party in the Legislative Assembly, which he headed for nearly twelve years, was a heterogeneous group; it consisted of independent members who had won their seats on their own, and after the election got together and elected Jinnah as their leader. Inevitably, the composition of the Independent Party changed after every election; in the early years it had very few Muslim members. Jinnah himself was elected from one of the constituencies in Bombay reserved for Muslims. The number of voters was small, only eight under the Reforms Act of 1909, and rose to nearly 5,000 by 1937. However, this presented no problem for him. His stock in Bombay, his adopted hometown, was high. He was re-elected to the Central Legislative Assembly in 1934 while he was in England. In a speech in March 1935 he took the House into confidence on the expenditure incurred by him on his election. He had, he said, sent a postcard to each of the 5,000 voters in his constituency, which cost him three to four hundred rupees.[1] Obviously, Jinnah's experience of electioneering was of little use to him when he set out in 1936 to lead the All India Muslim League in the first general election under the Reforms Act of 1935, which was due towards the end of the year. With the extension of franchise the number of eligible voters in the elections to provincial legislatures had risen from 3 to 10 per cent of the population. It was no longer enough for him to issue press statements from Bombay calling on the people to vote for the Muslim League.

It was only after his visit to Lahore in February 1936 that Jinnah began to tour the country, meeting local politicians and addressing meetings. An urgent problem for him was the revival of the Muslim League. As we have seen, he had been edged out of politics by a powerful group of politicians in the Punjab who had the backing of the government. In 1927, Sir Mohammad Shafi, Fazl-i-Husain and their friends in the Punjab rebelled against Jinnah's accord with the Congress and formed a rival organization — the All India Muslim Conference. This new party was treated by the government as the representative organization of Indian Muslims in the early 1930s as the All India Muslim League was a moribund party.

As we have seen, the All India Muslim League had been founded in 1906 after the historic Muslim deputation, which waited on Lord Minto, then Viceroy of India. In thirty years since its inception, it had failed to develop a popular base. In 1927 it had only 1,330 members. Jinnah had to adjourn the 1928 annual session because of factional clashes. The 1929 session was adjourned for lack of a quorum; the adjourned meeting was convened four months later in Delhi and ended in a pandemonium. The 1930 session at Allahabad, which was presided over by poet Sir Mohammad Iqbal, could not even muster the reduced quorum of seventy-five members. During the years 1931–33, the annual expenditure of the All India Muslim League did not exceed three thousand rupees. Attendance was less than 120 at the 1931 session in Delhi. In this session it was decided to improve attendance at the annual meetings by reducing the annual subscription for membership from 6 rupees to 1 rupee, abolishing the admission fee of 5 rupees and fixing the quorum at 50 instead of 75. No annual session was held in 1932, 1934 and 1935.

Jinnah was dismayed by the factional and personal rivalries within the political elite from whom the League drew its following, but he could do little about it. In practice, his role as 'working president' of the party was reduced to that of the chairman of a board of directors of a company; it was quite a problem for him to manage these annual gatherings, to reconcile opposing points of view and, in the last resort, to prevent the meeting from dissolving into chaos. For about two years, from mid-September 1931 to 1933, when the Muslim League was riven by dissensions, Jinnah was in retirement in England. Two years of squabbles and mutual recriminations and the danger of total fragmentation of the party at last drove the warring groups to bury the hatchet and invite Jinnah to take charge of the party.

In January 1934 Jinnah returned to India to resume leadership of the All India Muslim League. But it did not take him long to realize that his opponents were still after his blood; he decided to wait awhile before again taking a plunge into the whirlpool of Muslim politics. Of the inner tensions in Muslim politics at this time we get an intimate glimpse in the diary of Bhulabhai Desai, the leader of the Congress party in the Central Legislative Assembly. Desai had established a good rapport with Jinnah; this was the time when the Congress party and Jinnah's Independent Party in the Central Legislative Assembly were jointly inflicting defeats on the treasury benches.

The Diary of Bhulabhai Desai: 8 February 1935

> I attended the dinner given by the Mussalmans and the Aga Khan. Jinnah did not attend the dinner. He thought he was being eclipsed and he told me on the 13th that we [the Congress party] had assisted unconsciously in giving a representative position to the Aga Khan. He said the Aga Khan was a treacherous person.

17 February 1935

> I have kept Jinnah fully informed of my conversations with Sir Fazl-i-Husain and the Aga Khan so that he may not feel we are trying to negotiate with his opponents. He professed to be pleased, because he said that we were all together, and if extremists on either side were marginalized, it was all [the]

better. Of course he asked me not to trust the Aga Khan and Sir Fazl-i-Husain too much. Of course the Aga Khan will do more if the Government insisted, and Sir Fazl-i-Husain was undoubtedly largely influenced by personal ambitions.[2]

In 1936, Fazl-i-Husain could look back with satisfaction and even pride at the success of his efforts in securing in the new constitution all the safeguards he desired for Muslims. The terms of the British Premier's Communal Award issued in 1932, which embodied these safeguards and had been hailed privately, if not publicly, by Muslim leaders, had been incorporated in the new constitution.

For nearly twenty years, Fazl-i-Husain had been the most prominent Muslim politician in the Punjab reputed for his pro-British and communal proclivities. In 1931, he was appointed a member of the Viceroy's Executive Council and he won the confidence of Lord Willingdon. Fazl-i-Husain had the last word in the selection of Muslim delegates to the Round Table Conference, and was able to exercise remote but effective control over the Muslim delegation while the session was in progress in London. He had been largely responsible for the marginalizing of Jinnah and the Muslim League in the early 1930s. He clashed openly with Jinnah on basic issues pertaining to the imminent election under the new constitution. It seems surprising that in 1936, Fazl-i-Husain declared himself in favour of forming a non-communal party in the Punjab, and indeed in all provinces. His party, the Unionist Party, already included a few Hindus representing the rural constituencies in the East Punjab. Fazl-i-Husain was also of the view that provincial parties and not an all-India party could best devise strategies for contesting the elections. He reckoned that though the Communal Award had guaranteed a majority to Muslims in the Punjab legislature, the community constituted only 55 per cent of the population. There was no certainty that all the elected Muslim members would always agree; with the defection of even a few of them, an exclusively Muslim party could find itself in a minority. Therefore, the best course in the Punjab was to form a coalition in which Muslim dominance remained, but with the support of some Hindu and Sikh members. Such an arrangement would also help to allay communal tensions and contribute to the stability of the ministry. Fazl-i-Husain's arguments seem to have appealed to some influential Muslim leaders in Sind and the NWFP, which in any case had overwhelming Muslim majorities and there was no question of Hindu dominance.

It is a curious fact that though no love was lost between Jinnah and Fazl-i-Husain, they were reluctant to betray their mutual antipathy in public. In January 1934, Fazl-i-Husain even wrote to Jinnah welcoming him on his return to India to resume the leadership of the Muslim League. Two years later, Jinnah invited Fazl-i-Husain to preside over the annual session of the All India Muslim League. But Fazl-i-Husain had a different agenda and politely declined the honour. In April 1936 he sent an envoy to Jinnah to persuade him to keep the All India Muslim League out of the forthcoming elections to provincial legislatures. Jinnah did not agree and set up a Central Parliamentary Board of the Muslim League. Fazl-i-Husain was furious. He explained his stand in a letter to the Aga Khan and sought his support against Jinnah's 'mad scheme'.

Fazl-i-Husain to the Aga Khan, 22 June 1936

> The situation is something like this. Since last April the Unionist Party has been reorganized and a Unionist political organization of a non-communal type has been set going throughout the Punjab .... The sister communities have been taken by surprise and all their plans of upsetting the advantage to be secured by the Muslim community from the Communal Award have been disturbed .... You know perfectly well that the Punjab is the key to the Indian Muslim politics .... Sindh is following in our footsteps; the North-West Frontier Province is doing the same and to a minor extent Bengal and the U.P.[United Provinces] are coming into line. Thus Jinnah's Parliamentary Board is already broken up .... Hence the importance of strengthening the Punjab with a view to give the lead to Muslim India ....[3]

Fazl-i-Husain tried to convert leaders of the political parties in Sind, the NWFP and the United Provinces to his point of view. He was not worried much over the veto power vested by the constitution in the Governor of the province. He anticipated no difficulty in getting on with him. This line of thought appealed to other pro-British feudal leaders in the Muslim-majority provinces.

Jinnah did not give in to the demand of Fazl-i-Husain and other regional politicians that they should be left free to conduct the elections in their provinces; to accept such a demand would have meant the renunciation of the claim of the Muslim League being the representative body of the Muslims of India. Jinnah did not share the parochial perspective of regional politicians. He told the Bombay session of the Muslim League in April 1936 that it was not provincial autonomy that the people had been fighting for but the responsibility of the departments of the central government to be given to the elected representatives of the people of India.[4] He wanted all political parties to work the new constitution at the provincial level for what it was worth, but at the same time to carry on a constitutional agitation for real control of the levers of power in the provinces as well as in the proposed federation of India.

II

The sudden death of Fazl-i-Husain in August 1936 removed Jinnah's most formidable Muslim opponent from the political scene. He stepped up his electioneering campaign. He had already taken a leaf out of the book of the Indian National Congress, which had constituted a special committee for contesting elections to the legislatures. He got a resolution passed by the Bombay session for the setting up of a Central Parliamentary Board of the All India Muslim League with full powers to constitute a network of Provincial Parliamentary Boards. This provided him a powerful lever for the conduct of election campaigns. He nominated forty-six members from ten provinces to the Central Parliamentary Board. The first meeting of the Board was held at Delhi on 8 June 1936. Four hundred Muslim leaders and workers, besides the members of the Muslim League Central Parliamentary Board, had been invited to attend. Of the forty Bengal leaders and workers who were invited, only two, Ispahani and Abdur Rahman Siddiqui, attended. Only one worker came from Assam. Bombay sent a few. From the Punjab, Sir Mohammad Iqbal was present, but no one came from the Unionist Party. The largest contingent came from the United Provinces, but it had two factions. Nawabzada Liaquat Ali Khan dissociated himself from the Central Parliamentary Board along with the Nawab of Chhatari and Nawab Mohammad Yusuf because 50 per cent of the seats were not granted to the National Agriculturist Party, of which they were members. They suspected that Chaudhri Khaliquzzaman and his friends were in league with the Congress. This was a poor beginning. However, Jinnah went ahead to turn the Provincial Parliamentary Boards into his vanguard for electioneering in their respective provinces. By the end of August, Parliamentary Boards had been formed in the United Provinces, the Punjab, Madras, Bombay and Assam. In September Jinnah had a resolution passed by the Executive Council of the League authorizing him to take disciplinary action against recalcitrant members of the Parliamentary Boards. He cracked the whip immediately on no less a person than Fazlul Haq, a front-rank Bengali politician and leader of the Krishak Praja Party, who had backed out of an agreement for the formation of a united Muslim party in Bengal. Fazlul Haq was removed from the membership of the Parliamentary Board for 'breach of solemn agreement, insubordination, disloyalty and defiance of principles and policies laid down by the Board'.[5]

III

While Jinnah adhered to his platform of Hindu–Muslim unity and a joint front against British imposition of a new constitution on India, he was losing his patience at the failure of an adequate response from the Congress with which his relations had soured since the assumption of the Congress presidency by Jawaharlal Nehru. He resented the dismissive attitude of Nehru towards the Muslim leadership. He had never been able to hit it off with Nehru. He could never forget that Nehru was doing his political apprenticeship during the Home Rule movement at a time when he (Jinnah) was in the top leadership of both the Indian National Congress and the Muslim League. On his part, Nehru tended to question Jinnah's nationalist credentials; in his autobiography, published in 1936, Nehru had written that Jinnah 'had drifted away from the Congress .... and associated himself with the most reactionary elements in Muslim communalism'.[6] Nehru's speeches at the annual Congress session at Lucknow in April 1936 had disconcerted Jinnah. The election manifesto of the Congress denounced the roles of all communal parties, including the Muslim League, and even questioned the very existence of the communal problem:

> It is necessary to bear in mind that the whole communal problem, in spite of its importance, has nothing to do with the major problems of India — poverty and widespread unemployment. It is not a religious problem and it affects only a handful of people at the top. The peasantry, the workers, the traders and merchants and the lower middle class of all communities are in no way touched by it ....[7]

If the argument in the Congress manifesto, which bore the stamp of Nehru's views, was to be accepted, the Muslim League and its leaders would have become redundant. When Jinnah made a derogatory reference to Congress Muslims, Nehru retorted that 'there are Muslims in the Congress who can provide inspiration to a thousand Jinnahs.'[8]

'Historically speaking', Nehru declared, 'the present contest lies between imperialism and nationalism'. All 'third parties' and other groups have no real importance .... The Congress represents Indian nationalism ....'[9] It was impossible for Jinnah to accept such a proposition. With a stroke of his pen, Nehru had made the Muslim League and its leaders simply irrelevant in Indian politics. To dismiss the Muslim factor in Indian politics out of hand was to ignore the facts of recent history. Was Nehru suffering from amnesia? Had the Congress not negotiated with the Muslim League in 1916, 1927 and as recently as 1935?

Jinnah vigorously rebutted Nehru's arguments, and even ridiculed his political and economic solutions for India. 'I refuse to accept this proposition' he said, 'that there are only two parties in India — the Government and the Congress — and others must line up .... There is a third party in this country and that is Muslim India.' He contested Nehru's claim that the Congress was committed to the removal of poverty. 'Don't be misled by beautiful promises, claptrap and bamboozlement of electioneering campaign. I feel more than any man in this country the dire poverty from which our people are suffering. You are not going to change it overnight. Ours is not the only country that is suffering from it.'[10]

Jinnah's war of words with Nehru in the press soured relations between the Congress and the League. It distracted Jinnah from his main task because he had to mobilize Muslim voters over the heads of the provincial Muslim leaders, who dominated local politics. He made a frontal attack on the Unionist Party in the Punjab. 'I fear', he said, 'there is a caucus that is likely to be effective because they depend upon pocket boroughs, subsidized press and active interference in the elections on the part of the officials. If the intelligentsia of the Punjab is not vigilant, this caucus will succeed and a ministry will be formed which though in name will be Indian, yet in fact will carry out the behests of the Governor.'[11] A week later, Jinnah was in Peshawar and was taken in a procession through the city. The Chief Secretary of the North-West Frontier Province briefed the Home Department of the Government of India on Jinnah's visit to Peshawar in October 1936: 'Mr. Jinnah's departure was less triumphant than his arrival. Two days devoted to his "mission of unification" in Peshawar sent him to bed with high fever. He announced to the press that he had formed a committee, but many of the so-called members of the committee did not give their assent to even the use of their names. His only permanent achievement was the life membership of a college debating society.' Evidently, the British officials in the Muslim-majority provinces had an ingrained prejudice against Jinnah, but it was also true, as Jinnah was arraigned against the well-entrenched regional leaders who dominated Muslim politics and whom he could neither convert nor dislodge.[12]

In the course of his election campaign, as Jinnah travelled and talked to local politicians, it was borne upon him that with separate electorates, the extended franchise and the enormous expansion in the size of the electorate, a strictly secular approach might not work. Not surprisingly, in the last phase of his campaign his speeches increasingly acquired religious overtones. He visited the Masjid Nakhuda and joined the Friday prayers. Presiding over a meeting of 20,000 Muslims in Calcutta on 3 January 1937 on the death anniversary of Maulana Mahomed Ali, Jinnah said, 'Mahomed Ali was a great champion of Islam .... If he had been living today he would have fought for the Muslim League .... The Muslim League is the only political Muslim organization that counts. I appeal to Muslims to join and make it a strong and really representative body...that may speak with unchallenged authority on behalf of 80 million Muslims of the subcontinent .... I say Muslims should vote for Muslim League candidates ....'[13] Addressing Bengali Muslims, he said they could not neglect their brethren of other provinces; the faith of all Muslims bound them together. He warned the Congress to leave Muslims of Bengal alone. 'Mr. Jawaharlal Nehru is reported to have said that in Calcutta there are only two parties in the country, namely, the Congress and the Government, and others must line up .... we are not going to be dictated by anybody.'[14]

Chapter 19

THE MOMENT OF TRUTH

The election results came as a thunderbolt to Jinnah. In the Muslim-majority provinces, the Muslim League was literally routed. In Sind and the NWFP it did not win a single seat; in the Punjab it won two seats; in Bengal it won one-third of the Muslim seats and one-sixth of the total seats in the Legislative Council, but even in that province it did not occupy a commanding position. It turned out that the party alignments in the Muslim-majority provinces had cut across religious divisions. Sir Sikandar Hyat Khan in the Punjab, Fazlul Haq in Bengal and Sir Ghulam Husain Hidayatullah in Sind had not heeded Jinnah's appeal for Muslim unity under the banner of the Muslim League; they chose to be swayed by personal and class interests.

In the provinces in which Muslims were in a minority, the majority of the Muslim seats were won by Independents. In the lower houses of the legislatures of Bihar, the Central Provinces and Orissa the Muslim League did not win a single seat. It won eleven out of twenty-eight seats in Madras. Only in two provinces did it do well, winning twenty-seven out of sixty-four Muslim seats in the United Provinces and twenty out of twenty-nine Muslim seats in Bombay. All over India the Muslim League won only 105 out of 499 Muslim seats. With such dismal results, the Muslim League could hardly claim that it was the sole representative body of the Muslims in India.

This was the worst setback for Jinnah in his thirty-year-long political career. What was he to do? The easiest course for him was to opt out of active politics just as Annie Besant, C.P. Ramaswamy Aiyar, T.B. Sapru, M.R. Jayakar,

Bepin Chandra Pal, C.Y. Chintamani and other stalwarts of the Moderate era had done after Gandhi took over the helm in the Congress. Jinnah was, however, made of sterner stuff; he was not the man to accept defeat and let history pass over his head. This was not the first time he had to fight for his political survival. He had done it in the early 1920s after his exit from the Congress, and in the early 1930s, after his virtually forced retirement from politics and exile in England. In a rare moment of self-revelation, while addressing the League annual session at Bombay in April 1936, Jinnah had said he was not one of those who were disheartened easily. For him there was no despair. He gave the example of the spider 'which endeavoured to go up and fell, and again and again moved up ....'[1]

There was another option open to him. He could take the poll verdict in his stride, sit down to reconstruct his party, give it a mass base and retrieve his fortunes at the next election. After all, what had happened to him had happened from time to time to leaders of political parties in all democratic countries. This option had, however, its own problems. The Muslim League lacked a field organization; in the vast subcontinent it could not boast of branches even at the provincial level, not to speak of district and sub-district branches. Jinnah was already well into his 60s and in poor health; the re-building of the party was a herculean task. Gandhi had performed it for the Congress in the 1920s, but he was at that time not only much younger but had acquired experience of founding and running political parties in South Africa. Gandhi was lucky enough to draw under his wing able and loyal lieutenants with bases in their provinces, such as the Nehrus — Motilal and Jawaharlal — in the United Provinces, Rajendra Prasad in Bihar, Vallabhbhai Patel in Gujarat and C. Rajagopalachari in Madras. Jinnah had no able lieutenants of that calibre. What with his commitments as a practising lawyer in the High Court and his responsibilities as a leader of the Independent Party in the Central Assembly, he was barely able to manage single-handed a skeleton central office of the All India Muslim League from Delhi or from his residence in Bombay.

II

In the spring of 1937, it was clear to Jinnah that the moment of truth had arrived for him. Was it not a strange fatality that whenever he had tried to lead the Muslim League into the nationalist mainstream, forces beyond his control had not only frustrated his effort, but had driven him to a cruel choice between his political convictions and his political survival? He had begun his political career in 1906 by championing joint electorates for elective bodies regardless of caste and creed. But three years later, when the Minto–Morley reforms incorporating separate electorates for Muslims were approved by the British Parliament, he had to swallow his objections to separate electorates to ensure his election to the Imperial Legislative Council from a Muslim constituency in Bombay. By 1916, he became a fervent advocate of separate electorates and even persuaded the Indian National Congress to waive its principled objections to them. In the next four years he was able to forge his way to the highest echelons of both the Indian National Congress and the All India Muslim League. But, as ill luck would have it, the Khilafat frenzy and the Gandhian charisma in 1920 swept him from the centre of the national stage into political wilderness. He fell back on the Muslim League which henceforth was to be his constituency. In 1927 Jinnah resumed the role of a bridge-builder between the Congress and the League through the accord he initiated between the two parties, which seemed at the time a breakthrough in the solution of the communal problem in India. Unluckily for him, the accord was wrecked by some twists and turns of Indian politics triggered by the appointment of the Simon Commission, the convening of the All-Parties Conference and the debates on the Nehru Report.

As we have seen, Jinnah had to pay a high price for his initiative in seeking an accord with the Congress in 1927–28. He had unwittingly provoked an angry backlash from his co-religionists and caused the emergence, with the backing of the British bureaucracy, of the All India Muslim

Conference as a rival body to the Muslim League. Not until 1934 did he come out of the shadows and resume the leadership of the Muslim League. Undeterred by his bitter experience, he called for Muslim solidarity and Hindu–Muslim unity to form a united front against the British Government for imposing a flawed constitution on India. Indeed, he made it his election platform in 1936 which, to his dismay, was rebuffed by the Congress and rejected by an overwhelming majority of the Muslim electorate across the country.

The slanging match between Nehru and Jinnah during the election year helped to foster the impression that the general election in 1937 was in a sense a contest between the Congress and the Muslim League. The fact was that the Congress had contested only sixty-four seats out of 499 reserved for Muslims and won only twenty-seven. It was not the Congress but, what Jinnah described, the 'Muslim India' which had brought him to his sorry pass. For Jinnah the electoral verdict in the Muslim-majority provinces was the more galling. The election had confronted him with an unpleasant truth. His programme of Hindu–Muslim cooperation for a joint front against the British Government had not cut ice with the Muslim electorate. He had failed to foresee that most of the apolitical, pro-British regional leaders dominating Muslim politics in the provinces could not afford to get on the wrong side of the government. If he wanted their allegiance, he had to offer them something which they could accept. He could not convert them, nor could he dislodge them, so well entrenched were they in their own localities. The fact that his repeated attempts to bring the Muslim League on to the nationalist track had failed was proof enough that the politically conscious section of the Muslim community in India was impervious to appeals in the name of patriotism. Politics being the art of the possible, if he wanted the allegiance of his co-religionists he had to strike the right chord in them. Many years before, Shibli Numani, an eminent Arabic scholar, a poet and a colleague of Sir Syed, had written: 'The followers of the Prophet do not respond to the call of nationhood. Appeal to them in the name of religion and you will see what a splendid response you get.'[2] Whether or not Jinnah had heard of Numani and his view, his political predicament in the spring of 1937 led him to act upon it. So far he had not worn his religion on his sleeve. His visit to the Badshahi mosque in Lahore in February 1936 was his first experience of addressing a Friday congregation in a mosque; he had been pleased with it. The Islamic card could be the open sesame to the revival of his political fortunes after the disastrous election, but it involved a drastic reversal of his political stand and a total reorientation of his political credo. Henceforth, he would work for Muslim solidarity, but it was to be directed against the Congress and the Hindus, not against the British. He had to shed his life-long hostility to foreign rule and mend fences with the British bureaucracy; this would also facilitate his reconciliation with the well-entrenched Muslim leaders in the four provinces in which Muslims were in a majority.

Being a shrewd tactician, Jinnah realized that he had to play the Islamic card at the right moment. A sudden about-turn in his political posture after the rout of his party in the general election could leave him open to the charge of being a bad loser. It was prudent for him to wait until the Congress gave him some plausible reason for attacking it. If the Congress agreed to form ministries in the provinces in which it had a majority, such an opportunity was bound to arise. Immediately, his task was to prevent the demoralization of his party. He put up a brave face on the poor performance of his party at the polls. It was the first time that the All India Muslim League had fought an election at the centre without effective provincial or district-level organizations to back it. 'I am more than satisfied', he said, 'at the result of the first attempt'. He even went on to congratulate 'Muslims on this achievement after a work of only a few months!'[3]

III

Two decisions taken by the Congress after the elections were to serve as the ammunition for Jinnah's first salvo against the Congress. In a letter to Sir Stafford Cripps immediately after the results came out, Jawaharlal Nehru had acknowledged that, while in the general (non-Muslim) constituencies the Congress had carried all before it, it had made a poor showing in the Muslim constituencies, and the reasons for it, in Nehru's words, were 'our own timidity' and the 'burden of running over a thousand candidates in the general (non-Muslim) constituencies.'[4] The fact was that since the introduction of separate electorates in 1909, the Congress had been finding it difficult to make a dent in Muslim constituencies. In the 1934 elections to the Central Legislative Assembly, only two Muslims were elected on the Congress ticket, one of whom had contested a seat allotted to the universities.

After the general election in 1937, the Congress approved a campaign to educate Muslim masses through Urdu booklets explaining the political and economic programme of the Congress. The driving force for this campaign came from a few admirers of Nehru, such as K.M. Ashraf and Sajjad Zaheer, who had studied in British universities and were inspired by Marxist ideas. They felt that the Muslim masses needed to be lifted out of the communal rut and brought into the national mainstream.

The other decision of the Congress, which did not immediately draw much attention but has loomed large in the accounts of latter-day historians, was the failure of the negotiations between the Congress and the Muslim League for the formation of a coalition with the Muslim League in the United Provinces. Saleem M.M. Qureshi, a Pakistani historian, came to the conclusion that, with the failure of these negotiations, 'the dream of the Congress and Muslim League sharing power … was shattered … for all times to come'.[5]

The formation of a coalition in the parliamentary system is governed by two factors — the relative strength of the parties and the elements of convergence of their policies and attitudes. To get a balanced picture, it is important to see the negotiations for a coalition in the United Provinces in the political scenario after the 1937 election and the motives and aims of the two parties after the election.

The Congress had won overwhelming majorities in the legislatures of six provinces. However, for nearly four months it was not certain whether the Congress would accept office. The issue was fiercely debated within the Congress before and after the elections. Among those who opposed office acceptance was Nehru, the Congress President. He argued that nothing much could be got out of the new constitution, and that the Congress would have to bear the odium for becoming the apparatus of imperialism without being able to provide any tangible relief to the people. It was, however, evident that if the Congress abstained from forming ministries, reactionary elements favoured by the government would step in. Vallabhbhai Patel was in favour of office acceptance, not to work it, but to 'wreck it from within' by creating political deadlocks. In the end, Gandhi's view tilted the balance in favour of office acceptance. Gandhi had no ambition to be a legislator or a minister, but he wondered whether, with all its limitations, the new constitution could be used by the Congress to improve the lot of the people in India's villages, to encourage village industries, to ensure supply of clean water and an inexpensive nutritious diet, to extend education and to reduce the burdens on the peasantry. As a compromise between the opposing groups it was decided, at a joint meeting of the Congress members of the provincial legislatures and the members of the All India Congress Committee in March 1937, that the Congress should form ministries if the leaders of the Congress parties in the provincial legislatures were satisfied and were able to state publicly that the Governors would not use their special powers of interference, nor set aside the advice of the ministries in regard to their 'constitutional activities'. Official statements at first took the line that such an assurance would do violence to the constitution, and that the Governors could not act out of the terms of the Act of Parliament and the Instrument of Instructions issued to them. The Viceroy, Lord Linlithgow, told an Indian visitor that he could not change even a comma of the Government of India Act. Nevertheless, it became apparent to him that a large section of the Congress party was eager to accept office, but without some sort of assurance it was not possible for them to get a decision in favour of forming ministries.

The debate on assurances from the Governors was finally brought to an end by a long statement issued by the Viceroy, which was so phrased as to allay the fears of the Congress without surrendering any constitutional ground. Lord Linlithgow went on to say that the Governors would be anxious not only not to provoke conflicts but to avoid them. His statement, though vague, was conciliatory in tone. The Congress decided in July 1937 to form ministries in six provinces where it had a clear majority.

The assurance given by the government was not very explicit, and it was evident to the Congress leadership that much would depend on the strength and discipline of the legislative parties. The Congress approach to office acceptance was thus marked by a measure of caution. In the summer of 1937 no one could say how much cooperation the Congress would be able to get from the British bureaucracy, which, until recently, had been its arch enemy.

Much has been written on the protracted, abortive negotiations for a Congress–League coalition in the UP in 1937. The latest and perhaps the most penetrating account is by S.R. Mehrotra, who aptly describes Khaliquzzaman, an ex-Congressman, as a 'rather slippery politician who had a foot in almost every camp', who 'was torn between his old loyalty to the Congress and his new loyalty to the League, between his attraction of a ministership and fear of being repudiated by his colleagues in the Muslim League party.'[6] The Congress leaders got the impression that Khaliquzzaman was so keen to join the Congress ministry, that he was even prepared to leave the League party along with his supporters and join the Congress party. This explains the stringent terms offered by the Congress leaders. The parliamentary group of the League party was to abide by the decisions taken by the Congress both inside and outside the legislature and even to resign from the legislature or from the ministry if the Congress did so. The negotiations were protracted. When Khaliquzzaman first made overtures to the Congress in March his position was fairly strong. But as the relations between the Congress and the Muslim League deteriorated at the national level, Khaliquzzaman met with stout resistance to the Congress terms from a section of his own party in the UP. Meanwhile, Jinnah became suspicious of the goings-on in Lucknow. He issued a press statement that it was

> no use dealing with those men who are in and out of the Congress, and in and out of the League .... I am sure that Muslims of the U.P. will not betray the Musalmans of India .... I have been promised by Mr Khaliquzzaman, Leader of the Muslim League party in the U.P. Assembly that he will let me know what the situation is in the U.P. I sent reminders and I have been waiting to hear from him for the last three weeks and cannot understand the mystery of his silence. I only trust he will not enter into any commitments which may be repudiated not only by Muslims of his province, but by Muslims of the whole of India.[7]

On 25 April 1937, Khaliquzamman and his friends were taken to task by the Working Committee of the UP Muslim League Parliamentary Board. Jinnah visited Lucknow to assert his authority over the provincial party. He took the chair at a meeting of the UP Muslim League Parliamentary Board and made it clear that he would not permit any local and piecemeal arrangement with the Congress.

He declared that 'for the time being they would join hands neither with the Congress nor with the Government, but wait till they had gained strength by organizing the Muslims.'[8]

Jinnah did not trust Khaliquzzaman, but he did not take any action against him, as it could have split the League party in the UP. Legislative Council, which did not even have a majority of Muslim members. Khaliquzzaman persisted in his talks with the Congress and did not give up the trowel until 30 July. The negotiations with the Congress in the UP had been initiated by Khaliquzzaman and his friends; Jinnah had not taken any part in them. Even if Khaliquzzaman had succeeded in his negotiations with the Congress, it is likely that Jinnah would have vetoed him. In fact, the failure of these talks suited Jinnah more than their success. He could make it a grievance against the Congress. The induction of one or two League legislators into the cabinet of the government of one province out of 11 provinces and that too as junior partners in a Congress ministry made little sense to him. It could not solve Jinnah's formidable problems in the aftermath of the elections. He had to rebuild and rehabilitate the Muslim League, both in the four Muslim-majority provinces and seven Hindu-majority provinces. He had to placate, and secure the support of, the powerful pro-British feudal leaders of the regional parties in the Punjab, Sind and the NWFP, who had routed the Muslim League in the election. He had to soften the long-standing antagonism of the British bureaucracy towards him. The 'Islamic card' seemed to him to be the solution for all these problems and he decided to play it. We get a hint of Jinnah's evolving strategy in a letter written by Lord Brabourne, the Governor of Bombay, to the Viceroy six weeks before the Congress decided to accept office in six provinces having absolute majority in five provinces — Madras, Bihar, Orissa, the CP and the UP — and a near majority in Bombay.

Lord Brabourne to Lord Linlithgow, 5 June 1937

> Jinnah went on to tell me some of his plans for consolidating the Muslim League throughout India and how he is doing his utmost to awaken the Muhammedans to the necessity of standing on their own feet more than they do now. His policy is to preach communalism morning, noon and night and to endeavour to get the Muhammedans to found more schools, to open purely Muhammedan hospitals, children's homes, etc., and to teach them generally 'to stand on their own feet and make themselves independent of the Hindus'.[9]

Chapter 20

ON THE OFFENSIVE

Accompanied by his sister Fatima, Jinnah arrived in Lucknow on the evening of 13 October 1937 and was received by his hosts, the Raja of Mahmudabad and Khaliquzzaman, President of the Muslim League in the UP. On two previous occasions, in 1916 and 1936, when he had the honour of presiding over the annual sessions of the All India Muslim League at Lucknow, he was an ardent advocate of Hindu–Muslim unity and of a Congress–League accord as a joint front against the government. But in 1937 he was in Lucknow to announce the reversal of his political objective. Henceforth his target was the Congress, not the British bureaucracy. To symbolize the dramatic change in his political credo, he entered the pavilion for the League session wearing a long Indian coat, *shervani,* instead of his Saville Row suit, and a black *astrakhan* cap, which came to be known as the 'Jinnah cap' and became as famous as the Gandhi cap.

The session of the All India Muslim League began late in the afternoon of 15 October and continued till 9 pm. It had a record attendance of nearly 5,000, including 200 women. On the dais sat Sir Sikandar Hyat Khan, the Premier of the Punjab, Fazlul Haq, the Premier of Bengal, the Nawab of Chhatari, Maulana Shaukat Ali, Begum Shah Nawaz Khan, and the Raja of Mahmudabad, the chairman of the Reception Committee.

Jinnah began his speech by describing the League session as 'one of the most critical that has ever taken place during its existence for the last more than thirty years'. 'The Policies and Programmes' of this session, he said, were to decide 'the fate and the future of the Musalmans of India and the country at large.'[1] He held the leadership of the Congress responsible for alienating the Musalmans of India more and more by pursuing a policy which was 'exclusively Hindu'. In the seven provinces, he continued, in which they had formed governments, they had 'by their words, deeds and programme shown more and more that the Musalmans cannot expect any justice or fairplay at their hands.' Wherever the Congress was in a majority, it had refused to cooperate with the Muslim League parties and insisted on 'unconditional surrender and signing of their pledges'.[2] He accused the Congress ministries of wounding the feelings of Muslims by forcing Hindi on them, singing *Bande Mataram* as a national song and unfurling the Congress flag at public functions. Some Congress leaders, he said, were even asserting that there was no such thing as the minorities' question in India; others thought they could manage the Mussalmans by throwing a few crumbs to them in their 'present disorganized and helpless state'. However, he warned that the All India Muslim League was alive and would play its part in the realm of Indian politics; the sooner it was realized the better it would be for all concerned. He ridiculed the Congress proposal for a Constituent Assembly: 'To call for a Constituent Assembly on the basis of adult franchise is height of all ignorance. It shows lack of any sense of proportion. A Constituent Assembly can be called only by a sovereign authority and from the seat of power.'

Jinnah ended his speech on a grim note: 'There are forces which may bully you, tyrannize over you and intimidate you, and you may even have to suffer ....' The 'crucible of fire of persecution which may be levelled against you, tyranny that may be exercised, the threats and intimidations may unnerve you, but it is by resisting, by overcoming, by facing these disadvantages, hardships and sufferings that a nation will emerge worthy of its past glory and history .... Eighty millions of Musalmans ... have nothing to fear. They have their destiny in their hands ....'[3]

Jinnah's presidential speech set the tone for the rest of the session. A sense of grave crisis and deep resentment pervaded the speakers as well as the listeners in the conference hall. Typical was the threat by Fazlul Haq,

Premier of Bengal, that if the Congress did not change its policy of oppression of Muslims in the provinces ruled by it, he would retaliate in Bengal. Writing in the British-owned *Pioneer*, a Muslim observer graphically described the heated atmosphere in the meeting of the League:

> The doctrine of aloofness was preached *ad nauseam* in a most unrestrained and irresponsible language. Out of the clouds of circumlocution and confusion arose the cry of 'Islam in danger'. The Muslims were told that they were disunited and about to be crucified by the Hindus. Religious fervour was raised to a degree where it exhibited itself in blind fanaticism. In the name of Muslim solidarity Mr. Jinnah wants to divide India into Muslim India and Hindu India.[4]

A sense of crisis permeated the entire top leadership of the League the following morning when Jinnah chaired a meeting of the Executive Council. It had a record attendance. An account of its proceedings compiled by the central intelligence officer of the Home Department, which was enclosed with the Viceroy's letter of 27 October 1937 to the Secretary of State for India, indicates how Jinnah's speeches and statements in the preceding three months had shaken even the seasoned Muslim politicians and persuaded them to believe that Indian Muslims were in grave danger of falling under Hindu domination. According to the account, the first item on the agenda was the attitude to the Federation. Sir Sikandar described the proposed Federation as 'the ruination of the Mussalmans of India'. In British India they (the Muslims) were in a despicable minority. If the Indian states, which were predominantly Hindu, joined the Federation, the Mussalmans would be nowhere. The result would be that the Hindus would be in a strong position in the Federal Assembly, and Bengal, the Punjab, Sind, Assam and the North-West Frontier Province would be under perpetual subjection of the Hindu Raj at the centre.

Sir Sikandar went on to suggest an alternative scheme, with seven Federal states in India, to checkmate the Hindu majority. Maulana Hasrat Mohani feared that the

Congress would drive out both the Mussalmans and Englishmen from India. Similar misgivings were voiced by other leaders. The Executive Council resolved to oppose the Federal scheme embodied in the Reforms Act of 1935 and to appoint a committee to draw up an alternative scheme. The evening session of the Council was mainly devoted to the 'impeachment' of Sir Wazir Hasan, Jinnah's old colleague of the halcyon days of the Lucknow Pact. Sir Wazir tried to defend himself by saying that the salvation of Mussalmans lay in joining the Congress. He was opposed by Jinnah, Sir Sikandar, Fazlul Haq, Shaukat Ali and other leaders. Seth Yakub Hasan who was also present was hauled up for accepting a berth in the Congress ministry in Madras. He made a spirited reply to the charge, saying that he had contested the election on a Congress ticket. Jinnah and other members of the Council were of the view that there was a fundamental difference between the Congress and the Muslim League. As a member of the Council of the Muslim League it was his duty to stand on a League ticket. A vote of censure was passed by the Council against both Sir Wazir Hasan and Seth Yakub Hasan.

II

Sir Malcolm Hailey, a veteran of the Indian Civil Service, who had a long experience of observing the mindset of the Muslim political class as the Governor in two provinces, the Punjab and the United Provinces, noted in 1934 that 'Muslims had gained a great deal of their demands by the Communal Award which had removed their sense of danger that stood in the way of their reunion under a strong leadership.'[5] The general election of 1937 confirmed Hailey's judgement. The Muslim political class revealed a certain inertia born of complacency. Regional rather than religious affiliations determined the attitude of the Muslim electorate in the Muslim-majority provinces. In the Muslim-minority provinces, local rather than national issues influenced voting, resulting in the election of a large number of 'independent' Muslims belonging to no particular party. The Muslim League had made a poor showing.

The minatory tone of Jinnah's speeches at Lucknow was part of his new strategy, which was designed to retrieve what the ballot box had denied. After the Lucknow session, he did not rest on his laurels, but continued his crusade against the Congress as he toured the country. Referring to the Congress efforts for contacting Muslim masses, he said, 'We hear of mass contact. For what? To get hold of men who will be their creatures, who will sign their pledge, take up their programme and sing *Bande Mataram*.'[6] He warned the Muslim youth not to heed the rhetoric of Nehru and the Congress radicals who were exploiting the emotions of the youth in the country in the name of nationalism. He said Princes, Rajas and Maharajas had been dubbed by Nehru as blood-suckers. According to Nehru, the Congress was the only body which could remove hunger and poverty. But when and how? Somebody put that question to Nehru and he replied that it would be within his lifetime. Jinnah wished Nehru a long life so that when the Congress had been able to destroy everybody who was somebody in the present India, and turn the country into a desert, he might call a Constituent Assembly to frame a constitution. 'If you are not strong', Jinnah continued, 'if you are not united, if you do not build up your organisation ... you will be ... reduced to ... *Shudras* and Pariahs of the future.'[7] For instilling fear into the minds of his audience, he even made statements which were obviously untenable. 'When the Hindus blame us', he said, 'do you know what they mean? They want you (Muslims) to be reduced to a minority in the Punjab, Bengal, Sind and the NWFP. They have majority in seven provinces ... They know ... they can swamp the Muslim majority under the device of joint electorate.'[8] This was a curious argument. Separate electorates and Muslim majorities in all the Legislative Councils in the Muslim-majority provinces had been guaranteed in the new constitution and had indeed become a reality after the general election.

Jinnah had for the first time revealed his Islamic card at the Lucknow session. He had been encouraged by the response at the session, and thereafter his speeches and conduct acquired a new religious slant. In November 1937, when he arrived at Patna, he was escorted by a huge procession from the railway station through the city. When the procession reached the Jama Masjid, the Imam presented him with a sword and on behalf of the Muslims of Patna welcomed him and declared him in unequivocal terms to be the leader of the Muslims of India, 'in token of which', he said, 'we surrender our sword to you. Henceforth we shall be the faithful soldiers to the cause of the freedom of Islam and our country.'[9] Jinnah touched and kissed the sword.

Speaking on the occasion, he said the Muslims in the past had been in the 'no man's land'. Having no organization, no system, their leaders were exploited either by the British Government or the Congress to the fullest extent. It was only with the coming of the League that the Muslims had come into their own.[10] Some days later he said that all that he was doing was to ring the alarm bell. 'The bell is still ringing', he added, 'but I do not yet find the fire brigade. I want to produce this fire brigade, and with them, then God willing, I will be able to extinguish the fire.'[11]

While at Patna, Jinnah unfurled the Muslim League flag which he described as 'the flag of Islam', for, he said, 'you cannot separate the Muslim League from Islam. Many people misunderstand us when we talk of Islam, particularly our Hindu friends. When we say 'this flag is the flag of Islam', they think we are introducing religion into politics — a fact which we are proud. Islam gives us a complete code. It is not only religion but it contains laws, philosophy and politics. In fact it contains everything that matters to a man from morning to night. When we talk of Islam, we take it as an all-embracing word. We do not mean any ill will. The foundation of our Islamic code is that we should stand for liberty, equality and fraternity.'[12] He further said:

Surely our percentage is low but that alone should not give us any cause for anxiety. Thirteen hundred years ago, our Prophet (Peace be upon him) preached his faith when there was no Muslim. In 20 years time our Prophet (Peace be upon him) had spread not only his faith in Arabia, Egypt and Europe but also brought them under his suzerainty. If a single Muslim can do all this, what is it which 9 crores of Muslims cannot do. If the Muslims have ever been discomfited, it was by another Muslim. And I say if you stand united there is no power on earth which can suppress or oppress you.[13]

Jinnah's adoption of the role of the saviour of Islam in India evoked an immediate response. In the general election in the beginning of 1937, his party had not won a single Muslim seat in the Bihar Legislative Council. By the end of the year his stock rose sky-high in this province. The religious idiom clicked wherever Jinnah went. On the morning of 1 January 1938, when he arrived by the Doon Express at the Gaya railway station, according to the correspondent of *Star of India:*

The crowd of tens of thousands had gathered to receive him. He was driven in a decorated car, amidst cries of 'League *Zindabad*' and 'Islam *Zindabad*'. The procession which was preceded by a pilot motor cycle with the League flag waving over his head volunteers on horseback volunteers in uniform volunteers carrying shining swords, it took over three hours to pass through its route. The *pandal* [pavilion] [had a capacity of over] 50,000 people from Gaya. Mr. Jinnah passed through a guard of honour presented by the Muslim National Guards who were equipped with swords.[14]

Six months later, when Jinnah performed the flag hoisting ceremony at Bombay, he said the flag of the Muslim League 'was not a new flag. It was several centuries old and was given to them by the Prophet'. 'No power on earth', he added, 'could bring their flag down'.[15]

Chapter 21

THE CONGRESS RESPONSE

By the end of 1937, relations between the Congress and the League had reached an all-time low. The Congress leaders were alarmed by the widening communal rift and discussed all its aspects, from the choice of Muslim ministers in the Congress-ruled provinces to that of the national anthem. How far the Congress leadership was prepared to go to soothe Muslim sensitivities is shown by the fact that soon after the Lucknow session of the Muslim League, the Congress Working Committee constituted a sub-committee consisting of Gandhi, Jawaharlal Nehru, Vallabhbhai Patel, Maulana Azad and Subhas Chandra Bose to go into the question of the national anthem and, on its recommendation, decided that out of deference to Muslim susceptibilities, only the first two stanzas should be sung on ceremonial occasions.

As the New Year dawned, there were hints of a thaw in relations between the Muslim League and the Congress. In one of his speeches at Calcutta, Jinnah threw a challenge to Nehru 'to come and sit with us and formulate a constructive programme'. In January Maulana Azad called on Jinnah at his residence in Bombay to discuss the inclusion of a second Muslim minister in the Congress ministry in Bombay; he carried away the impression that Jinnah wished to meet Gandhi and was 'waiting for a suitable opportunity'.[1] About the same time Nawab Ismail Khan, president of the UP Muslim League and a member of the Executive Council of the All India Muslim League, wrote to Nehru urging him to meet Jinnah and to assist in reducing the tension between the two communities.[2] Nehru took it as a feeler from the League leadership, and replied at great length to the Nawab, clearing doubts about Congress policies on such issues as 'the mass contact movement', the national anthem, the national flag and the Wardha scheme of education, which had become the targets of League criticism. The Congress 'mass contact movement', Nehru told the Nawab, was not directed against the Muslim League; it had never been thought of in terms of Muslims alone, nor was it confined to them. The Congress had worked among the Hindu masses and 'disabled' the Hindu Mahasabha 'politically'; it had carried out effective and successful work among the Christian masses in the South, and among the Parsis, the Jews and the Sikhs. The *Bande Mataram* song, Nehru recalled, had first become popular during the agitation against the partition of Bengal, when it came to be regarded by the British as a symbol of sedition. From 1905 to 1920, the song had been sung at innumerable meetings, at some of which Jinnah himself was present. The Congress flag was born during the early days of the non-cooperation movement, and its colours had been determined to represent the various communities: saffron for Hindus, green for Muslims and white for other minorities. Had not Maulana Mahomed Ali, the Khilafat leader, delivered scores of speeches on the national flag as representing the unity of India? As for the Wardha scheme of 'basic education', it was no diabolical plot against Muslim children; it had in fact been devised by two eminent Muslim educationists, Dr Zakir Husain and K.G. Saiyaddain, to substitute coordinated training in the use of the hand and the eye for a notoriously bookish and volatile learning which village children unlearned soon after leaving school.

Among those who suggested to Nehru to meet Jinnah was Khaliquzzaman, the leader of the Muslim League party in the UP legislature. Both Gandhi and Nehru welcomed the idea of contacting the League leader. Nehru wrote to Jinnah that it would be helpful if the disputed issues were first defined so that they could come to grips with them when they met. This elicited a stinker from Jinnah: 'You [are] insisting upon the course', he wrote to Nehru, 'that I should formulate the points in dispute and submit to you for your consideration and then carry on correspondence with you .... The method you insist upon may be appropriate between two litigants and that is followed by solicitors on behalf of their clients but national issues cannot be settled like that.'[3] Jinnah administered a similar rebuke to Gandhi when he wrote to him that Maulana Azad would open the talks on behalf of the Congress. 'I find', Jinnah wrote, 'that there is no change in your attitude and mentality when you say you will be guided by Maulana Abul Kalam Azad'.[4]

After Jinnah had expressed his inability to break his journey at Wardha or even at Delhi to see him, Gandhi agreed to travel to Bombay to meet him. The meeting took place at Jinnah's residence on 28 April 1938. It lasted three-and-a-half hours; Jinnah did most of the talking. It was a depressing experience for Gandhi. Jinnah did not budge an inch from his publicly stated position. Gandhi did not feel like arguing with him, and took down notes of his talks, which he passed on to Subhas Chandra Bose who had just succeeded Nehru as the president of the Congress. Gandhi was not very optimistic, but he telegraphed Bose, urging him to hold formal negotiations with Jinnah and advised Nehru and Azad to make themselves available at Bombay.

Bose called on Jinnah at his residence on 14 May for a preliminary discussion. He told Jinnah that the members of the Working Committee, who were present in Bombay, would accompany him at the discussion with the League leadership. Jinnah stipulated that the conversations should be held on the understanding that the All India Muslim League was the authoritative and representative organization of Indian Muslims, and that the Congress was the authoritative and representative organization of the solid body of Hindu opinion. Bose gave a note to Jinnah explaining why the Congress could not possibly consider itself or function as if it represented one community only, even though it might be the majority community in India. Its doors 'must invariably remain open to all communities' and it must welcome all Indians who agreed with its general policy and methods. At the same time the Congress was perfectly willing to confer and cooperate with other organizations, which represented minority interests. The Congress recognized that the Muslim League was an organization representing a large body of Muslim opinion, which must carry weight, and indeed it was for this reason that the Congress wanted to understand the viewpoint of the League and to come to an understanding with it. The Congress could not, however, accept, either explicitly or implicitly, the status of the League as the 'authoritative' Muslim organization of India.

On 15 May, Bose wrote to Jinnah suggesting that they should proceed to the next stage of negotiations — the appointment of two committees for the conference which would jointly settle the terms of understanding. Jinnah replied to Bose the following day, saying that he proposed to place the matter before the Executive Council of his party at a meeting to be held in Bombay in the first week of June. On 5 June Jinnah informed Bose that it was not possible for the Muslim League to negotiate with the Congress except on the basis that the Muslim League was the 'authoritative and representative organization of the Mussalmans of India'. He added two further preliminary conditions — no Muslim was to be included in the Congress delegation in the conference, and the League could consult the 'other minorities' to safeguard their interests.

The Congress leaders could hardly wait for three weeks for the decision of the Executive Council of the League. They had come all the way to Bombay in an all-out effort to reach an understanding with the League, but the negotiations could not even take off. Meanwhile, Gandhi, who had stayed on in Bombay for a few days for a little rest, called on Jinnah on 20 May, and wrote to Amrit Kaur, his secretary at the Sevagram Ashram, that Jinnah was 'a very tough customer. If the other members of the [Muslim] League are of the same type a settlement is an impossibility'.[5] There was no need for Jinnah to call a meeting of the Executive Council for advice. He had already broached the subject at a meeting of the Council. He had also received a letter from Jawaharlal Nehru proposing a meeting with him. He asked the members of the Council to suggest the lines on which discussions should take place. According to an authentic report, a member of the Council wanted to know the contents of Nehru's letter, but Jinnah regretted his inability to take the Council into confidence on the contents of this letter and his reply to it; he said that they were 'confidential'. Nevertheless, the Executive Council, all of whose members were his nominees, unanimously gave Jinnah full powers to hold discussions with Nehru on any lines he thought fit.[6]

Some members of the League Executive Council had made themselves believe that the estrangement between the two parties was a passing phase, and that Jinnah would be open to rapprochement with the Congress after the abortive attempt in May 1938. The fact was that at this stage Jinnah did not want to hold any serious talks with the Congress. He was playing for higher stakes. He had deliberately held out an olive branch to the Congress leaders, made them come down to Bombay and then stipulated conditions for substantive talks, which he knew the Congress would not accept. From the standpoint of the Congress leaders, it was a wholly futile exercise, but from that of Jinnah it was a brilliant tactical move. It was edifying for his colleagues in the Executive Council and the rank and file of his party, but intriguing and humiliating for the Congress leaders.

John Gunther, an American journalist and the author of the best-seller, *Inside Asia,* and his wife, Frances Gunther, were in India in 1938, and had easy access to Indian political leaders as well as to the Viceroy and senior British officials. Frances recalled her discussions with Jinnah in a weekly paper:

In 1938, John Gunther and I spent a three-hour lunch with Mr. Jinnah, leader of the Muslim League, asking for a concrete example of a Muslim grievance against the Indian [National] Congress; he could not offer a single one. In 1940, Sir Stafford Cripps asked Jinnah the same question; Jinnah was now prepared. He gave Cripps one grievance. Cripps made a point of personally investigating the case, and, as he reported later in New York, found 'nothing of any substance in it at all'. Yet in September 1942, Herbert Matthews reports to the *N.Y. Times* from New Delhi that Muslim leaders (he does not quote Jinnah) now tell him that they have been 'through hell'.[7]

In retrospect, it would seem as if the precondition for the recognition of the Muslim League as the *sole* organization representing *all* Indian Muslims had been laid down by Jinnah to avoid coming to the negotiating table. In March 1938, when Nehru urged the League leader to spell out the demands of the League, all that he could do was to refer Nehru to the 'Fourteen Points', to an anonymous article in the *NewYork Times* of 1 March 1938, and to a statement of M.S. Aney, the Nationalist Party leader. The fact was that almost all the political demands of the Muslim community embodied in the 'Fourteen Points' had been conceded in the constitution, which had come into force in 1937, and Jinnah had as yet no new demands to make on the Congress. This interpretation is supported by the confession in his memoirs by Khaliquzzaman, who in 1938 had urged Nehru to meet Jinnah — he believed that Jinnah was not serious about a settlement with the Congress:

> It was a piece of good luck for us that Congress fought shy of accepting the Muslim demand for the recognition of the League as an authoritative representative organization of Muslims on such a flimsy pretext while yet at the same time wooing and running after the League. If Congress had accepted the position at the time when the demand was made by the League, I wonder what positive demands we could then have made.[8]

In the opinion of Pakistani historian Khalid bin Sayeed, Jinnah's aim in the negotiations with the Congress was simply to discredit its claim that it represented both Hindus and Muslims, and that he was not interested in a settlement as in 1938 the League had yet not reached the organizational strength to establish its claim that it was an 'authoritative and representative body' of Indian Muslims. A settlement with the Congress at that time did not suit Jinnah; the most that he could get from these talks was the concession of a few seats for the Muslim League in the Congress ministries, but the acceptance of such a concession would have taken the wind out of his sails.[9]

The fact is that Jinnah's decision to play the Islamic card in 1937 had necessitated a radical change in his political orientation. He gave up his opposition to the Reforms Act of 1935. He was no longer a critic of the Imperial power; in fact, it was part of his strategy to seek its support against the Congress. He could not take up the cause of the people of the Indian States against their autocratic rulers; it would have created problems for some Muslim rulers, such as those of Hyderabad and Bhopal. He could not put forward any radical social and economic programme for British India because his party was dependent upon the powerful, feudal landowning politicians in the Punjab, Sind, the UP, the NWFP who dominated the Muslim League. So the only programme which seemed practicable to him was to slam the 'Congress tyranny', make allegations of establishing a 'Hindu Raj', and call upon Indian Muslims to come under one flag — 'the flag of the Muslim League — the flag of Islam — so that we all may be one.'[10]

II

One of the main items on the Congress agenda for discussion at the joint meeting with the League leaders — which did not come off — was Jinnah's allegations of 'injustice' and 'atrocities' committed against Muslims in the Congress-ruled provinces. Jinnah had started levelling these charges soon after the Congress took office in July 1937, but it was not until the end of 1938 that the Muslim League published reports of the Pirpur Committee and the Shareef Committee listing the grievances of the Muslims in the Congress-ruled provinces. Some of these grievances were of a general character, such as the singing of the national anthem and the hoisting of the Congress flag on public buildings. One of the charges against the Congress was that excessive reverence was paid to Gandhi and that his birthday had been declared a holiday. 'To declare my birthday as a holiday', Gandhi wrote, 'should be classified as a cognizable offence'. As for the national anthem and the national flag, Gandhi's advice to Congressmen, through the pages of his weekly paper *Harijan,* was to respect Muslim susceptibilities and not sing the anthem or hoist the flag if a single Muslim objected. So far as the Wardha scheme of Education was concerned, the complaint that it did not provide for religious instruction for Muslim children had little meaning because the curriculum did not include such instruction for children of any religious community.

The reports issued by the League accused the Congress ministries of launching a systematic persecution of Muslims. The Shareef Committee report[11] went so far as to say that in Bihar 'Muslims will have to decide soon whether they should migrate from this province or face annihilation'. The Congress ministries refuted the allegations made in the Pirpur and Shareef reports against them both in and outside the provincial legislatures. The Bihar government gave a detailed and reasoned reply to the charges, which was issued in the form of a pamphlet. Nehru appealed to Jinnah to agree to an impartial enquiry. Rajendra Prasad, who was Congress president in 1939, suggested an enquiry by Sir Maurice Gwyer, the Chief Justice of the Federal Court. This proposal was rejected by Jinnah on the ground that the matter was 'under His Excellency the Viceroy's consideration'. In December 1939, Jinnah called for a Royal Commission to investigate the charges — a demand which the British Government could hardly concede in wartime and for raking up such a controversy. 'It has been our misfortune', Nehru wrote to Jinnah, 'that charges are made in a one-sided way and they are never inquired into or disposed of. You will appreciate that it is very easy to make complaints and very unsafe to rely upon them without due enquiry.'[12]

What Nehru and other Congress leaders did not know was that under the instructions of the Viceroy, the Governors of the Congress-ruled provinces were keeping a vigilant eye on the working of their ministries. While isolated acts of petty tyranny by local officials may have occurred in remote villages and towns in the Congress-ruled (as well as in other) provinces, the theory of a concerted tyranny directed against the Muslim community was unsustainable. It is important to recall that during these years nearly half the members of the ICS were British and they occupied key positions in the provincial secretariats as well as in the important districts. Almost all the Inspectors-General of Police were British, and so were most of the Superintendents of Police. There was a fair sprinkling of Muslims and Christians in the Indian Civil Service and in the Indian Police Service, and Muslims were well represented in the middle and lower ranks of the police. There is no evidence in the records of the Home Department of the Government of India of that period to support the theory of establishing a 'Hindu Raj' in the Congress-ruled provinces. It was true that law and order had become a provincial subject, but the secret channels of communication between the Viceroy and the Governors and the Chief Secretaries of the provinces had not dried up. The Viceroy was calling for and receiving reports from the Governors on the treatment of the Muslim minority by the Congress ministries. As we read these reports today, they make a telling commentary on Jinnah's propaganda campaign. It was fortunate for him that this correspondence between the British Governors and the Viceroy was confidential; its leakage would have taken the bottom out of his case against the Congress.

It is a curious fact that the British Governors, whose lifelong task had been to contain and suppress the nationalist movement spearheaded by the Congress, did not lose their objectivity when judging the performance of the Congress ministries. Among the Congress ministries which drew the greatest flak from the League were the ministries in the United Provinces, Bihar and the Central Provinces.

Sir Harry Haig, Governor of the United Provinces, could not be accused of having a soft corner for the Congress. In March 1934, when he was Home Secretary under Lord Willingdon, he had written: 'For the Congress party to achieve power at the outset of the new constitution would be dangerous. We should recognize that the Congress are and for a long time will remain our enemies.'[13] Four years later, he wrote to the Viceroy that these attacks by the Muslim League on the Congress ministries were 'very unfair'. The allegations that the Ministry had not taken all reasonable steps to maintain law and order and that the local officers did not act impartially were, in Haig's opinion, a 'deliberate falsity to a degree which even the manoeuvres of politics can hardly excuse'. 'There was no truth', he wrote, 'in the allegation that the right type of Muslims were not getting Government appointments. The Congress, though consisting predominantly of Hindus, always professes and to a large extent pursues a non-communal policy.'[14]

Sir Maurice Hallet, Governor of Bihar who had also served as Home Secretary in the Government of India, pronounced the League's charges against the Congress ministries as 'vague and indefinite'. He reported to Viceroy Linlithgow that 'he did not know of any case in which government or local officials had failed to take action against aggressors in communal riots. 'Muslims whom I met', he wrote, 'admitted their inability to bring any charges of anti-Muslim prejudice against the [Congress] government. Speaking from my experience, both of Bihar and the United Provinces, I cannot see that any orders passed by Government have been really detrimental to Muslim interests.'[15] The experience of Sir Francis Wylie, Governor of the Central Provinces and Berar, was similar. He told Linlithgow that he did not find much substance in the League's charges against the Congress ministry in his province. As regards the introduction of the Wardha syllabus in primary schools and the establishment of Vidya Mandirs, which was the target of bitter attacks by the League, he pointed out that its syllabus was devised to impart elementary education by means of a 'basic craft', such as *charkha,* and to tackle the problem of mass illiteracy in rural areas. He added, 'I keep an eye out at all times for any genuine Muslim grievances there may be, and so far I must confess that, apart from the feeling of dissatisfaction already referred to, ... there is little that is concrete to go on. A colourable pretext is however all that is needed and the Vidya Mandir scheme may yet provide the necessary peg for a considerable agitation.'[16]

Four months later, Wylie dealt exhaustively with the instances of grievances of the Muslims of the Central Provinces contained in a letter written by the Vice-Chancellor of Aligarh Muslim University. He came to the conclusion, after the examination of the allegations, that 'there may have been pinpricks but of really serious injustice there is no evidence as yet. There might be resentment among Muslims against the perpetual domination of their communal opponents — which leads them to make baseless accusations — as in the Pirpur report.' Wylie stated that in his province the necessity of exercise of his individual judgement (reserved power) had not yet arisen.[17]

III

'The door is closed', Gandhi wrote to Vallabhbhai Patel.[18] The Congress leadership came to the conclusion that there was no hope of reaching an understanding with the

League. All that they could do was to reaffirm the policies of equal treatment of all citizens irrespective of caste, creed and religion guaranteed in the resolution passed by the Indian National Congress at its Karachi session in 1931 on fundamental rights. However, the Congress ministries were asked to be doubly vigilant about the redressal of any real Muslim grievance. The ministries were instructed to reply to the charges of discrimination against Muslims, both inside and outside the provincial legislatures.

The reaction of the Congress leadership to Jinnah's intransigence struck Subhas Chandra Bose as too passive. He came to the conclusion that Jinnah was 'unreasonable and intransigent', and that the best way to deal with him was to practise realpolitik. Bose hailed from Bengal where the Hindus were in a minority; his political approach was somewhat different from that of the other Congress leaders. He was confident that it was possible to put up a coalition ministry in Bengal, including the Congress party, and that the formation of such a ministry would be a step towards Hindu–Muslim amity. An opportunity came when the ruling Krishak Praja Party headed by Fazlul Haq split; half of its members, headed by Syed Nausher Ali, parted company with Fazlul Haq and went into opposition and were in the same position as the Congress. Sarat Chandra Bose, the brother of Subhas Chandra Bose, was the leader of the Congress party in the Bengal Legislative Assembly. Subhas Chandra Bose sought permission of the Congress High Command to work for a coalition ministry in Bengal. What irked him was that, although he was the president of the Indian National Congress and also the head of the Provincial Congress Committee in Bengal, his proposal was turned down by Gandhi on the advice of Abul Kalam Azad who did not want the Congress to meddle in the politics of Muslim-majority provinces. Bose was furious; he felt that the Congress was losing an opportunity of paying the League back in its own coin. The Congress leaders did not want to further exacerbate the antagonism of the Muslim League regardless of what the League was doing;

they were anxious to lower the communal temperature. In the Shia–Sunni conflict in Lucknow, for example, the Congress tried to heal the breach between the two sects and to calm the situation. The Congress was opposed to separate electorates in principle. When a Shia leader of the UP wrote to Nehru pleading for Congress support for the grant of separate electorates for the Shia community, Nehru replied that the suggestion was in the interest of neither the Muslim community nor the country.

IV

The Congress leaders could take Jinnah's propaganda campaign against the Congress and the Hindus in their stride, but they could not ignore its results. In 1938 there was an outbreak of communal riots. Haig, Governor of the UP, told the Viceroy: 'Finding themselves unable to achieve much by parliamentary methods, they [the Muslim League] were inevitably tempted to create unrest and disturbance outside the legislature.'[19] We get an inkling of the deteriorating communal situation from the periodical reports of the Chief Secretaries of the provinces to the Home Department of the Central Government. This was especially so in the UP and Bihar. The Chief Secretary of the United Provinces reported a hostile demonstration at Jaunpur when brickbats were thrown at a car carrying a Congress minister who was accompanied by the Commissioner and the Collector of the district.[20] By April 1938, Govind Ballabh Pant, Chief Minister of the UP, was complaining that the Muslim League was 'taking now more and more to the ways of violence'.[21] The Chief Secretary of Bihar reported to the Home Department of the Central Government that objectionable speeches were often delivered in mosques where shorthand writers were not allowed and where even their presence as spectators was resented.[22]

In August 1938, the Chief Secretary of the United Provinces wrote that the Muslim League was installing its flags on public buildings, that its meetings were marked by violent speeches, and that it was organizing processions of uniformed volunteers. It was openly being said that Muslims would not confine themselves to non-violent activities.[23] The Urdu press was publishing inflammatory articles. The atmosphere was charged with tension in Allahabad city; the discovery of a pig's head in a mosque had led to cases of stabbing of Hindus by Muslims. A company of troops had to be called in to prevent the trouble from spreading.

The communal situation in the UP was so disturbing that, in May 1939, Secretary of State Zetland suggested to Linlithgow that if Nehru was willing to consider the possibility, he was likely to make a good Prime Minister of the UP. With him as Prime Minister and with Kidwai as one of his colleagues, the situation might improve.[24] Linlithgow welcomed the idea. Interestingly, Gandhi had also suggested to Nehru to take charge of the province to restore peace. Sir Roger Lumley, Governor of Bombay, wrote to the Viceroy on 1 May 1938 about a riot in Bombay city: 'The origin of this outbreak was attributed to a quarrel over a game of cards between a Muhammedan and three Hindus. No damage or casualty resulted from this trivial incident, but rumours quickly spread and very soon the two communities ... were in a state of excitement [resulting in] stone-throwing and stabbing assaults. The total casualties have so far been — 14 dead and about 100 injured.' 'The measures taken by the Ministry', according to Lumley, 'were prompt and effective .... Nearly 2,500 persons were arrested for disobeying ... orders.[25]

The Congress ministries were directed by the Parliamentary Committee, which came to be known as the Congress High Command, to take strong action to quell communal riots. Curiously enough, the origin of some of these riots was often trivial. By mid-July 1939, Nehru confessed in a letter to Rajendra Prasad, the Congress president, that the Muslim League propaganda against the Congress had succeeded, and that there was more general ill will than at any time in the past between Muslims and Hindus. It was true that the Congress had more than 100,000 Muslim members on its roll and a solid core of nationalist Muslims, 'but there is no doubt that it has been unable to check the growth of communalism and anti-Congress feelings among Muslim masses.' It was, therefore, practical politics to dissolve the 'mass contact committees' formed in 1937. Nehru also noted that the nationalist Muslims were getting demoralized by the attacks on them in public meetings and in the Muslim press. They were targets of social boycott by their political opponents. Syed Mahmud, Nehru's friend of college days, who was a Congress minister in Bihar, unburdened himself to Nehru by narrating his bitter experiences in arranging the burial of his mother-in-law, as his family was regarded a Congress family:

> Here Muslim League people canvassed that nobody should take part in the burial of my mother-in-law as mine was a Congress family .... Only 15 or 20 people of the family took part in it. Yesterday was *Fateha* and they made the same attempt .... The limit has been reached .... My poor wife is feeling this very much. Amongst the Mussalmans this is the greatest form of insult conveivable.[26]

Chapter 22

BRITISH RESPONSE

The poor performance of the Muslim League in the general election in 1937 did not come as a surprise to the government. Official forecasts had predicted victory for the regional Muslim parties against the Muslim League. Jinnah's election platform — denunciation of the new constitution and appeal to like-minded parties, and especially to the Congress, to get together to agitate against the retrograde Act of 1935 — had not endeared him to the British authorities. In September 1937, when Jinnah called on the Viceroy, he struck him as a failed politician. 'My talk with Jinnah', Linlithgow wrote to Zetland, Secretary of State for India, 'covered a good deal of ground. I do not quite frankly feel any deep confidence in him, and I suspect he is one of those political leaders who can play a personal hand, but no other, and whose permanent control on the allegiance of their followers is frequently open to question.'[1]

Six weeks after his meeting with the Viceroy, Jinnah unleashed his propaganda offensive against the Congress at the Lucknow session of the Muslim League and it became obvious that his target henceforth was going to be the Congress and not the British Government. Linlithgow sent an account of the proceedings of the Muslim League Executive Council — obtained through central intelligence — which indicated that Jinnah was trying to bolster his position after his electoral disaster by seeking support from Sikandar Hyat Khan, the Premier of the Punjab and the leader of the Unionist Party in the Punjab, and Fazlul Huq, the Premier of Bengal and the leader of the Krishak Praja Party in Bengal, which had routed the Muslim League at the election.[2] Linlithgow saw possibilities of realignment in Muslim politics, but in the post-election scenario in 1937, the pressing problem for the government was how to deal with the Indian National Congress which had won overwhelming majority in five provinces and a simple majority in one province. The reaction of the government to the offensive which Jinnah had launched against the Congress after the general election was bound to be influenced by the decision of the Congress on acceptance of office. It is important therefore to trace the evolving relationship between the Congress and the government during the next two years in order to get an insight into Linlithgow's policy towards the Muslim League and its leaders.

II

After the election results were out, the Congress was still undecided whether it should accept office in the provinces in which it had won a majority. Boycott of the Legislative Councils had been an important plank in Gandhi's civil disobedience movement. In 1920 he had declared that his faith in obtaining political freedom through constitutional methods had been shaken. However, 17 years later it seemed to him that provincial autonomy under the new constitution gave enough scope to the legislatures to improve the lot of the people. 'The boycott of the legislatures, let me tell you', he wrote in *Harijan,* 'is not an eternal principle like that of truth and non-violence. My opposition to it has lessened. The question is that of strategy and I can only say what is much needed at a particular moment.'[3] The need of the moment, Gandhi felt, was 'constructive' work. Since the suspension of civil disobedience in 1934, he had been preoccupied with activities which, though non-political in common parlance, were nevertheless important for the masses, such as a clean water supply, cheap and nutritious diet, a sound educational system and a self-sufficient and healthy economy for villages. He wondered whether, with all its deficiencies, the new constitution could further a programme of village uplift. There was no reason, he said, why Congress ministries could not encourage village industries, introduce prohibition, reduce debt burdens on the peasantry, promote the use of home-spun cloth, extend education and combat untouchability.

Another consideration seems to have weighed with Gandhi. During the previous two decades he had launched three major civil disobedience campaigns. He had seen the country vibrate to a new political consciousness under their impact, but he had also seen that the spirit of non-violence had been slow in permeating the people, and that even his closest colleagues chafed at the self-imposed restraints of *satyagraha*. And violence seemed not only latent, but near the surface, erupting unexpectedly; the requisite atmosphere for the launching of a *satyagraha* campaign was not easy to create and maintain. At the same time, the discontent in the country was growing. The new constitution under the Act of 1935 was far from offering political freedom to India, but it had created an electorate of 30 million; the condition of these millions, and the many millions who had still to get the vote, could all be affected by the policies of the provincial governments. The new constitution could be construed, wrote Gandhi, as an attempt, however feeble and limited, to replace the rule of the sword by the rule of the majority. 'If the Congress worked the new constitution', he suggested, 'to achieve its goal of independence, it would avoid a bloody revolution and mass civil disobedience movement.'[4]

Linlithgow had told an Indian visitor in August 1936 that he could not change even a comma of the Government of India Act.[5] This was true so far as it went, but, as Gandhi saw it, it was not a catastrophic limitation; the constitution by which the British themselves were governed flowed not from a legal document but from a series of conventions developed in the actual working of their constitution. Gandhi's own approach to the new constitution was not that of a constitutional lawyer, not even that of a political strategist. He wrote in *Harijan* : 'I had not studied the Act (the Government of India Act, 1935) when

I advised office acceptance. I have since been studying *Provincial Autonomy* written by Prof. K.T. Shah .... I see nothing in the Act to prevent Congress ministers from undertaking the programme suggested by me. The special powers and safeguards come into play only when there is violence in the country or a clash between the minorities and the so-called majority community, which is another word for violence.'[6]

Ultimately, Gandhi's view prevailed at the crucial meeting of the Congress Working Committee, the highest executive organ of the party. Of the 14 members present only three followed Jawaharlal Nehru, the Congress president, in voting against office acceptance. It was decided that the Congress should agree to form ministries in the provinces where it had won a majority, provided the leaders of the Congress legislative parties were satisfied and were able to state publicly that the Governors would not use their special powers of interference or set aside the advice of the ministers 'in regard to their constitutional activities'.[7]

Nehru was extremely disappointed and he described the decision of the Congress Working Committee as 'unfortunate' ... which, he said, was attended with risks and dangers.[8] It was always dangerous, he argued, to assume responsibility without power even in democratic countries; it could be far worse in an undemocratic country, 'where we have to follow the rules and regulations of our opponents' making .... The big things for which we stand will be forgotten and petty issues will absorb our attention.'[9] Gandhi and the leaders of the Congress, who had supported office acceptance, were also conscious of the risks involved. This was why most of the senior leaders of the party kept out of provincial politics, and a parliamentary sub-committee, consisting of Vallabhbhai Patel, Rajendra Prasad and Abul Kalam Azad, was appointed to guide the Congress ministries. At Gandhi's instance, instructions were issued to the Congress Premiers to avoid social intercourse with British officials and not to attend parties given to incoming and outgoing governors. Titles and honours from the government were not to be accepted. The ministers were not to draw a salary of more than Rs 500 per month. Gandhi went on issuing his 'moral directives' to the Congress ministers through his weekly *Harijan*. The ministers were enjoined not to take to the Western style and incur expenditure on the Western scale. Congressmen had been disciplined during the past 17 years in rigorous simplicity; the ministers were enjoined to introduce that simplicity into the administration of their provinces.

It was not only the Congress which was cautious in its approach to office acceptance. Linlithgow was anxious about the repercussions of Congress entry into provincial administration. In March 1937, he wrote to Zetland: 'We have ample proof that the ultimate purpose of Nehru and Gandhi is to make for the overthrow of Government by organization of agrarian mischief on a good scale.[10] Linlithgow's first impulse was not to yield to the Congress demand for 'assurances' regarding the exercise of reserved powers by the Governors. However, some of the Governors, such as Lord Erskine, the Governor of Madras, represented that it would be a good thing if the Congress formed ministries because the Congress was very vulnerable at the provincial level.[11] Top Congress leaders, except for C. Rajagopalachari in Madras, were keeping out of the Congress ministries, and the local Congress leaders in the provinces were keen on acceptance of office. 'If they are given only three months or so', Erskine wrote, 'in which to intrigue against themselves, a sufficient number then may break away from the Congress and support a ministry in order to avoid [the legislature] being dissolved.'[12] Erskine's strategy of bypassing Nehru and the national leaders and concentrating on local Congress leaders appealed to Secretary of State Zetland who told the British cabinet that it might be possible to break political deadlock with the Congress by encouraging its right wing to break away from 'the tyranny of the [national] caucus'.[13]

As we have already seen, the problem of assurances was solved once it became clear that the Congress was keen to form ministries. Linlithgow had already told the Governors of the provinces that so long as the Congress was the largest party in a legislature, it would be the government's objective to secure the help of the Congress in carrying on the administration. 'That the Congress in office may confront us with real and serious difficulties', he wrote, 'I fully accept. Those dangers were foreseen when the Act was framed.'[14]

III

Linlithgow had taken charge as Viceroy in July 1936. For a whole year he had not taken notice of Gandhi. However, soon after the installation of the Congress ministries, he thought it prudent to invite Gandhi to meet him. The meeting took place at Simla on 4 August 1937 and lasted for two hours. Linlithgow had intended it to be a courtesy call, and so there was no business agenda. In a detailed note of the conversation running to nearly 3,000 words, Linlithgow wrote that though they did not find themselves in agreement on all points, the interview was 'extremely friendly in character'. He tried to persuade Gandhi not to impose restrictions on the Congress ministers' social relations with the Governors and high officials. However, Gandhi was firm and he frankly told the Viceroy that, while these social contacts could be useful, they represented a real contribution to 'the strengthening of imperialism' and therefore the risks involved were such as he would not take.

Gandhi seemed to Linlithgow to be in good health; he recorded: his voice was firm, his mind was extremely quick and alert, his sense of humour very keen. It was impossible not to be impressed by his general quality. The strong impression upon my mind was that of a man implacably hostile to British rule in India, and who would in no circumstance hesitate (while at all times behaving with perfect good manners) to take advantage of any person or circumstance in order to advance the process, to which every fibre of his mind is entirely devoted, of reducing British power, influence and prestige in the Subcontinent.[15]

When the Congress ministries took office in the provinces in July 1937, neither the Congress leaders nor the government could foresee how their partnership in the provinces would actually work out. It was not easy for either side to leave the history of its long conflict behind, but association in day-to-day problems began to break some of the barriers. Of the ICS officers serving in the provinces, nearly half were Europeans. Though their salaries were heavy on the revenues of the provinces and their careers were protected by the constitution, many of them tried to adjust themselves to provincial autonomy and to their new bosses. The tempo quickened all round; in the provincial secretariats, the Congress ministries busied themselves in drafting new measures of social and economic reforms with unwonted speed; in the districts the new democratic structure made increasing demands on the time of executive officers. There was in the beginning some meddling in the day-to-day administration by local politicians. However, the British officers who had been able to adapt themselves to the system of dyarchy during the 1920s tried to adjust themselves to provincial autonomy, even if it required visibly greater effort. The regime of benevolent despots in the districts conferring titles and offering lands and jobs for loyalty to the Raj was no longer unquestioned. This was something that could not have been easy to accept by those who had been reared in the Imperial tradition. As Philip Mason, a former member of the ICS, put it, 'it is hard to serve where you have ruled'.[16]

Nine months after the Congress took office, Satyamurti, a senior member of the Congress ministry in Madras, in an interview to *The Times of India* claimed that the Congressmen had been running the administration of the provinces with sagacity, statesmanship, tact and firmness. The services were playing the game loyally; the Governors and their ministers were hitting it off well. The facts ought to certainly remove all bona fide fears on the part of the British conservatives of any danger in the Congress being entrusted with the task of administration in the centre.[17]

C. Rajagopalachari, the Premier of Madras, got along famously with Governor Lord Erskine, and acknowledged publicly that he had had no problem in carrying out the Congress programme. In reply to an address presented to him by the Congress Committee of Madras, he said: 'British imperialism is like a snake, and I am a snake charmer. With the power of "mantra" you have given me by your support, I can assure you of the realization of our ideals of Swaraj.'[18] It would seem that Rajagopalachari himself was also charmed; he wrote to Erskine on his retirement, 'You are leaving behind in me a memory of cooperation of the most cordial, frank and friendly type.'[19]

There was an inherent contradiction between the popular governments in the provinces and a completely authoritarian government at the Centre, and this contradiction led to curious anomalies. For example, Govind Ballabh Pant, the Premier of the UP, drew the attention of the Home Department of the Government of India that the Central Intelligence Department continued to censor the correspondence of Jawaharlal Nehru, who was at the time president of the Congress.[20] However, it did not take long for the relations of the Congress ministers and the Governors to be stabilized. The Governors usually found their ministers earnest and competent; the ministers generally found the Governors very fair and helpful.

Jawaharlal Nehru wrote in his book, *The Discovery of India* (1946), that 'between Indian nationalism and an alien imperialism, there can be no final peace'. In the spring of 1939, however, a rupture between the Congress and the government seemed improbable. During the two years the Congress was in office, its ministries had been occupied with their socio-economic agenda, including legislation for reduction in rent, land revenue and burden of rural debt, grant of loans to industrial workers, prohibition of intoxicating liquor and drugs, removal of illiteracy, improvement in elementary education and promotion of adult and female education. In June 1939,

Jawaharlal Nehru, as Vice-Chairman of the non-official 'National Planning Committee' appointed by the Congress president, wrote to Sir Jagdish Prasad, a member of the Viceroy's Executive Council, seeking cooperation in collecting data. The Government of India nominated its Economic Adviser, Dr Gregory, to attend the meetings of the National Planning Committee of the Congress and supply it such information as it required.

A breach between the Congress and the Government may have been inevitable in the long run, but it might have been postponed, if not averted, by the Congress ardour for social and economic reforms and the government's anxiety not to disturb stable administrations in the provinces in a period of acute international uncertainty.

There were occasional differences between the Congress ministries and the Governors, such as in February 1938 on the question of the release of political prisoners in the UP and Bihar. The respective Governors of these provinces, Sir Harry Haig and Sir Maurice Hallet, at the instance of the central government, invoked their special powers and refused to accept the recommendation of the ministers for the release of all political prisoners. The crisis lasted for ten days, but an agreement was reached after discussions between the Governors and the Congress Premiers. The latter accepted (with Gandhi's approval) the principle of the examination of each individual case before ordering release.

It is significant that as late as February 1940 — when relations between the Congress and the British Government were on the verge of a rupture — Secretary of State Zetland, in an interview with Crozier, the editor of *The Manchester Guardian,* commended the performance of the Congress ministries. He said that the relations between the British Governors and the Congress ministers had been cordial, that there had been frank discussions and resolution of differences in the spirit of give and take, that the existence of the reserved powers of the Governors had been a more powerful influence upon the administration than the actual employment of them.

Zetland told Crozier that investigations had shown that the charges, such as the singing of *Bande Mataram* in schools and the unfurling of the Congress flag on public buildings, levied by the Muslim League against the Congress ministries were almost 'wholly psychological'. Years later, long after the parting of ways between the Congress and the government, Prof. Coupland conceded that taken as a whole the record of its ministries was one in which the Congress could take reasonable pride. Its leaders had shown that they could act as well as talk, administer as well as agitate.

By the beginning of 1938, there was no more talk of 'wrecking the constitution'; the Congress leaders were too busy with legislation for the promotion of primary education and village industries, agrarian reforms and settlement of industrial disputes. They were also trying to keep the left wing in the Congress party at bay. The Viceroy and the Governors of the eight (out of eleven) provinces in which the Congress party was in power were aware of the left-wing pressure within the Congress and how the right wing, with Gandhi's backing, was withstanding it. In April 1938, Lord Brabourne, Governor of Bombay, wrote to Sir Alexander Hastings, who was on the staff of the King: 'As you suggest, I am writing today to His Majesty to give him a short account of my interview with Gandhi .... How right you are when you say that Gandhi's demise might be a source of regret. Were he to die at the present moment, it would really be a great blow, because he has come to realize the danger of extremists in the Congress getting the upper hand, and he is doing all he can to back the right wing.'[21]

Gandhi's stock was high in 1938 in official circles. This comes out well in a letter written to Nehru by Frances Gunther:

Frances Gunther to Jawaharlal Nehru, 13 February 1938:

> Nothing encourages the British so much as thought of a split between you and Gandhi .... Gandhi is practically considered

the King-Emperor's personal representative in Congress, the Grand Old Man of British politics — simply adored by the mighty — [I] would not be surprised if they offered to bury him in Westminster .... You, on the other hand, are considered so dangerous that if the British Empire ever falls, it will all be laid on you. Who knows? They might be right. They often are. Whenever we meet, interest — and fear — is centred on you, your thoughts, your plans, your projects and your influence.[22]

That the government was really beginning to look upon Gandhi as a constructive and steadying influence on Indian politics is confirmed by a letter written by Brabourne, who was acting as Viceroy in the summer of 1938, to Zetland, saying that 'it is becoming more and more obvious that there is a very strong party in the Congress which is prepared to accept Federation, with the idea that in practice the safeguards and the special responsibilities of the Governor-General will prove no more of an obstacle to the carrying out of Congress policy than they have [been] in the provinces, but whether this party will carry their point without a definite split with the left wing, I think that no one can yet prophesy.'[23]

About the same time, Agatha Harrison, a member of the Conciliation Group in London which, inter alia, kept politicians of Labour and Liberal parties in Britain informed on the views of Gandhi and the Congress, was in India, shuttling between Simla and Gandhi's ashram in Sevagram. It was at her request that Bhulabhai Desai, the leader of the Congress legislative party in the Central Legislative Assembly, ascertained from Gandhi the minimum conditions and changes in the constitution in the Act of 1935 which he would desire before he could commend participation in the Federation to the Congress. Gandhi made it clear that no negotiations were possible until the question of the election of the Princely states' representatives to the Federal legislature, instead of nomination by the rulers, was settled; after this no large-scale alteration of the constitution would be required. However, some agreed amendments could be carried through by the British Parliament, notwithstanding the prevailing critical conditions in England and Europe. Gandhi described it as a 'working arrangement', until a Constituent Assembly could be convened to draw up a constitution to replace the Act of 1935.[24]

Linlithgow was aware that even this or any 'working arrangement' with the Congress for launching a federal centre under the second part of the Act of 1935 required the cooperation of the Muslim community. His own assessment, on the basis of the reports he had received from the Governors, central intelligence officers and his own personal enquiries, was that Jinnah's charges against the Congress ministries were highly exaggerated and he made no secret of his opinion of Jinnah.

Linlithgow to Zetland, 2 October 1939:

> I have never taken these complaints [against the Congress ministries] seriously. Regarding the offer of Rajendra Prasad on behalf of the Congress Working Committee of a judicial enquiry into Muslim greviances and Jinnah's refusal of the offer on the ground that the matter was before the Governor-General, I have now no desire to shoulder any of Jinnah's responsibilities or to be left as a middleman between Muslims and the Congress in matters such as these. In actual fact, as you will have gathered from the account of my interview with Jinnah, we did discuss in general terms the Muslim grievances against Congress governments, and I indicated to him my feeling that they were 'psychological rather than material, a view which he said he at one time had been disposed to accept, but from which he was now tending to resile in the light of further experience.'[25]

IV

In the summer of 1938, Linlithgow decided to visit England on a short vacation. He used this visit not only to acquaint himself with the currents of British politics, but with the fast-developing international situation. The clouds of war were hovering over Europe. The totalitarian regimes in Germany, Italy and Japan, which had crushed all opposition at home, were preparing for adventures abroad. With the invasion of Abyssinia by Italy and occupation of the demilitarized zone, the annexation of Austria by Germany and Italian intervention in the Spanish civil war, the system of collective security through the League of Nations had virtually collapsed. The smaller nations of Europe were living in daily dread, not knowing when and where the next blow would fall. Britain and France belatedly had awakened to the need for rearmament against the threat of war; in the autumn of 1938 they were barely able to buy peace by permitting Germany to annex part of Czechoslovakia. The British political parties, the press and the Parliament were concerned about the international situation and the problem of defence of Britain and its far-flung empire.

It so happened that Jawaharlal Nehru also visited Europe at this time to study the critical international situation. Linlithgow invited him to lunch. It was their first meeting. 'Would you believe it', Nehru wrote home to J.B. Kripalani, General Secretary of the All India Congress Committee, 'that in the course of two hours of very frank and friendly conversation, there was no mention of Hindu–Muslim affairs or even of federation, so far as I remember. Our conversation covered a wide range of subjects .... We talked of independence and the Constituent Assembly and economic questions and the present international situation .... This will indicate to you what the basis of my talk has been.'[26]

On return to India in October 1938, Linlithgow decided to accelerate the process for the implementation of the second part of the Act of 1935, and to set up the Federation incorporating the provinces and the Princely states. In October 1938 he wrote to Neville Chamberlain, the British Prime Minister: 'I am now even more hopeful than I was three months ago about my prospects of securing Federation early without a serious row. I will be busy to put India into the best fighting shape in case of war.'[27]

During the latter half of 1938 and the first half of 1939, there were indications of the narrowing of the gulf between the Congress and the government after long years of distrust and conflict.

Some right wing Congress leaders, such as K.M. Munshi, a minister in the Bombay Congress ministry, believed that 'if the Act [of 1935] were worked properly, the transition to full-fledged dominion status for the whole of India would have been easy with the executives in the provinces being made responsible to their respective legislatures.'[28] In June 1938, B.G. Kher, the Premier of Bombay, arranged a meeting between Sir Roger Lumley, who had succeeded Lord Brabourne as Governor, and Vallabhbhai Patel. The meeting lasted for an hour. Patel told Lumley that the Congress had decided in 1937 to accept office 'against their better judgment' for two reasons. One was to prevent the administration passing into the hands of 'reactionaries', and the other was to show Britain that Congressmen could govern, and he hoped that this would have the effect of making Great Britain willing to advance further than the Government of India Act of 1935.

In May 1939, Linlithgow told Zetland that it would be a good idea to include in the British delegation to the League of Nations a Congress representative like K.M. Munshi. In June 1939, the Viceroy was impressed by Rajendra Prasad, whom he had invited to meet him in connection with a strike in an oil company in Assam. In July 1939, Linlithgow conveyed to Zetland Lord Erskine's appreciation of the very positive and practical outlook of C. Rajagopalchari. Erksine was hopeful about the Congress attitude if the war broke out. He quoted K.M. Munshi's comment to Low of the *Times of India,* 'If war comes Gandhi will find a formula'.

V

While Linlithgow was cultivating the Congress leaders, he was also trying to rope in the Muslim League into his federal plan. The Muslim League was not in power in any province, but with its appeal for Muslim solidarity at the national level, Jinnah had been able to secure the backing of the Premiers of three Muslim-majority provinces, viz., the Punjab, Bengal and Sind. Linlithgow had met Jinnah several times. Brabourne, during his term as Governor of Bombay, had kept Linlithgow and Zetland informed on Jinnah's political moves and the state of Muslim politics. In August 1938, he wrote to Zetland that Jinnah had met him and ended the conversation with the 'startling suggestion that we [the British] should keep the centre as it is now, that we should make friends with the Muslims by protecting them in the Congress provinces and if we did that the Muslims will protect us at the centre.' Surprising as it may seem, neither the Viceroy nor the Secretary of State jumped at Jinnah's offer. Their hearts were set on the installation of a popular government at the centre within the Act of 1935, and this required the cooperation of all parties, and especially of the Congress and the Muslim League, to prepare India for the critical times ahead. The fact was that Brabourne was no more convinced than Linlithgow by the catalogue of Muslim grievances against the Congress ministries which Jinnah was reeling off at every meeting, such as Muslim schoolchildren having to sing *Bande Mataram,* inadequate arrangements for teaching of Urdu and inadequate Muslim representation in local bodies. Brabourne felt that some of the grievances were probably true, but there was 'a great element of exaggeration in the allegations'.

In February 1939, Linlithgow sent for Jinnah to ascertain his views on the launching of his Federal plan. Jinnah did not reject the proposal outright, but told the Viceroy that the Federation had to be such as to ensure an adequate 'equipoise between Muslim and Hindu votes', and an 'appropriate balance between the communities'. When Linlithgow asked him how he proposed to achieve this balance, Jinnah replied that he had in his mind the 'manipulation of territorial votes and the adjustment of territorial divisions'. This was the first time that Jinnah hinted to Linlithgow that carving up of India could solve the communal problem. Linlithgow put it bluntly to him whether he wanted the British to stay on. Jinnah replied that 'it looked very much that this position was to emerge'. Linlithgow said that the Act of 1935 had been passed after ten years of endeavours, with the help of Indian opinion, to devise a workable scheme, but Jinnah was switching on to something entirely different. In his record of this interview, Linlithgow wrote that, though friendly, Jinnah was 'not too constructive', and added that 'one has of course always to take what he says with a good deal of reserve, and to make the fullest allowance for his defensive tendency to exaggerate and to pave the way for accommodation by the most extravagant claims.'[29]

Two months later, Linlithgow wrote that he was 'distressed' by the Muslim attitude: 'the community was 'completely puzzled as to the wise course to adopt and ... Jinnah, though clever, keeps things too much in his own hands and is too much concerned to run a purely personal policy on the basis of mystery.'[30] Such was Linlithgow's lack of trust in Jinnah that in April 1939 he passed on to Zetland an intelligence report revealing that Jinnah had directed Khaliquzzaman and Abdur Rahman Siddiqui, who were Muslim League's envoys in London for a conference on the Palestine problem, to get in touch with Hitler and Mussolini and put before them the case of Indian Muslims.[31] Zetland at once asked British intelligence to track the movements of the Muslim League envoys in Europe after the London conference. It turned out that Khaliquzzaman and Siddiqui had indeed gone to Geneva where they contacted the Italian Counsul-General, who received them warmly and sent them on to Rome to meet Mussolini or Count Ciano, but they returned disappointed and 'took the dust of Rome off their feet'.

In his memoirs, *Pathway to Pakistan,* Khaliquzzaman gives an account of his visit to Rome and his failure to get an interview with Mussolini or Count Ciano, but he does not reveal the real purpose of the visit — whether it was about the Palestine problem or about the Muslims' predicament in India.³² In either case, it is astonishing that such a visit should have been undertaken by envoys of the All India Muslim League at a time when Great Britain's relations with Germany and Italy were on the verge of a breakdown.

Linlithgow's reaction to the various Pakistan schemes for territorial adjustment and partition, which were being talked about in the Muslim League meetings in 1939 was one of lively scepticism. He was not unduly perturbed, he wrote to Zetland, because he did not believe that any of the schemes which had so far been 'ventilated' had 'the least chance of surviving critical examination'.³³ He sounded out the provincial Governors on the prospects of drawing Muslims into his plan for setting up the Federation. Sir Roger Lumley, who had succeeded Brabourne as Governor of Bombay, assured him that the Muslims in Bombay province were not 'sufficiently strong or united to do anything effective against the Federation'.³⁴ Sir Henry Craik, Governor of the Punjab, pooh-poohed the idea of any effective Muslim interference in the way of the launching of the Federation. In June 1939, Linlithgow's considered view was: 'I do not myself see in what way the Muslim League could effectively torpedo Federation'.³⁵

VI

While the Viceroy was trying to rope in the political parties into his scheme for Federation, there was a virtual revolt in his Executive Council. General Cassels, the Commander-in-Chief, submitted a memorandum requesting the Viceroy to hold a private meeting to which only he (C-in-C), Sir James Grigg, the Finance Member, and Sir Reginald Maxwell, the Home Member, should be invited. At this meeting held in the Viceroy's House on 20 February 1939, General Cassels sounded a note of warning: if the Congress were allowed to pursue their announced policy for very much longer, their hold on the country would proportionately increase and it would be very difficult to deal with them when the government would be forced to accept their challenge.[36]

Grigg concurred with the Commander-in-Chief's 'general diagnosis' and said that the commendations of the Congress ministries by the British Governors, by European businessmen, and by 'Cook's tourists' of the liberal politician type were quite unjustified. The Congress, in his judgement, had skilfully pursued the policy of wrecking the constitution from within. He suggested that the government's attitude with regard to the retention of Congress ministries in office as the prime object of the British endeavour should be abandoned, and that an authoritative statement should be issued that no amendment of the Act of 1935 involving the abandonment or attenuation of any powers reserved under it would be made. Maxwell, the Home Member, went further and said that in the event of any serious threat from the Congress, at a time when Britain was preoccupied elsewhere, 'two trump cards were available to the government: making terms with the Muhammedans and making terms with the States', and either course would involve the abandonment by the government of its constitutional policy but it would checkmate the Congress, and perhaps the prospect of either would bring the Congress to terms.

Linlithgow was somewhat taken aback by the revolt in his own backyard. He reserved his own judgement, but promised to convey the views expressed at the meeting to the Secretary of State. But undaunted by this pressure of the senior members of his Executive Council, he persevered in his effort to set up a popular government at the centre.

As the summer of 1939 wore on, Linlithgow was getting desperate about his plan. He wrote to Zetland: 'The moment we weaken in our resolve to push Federation we shall find ourselves without a policy and without a future.' He urged Zetland to take the earliest opportunity to declare in the House of Lords that an early Federation under Part II of the Act of 1935 remained as strong as ever the policy of His Majesty's Government.[37]

While Linlithgow was talking to the leaders of the Congress and the League, he was also trying to get the consent of the rulers of the Princely states as the third party of the Federal set-up. The negotiations with the Princes had been prolonged because of their demands of concessions on excise, customs and corporate tax, not due to them under the Act of 1935. Zetland did not like the idea of 'bribing' them, but Linlithgow yielded to their demands and during his visit to England persuaded the Home Government to amend the Act of 1935 to accommodate the Princes. All this took time. Not until January 1939 was Linlithgow able to arrange for the offer of the terms of accession to the federation to be sent to the Princes. They were given six months to reply, but as the requisite number of acceptances had not come in till July, the date for acceptance of the offer was extended to 30 September. But the war broke out on 3 September, and Linlithgow announced that Britain had 'no choice but to hold in suspense the work in connection with the preparation for Federation'.

The outbreak of the war was to make short work of Linlithgow's federal plan, but he had lost valuable time during the first two years of his term and failed to prod the Princes towards a positive decision. The Princes, with their 18th century mindset, wanted to hold on to their autocratic regimes; they had been put off by the Congress demand that the native (Princely) states should be represented in the federal legislature through election and not by nomination by the rulers. Their insistence on their treaty rights had the support not only of the Political Department of the Government of India but of Tory diehards of the ruling Conservative Party in Britain.

Chapter 23

INCHING TOWARDS PARTITION

Pakistani historian Saleem Qureshi dates the beginning of Muslim separatism in India (which in the 1940s came to be termed Muslim nationalism) to 1885 when the Indian National Congress was founded. 'The history of Muslim nationalism in India', he says, 'is largely a history of reaction to the Congress'.[1]

Qureshi's thesis is supported by several other Pakistani historians who have hailed Sir Syed Ahmad Khan as the 'father-figure' of Pakistan. The political concept of Pakistan, as it came to be formulated in 1939–40, was inconceivable in the last quarter of the 19th century, but there was much in the writings and speeches of Sir Syed to nourish its psychological roots in the Muslim elite. That the Muslims, the former rulers of the Indian subcontinent, had been the victims of history, that the Hindus had stolen a march over them in education and employment, that the Muslim youth must be educated separately from the Hindus under Muslim auspices, that for the Muslims to compete with the Hindus for public services and elective bodies was a hopeless task, that any democratic polity must result in Hindu domination, that the British Raj was preferable to Hindu domination, were all assumptions of Sir Syed which grew into the dogmas of Muslim separatism during the next half a century.

Sir Syed Ahmad Khan was highly respected as a religious and social reformer. He exerted powerful influence in favour of the isolation of Muslims from the nationalist movement just when it started, thus raising the great question which was to hang over Indian politics during the next 50 years: what would be the position of the Muslim community in independent India?

Twenty years later, in 1906, when an influential deputation of Muslim leaders headed by the Aga Khan presented a memorial[2] to Lord Minto, the then Viceroy of India, to oppose the extension of the elective system to legislatures, it sought some means of offsetting the numerical inferiority of Muslims in the population of India and pleaded for 'due consideration to the position which they (Muslims) occupied in India a little more than a hundred years ago... and of which the traditions have naturally not faded from their minds.'[3] Lord Minto in his reply to the deputation greeted them as the 'descendants of a conquering and ruling race'. The self-image of the Muslim elite as the former rulers of India became a block in the way of their identification with the Indian National Congress. The fact is that the demands of the Indian National Congress as voiced in its annual sessions — such as the Indianization of higher services, equitable financial burdens between India and Britain, reduction in military expenditure, reduction in land revenue, separation of executive and judiciary — did not excite the Muslim elite who were happy enough with the status quo and the patronage of the British officials with whom they came into contact. The British bureaucracy, on its part, tended to look upon the Muslim community, as it did in the case of the rulers of the Princely states, as the pillars of the British Raj.

During the next two decades the anxiety of the Muslim elite to offset the Hindu majority in India found expression in a number of demands such as the creation of more Muslim-majority provinces by separating Sind from Bombay, by upgrading the status of the North-West Frontier Province, by seeking statutory Muslim majorities in the legislatures of Punjab and Bengal, and by insisting on weighted reservation (33 per cent as against their population of 25 per cent) for Muslims in the central legislature. The appointment of the Simon Commission in

1927, followed by the Round Table Conference in London in 1930, kept Muslim demands for 'safeguards' in the new constitution at the forefront. In 1932, Prime Minister MacDonald's 'Communal Award' conceded practically all Muslim demands vis-à-vis Hindus for incorporation in the new constitution.

It is significant that Maulana Mahomed Ali, the Khilafat leader and a close comrade of Gandhi during the Khilafat and non-cooperation movements in the early 1920s, wrote in 1930, a few months before his death, to the Private Secretary to the Viceroy Lord Irwin:

> Separate electorates and weightage in the Hindu-majority Provinces were not sufficient safeguards ... under a so-called democratic and nationalist constitution. What we need is the strengthening of our position in the Provinces in which we constitute a majority, such as in the reformed [North-West] Frontier, in the separated Sind, in the 56% of Punjab and 55% of Bengal. The strengthening of our position there would protect the Muslim minorities in other Provinces far more effectively than mere weightage or even separate electorates.[4]

Five years later, the Aga Khan who had been the de facto leader of the Muslim delegates in the Round Table Conference wrote to Mian Fazl-i-Hussain that the Muslims in India were in a minority of the population (not even one-fourth of the population) and, whether they liked it or not, for all time they would have to live in India and for all time they would have the Hindu majority by their side. The Muslim position would have been desperate and hopeless if they were 25 per cent all over the country, and Hindus everywhere in majority. But fortunately, the Aga Khan wrote, things were not so bad. We have 'the vast Pakistan bloc on one side where we are in a positive majority and which is a frontier province, touching independent Moslem States as well as the sea. Again in Bengal, which is a frontier and maritime province, we have a majority .... Our position is neither hopeless nor desperate. Where we are small minorities (as in the South and Centre) we must frankly accept the position, similar to that of the Jews in Europe or the Parsees and Christians in India.'[5]

When the Aga Khan wrote to Fazl-i-Hussain about a 'Pakistan bloc' in 1935, the word had not yet gained currency. It had been coined by Rahmat Ali, a young Punjabi who had studied at Cambridge and published a pamphlet, *Now or Never,* in 1933. In this pamphlet he had castigated the Muslim delegation to the Round Table Conference for agreeing to an all-India Federation, 'thereby signing the death warrant of Islam and its future in India'. He averred that Hindus and Muslims were followers of two essentially different religious systems, and Muslims must, therefore, demand from the British Government the recognition of a separate national status and the grant of a Federal constitution separate from the rest of India.[6]

Rahmat Ali had timed the publication of his pamphlet so as to synchronize with the first meeting of the Joint Parliamentary Committee in London in 1933, which was discussing the draft of the new constitution for India. After the members of the Muslim delegation had given their evidence and endorsed the proposal of an all-India Federation, Sir Reginald Craddock, a former Home Member of the Viceroy's Executive Council, drew their attention to Rahmat Ali's pamphlet. One Muslim delegate dismissed Rahmat Ali's scheme as 'only a student's scheme and one which no responsible people have put forward'. Another described it as 'chimerical and impracticable'.[7] Craddock was however so taken with Rahmat Ali's scheme that he said: 'you advance very quickly in India, and it may be when these students grow up it will be put forward; the scheme must be in the minds of people anyhow.'[8] Craddock's comment unwittingly revealed a basic factor in Indian politics: the proclivity of the British bureaucracy for encouraging Muslim separatism as a counterweight to Indian nationalism. Another British official, Coatman, who had served as a publicity officer in the central government, wrote in his book *Years of Destiny* (1932), that 'the creation of a strong, united India, including the whole of British India and the Indian States and the borderland in the North-West,... was in day by day, being made impossible, and in its place it seemed that 'there may be brought into being a powerful Muhammedan State in the north and north-west, with its eyes definitely turned away from India, towards the rest of the Muslim world, of which it forms a fringe.'[9]

A Turkish writer, Halide Edib, who visited India in the mid-1930s, wrote in her book *Inside India* that she had questioned a large number of Muslims in or out of politics, but found adherents of the 'Pakistan National Movement' only among Muslim students who had lived abroad.[10] Jinnah had refused to see Rahmat Ali. At the Round Table Conference he had stoutly fought for safeguards for Muslims. His 'Fourteen Points' may have seemed too high in 1929, but were virtually conceded in the Communal Award by Prime Minister MacDonald in 1932. Jinnah realized that the Communal Award had conceded almost all that Muslims had wanted as safeguards. He was more worried about British reluctance to part with power. He had taken no notice of Rahmat Ali's scheme and were it not for the disastrous election of 1937 which led to a drastic reversal of Jinnah's political stand, Rahmat Ali would have faded into history as a political maverick.

II

As we have seen, Jinnah had first revealed his Islamic card at the Lucknow session of the Muslim League in October 1937; within a year it did wonders for him and his party. The Muslim members of the provincial legislatures in the Hindu-majority provinces, who had won their seats as independent candidates in 1937, joined the Muslim League party. In the Central Legislative Assembly, for the first time, a Muslim League party was formed. While addressing the members of this party in August 1938, Jinnah chose to comment adversely on the democratic system. 'I do not know', he said, 'how far this machine [democratic parliamentary government], which is now planted here [in India] when every other country... has given it up will succeed. The question is whether a system of government which developed in England for six centuries is suited to the genius of the Indian people. 'Can this democratic parliamentary government succeed in this country?' It 'is not a democratic majority in seven Congress provinces ... it is the permanent Hindu majority.'[11]

Two months later, at the Sind Muslim League Provincial Conference, Jinnah said, 'the Sudeten Germans were forced under the heel of the majority of Czechoslovakia who oppressed them, suppressed them, maltreated them and showed a brutal and callous disregard for their rights and interests for two decades hence the inevitable result that the Republic of Czechoslovakia is now broken up and a new map will have to be drawn. Just as the Sudeten Germans were not defenceless and survived the oppression... so also the Musalmans are not defenceless and cannot give up their national entity and aspirations in this great continent.'[12]

Jinnah's remarks seem strange as he was speaking just after the Munich Pact in October 1938 when the whole free world was torn between a sense of relief at the war having been averted and a feeling of anguish at the sacrifice of the Czechoslovak Republic. Jinnah compared the lot of Indian Muslims to that of Sudeten Germans, and drew his own inference from it. It is difficult to believe that he did not know that the Sudeten Germans were mere pawns in Hitler's war game to break up Czechoslovakia and it was in a bid to dominate Europe and indeed the world. Evidently, Jinnah's speech was directed only to his co-religionists; he did not seem to be concerned about the totalitarian threat to democracy in Europe; he put a question mark on the suitability of a democratic polity in India; his campaign against the Congress and the spectre of Hindu Raj was bringing him to a 'surgical' solution of the communal problem in India.

III

The Sind Muslim League Conference, with Jinnah in the chair, passed a resolution recommending to the All India Muslim League that it devise a scheme of constitution under which the Muslim-majority provinces, the Moslems of 'Native States' and the areas inhabited by the majority of Moslems may obtain full independence in the form of a Federation of their own with permission to any other Moslem States beyond the Indian frontiers to join the Federation and with such safeguards for non-Moslem minorities as may be conceded to Muslim minorities in the non-Muslim Federation of India.[13] This resolution posed a challenge to the prevalent beliefs of not only Hindus but of the British, and indeed even of many Muslims. It was at this conference that Fazlul Haq, Prime Minister of Bengal, said: 'If Mohammad-bin-Qasim, an eight-year-old lad, with 18 soldiers, could conquer Sind, then surely nine crore Muslims can conquer the whole of India.'[14]

Two months later, in December 1938, at the annual session of the All India Muslim League at Patna, Jinnah said that he would have to come to the rescue of Muslims in the native (Princely) states in the event of their being exploited by other parties. In the same month, the Muslim League Executive Council passed a resolution to counter the Muslim mass contact movement launched by the Congress, and instructed its 'propaganda committee' to ensure that

> In every province and district where the spiritual influence of the *ulemas* could be utilized for the purpose, brief fatwas and manifestos should be issued on behalf of the ulemas in which Muslims should be warned against joining the Congress, and the disadvantages from the religious point of view of any assistance to the Congress should be clearly and emphatically explained to them. These *Fatwas* should be published under the authority of the All India Muslim League through the local League in each district.[15]

According to Waheed Ahmad, the author of the series *The Nation's Voice,* it was on 12 April 1939 that Jinnah for the first time used the word 'nation' in emphatic terms in relation to Indian Muslims, though three years earlier, in 1936, he had stated that he believed that Muslims could arrive at a settlement with Hindus as two nations being as partners. 'I make no secret of the fact that Muslims and Hindus are two nations and Muslims cannot maintain their status as such unless they acquire national self-consciousness and national self-determination. The Muslim mind suffers from defeatism. Fear, demoralization and mediocrity haunt the minds of many of us. We are going to live as a nation and play our part as a nation.'[16]

The pitch of the League significantly rose at its Patna session in December 1938 when Jinnah declared: 'I say the Muslim League is not going to be an ally of anyone, but would be ally of even the devil if need be in the interest of Muslims.'[17]

In August 1939, some professors of Aligarh Muslim University proposed the creation of three sovereign states in British India:

1. North-West India or Pakistan,
2. Bengal, and
3. Hindustan.

The principalities (Princely states) within those states or exclusively on the frontier of one of them were to be attached automatically. But Hyderabad was to recover Berar and Karnataka to become, with these territories, the fourth sovereign state, 'the southern wing of Muslim India'. Both Pakistan and Bengal were to be Muslim states. Within Hindustan, Delhi and Malabar would be two autonomous provinces with strong Muslim minorities. This was the only scheme which Jinnah mentioned to Linlithgow during his talks with him in 1939.

In his presidential address to the League session in 1930, Iqbal had propounded what he called a 'territorial solution of the Indian problem'. He argued that the criterion of autonomous states based on unity of language, race, history, religion and identity of economic interests is the only possible way to secure a stable constitutional structure in India.

Iqbal was not, however, advocating partition of India. By 'autonomy' he did not mean full independence. He was not thinking primarily of Muslim consolidation. He wanted to unite the Punjab and its neighbours in a consolidated 'North-West Indian Muslim State'. He did not propose that the Muslim State should be carved out from the rest of India; it was to be one of the several similarly constituted states which would be linked together in a loose all-India federation.

Jinnah had taken little notice of Iqbal's proposal when it was first made in 1930. Frank Moraes, a Bombay-based journalist, tells us that Jinnah referred to Iqbal 'as a visionary and a poet'.[18] However, seven years later Iqbal's ideas began to make sense to Jinnah after he had decided to play his Islamic card. In March 1937, Iqbal wrote to Jinnah to hold an all-India Muslim convention and invite to it members of the new provincial assemblies and restate strongly the political objective of Indian Muslims as a distinct political unit in the country. It was absolutely necessary to tell the world both inside and outside India that the economic problem was not the only problem in the country; from the Muslim point of view the cultural problem was of greater consequence. 'The enforcement and development of the Shariat of Islam was', Iqbal wrote, 'impossible in this country without a free Muslim State or States'. It was the only way to solve the problem of bread for Muslims as well as to secure a peaceful India. If such a thing was impossible in India, the only other alternative was a civil war which, as a matter of fact, had been going on for some time in the form of Hindu–Muslim riots.

Iqbal was talking of civil war even before the Congress accepted office, indeed at a time when it had decided not to accept office! Iqbal recommended to Jinnah that Muslims of north-west India and Bengal ought to ignore Muslim-minority provinces; this was the best course to adopt in the interest of both the Muslim majority and Muslim-minority provinces. He suggested that the next session of the League should be held in the Punjab and not in a Muslim-minority province.

Jinnah did not follow Iqbal's idea of 'sovereign' Muslim states becoming part of a large federation, but he accepted Iqbal's idea of ignoring Muslim-minority provinces and concentrating on the Muslim-majority provinces. He could not recommend democratization of Princely states because he did not want to antagonize rulers of Muslim states, such as Hyderabad and Bhopal. Nor could he spell out any radical proposal on economic policy, as it would affect the landowning Muslim elite of Punjab, Sind and the NWFP. He concentrated only on slamming the Congress.

IV

It was at this time in March 1939 that Choudhary Khaliquzzaman, with a member of the Muslim League Executive Council, called on Col Muirhead, Under-Secretary of State for India, who told them:

> You say that the British democracy does not suit you and I see that it does not, but we do not know of any other kind of democracy. We apply the same principle in India which we apply in our own country, and you do not suggest any alternative.[19]

Chapter 24

DECLARATION OF WAR

On 3 September 1939, the *Gazette of India* carried a grave announcement: 'I, Victor Alexander John, Marquess of Linlithgow, Governor-General of India and ex-officio Admiral, therein being satisfied thereof by information received by me, do hereby proclaim that war has broken out between His Majesty and Germany.'

'One man, and he a foreigner', wrote Jawaharlal Nehru in the *Discovery of India*, 'plunged four hundred millions of human beings into war without the slightest reference to them.'

Linlithgow had failed to take Indian leaders into confidence before declaring India belligerent, but he endeavoured to make up for this soon thereafter. He sent telegrams to Gandhi and Jinnah inviting them to meet him on 4 September. Jinnah arrived at the Viceroy's House at Simla in high spirits. This was the day for which he had been waiting for two long years. What particularly struck him was that he had been invited on the same day as Gandhi. As he publicly recalled later:

> Up to the time of the declaration of the war, the Viceroy never thought of me, but of Gandhi and Gandhi alone. Therefore, when I got this invitation from the Viceroy along with Mr. Gandhi, I wondered within myself why I was so suddenly promoted, and then ...' the answer was 'The All India Muslim League ....'[1]

Linlithgow told Jinnah that he was anxious to see leaders of all parties in connection with the outbreak of hostilities between Germany and Britain, that he had seen Gandhi earlier in the day, and proposed to see other leaders during the course of the week. His object was to do all in his power to render India's part in the war effective in terms of both her own defence and her share in the general effort of the British Empire.[2]

Jinnah expressed his 'whole-hearted' loyalty and readiness to give full support to the government on behalf of his party, but he also had some reservations and demands. He urged the government to recognize that the democratic form of government did not suit India, and that the constitution under the Act of 1935 needed to be overhauled and reshaped. He pleaded for the protection of Muslims in the Congress-ruled provinces 'in the enjoyment of their life, their property and their culture'. When Linlithgow asked him point blank: 'Do you want us to turn the Congress ministries out?' Jinnah replied: 'Yes! Turn them out at once. Nothing else will bring them to senses. Their object, though you may not believe it, and though I did not believe it till two years ago, is nothing less than to destroy both you, British, and us, Muslims. They will never stand by you.'[3]

Linlithgow asked Jinnah, if democratic government was unsuitable to India, how was she to obtain her goal of self-government? Jinnah replied that the solution was in the adoption of the partition of the country. While pledging support of the Muslim League to the government, Jinnah sought Linlithgow's good offices to strengthen his party by advising Sikandar Hyat Khan and Fazlul Haq, the respective Prime Ministers of Punjab and Bengal, not to act independently but to follow the lead of the Muslim League on national issues.

It may seem surprising that in his very first meeting after the outbreak of the war Jinnah should have placed on the Viceroy's table all the cards he had held close to his chest for two years since his electoral disaster at the polls in 1937. Evidently, he reckoned that the government and the Congress would not be able to agree and sooner or later the government would have to lean on the Muslim League.

Linlithgow gave a patient hearing to Jinnah, but was cautious in responding to him. For one thing, he was cultivating Gandhi and other leaders of the Congress and hoped to secure their cooperation in coping with the emergency which had arisen. For another, he was not sure of Jinnah's credentials to speak on behalf of Indian Muslims. Shortly before Jinnah's arrival for the meeting, Sikandar Hyat had sent a message to Linlithgow that nothing should be done to 'inflate' Jinnah or to make him more difficult to deal with, because the Punjab and Bengal were already wholly behind the government for the prosecution of war, irrespective of Jinnah's opinion.[4]

Linlithgow's comments on this meeting with Jinnah to the Secretary of State show that he did not take Jinnah's claims seriously:

> I found him a little more sticky and rather more disposed to bargain; but his own position is not too strong. It is obvious that a section of Muslim opinion represented by Sikandar, and, to some extent, by Fazlul Haq is increasingly restive of control by the Muslim League under Jinnah's leadership. The existence of this state of things in Muslim politics makes the support of or the lack of support of Jinnah of somewhat less consequence than would otherwise be the case.[5]

II

Jinnah had to wait for a month for the next call from the Viceregal Lodge. It was a period of uncertainty and tension for him after his first meeting with the Viceroy. He knew that the Viceroy was engaged in negotiations with Gandhi and other Congress leaders to win them over and that the outcome of these negotiations would affect the government's attitude to the Muslim League.

Linlithgow was keen on bringing together the Congress, the Muslim League and the Princes into an interim political and administrative arrangement which would strengthen the hand of the government during the emergency which had arisen. He had achieved a good rapport with Gandhi during the previous two years. He was satisfied with the functioning of the Congress ministries in eight out of eleven provinces, and he had of course no problem with the loyal governments of three Muslim-majority provinces of Punjab, Sind and Bengal. He believed on the basis of information he had been receiving from the British Governors and the central intelligence of the Government of India that the Muslim League's charges against the Congress ministries were 'psychological and not material'. He felt it would not be difficult for him to get the necessary assurances from the Congress to induct the League into an arrangement for a functioning federal centre during the war.

Linlithgow had been slow to realize the implications of the international situation in 1938–39, of which most British politicians, not only of the opposition parties but even of the ruling Conservative Party, were becoming aware. He had been the chairman of the Joint Parliamentary Committee, which had dealt with the passage of the Act of 1935 through the British Parliament in its final stage. His vision was limited by that experience; he believed that a fuller implementation of that constitution would provide a practical solution for the effective prosecution of the war.

As the Viceroy's talks with Congress leaders in September 1939 did not go as well as he had hoped, he decided to soften his attitude towards Jinnah. He had not taken the League leader seriously at their first meeting after the outbreak of the war, but a month later, when Jinnah called on him, he was more cordial and forthcoming. Jinnah thanked him for what he had done to help him keep his party together; Linlithgow had reined in Sikandar Hyat and Fazlul Haq and exhorted them not to question Jinnah's standing in national politics. In his talks with Jinnah, Linlithgow rationalized his intervention in Muslim politics with the remark that 'it was clearly unsatisfactory that while one of the two great parties [the Congress] was well-organized and well-equipped to pursue its objectives and express its aims, the other [the Muslim League], equally of great importance, should be prevented from securing its full expression by any failure to secure an adequate mouthpiece. It was in the public interest that the Muslim point of view should be fully and competently expressed.'6

Encouraged by the Viceroy's sympathetic attitude at this meeting, Jinnah brought up the question of the treatment of Muslims in Congress-ruled provinces and made a fundamental proposition. He told Linlithgow that he had received representations from a group of professors of the Aligarh Muslim University urging him not to reach an agreement either with the Congress or the government, unless the plan to create a united India was abandoned, and effective protection was afforded to Muslims in Congress-ruled, Hindu-majority provinces.7 Linlithgow's response was the same as in his previous meetings with Jinnah: he had personally gone into the allegations against the Congress ministries 'most carefully', but it had been 'extremely difficult to find any positive instance of real oppression or the like by them'. He thought the true explanation for these charges was that the allegations were very largely 'psychological', arising out of the feeling of inferiority on the part of these Muslim minorities, and their apprehension that a Hindu Raj lay at the back of the minds of the Hindus in the Hindu-majority provinces — an idea which the superiority complex of Hindus in these provinces might well contribute to foster.8

III

While the talks between the Congress and the government were going on, there was a strange interlude in the third week of October 1939 of a friendly overture to the Congress from Jinnah. Raghunandan Saran, a Delhi businessman, who was on friendly terms with both Nehru and Jinnah, received a message from Nawabzada Liaquat Ali Khan that Jinnah would like to settle the Hindu–Muslim problem and would welcome a discussion with Nehru. Raghunandan Saran met Jinnah on 17 October, and on the same day wrote to Nehru:

> He received me with utmost courtesy and warmth of feelings and opened the conversation on the note of reminiscence carrying us to the year 1922 when I used to meet him and his wife. He seemed to be in a particularly good mood and humour. At the outset he asked me to warn you against lies and gossip ... he said that it was simply unthinkable that he should have told anyone that he had no confidence in the members of the [Congress] Working Committee. On the contrary, he said that he held most of them in high esteem and regard. Talking about you he said that he had affection for you coupled with high regard for your character and integrity, etc. Then he said to me that, having said all that, he had to see [the] Hindu–Muslim problem from his own stand point. He said that he would welcome resumption of conversations with you.[9]

On receipt of Raghunandan Saran's letter, Jawaharlal Nehru hastened to write to Jinnah. 'I entirely agree with you', Nehru wrote, 'that it is a tragedy that the Hindu–Muslim problem has not so far been settled in a satisfactory way .... With your goodwill and commanding position in the Muslim League a solution should not be as difficult as people imagine .... For, after all, the actual matters under dispute should be, and indeed are, easily capable of adjustment.' He pleaded with Jinnah to join the Congress in protesting against India being plunged into the war without her consent. He appealed to Jinnah's patriotism: 'our dignity and self-respect as Indians have been insulted by the British government'.[10]

For once Jinnah seemed interested and even cordial, but he did not commit himself to any course of action, agreeing only to continue the discussions. Jinnah's overture at this juncture to the Congress and its leadership is difficult to explain. Was it a case of 'double speak' or a tactical move to keep the lines of communication with the Congress open in the remote possibility of a rapprochement between the government and the Congress? From Jinnah's exchanges with the Viceroy we know that he had burnt his bridges with the Congress. Nehru and the Congress leaders were naive enough to take Jinnah at his word. The correspondence between Nehru and Jinnah initiated in October 1939, though friendly, did not yield any result and ended abruptly two months later when Jinnah announced celebration of a 'Deliverance Day' on the resignation of the Congress ministries. Jinnah's abrupt and aggressive gesture against the Congress was due to the knowledge that the negotiations between the Congress and the government had broken down. It was this outcome which Jinnah had hoped for for four months. It is important to understand the conflicting policies of the Congress party and the government, which were also to determine the policies of Jinnah and the Muslim League during the next six years.

IV

The Indian National Congress, though only a political party, had a 'foreign policy'; its approach to international affairs had been largely shaped by Jawaharlal Nehru. In the summer of 1938 when Nehru was in London during the critical days preceding the Munich crisis, in a letter to the *Manchester Guardian* he had sharply criticized the British Government's policy of 'appeasement' of the totalitarian powers. Gandhi himself reacted to the Munich Pact with the question: 'Is it a triumph of organized violence? Has Herr Hitler discovered a new technique of organizing violence which enables him to gain his ends without shedding blood?' The Congress had voiced its sympathy with the victims of the totalitarian powers' aggression, even though some of its leaders, such as Subhas Chandra Bose, doubted the wisdom of antagonizing powerful nations such as Germany, Italy and Japan, for the sake of Abyssinia, Czechoslovakia and China, whose fate in any case seemed to be sealed.

On receipt of a telegram from the Viceroy, Gandhi took the first train to Simla and arrived on the morning of 4 September. He told the Viceroy that his sympathies were with England and France, although, as a man of non-violence, he himself could only offer his moral support to the Allied cause. As he discussed the war and pictured the possible destruction of the House of Commons and Westminister Abbey, he broke down. Though Gandhi's own position was anchored to his pacifism, he recognized, as he had done in 1914, that the proposal that India should defend herself against foreign aggression with non-violence was one which few Congressmen in India would accept as a practical proposition. After all, the Indian National Congress was not a body of pacifists; Nehru, Patel, C. Rajagopalachari, Abul Kalam Azad, indeed virtually the entire Congress leadership, were in favour of fighting for the Allied cause. The Congress had accepted non-violence in the struggle for freedom, but not as a creed for all times and in all situations. However, when it came to conducting negotiations with the government, the Congress leaders wanted Gandhi to conduct them on behalf of the party. And Gandhi agreed to do so.

The attitude of the Congress Working Committee to the war was explained in its resolution of 14 September 1939, perhaps the longest in its history, running to more than 2,000 words. The committee expressed its sympathy for victims of Fascist and Nazi aggression and offered cooperation of the Congress to Great Britain, but on the condition that cooperation would be between equals by mutual consent for a worthy cause. Since wars were no longer bouts between professional armies in distant battlefields and whole nations were likely to be mobilized as workers or soldiers, it was for Great Britain to release India's energies by treating her as an equal partner in a common struggle to enable her to play her full part in the world struggle. Thus, at an early stage in the war, the Congress asked the government to define the shape of the order for which the war was being waged, and to give

India a foretaste of the freedom and democracy for which she was being called upon to fight. Unlike the Viceroy and the Congress leadership, Jinnah did not seem to be worried about the threat posed by the aggressive totalitarian powers to democratic nations in Europe and even to India which was part of the British Empire. Jinnah's speeches and writings in the months immediately preceding the war did not betray any concern at the worsening of the international situation. His eyes were focused on Indian politics; his one-point programme was to checkmate the Congress; it was as if the real threat to India and the world did not emanate from Hitler, Mussolini and other Fascist powers but from Gandhi, Nehru and the Congress. Jinnah was perhaps the only important political leader in India who welcomed the outbreak of hostilities in Europe. As he recalled later (in 1945): 'There was going to be a deal between Mr. Gandhi and Lord Linlithgow. Providence helped us. The war which nobody welcomes proved to be a blessing in disguise.'[11] While the government and the Congress were agonizing over the search for a formula to cooperate for effective prosecution of the war, Jinnah was hoping against hope that their talks would fail, leaving the field clear for him.

There was no doubt at the beginning of the war that the Viceroy as well as the Congress leaders were keen on an understanding. On 21 September, Sir Harry Haig, Governor of the United Provinces, called at Anand Bhawan, the Nehrus' residence, ostensibly to see Vijaylakshmi Pandit, a member of the UP cabinet. She told Haig that her brother was in the house and would be glad to meet him. After a 'frank and friendly talk' for an hour, Haig was left with a 'strong impression' that Nehru was personally anxious to assist to the full in the prosecution of the war. Nehru told Haig that the Congress demand for a declaration of war aims and some guarantee of how they would be applied in practice might be represented as 'bargaining', but it was no use for him or for Gandhi to pledge full support to Great Britain, howsoever much they might like to do so, unless they could carry the country with them.[12]

Five days later Gandhi met the Viceroy and had a long discussion, but he drew a blank on the main issues, i.e. the declaration of British war aims and the arrangements during the war for popular participation in the war effort. Linlithgow enumerated various hurdles, such as the opposition of the Princes and the scheduled castes to the Congress demands. He saw 'no prospects whatsoever of any amendment of the Act of 1935 or of creating a *kutcha* [temporary] war centre within the existing law'.[13]

V

Gandhi was disappointed with his interview with the Viceroy on 26 September. He felt there was not sufficient meeting ground between them, but he did not throw in the trowel. Linlithgow was also willing to explore with the Congress leaders for a possible *modus vivendi*. At Gandhi's instance, Nehru called on the Viceroy on 3 October; he followed up his talk with a cordial letter to tell Linlithgow: 'how much I desire that the long conflict of India and England should be ended and they should cooperate together. I have felt that this war with all its horrors has brought this opportunity to our respective countries and it will be sad and tragic if we are unable to take advantage of it.'[14]

On the following day Vallabhbhai Patel called on the Viceroy. Linlithgow found him 'as a man of considerable shrewdness, a quick and active brain in addition to his strong and somewhat dominating personality'. Patel told Linlithgow that 'this was really a business between him and Gandhi'. Rajendra Prasad, the Congress president, had already met Linlithgow when he had accompanied Gandhi. Linlithgow and Zetland, Secretary of State, were still hoping for an understanding with the Congress when the Congress Working Committee, at its meeting at Wardha on 23 October, decided that the Congress ministries should tender their resignations.

In his meeting with Linlithgow on 2 November, Gandhi made it clear that his own difficulty and that of the

Congress were 'fundamental'; they hinged on a declaration of British war aims. The justification for this stand by the Congress was given at length in a resolution passed by the All India Congress Committee but it was succinctly summed up by Vallabhbhai Patel and relayed to the Viceroy by Lumley, the Governor of Bombay. The Congress was not convinced that the British Government meant to part with power, and as long as that uncertainty remained, it was useless for the Congress to 'try and reach an agreement with the minorities, and the Princes since they will continue to dig their toes in as long as they have the British Government behind them.'[15]

In his negotiations with the Congress, Linlithgow was harping on the opposition not only of the Muslims but other minorities in which he included even scheduled castes and Europeans. The Congress suspected that this was a trap; it was impossible for it to placate so many interests, which were dependent on the government and desired to maintain British rule in India.

By December 1939 Linlithgow was at the end of his tether. He had not been able to persuade the Congress to come to a settlement within the parameters of the Act of 1935, and in fact he said so in a letter to Zetland in December 1939:

> After all we framed the Constitution as it stands in the Act of 1935, because we thought that was the best way — given the political position in both countries — of maintaining British influence in India. It is no part of our policy, I take it, to expedite in India constitutional changes for their own sake, or gratuitously to hurry the handing over of the controls to Indian hands at any pace faster than that which we regard as best calculated, on a long view, to hold India to the Empire.[16]

VI

Zetland had been backing Linlithgow for three years; their rapport had helped their smooth sailing in Whitehall. By

December 1939, Zetland came to the conclusion that in the situation created by the war, an imaginative policy was required to enlist the support of the Indian people, and especially of the Congress, the largest political party. When he could not convert Linlithgow to his view, Zetland decided to go ahead on his own. He was able to convince Neville Chamberlain, the Prime Minister, that a 'closer accommodation' to the Congress was required and for this purpose Britain should agree to the principle that India would be conceded the right to frame its own postwar Dominion (Status) constitution, subject to agreement amongst the political parties on the composition of a Constituent Assembly. Zetland feared that the failure of the talks with the Congress would mean civil disobedience which 'Britain could contain only by methods which will expose our general motives of the war to the most effective criticism, not the least in America.'[17] Chamberlain saw Zetland's point; he was hopeful of getting the support of Halifax (Lord Irwin) who had signed the Gandhi–Irwin Pact in 1931 and Sir Samuel Hoare who had piloted the Act of 1935 through Parliament, but Churchill's opposition was likely to be a problem. And this is exactly what happened. Churchill did not see why the government wanted to encourage unity between Hindus and Muslims. Such a unity, he said, was, in fact, 'almost out of the realm of practical politics', and if it came about the result would be that both 'Hindus and Muslims would join together in showing the British the door'. The War Cabinet was divided on this issue, Zetland's proposal was still-born, and the Viceroy was asked to talk to Gandhi and offer a constitutional package which he had already been unable to accept. Linlithgow was unable to make any headway. He felt it was no use 'running after Gandhi'; the best thing was 'to lie back for the present'.

VII

By the beginning of 1940, the government needed Jinnah as much as Jinnah needed it. Linlithgow was in touch with Lumley, the Governor of Bombay, regarding Jinnah's attitude and advised Lumley 'if he [Jinnah] can hold his team behind him, his importance, and the importance for that matter of the Muslim community in these political negotiations, will be immensely increased.'[18]

The gulf between the Congress and the government remained unbridged. After a prolonged interview on 5 February, Gandhi told the Viceroy that the discussions which had taken place between them had revealed that there was not sufficient common ground to render further discussions 'profitable at that stage'.

On the following day, when Jinnah came to the Viceroy's House, Linlithgow informed him that his talks with Gandhi had proved abortive. Towards the end of this meeting Linlithgow advised Jinnah that the Muslim League should not maintain a purely negative position. Jinnah said that he and his friends were disposed on the whole to take the view that to publish in full their formulated opinions as to the constructive steps to be taken for the future would, from their stand-point, at this stage be inadvisable since it would needlessly expose them to criticism. Linlithgow told Jinnah that, howsoever convenient his position from the tactical point of view, it was impossible to educate public opinion in Great Britain, and more particularly the 600-odd representatives of the constituencies in the House of Commons by the submission of a formal memorandum to His Majesty's Government, or by leading evidence before some committee on the eve of a critical decision. If he [Jinnah] and his friends wanted to ensure that the Muslim case should not go by default in the United Kingdom, it was really essential that they should formulate their plan in the near future; it was quite useless to appeal for support in Great Britain for a party whose policy was one of sheer negation.[19]

Jinnah took the hint and told the Viceroy that he would probably be wise to make public at any rate 'the outlines of their position in time to allow them to explain their position both in Great Britain and in India'.[20]

It so happened that on the very day of this meeting between Linlithgow and Jinnah, the Working Committee of the Muslim League was in session at Delhi. The minutes of this meeting indicate the last resolution approved was on the outline of a scheme for the partition of India. The resolution itself was to be drafted on the second day of the annual session of the All India Muslim League at Lahore in March.

Chapter 25

THE DIE IS CAST

While travelling by train with his sister Fatima from Bombay to New Delhi in the second week of March, Jinnah complained of pain in the middle of his back and spinal chord. He was examined by his doctor and was told that he was suffering from pleurisy and required bed-rest for at least a fortnight. He did not follow the doctor's advice in order to keep an appointment with the Viceroy on 13 March. This was just a week before he was scheduled to leave for Lahore to preside over the annual session of the All India Muslim League. As luck would have it, on 19 March a procession of Khaksars, members of an Islamic paramilitary organization, armed with spades, symbolic of their organization, clashed with the police at Lahore while defying a ban imposed by the Punjab government under the Defence of India Rules. The Khaksars were ordered to disperse; they replied by attacking the police with their spades. The police opened fire; 30 Khaksars were killed, two policemen lost their lives, two police officers were injured, one of whom subsequently died. The incident roused public indignation not only against the police, but also against Sikandar Hyat Khan, the Premier of the Punjab, who was the *bête noire* not only of the Khaksars, but of the adherents of the Muslim League in the Punjab. Sikandar Hyat telephoned Jinnah to tell him that the situation at Lahore was tense, and that the Khaksars and their supporters were threatening to disrupt the proceedings of the League session, and suggested that the session be postponed. Jinnah did not agree and told Sikandar Hyat that the session must be held as planned, but the plan for the procession to welcome him should be abandoned.

Jinnah's handling of the situation after his arrival at Lahore was masterly. He motored down straight from the railway station to the general ward of Mayo Hospital to inquire about the condition of the wounded Khaksars. He addressed a public meeting of Muslims and assured the aggrieved relatives and supporters of the Khaksars that he would see that justice was done. Although on the first day of the League session the Khaksars held a demonstration and shouted *Sikandar murdabad* (death to Sikandar), they did not create any disturbance and dispersed peacefully. On the last day of the session Jinnah moved a resolution from the chair, rather than having it come from the floor, and permitted neither the seconding of it nor any discussion on it. The resolution expressed sorrow for the shooting and sympathy with the relatives of the victims, demanded an impartial investigation by a committee to be appointed by the provincial government, and authorized the Working Committee of the All India Muslim League to take further action; it appealed to the government to revoke the order declaring the Khaksar organization an unlawful body. The resolution was thus designed to defuse the situation and at the same time to head off Sir Sikandar's critics among the Khaksars and in the Muslim League. All in all, the crisis over the tragic incident was over; the session began and ended without any major disturbance.

The *pandal* (the large enclosed tent) for the annual session of the All India Muslim League had been erected in Minto Park close to the centre of the city. The ramparts of the Lahore Fort, in which British troops were stationed by the government as a precautionary measure for the entire period of the session, looked straight down on to the League's meeting from one direction. From another direction, the minarets of Lahore's largest mosque cast their shadows on the venue of the meeting. The *pandal* wore a festive appearance; it was decorated with banners, with white lettering on green background, inscribed with verses from the Quran. There was also green bunting around the dais.

Accompanied by the Nawab of Mamdot, the chairman of the reception committee, Jinnah, wearing an achkan and chooridar (close fitting pyjamas), entered the *pandal* at 2.25 pm amidst shouts of *Jinnah zindabad* (long live Jinnah) in a solemn procession which was headed and followed by Muslim National Guard volunteers dressed in green and armed with drawn swords. Jinnah was seated on a regal throne. Beside him sat prominent leaders of the Muslim League from the provinces, and some distinguished Muslim ladies such as Jinnah's sister Fatima, Begum Mahomed Ali, the widow of Maulana Mahomed Ali of the Khilafat fame, Begum Liaquat Ali, Lady Shahnawaz and Lady Haroon. To the right of the speaker's stand was a platform, duly screened, to seat nearly 500 women visitors in *purdah*.

The proceedings began with recitations from the Quran and the singing of poems. One of the poems was by Sir Muhammad Iqbal: '*Muslim hain hum, watan hai sara jahan hamara*' (we are Muslims, the whole world is our homeland). A poem by Hafiz Jullundhari described Jinnah as 'the smoke of the fire that was burning in India'. The audience numbered about 60,000, but if the overflow from the *pandal* was taken into account, it was close to 100,000.

After the Nawab of Mamdot, the chairman of the Reception Committee, had introduced him, Jinnah started speaking in Urdu. He said, 'I thank you from the bottom of my heart for the affection and respect you have shown me since I came to Lahore. The world is watching us and so let me have your permission to speak in English.' It was an extempore speech for nearly 100 minutes, a fighting speech, a remarkable performance by a man in fragile health. Most of those present did not understand English but they heard Jinnah in pin drop silence.[1]

Jinnah began on an optimistic note about the growth and consolidation of the Muslim League organization. He announced that provincial branches of the All India Muslim League had been formed. The League had won every single by-election. A committee of women had been set up; women could do a great deal within their homes, even in *purdah;* 'they could participate in our struggle for life and death'. He then went on to attack the Congress on its two-year' rule in the Hindu-majority provinces. He condemned the singing of *Bande Mataram* despite Muslim objections and 'the dangerous scheme of Wardha' for education of primary schoolchildren. There had been a gentleman's agreement between the Congress and the government, and the protests by Muslims had been ignored. However, providence had come to their rescue. The war broke out and the agreement between the Congress and the government came to an end. Jinnah, to the delight of his audience, aimed some barbed shafts at the Congress and especially at Gandhi. 'Why then all this camouflage? Why all these machinations? Why [do you] not come as a Hindu leader, proudly representing your people and let me meet you proudly representing the Mussalmans?' Gandhi had called him his brother, but the difference was that 'brother Gandhi had three votes, and he [Jinnah] had only one'. Why did not Gandhi honestly acknowledge that the Congress was a Hindu Congress, that he did not represent any body except the solid body of Hindus?[2]

Jinnah ridiculed the Congress demand for a Constituent Assembly. Was it not 'absurd to ask a ruling power to abdicate in favour of a Constituent Assembly'? After taking the Congress to task for its acts of commission and omission, Jinnah came to the fundamental issue. The problem in India, he averred, was not only between two political parties, but between two cultures and indeed between two religions.

> They [Hinduism and Islam] are not religions in the strict sense of the word, but they are, in fact, different and distinct social orders. Hindus and Muslims belong to two different religious philosophies, social customs and literatures. They neither intermarry, nor inter-dine together and indeed they belong to different civilizations which are based mainly on conflicting ideas and concepts .... They derive their inspiration from

different sources of history. They have different epics, their heroes are different. Very often the hero of one is a foe of the other, and likewise their victories and defeats overlap. To yoke together two such nations under a single state, one as a numerical minority and the other as a majority, must lead to growing discontent and final destruction of any fabric that may be built up for the government of such a state ...[3]

History has shown to us many geographical tracts much smaller than the subcontinent of India, which otherwise might have been called one country, but which have been divided into as many states as there are nations inhabiting them. Balkan Peninsula comprises as many as 7 or 8 sovereign states. Likewise, the Portuguese and the Spanish stand divided in the Iberian Peninsula.[4]

Jinnah argued that the history of the previous 1,200 years had failed to achieve unity, and that 'the present artificial unity of India' dated back only to the British conquest and had been maintained by the British bayonet. India was always divided into Hindu and Muslim India, and the termination of the British regime, which was implicit in the recent declaration of the British Government, will be the herald of the entire break-up, with worse disasters than had ever taken place during the last 1000 years under Muslims. Muslim India would not accept any constitution which resulted in a Hindu-majority Government. Mussalmans were a nation according to any definition of a nation; and they must have their homeland, their territory and their state. He concluded his speech with an appeal to the Muslim intelligentsia to come forward as 'servants of Islam' strengthen the Muslim League, consolidate all the Muslims in India and anchor the Muslim masses.

II

The Lahore resolution of the League or the 'Pakistan resolution' as it came to be known, demanding a separate independent state for Indian Muslims, came as a bombshell to most people outside the inner circle of the Muslim League. The reaction of the Congress leaders was predictably critical. C. Rajagopalachari called it a 'medieval conception'. Abul Kalam Azad described it as 'meaningless and absurd'.[5] Jawaharlal Nehru's reaction was sharp: 'All the old problems ... pale into insignificance before the latest stand of the Muslim League leaders at Lahore. The whole problem has taken a new complexion and there is no question of settlement or negotiations now.'[6] Abdul Qaiyum Khan, from the North-West Frontier Province, declared that his province would resist the partition of the country with its blood.[7] Syed Habibul Rahman, a member of the Krishak Praja Party in Bengal, condemned the proposal as 'absurd, chimerical, and visionary, [which] will remain for ever a castle in the air'.[8]

There was no doubt that the Pakistan resolution had given a new twist to the communal problem. Solutions hitherto thought of, such as separate electorates and coalition cabinets, suddenly became irrelevant. 'For the moment', wrote the *Manchester Guardian,* 'Mr. Jinnah has re-established the reign of chaos in India.'[9]

Curiously enough, Gandhi's reaction was not outright dismissive but at once restrained, reasoned and conciliatory. He knew, he wrote, that he had become 'as a red rag to the bull today to Muslims', but he analyzed the issues raised by the Lahore resolution in a series of articles in the *Harijan.* He described the two-nation theory as an 'untruth', the strongest word in Gandhi's dictionary. The vast majority of Muslims in India were, he wrote, converts to Islam or descendants of converts. They did not become a separate nation as soon as they became converts. A Bengali Muslim spoke the same tongue as that of a Bengali Hindu, ate the same food, had the same amusements as his Hindu neighbour; and dressed alike. The same phenomenon was more or less true in southern India among the poor, who constituted the masses of India. Gandhi pointed out that communal riots in India were mostly provoked by slaughter of cows or by religious processions before mosques; this meant that 'our superstitions create trouble and not our separate cultures'. Religion could not be the sole basis of nationality. Europe was Christian, but Germany and England, so much alike in culture, were grimly at one another's throats.[10] However, Gandhi conceded that there was no non-violent method of compelling the obedience of eight crore Muslims to the will of the rest of India, howsoever powerful a majority the rest might represent; the Muslims had the same right of self-determination as the rest of India had. 'We are at present', he wrote, 'a joint family'. 'Any member may claim a division.'[11]

Gandhi had an instinctive feeling that partition would not solve the communal problem and would have disastrous consequences. In March 1939, exactly a year before the Lahore session of the Muslim League, Linlithgow at the end of an interview with Gandhi broached the subject of partition and wrote to Secretary of State Zetland:

Linlithgow to Zetland, 15 March 1939.

> Before we concluded, I thought it well to mention the Pakistan project to him [Gandhi], and to ask him whether he thought it had any life in it. He said, he understood, not, but that that might come ... he doubted if it [the Pakistan project] would stand any detailed examination, though it had no doubt wide possibilities. I asked whether by that he meant that it might represent an upsurge running back into the depths of the Muslim world. He said that might indeed be the case in certain circumstances, but even if Pakistan admitted of realization, it would never settle the communal question in India, or represent more than a sharp division which might in due course give rise to a major calamity.[12]

III

Adverse reactions to the proposal for partition of India were not confined to Congress leaders. A week after the Lahore session of the League the Governor of Bombay, Sir Roger Lumley, apprised the Viceroy of the situation in Bombay, which was Jinnah's political base:

> The Muslim League meeting at Lahore has undoubtedly shocked all communities, including the Muslims. Although the idea of partition of India is not a new one, nobody here had hitherto taken it very seriously, but the fact that it has now been sponsored for the first time by a great party has come as a considerable shock. Hindus of all kinds are angry about it. Parsis do not like it, and the best that any Muslim has said is that Jinnah cannot mean it and is only using it as a bargain.... Among local Muslims there is considerable dismay, which is natural, as they see little in Jinnah's scheme which will bring advantage to Muslims in this province. Jinnah's speech in Lahore is likely to lose a good deal of sup-port from educated Muslims here.[13]

Some of the Muslim leaders who had attended the Lahore session had grave misgivings about the turn the League politics had taken. Sikandar Hyat Khan, who had toed Jinnah's line against his better judgement at the Lahore session publicly, expressed his apprehensions a few months later in an interview to *The Tribune*.[14] He explained that he was associated with the drafting of the Pakistan resolution for the 'Subjects Committee', but the draft was amended and the clause for constitutional arrangements for coordination between various independent federations was deleted. Sir Ghulam Hussain Hidayatullah, the Premier of Sind, rejected the idea of partition.[15] Khan Bahadur Allah Baksh, the leader of the opposition and a former Prime Minister of Sind, presided over a well-attended All India Azad (Independent) Muslims Conference at Delhi on 29 April 1940.

In his presidential address, Allah Baksh disputed Jinnah's contention that he was speaking for the Muslims of India. No responsible minister of the Unionist government, the ruling party in the Punjab had cared to lend the slightest support to his scheme. The ruling parties in the Muslim-majority provinces of North-West Frontier Province and Sind enjoyed comfortable majorities in the autonomous provinces; they were helped by the centre financially and had no incentive to exchange their existing position for that of minorities in a larger unit, though overwhelmingly

Muslim. He feared that the Pakistan proposal would lead to the creation of another Palestine under a British mandate. The proceedings of this conference were not only widely covered in the national press but the British-owned *Statesman* and *The Times of India* noticed it. *The Times of India* (30 April 1940) discerned in the conference the signs of a 'striking mobilization of moderate patriotic opinion', in no way committed to the intransigence of the Congress and the Muslim League. At the same time, *The Statesman* wrote that there were 'large numbers of Muslims who were outside the League and firmly opposed to the idea of partition'.

In December 1940, Purshotamdas Thakurdas, a Bombay magnate who had been a member in the 1930s of the Independent Party headed by Jinnah in the Central Assembly, called on Nawabzada Liaquat Ali Khan at Delhi and gathered the impression that 'it was not a question so much of pressing Pakistan — which is another name for the Lahore Resolution — as to ensuring that the Mohammedans will get freedom from what Muslims call *zabardasti* (high-handedness) of Hindus.'[16]

The League session was a resounding success. Never before had Jinnah witnessed a massive gathering of 60,000 at an annual session of the League. Never before had hundreds of *purdah-nasheen* (veiled) women attended the session. Gone were the days when the leaders had to wait for completion of the quorum of 75 before commencing the meeting. His relentless campaign against the Congress and the 'Hindu majority' had succeeded in stirring the politically conscious class in the Muslim community. It had also instigated a religious revival. Phillips Talbot, an American scholar, who was a witness to the changing political scene at the national and local level at this time, noted that the educated Muslims in Lahore were being drawn towards the study of their religion, and wrote:

> ... the urban environment of Lahore is drawing many educated city Muslims to a new fact that is displacing the sceptism that accompanied the first impact of Western knowledge ....

the new stirrings in Islam can be seen in the mosques, in the publication of books on religious matters. Now-a-days sermons are read everywhere in Urdu, the language of the people .... Weekly study circles have been established in numerous neighbourhoods. In addition to stimulus of politics and education, there is a direct religious revivalism ... the poems and preachings of Muhammad Iqbal have instilled into a growing number of educated Muslims a new fervor in the faith.[17]

Curiously enough, this religious revival was also triggering in Indian Muslims a conflict between their patriotism and their religious faith. Striking evidence of this identity crisis comes through letters written in May 1940 by Tahira, the 16-year old daughter of Sikandar Hyat Khan, to Jawaharlal Nehru. She had met Nehru at a dinner at Lahore, but did not get a chance to talk to him. She had also had opportunities to meet Jinnah when he visited Lahore. We get a glimpse of the goings-on in the families of the uppermost section of the Muslim elite from the following letter:

Tahira to Jawaharlal Nehru, 28 April 1940

... Mr. Jinnah told me that Muslim League was fighting to achieve independence, while the next time he criticizes Swadeshi goods and objects to my wearing them just because there are more Hindus working in the factories. He scolded me for having these views and asked me to change my ideas. I told him that I would have gladly stood with him, if he was a national leader, but as he is a communalist, I refused. I do not know why Mr. Jinnah thinks that people who join the Congress are fighting against Islam ....

Panditji, let me tell you how Muslim children are taught, though I am sure you must be knowing. When they are young and their minds have not yet developed, they learn Quran from a maulvi and he tells them all sorts of rubbish; that the Hindus curse our Prophet, they do not believe in Quran, they are our enemies and that they eat ham. Even my younger sisters and brothers are taught in the same way, but I cannot say anything, and if I do sometimes, I am called a Hindu.

Well, that is suppose(d) to (be) an insult ....
Why should Daddy object to my praising Congress. They (Daddy's friends) always answer that 'you and your comrades want Hindu Raj.' Well, Panditji, I have told them so many times that only a lunatic can think that Hindus can dominate martial races like Sikhs and Muslims ...
... I have been taken out of Queen Mary's College because of my views. Miss Cocks (our Principal) scolded me and said that several parents have been complaining that I had converted their daughters to my views.[18]

Jinnah was too seasoned a politician to imagine that he had won the battle for partition by blowing the bugle at Lahore He was watching the moves of all the parties involved in the triangular contest between the Congress, the British and the Muslim League. Most important of these was the British attitude. The alliance with the British had been part of Jinnah's plan for two years, but it was only in 1940 that it became possible. We get a glimpse of Jinnah's strategy in a note recorded by Sir Girja Shankar Bajpai, a member of the Viceroy's Executive Council, on 18 April 1940.[19]

I was with him for an hour and three quarters, practically all the time in the role of a listener. I have never known Mr. Jinnah suffer from diffidence. The impression he gave me yesterday was that he felt himself to be on the 'top of the world'. Doubtless the volume and unanimity of applause that he received during the recent session of the Muslim League at Lahore had contributed to this sense of exaltation.
Mr. Jinnah's main topic was the proposal to Balkanise India, which the League, under his leadership, has now publicly adopted as its goal.
What had been looked upon as a day-dream, when the late Sir Mohammad Iqbal commended it to Indian Muslims, was now, of course with the improvements that Jinnah had introduced, in his opinion the only logical and practical solution of the Indian problem. Muslims, he claimed, represented a distinct religious and social entity and would never tolerate the idea of Hindu domination, which was an essential feature of an all-India Federation.

He said India was more comparable to Europe than to any other political unit. If the political unity of Europe was a mere dream, how could it be anything else in the case of India? A unity inspired by sincere allegiance to common ideals was quite out of the question for a subcontinent with so many heterogeneous nationalities as Muslims, Hindus of Aryan origin and Hindus of Dravidian stock. The Muslim claim for separate states was similar to that of the Telegus in south India, who wanted a separate linguistic province of their own; if such a demand was legitimate, why should the former be looked upon as inimical to Indian interests?

Mr. Jinnah had, however, the following 'concessions' in mind vis-à-vis His Majesty's Government:

1. That the conglomeration of Sovereign States which India, if divided, would constitute, should remain within the British Commonwealth of Nations.
2. That the transfer of Defence should be a slow process, extending, possibly, over 40 or 50 years.
3. That the transfer of Defence should be effected, not to the legislature of any of the proposed Sovereign States, but to their Executives.

As for Mr. Jinnah's attitude towards the Congress, it could be summed up as follows.

1. A profound distrust of Mr. Gandhi. With bitter but vivid reminiscence he described how, on several occasions in the past, Mr. Gandhi had frustrated all of Mr. Jinnah's constructive efforts to advance India on the path of Dominion Status. Mr. Jinnah could no longer treat the Mahatma as a sane leader.
2. An arrogant contempt for the Congress High Command. He described the majority of them as a collection of 'crooks'.

A few weeks after Jinnah's meeting with Sir Girja Shankar Bajpai followed Hitler's invasion of Belgium and France and British reverses. There was an immediate reaction in Britain. Chamberlain resigned and Churchill took over as Prime Minister. Luckily for Jinnah, these changes were to work in his favour as we shall see later.

IV

On 2 February, Zetland acquainted the Cabinet with the package with which Linlithgow hoped to secure Gandhi's cooperation: the promise of Dominion status as soon as possible; the enlargement of the Viceroy's Executive Council to include politicians; the inauguration of federation as soon as the (Princely) states could be brought in; and subsequent consultation with Indians on the revision of the constitution. Zetland, firmer in his conviction than he had been previously about the changed position in India, argued that there was 'no chance of this plan proving the basis of fruitful discussion' in India. Gandhi would reject it for not fulfilling the demands of the Congress. Muslims would ask for changes in the federal constitution that the Congress would oppose. If the talks with Gandhi were not 'to break down almost as soon as they start, the Viceroy must be prepared to offer a closer accommodation to the Congress point of view'. He asked the Cabinet to endorse, as its provisional view, the policy that India should be conceded the right to frame its own post-war Dominion constitution, subject to agreement among the parties on the composition of a constituent assembly and the conclusion of a treaty. Zetland warned that the result of the failure of Linlithgow's talk with Gandhi would be civil disobedience, which Britain could contain 'only by methods which would expose our general motives in the war to the most effective criticism', not least in America.

Zetland failed to carry his proposal through the Cabinet. It merely approved of Linlithgow's discussion with Gandhi. If the approach failed, Linlithgow was not to go any further. In specifying Britain's objectives he must avoid the phrase 'independence within the Empire' in favour of 'self-governing, or autonomous, communities within the Empire', which was less likely to be construed as implying a right of secession. The opposition to Zetland was led by Winston Churchill and Sir John Simon. Churchill advocated a firm stand against the Congress. Since the resumption of official control, he said, 'for the first time for several years the Congress Provinces had been properly administered...'

> ... he did not share the anxiety to encourage and promote unity between the Hindu and Muslim communities. Such unity was, in fact, almost out of the realm of practical politics, while, if it were to be brought about, the immediate result would be that the united communities would join in showing us the door. He regarded the Hindu–Muslim feud as the bulwark of British rule in India.

Simon argued that 'there was every reason for not going any faster than we are obliged to'. Anderson was opposed to offering Congress anything beyond Linlithgow's proposal, and Chamberlain decided to look no further forward for the moment. Only Halifax, who as Lord Irwin had signed a pact with Gandhi in 1931, supported Zetland's view.

The Linlithgow–Gandhi talks proved abortive despite Linlithgow's assessment that 'if Gandhi is prepared to be reasonable then there is ... some chance of a settlement' on the Cabinet's approved basis'. Gandhi, however, reiterated the claim for a constituent assembly and rejected the (proposal of) provincial coalitions. On 6 February Linlithgow advised Zetland that the Congress seemed to be gambling that British 'calamities in the field', or 'pressure from public opinion at Home', would produce a better offer. He concluded that there was 'nothing for it now but to lie back for the present'. A week later, he confirmed that it was best to 'refrain from action' to avoid 'running after the Congress'.

Gandhi's abrupt termination of negotiations on 6 February left Zetland with no opening for referring back to the Cabinet.[20]

V

As we have already seen, in February 1940 Zetland had been unable to carry the War Cabinet with him on a constitutional package which had a chance of securing the cooperation of the Congress. In May, when Churchill took over Prime Ministership, he reconstituted the Cabinet and Leopold Amery replaced Zetland as Secretary of State for India. Amery was receptive to the revival of Zetland's proposal for post-war Dominion status, constituent assembly and a treaty with India. It took him some effort to bring round Linlithgow to his point of view. Linlithgow agreed to do what he had resisted for seven months; he suggested that Amery should seek the Cabinet's approval for a declaration that the British aim in India was Dominion status, that the Act of 1935 would be open to discussion at the end of the war, and that the government would abide by the decisions on which various political parties agreed. Amery placed Linlithgow's recommendations before the Cabinet for its approval. Amery wanted to propose no less than full and immediate post-war dominionhood for India, provided Indians agreed upon a constitution. It was no easy task to secure acceptance of the War Cabinet which had been reconstituted by Churchill. When the Cabinet considered the proposal on 12 July, Churchill strongly opposed any new declaration of intent. He had thwarted the attempt by Zetland to make a bold move for post-war constitutional changes in India in February 1940; he did the same to the new proposal put forward by Linlithgow at the instance of Amery. Amery was supported by two Labour members of the War Cabinet, Attlee and Greenwood. Halifax, who had supported Zetland's proposal, was absent. Churchill made no secret of his disapproval of the new proposal. He rebuked Amery 'for misleading his colleagues into the belief that the proposal had come from the Viceroy'. He cabled direct to Linlithgow questioning the wisdom of any declaration when the invasion of Britain was imminent, and a parliamentary discussion of 'the issues involved in such a far-reaching departure was impossible'.[21] Linlithgow was shaken by the Prime Minister's reprimand and apologized to him. On 28 July Churchill cabled him that it was not possible for the War Cabinet to promise in advance to accept 'a body to frame the main structure of the constitution at the end of the war. We should know before-hand what this body was and feel assured that it represented not only Hindus and Muslims, but the Princes, the Depressed Classes, the Sikhs, the Anglo-Indians and others.' Further, it was impossible 'to pledge in advance the attitude of a future Parliament called into being in the unforeseeable conditions which will follow the war'; the fixing of a particular date for the achievement of Dominion status was not advisable.[22] In the circumstances, the War Cabinet approved Churchill's proposal, reaffirming the expansion of the Viceroy's Executive Council and the setting up of a War Advisory Committee, recommended by the Viceroy. Churchill was authorized to redraft the declaration on the lines 'dictated by him' for approval of the Cabinet. The result was the declaration of 8 August 1940 announced by Linlithgow which reiterated Dominion Status as the goal and spelt out the British obligation to minorities, a veto on the constitution:

> It goes without saying that [His Majesty's Government] could not contemplate the transfer of their present responsibilities for the peace and welfare of India to any system of government whose authority is directly denied by large and powerful elements in India's national life.

The Muslim League Executive Council meeting noted 'with satisfaction' that the 8 August 1940 offer of the British Government 'practically met the demand of the League for a clear assurance to the effect that no future constitution, interim or final, should be adopted by the British Government without their approval and consent.'[23]

The All India Congress Committee declared that Britain had 'no intention to recognize India's independence, and would, if they could, continue to hold this country indefinitely in bondage for British exploitation.' The Viceroy advised, and the Cabinet agreed, that in the circumstances he should not proceed to enlarge his council or set up the Consultative Committee.[24]

R.J. Moore, a British historian who has written extensively on the last phase of British rule in India, has graphically described the consequences of Churchill's frustration at Linlithgow's belated initiative in July 1940 which might have averted partition and changed the course of history:

> It would be fanciful to cast [Churchill] the arch-diehard as an unwitting architect of Pakistan. But by his intervention in July 1940 the bricklayer of Chartwell did help to build the foundations for the wall of partition.[25]

Chapter 26

PHANTOM TO REALITY

After the August 1940 declaration by the Viceroy of British policy, Congress leaders realized that the British Government, headed by Winston Churchill, was neither prepared to pledge itself to Indian freedom after the war, nor to take the Congress into effective partnership in the struggle against the Axis Powers. All that the Congress was offered was membership of advisory committees and certain seats in the Viceroy's Executive Council without an effective voice in the administration. This was a passive role which a nationalist party, with 20 years of struggle behind it, could not accept. The Congress could hardly sit back with folded arms as a spectator of events while the future of nations was at stake. Pressures began to build up within the Congress for a mass civil disobedience movement. Gandhi resisted these pressures as long as he could, and then diverted them into the relatively innocuous channels of a campaign of 'individual satyagraha'. This was conceived as a token protest without seriously embarrassing the war effort. The instructions which Gandhi issued for the *satyagrahis* and sportingly communicated to the Viceroy that ruled out public excitement and harassment to the authorities are remarkable for the restrains imposed on his followers. Gandhi insisted on personally approving the lists of *satyagrahis*, who were enjoined to intimate the district magistrates in advance of the time and place for the offering of satyagraha. Public meetings were to be discouraged in towns.

The movement began on 17 October 1940 with an anti-war speech by Acharya Vinoba Bhave, one of Gandhi's saintly followers, who was arrested. Jawaharlal Nehru had been chosen to follow Bhave; he was sentenced to four years' imprisonment. By the end of the year nearly 400 Congress legislators, including 29 ex-ministers, were in jail. By 15 May 1941, according to official records, 25,069 convictions had been made for offering civil disobedience.[1] There was, however, very little excitement, thanks to the manner in which Gandhi had conducted this 'symbolic' campaign; he would not agree to its extension into a mass civil disobedience movement.

When the *Hindu* newspaper pointed out that the movement had produced no appreciable impression on the war effort, Gandhi replied that it was not intended to hamper the war effort.[2] He got no thanks for his studied restraint from the government or from Jinnah. Amery, Secretary of State for India, wrote that the movement was 'as regrettable as irrational, which was proceeding languidly and without invoking much interest'. Linlithgow agreed with Amery that 'Gandhi has been an "intolerable nuisance" since the beginning of the war, that he wants our enemies to win the war ... what he is really concerned to do is to maintain his nuisance and his bargaining value at as high a level as possible, with a view to the post-war designs ... his desire is to keep the pot simmering but not boiling. I feel very strongly that the only possible answer to the declaration of war by any section of the Congress in the present circumstances must be a declared determination to crush that organization as a whole. In that view I hope you and your Government will concur.'[3]

II

Jinnah's comments on Gandhi's symbolic protest were sharp. He feared the critical war situation might lead the British Government to accommodate the Congress point of view and leave the Muslim League high and dry. So he hit out at both the Congress and the government. The Council of the All India Muslim League passed a resolution warning that if any concession was made to the Congress which adversely affected or militated against Muslim de-mands, 'it would be resisted by the Muslim League with all the power it can command and the party would not hesitate to intervene ... for the protection of the rights and interests of the Mussalmans in the country.' Jinnah criticized the British press which was suggesting that the government should secure cooperation of all parties in India, and especially of the Congress, to cope with the menacing war situation. He accused the British press of 'playing into the hands of the Congress and the Hindu propaganda. I ... do not know who is responsible, His Excellency the Viceroy, the Secretary of State for India or His Majesty's Government or whether Parliament or whether it is the King.'[4] '... I want the British government not to force Muslim India to fill Indian jails ... Pakistan is now our sacred creed, an article of faith, and any declaration by the British government or the Prime Minister which, in any way, will militate against it ... would be resisted with all the power it can command.'[5]

While Jinnah was firing his barbed shafts indiscriminately at both the Congress and the government, in an unguarded moment of self-revelation he revealed his basic strategy during the war: he enjoined Muslims to let the Congress and the Government 'fight it out'!

III

The entry of Japan into the war brought it almost to India's door. With the American fleet crippled, the Japanese swept quickly through the Western Pacific. On 15 February 1942 Singapore fell and the Bay of Bengal lay exposed to the Japanese fleet. The British command of the sea had gone. The tide of the Japanese conquest, after overwhelming Malaya and Burma, threatened to engulf eastern and southern

India. The rapidity with which the Japanese advanced was evidence not only of their superiority in numbers and strategy, but also of the lack of will of the people to resist in the countries invaded by them.

Gandhi condemned the Japanese slogan of 'Asia for Asiatics' and even favoured the boycott of Japanese goods as a mark of sympathy with China which had been invaded by Japan. Nehru's sympathy for China was well known. The danger in 1942 was not so much of active collaboration by sections of Indians with the Japanese as of defeatism and passivity on the part of the people, which might enable the Japanese to consolidate themselves if they managed to land and win one or two initial battles. The demand of the Indian National Congress, therefore, was that the people should be given a stake in an all-out resistance to the Axis Powers.

Gandhi's initial reaction to the Viceroy's gesture in releasing the prisoners convicted for individual civil disobedience in the beginning of December 1941 had been far from enthusiastic; it did not, he declared, 'evoke a single responsive or appreciative chord' in him. Events, however, were moving fast, faster than anticipated by the Congress as well as the government. In the winter of 1941–42, the war situation was critical for the Allies as it had been in the summer of 1940 after the fall of France. Once again a section of Congress leaders led by C. Rajagopalachari proposed an immediate settlement with the British Government for making a united front against the Japanese.

Meanwhile, the critical war situation had made its impact on the British Government. Prime Minister Churchill was a 'diehard' so far as Indian independence was concerned, and his views in 1941 were no different from those he held in 1931. However, the pace of the Japanese advance persuaded him to seek a way out of the political deadlock by sending to India a member of the British Cabinet. Stafford Cripps was selected for this momentous mission. His sympathies with the cause of Indian freedom were known. He personally knew some front-rank leaders of Indian opinion. He had reason to be optimistic when he arrived at New Delhi on 22 March. The 'Draft Declaration' which he brought with him contained proposals for the solution of India's political problem. Immediately after the war elections were to be held to provincial legislatures; members of the lower houses of these legislatures were to elect a constitution-making body which was to be charged with the task of framing a constitution for a 'Union of India', 'a full-fledged Dominion with the same full status as the other Dominions'. The Indian Princely states were to be invited to nominate representatives to this body. The Union of India was to have the right to opt out of the British Commonwealth. The British Government undertook to implement this constitution subject to '... the right of any Province of British India that is not prepared to accept the new Constitution to retain its present constitutional position, provision being made for its subsequent accession if it so decides'. Attlee, who was then the leader of the Labour Party, later recorded that the Draft Declaration struck him as a bold plan, which reflected credit on those members of the Government who were not sanguine as to the feasibility of Indian self-government and especially on the Prime Minister whose views were very strong.[6]

Against this exuberant confidence of British leaders may be set the misgivings with which the plan was received by Congress leaders. Gandhi — whom Cripps had summoned from Wardha by telegram — after reading the proposals advised Cripps to take the next plane home. Jawaharlal Nehru confessed to a 'profound depression' when he read the proposals for the first time; the more he read and pondered over them, the more depressed he felt. It was true that India's right to self-determination had been definitely conceded by the British Government for the first time, and both the time and the machinery for exercising this right had been clearly specified. But the right of non-accession given to the provinces and the Indian Princely states threatened to convert the country into a political chequerboard containing scores of 'independent states', which could make short work of India as a political and economic entity. The right of non-accession was evidently given to the provinces to meet the Muslim League's demand for Pakistan half-way.

The Congress, in spite of its serious objections to the long-term proposals, was willing to put that complicated problem in cold storage and concentrate on the immediate task of mobilizing the country against the Japanese peril for the defence of India. The Congress leaders, who had parted company with Gandhi on the issue of non-violent defence of India, were thinking in terms of a last-ditch fight against the Japanese, and of building up new armies, militia and home guards. There were a series of discussions between the Congress leaders on the one hand and Cripps and Lord Linlithgow, the Viceroy, on the other regarding the functions of an Indian Defence Member of the Viceroy's Council. These discussions, in which Colonel Louis Johnson, the personal envoy of US President Roosevelt, also joined, broke down not on the demarcation of duties between the Indian Defence Member and the British Commander-in-Chief, but on a much wider issue — the nature and authority of the interim government as a whole.

IV

In December 1941 when Churchill visited Washington, President Roosevelt referred to the Indian problem. 'I reacted so strongly', Churchill later recalled, 'and at such length that he never raised it verbally again'. However, it was the pace of the Japanese advance and American pressure which led Churchill to take an initiative and approve of the Cripps mission to India. On 25 February, ten days after the fall of Singapore, Churchill appointed a sub-committee of the War Cabinet to study the Indian problem and to suggest a solution. Of the members of this study group, Sir John Simon and Clement Attlee had been members of the Statutory Commission, and James Grigg and John Anderson had held high offices in India. Stafford Cripps was well acquainted with Indian leaders and politics and with Amery. On 11 March, Churchill was able to report to the House of Commons that the War Cabinet had come to a unanimous decision on the Indian question, and that Stafford Cripps, the leader of the House of Commons, was proceeding to India to discuss the proposals with Indian leaders.

The immediate and declared objective of the Cripps mission was to evolve a scheme to resolve the political deadlock, which would make it possible to induct political leaders into government and organize public resistance against the Japanese if they invaded India.[7] The Cripps plan, as framed for approval by the War Cabinet, was a compromise plan. It was the result partly of the prodding by President Roosevelt and partly of the pressure in Britain itself which led a reluctant Churchill to take the initiative. However, Amery wrote to the Viceroy on 2 March 1942 that 'in the Cripps Plan we have safeguarded the Muslims over Pakistan ...' In his telegram of 10 March 1942 to Linlithgow, he wrote: 'the nest (Cripps Plan) contains the Pakistan Cuckoo's egg ... it is for the Congress to find a compromise which will induce the Muslims to drop Pakistan'.[8] A fortnight later, in his letter of 24 March 1942 to Linlithgow, Amery was more explicit: 'Jinnah, I shall have thought, will be content to realize that he has now got his Pakistan in essence'.[9]

Amery had correctly anticipated Jinnah's response. After Jinnah read the 'Plan', according to Cripps, he appeared rather surprised 'on the distance it went to meet the Pakistan case'. The fact was that Churchill, Amery and Linlithgow reckoned that the establishment of Pakistan de facto, coupled with the Princely states becoming independent, would emasculate the 'Indian Union State'. Amery went on to say that with the formation of Pakistan, the entire country would be broken up, the Central Government would not be strong, and it would be impossible for the divided units 'to maintain their military, naval and air-strength'. Therefore, Amery added, 'once again the Indians will become dependent on the British'.

V

President Roosevelt had been anxiously watching the progress of Cripps's negotiations and was receiving first-hand reports from Louis Johnson, his personal envoy at New Delhi. He sent a message to Churchill that the American public could not understand why, if there was willingness on the part of the British Government to permit the component parts of India to secede from the British Empire after the war, the British Government was unwilling to permit Indians to enjoy during the war what was tantamount to self-government.

Roosevelt sent his old friend William Phillips to India, who, to his surprise, espoused the Congress party's viewpoint. Although Roosevelt did not back Phillips, he did cite his view to prod Churchill, then in Washington. Churchill retorted, 'Take India if that is what you want! But I warn you that if I open the door a crack there will be the greatest blood bath in history.'

Roosevelt replied to Churchill the same day:

> I am sorry to say that I cannot agree with the point of view ... that public opinion in the United States believes that the negotiations have failed on broad general issues. The general impression here is quite contrary. The feeling is almost universally held that the deadlock has been caused by the unwillingness of the British Government to concede to the Indians the right of self-government, notwithstanding the willingness of the Indians to entrust technical, military and naval defense control to the competent British authorities .... Consequently would it not be possible for you to have Cripps postpone his departure on the ground that you personally have sent him instructions to make a final effort to find a common ground of understanding?'[10]

Churchill then dug in his heels. His reply, dispatched the next day, ran as follows: 'You know the weight I attach to everything you say to me but I did not think I could take responsibility for the defence of India if everything is again to be thrown into the melting pot at this critical juncture.' Besides, he pointed out, Cripps had already left India.[11]

Colonel Louis Johnson's presence in New Delhi during the Cripps mission had given the US President a trustworthy source of information on the events that created doubts in his and Secretary of State Cordell Hull's mind whether or not Churchill had really wanted the mission to succeed. On 4 April, Johnson had wired the following message to Hull: 'Unless the President feels that he can intercede with Churchill it seems the Cripps mission is doomed to failure', adding that 'Cripps so believes too'. And as the negotiations collapsed on 11 April, Johnson informed Hull: 'Cripps with embarrassment told me that he could not change [the] draft [of the British offer] without Churchill's approval'. He added that 'Churchill had cabled him that he will give no approval unless Wavell [the commander-in-chief in India] and Viceroy endorsed the change'. Johnson then concluded: 'London wanted a Congress refusal'. He also added that the 'Muslim League [was being] used by Britain as a counterforce to [the] Congress' and that 'Wavell hates and distrusts Nehru'.[12]

VI

The Muslim League Council in a resolution expressed gratification that the possibility of Pakistan was 'recognized by implication' but stated that 'the only solution of India's constitutional problem was the partition of India into independent zones; and it would, therefore, be unfair to Moslems to compel them to enter such a constitution-making body whose main object is the creation of a new Indian Union.' However, the proposals for the future were considered unacceptable and no useful purpose would be served to deal further with the question of the immediate arrangements.[13]

Results of the Cripps Mission and the Quit India Movement

A Pakistani historian has correctly summed up the results of the Cripps mission. The Muslim League and the British

Government had benefited from the Cripps mission, while the Congress had suffered a setback. Only two years previously, the birth of the idea of Pakistan had been greeted with derision. The British Government had now officially declared it to be an acceptable possibility. Well might Jawaharlal Nehru complain that his old friend, Cripps, had 'allowed himself to become the devil's advocate'.[14] The British Government had valued the Muslims as a counterpoise to the hostile Congress from the very beginning of the war, but now looked upon the Muslims even more benignly than before. And shortly afterward, by starting the Quit India movement and courting internment, Gandhi had left the field clear for Jinnah to boost the already growing strength of the Pakistan movement.[15] The understanding of the Congress of the implications of the Cripps mission plan, as Azad told Cripps, was the same: that his plan had prejudiced any more favourable solution to the problem and had made it more difficult for any agreement between the Congress and the Muslim League. Azad was prescient. With Pakistan within Jinnah's grasp, there was no need for him to compromise with the Congress in any future negotiations for a political settlement.

VII

The Quit India resolution passed by the All India Congress Committee on 9 August 1942 envisaged a free India resisting Nazi aggression with all the armed and nonviolent forces at its disposal in cooperation with the Allied powers. However, in this fateful confrontation with the British Government in August 1942, Gandhi made a serious, almost inexcusable, miscalculation. He assumed that Viceroy Linlithgow would react to the Congress ultimatum as his predecessors had done in 1921 and 1930, and thus give him time to negotiate with the government to elucidate his stand and to regulate the form and range of civil disobedience. Linlithgow had, however, no intention of playing the game according to the Mahatma's rules. The fact is that the Viceroy with the backing of Churchill had decided two years earlier, in August 1940, to crush the Congress if it threw down the gauntlet to the government during the war.

In planning a knock-out blow at the Congress in the event of hostilities, Lord Linlithgow had taken a leaf out of his predecessor's book. When the movement of defiance of authority was actually initiated, it was to be regarded as a 'hostile action intended to assist the King's enemies'. 'Past experience', he wrote, 'had shown the advantage of depriving the organizers of such a movement of the initiative at the earliest moment'. So it was the 'intention of the Government of India that as soon as such a movement becomes recognizable, the whole resources of the Government would be employed to crush it at the outset and to prevent it from obtaining any momentum whatsoever'. Within hours of the passage of the Quit India resolution, almost all the leaders of the Congress, not only at the all-India but also at the provincial and even district levels, were arrested. This was designed to disable the whole Congress organization from functioning.

If Gandhi was guilty of a serious miscalculation, so was Linlithgow; the pre-emptive strike, far from preventing trouble, provoked a violent explosion which shook the Raj. There were clashes with the police in Bombay, Delhi, Pune, Kanpur, Allahabad and many other towns, and countless cases of firing by the police. There were strikes by mill workers in Bombay, Jamshedpur, Ahmedabad and Bangalore; students walked out of schools and colleges. Seventeen newspapers in English and Indian languages suspended publication. The gravest developments from the British standpoint, however, were the uprisings in the countryside in Bihar, UP and Bombay. Most of them were instigated by students who led mobs in attacks on the nearest police stations, post offices, court and school buildings, roads and railways — indeed on all the visible symbols of foreign rule.

On 31 August 1942, the Viceroy informed Churchill that he was facing 'the most serious rebellion since that of 1857'. The comparison was not quite apt. The Indian sepoys who mutinied in 1857 had some arms and ammunition and training; the simple village folk of Ballia, Sahasram and Azamgarh and other small towns and villages in Bihar and UP, who had risen in revolt at the bidding of boys fresh from schools and colleges, wielded nothing more lethal than sticks and stones; their violence was sporadic, unplanned and suicidal. The British response was predictably ruthless. According to official figures, which could well be underestimates, by the end of 1942 over 66,000 persons had been convicted or detained and the military had fired on 538 occasions.[16]

Gandhi had stressed non-violence as the basic premise of the struggle, but his advice remained unheeded between the frenzy of the people and the hammer-blows of the government. Though the British recalled the revolt of 1857, the outbreak in 1942 was the result of violence as spontaneous as it was suicidal.

There was, of course, the underground movement which on a low key started from 9 August and went on fitfully for more than two years. It was led by Congress socialists, members of the Forward Bloc, revolutionary terrorists and even some Gandhians. Mobs staged strikes, burnt government buildings, damaged railway tracks and bridges, cut telegraph and telephone wires and stole or burnt postal boxes. Then there were the parallel governments, such as in Midnapore and Satara districts, which revealed great ingenuity and organization. Doubtless there was in this underground movement ardent patriotism, individual heroism and even romance, but it did not affect the war effort, much less posed a serious challenge to the British Raj.

When Lord Linlithgow left India in 1943, he had no doubt that he had crushed not only the 'rebellion' but the Congress. Little did he know that he had hastened the liquidation of the Raj. In his arrogance he had taken a risk which none of his predecessors had dared to take — that of Gandhi's death in jail when the Mahatma embarked on a 21-day fast to protest against the charge that he was responsible for the violence of the Quit India movement.

VIII

Lord Linlithgow justified his siding with the Muslims openly. 'To those who may be tempted to regard the establishment of Congress Hindu Raj', he wrote, 'as a lesser risk than infuriating the Muslims', the answer is that it was not only a question of irritating 90 million of Muslims, communal outbreaks of a serious kind would certainly damage very dangerously the Indian army, and, if protracted, 'might well lead to the disintegration of a large and important part of our forces in Egypt and the Middle East, as well as in India.'[17]

Jinnah declared that the Quit India movement was not only a war against the British but a 'civil war' inasmuch as it was a fight for the Congress demands which were inimical to and destructive of Muslim rights. 'What would the British government gain', he asked, 'by appeasing the Congress?' It would only antagonize other elements and cause more trouble. If Muslims had joined the Congress movement in the name of freedom and independence, Mr Gandhi would have represented to England and America and the world that he alone represented the whole of India and that his demand was also supported by Muslim India. A greater folly and a more serious blunder the Muslims could not have committed if they had fallen into this trap. 'If we had any belief', he said, 'in the *bona fides* and honesty of the British, ordinarily we would have joined them to crush the movement which was aimed against us equally.' 'But I regret to say', he went on, 'we cannot trust the British either. They are playing their own game and, therefore, we only asked the Muslims to keep aloof from this movement.' 'This is one of those cases', he said, 'where neutrality is the most effective policy on our part.'[18]

The policy of a plausible argument for 'neutrality' suited Jinnah's strategy of achieving the maximum gains at the lowest cost. The fact was that he was in no position to oppose the government. So he imposed impossible conditions for his cooperation during the war. He knew it was dangerous for him to obstruct the conduct of the war. Many of the recruits in the army came from the Punjab where he had little influence; he therefore concentrated his attack on the Congress. The Muslim League Working Committee denounced the 'Quit India' movement as an attempt 'to establish Hindu Raj' and 'to deal a deathblow to the Muslim goal of Pakistan'. The League's tirade against the Congress was useful to the government which was aiming the full force of its war-publicity machine at the Congress to represent it as anti-British, anti-national and pro-Axis.

With the Congress outlawed, its leaders in prison, its publicity media silenced, the stage was clear for the Muslim League. 'The Government have no love for the League', a Congress leader wrote, 'less for its leader. For them, the League and its leader are the enemy's enemy, the common enemy being the nationalist forces represented by the Congress.' Engaged in the task of an all-out offensive against the Congress, the British Governors and officials were glad to see an ally in the most vociferous opponent of the Congress.[19]

The political gains of the League's new position were not long in coming. In August 1942, Sir Saadullah Khan formed a League ministry in Assam. A month later, Allah Baksh, the Premier of Sind, whose sympathy with the Congress was an open secret, was dismissed from office even though he commanded a majority in the Sind Legislative Assembly, and a League ministry was formed. In March 1943, Nizamuddin, Jinnah's loyal supporter in Bengal, formed a ministry with the help of the European group. In May 1943, the League was able to form a ministry in the North-West Frontier

Province, as most of the Congress members of the provincial legislature were in jail. It was only when the estrangement between the Congress and the government reached its peak that the dividends to the League were the highest in the form of League ministries in the provinces which it claimed for Pakistan.

IX

The death of his secretary and beloved wife in the Aga Khan Palace where he had been interned had sombre associations for Gandhi. His health was becoming a cause of concern to the government early in 1944. He had contracted malaria and was running a high fever. The tide of the war had already turned in favour of the Allies, and the risks of Gandhi's release seemed to the government immeasurably less than those of his possible death in jail. His premature release on 6 May 1944 did not please Gandhi; he even felt ashamed that he should have fallen ill in jail.

Gandhi knew that his stock in official circles was not high, that his own *bona fides* and those of the Congress were questioned, and that with a British Cabinet presided over by Churchill, the scales were heavily tipped against him. In spite of this, he took the initiative in an attempt to break the political deadlock. On 17 June 1944 he wrote to the Viceroy, Lord Wavell, seeking permission to meet members of the Congress Working Committee and requesting him to see him before deciding. The Viceroy turned down his request; he did not see any advantage in meeting with Gandhi 'in consideration of radical differences' in their viewpoints. In an interview with Stuart Gelder of the British journal, *The News Chronicle,* Gandhi suggested the formation of a 'National Government' at the centre, chosen by the elected members of the Central Legislative Assembly. This proposal was described by the Viceroy as 'quite unacceptable to His Majesty's Government'.

Having failed to make any headway with the government Gandhi sought an accord with Jinnah. He did not accept the two-nation theory, but he was prepared to recognize the psychology which had commended this theory to the Muslim intelligentsia. The basis on which he proposed to negotiate with Jinnah was the 'Rajaji formula', devised by C. Rajagopalachari, the ex-Premier of Madras who, while having had differences with his colleagues in 1941, was one of the keenest intellects in the Congress. Rajagopalachari had suggested that if the Muslim League endorsed Congress demands for national independence and formation of a provisional government during the war, it would agree to a demarcation of contiguous Muslim-majority districts in the north-west and north-east of India, and to a plebiscite of all adult inhabitants in these areas to decide whether they would prefer to remain in a free united India or in separate states. And if, ultimately, separation was agreed upon, the two states were to devise mutual agreements for defence, communications and other essential matters.

The terms offered by Gandhi to Jinnah in September 1944 would have been unthinkable four years earlier when he had described Pakistan as an 'untruth'. Gandhi not only recognized the principle of partition, but even suggested a mechanism for it. It is important to note that, while Gandhi suggested links between the two states, he did not insist on a central government. He was content to have 'a Board of Representatives of both the States' for certain common purposes and services. He could not, he confessed to Jinnah, envisage the two (successor) states after the partition 'as if there was nothing common between . . . [them] except enmity'. The search for cultural and economic autonomy was legitimate enough, but some safeguards were imperative to prevent an armament race and an armed conflict between the two states.

Jinnah rejected Gandhi's offer out of hand. The demarcation of boundaries by districts was unacceptable to him, though he was to accept it in 1947. He would have nothing less than the 'full' six provinces for Pakistan, even though in two of them (Punjab and Bengal) the Muslim majority was marginal, and in one province, Assam, it was non-existent. Jinnah did not see why the non-Muslim population in these provinces should have a voice in determining their fate: if there was to be a plebiscite or referendum, it was to be confined to Muslims. Nor would Jinnah agree to any common links between India and Pakistan in such matters as foreign affairs, defence or communications. He would not agree to Gandhi's proposal that 'marriage should precede divorce', that the partition should come, if at all, after the British departure and after the two communities had an opportunity to coexist. The fact that Gandhi had knocked at his door raised Jinnah's prestige in the eyes of Indian Muslims.

The Gandhi–Jinnah talks began on 9 September 1944 and concluded on 27 September. The optimism which they aroused at the time did not derive from any real prospects of an agreement between the two leaders, but only reflected public weariness of the political deadlock, and an almost universal desire for concord between the League and the Congress. On his return from the first interview, Gandhi was asked if he had brought anything from Jinnah. 'Only flowers', he replied. The subsequent meetings registered no more tangible gains. Jinnah questioned Gandhi's credentials. It was true that since 1933 Gandhi had ceased to be a member of the Congress, but Jinnah knew very well that Gandhi's influence on the counsel of the Congress did not depend upon a membership card or on the holding of any office. The League leader's approach was doctrinaire. He wanted Gandhi to recognize that the All India Muslim League had the exclusive right to speak on behalf of Indian Muslims. He wanted the idea of Pakistan to be conceded in principle before he would define its geographical boundaries or discuss its details. He would not hear of non-Muslims in Muslim-majority provinces participating in the plebiscite which was to determine their future; the right of self-determination in these areas could only be exercised by Muslims.

Gandhi suggested that the demarcation of boundaries and the plebiscite should follow and not precede the transfer of power from Britain to India he hoped that after the departure of the British the two communities would learn, in the bracing climate of freedom, to make mutual adjustments, and the need for partition of the country might never arise. What was Gandhi's hope was Jinnah's fear. Jinnah did not want to take any risks and so made partition a precondition of Indian independence. To Gandhi the prospect of two states carved out on the basis of religious affiliation alone was disconcerting.

While these conversations were no more than a kind of re-eduction for Gandhi, to Jinnah they brought an accession of political gains. For four years the Muslim League had not swerved an inch from the position Jinnah had adopted in March 1940; events had shown that his intransigence had worked in his favour. The 'Rajaji formula', which had formed the initial basis of the negotiations, did not concede all that Jinnah demanded, but at least it recognized the possibility of the partition of the country. The fact that Gandhi, who had once described the division of India as a sin, had relented so far as to discuss the machinery for the exercise of the right of self-determination by Muslims was a feather in Jinnah's cap. Viewed in the long-term strategy of the campaign for Pakistan, the Gandhi–Jinnah talks were another milestone, marking further progress from the offer of Lord Linlithgow in August 1940 and the Cripps Mission in 1942.

The conclusion is inescapable that Jinnah was not interested in a compromise; he did not think the time for agreement was opportune; in any case, an understanding with the Congress had little attraction for him when he could hope to get better terms from the government.

As the war drew to a close, the need for a fresh move in India was keenly felt. The Simla Conference was a recognition of this need. The war in Europe ended in May 1945; Japan surrendered in August. The first post-war elections in Britain returned the Labour Party to power. The new

Secretary of State for India, Lord Pethick-Lawrence, spoke of 'equal partnership' between Britain and India. Lord Wavell had already announced that elections would be held 'as soon as possible' to the Central Legislative Assembly and the provincial legislatures, which had been in existence since 1934 and 1937 respectively. In September 1945, after a visit to London, the Viceroy announced that 'in the spirit of Cripps offer' the Government proposed to convene a constitution-making body. The announcement did not arouse much enthusiasm. The Labour Government decided to send an All-party Parliamentary Delegation to study the situation in India and to convince her people that self-government was within their grasp.

Two further efforts at a short-term solution met with no more success. Early in 1945, the 'Bhulabhai Desai–Liaquat Ali Pact' for Congress–League cooperation in the formation of an Interim Government at the centre was published, but Liaquat Ali backed out. Desai burnt his fingers in these parleys; the Pact was rejected out of hand by Jinnah, but it introduced the idea of parity between the Congress and the League, agreed to by Desai for the formation of a national government. At the Simla Conference, convened by Lord Wavell in June 1945, this parity was almost taken for granted. By the time the conference ended, Jinnah had raised his price by demanding parity between the Muslim League and all other parties. The Simla Conference broke down because Jinnah would not permit the Viceroy to nominate to his Executive Council any Muslim member — not even a non-Congress Muslim representative of the Unionist Party which was in power in the Punjab but did not owe allegiance to the League.

Chapter 27

TOWARDS TRANSFER OF POWER

Some Pakistani historians have tended to seek the causes of partition in particular episodes during the months and years immediately preceding it. In fact partition was the culmination of a movement of Muslim separatism which had been gathering momentum at least since 1877 when the M.A.O. College was founded. Its founder, Syed Ahmad Khan, vigorously opposed the Indian National Congress when it was still in infancy. Highly respected as he was as a religious and social reformer in his community, Syed Ahmad Khan exerted a profound influence in favour of isolation of the Muslims from the nationalist movement. He raised the question mark that was to cast its shadow over Indian politics during the next 60 years. What would be the position of the Muslim community in a free India? He was the one who put forward the idea which found wide acceptance among the Muslim elite of the day that, although fellow inhabitants of the Hindus and other communities, the Muslims in India constituted a nation separate from the rest and had their own special interests to protect and promote.

Syed Ahmad Khan has been hailed as a father-figure by Pakistani scholars. The political concept of Pakistan, as it was formulated by the Muslim League in the 1940s, was inconceivable in the last quarter of the 19th century. There was, however, much in the writings and speeches of Syed Ahmad Khan to nourish the psychology of Muslim separatism. That the Muslims, the former rulers of the subcontinent, had been the unjust victims of history, and especially of the events of 1857, that the Hindus had stolen a march over them in education and employment, that the Muslim youth must be educated separately from the Hindus under Muslim auspices, that for the Muslims to compete with the Hindus for entry into public services and elective bodies was a hopeless task, that any democratic polity must result in Hindu domination, that the British Raj was preferable to Hindu dominance inevitable in a representative form of government, were all Syed Ahmad Khan's assumptions. These assumptions became the dogmas of Muslim separatism during the next half century.

The long rule of the Sultans of Delhi and the Mughal Emperors had ingrained in the Muslim elite a certain pride and faith in its destiny to rule over India. This belief survived the disintegration of the Mughal Empire and the advent of British rule. In his writings and speeches, Syed Ahmad Khan made it a point to remind his co-religionists that they were the descendants of the former rulers of India. Twenty years later, in 1906, when an influential Muslim deputation headed by the Aga Khan waited on the Viceroy, Lord Minto, it pleaded for 'due consideration to be paid to the position which Muslims occupied in India a little more than a hundred years ago and of which the traditions have naturally not faded from their minds.' Lord Minto was chivalrous enough to greet them as 'the descendants of a conquering and ruling race'. This self-image of the Muslim elite as the former rulers of India became a block in the way of their identifying themselves with the Indian National Congress. The signatories to the memorial to Minto described themselves as 'nobles, jagirdars, taluqdars, zamindars, lawyers, merchants and others'. Consisting as it did largely of the titled and landed gentry, with a sprinkling of professional classes and retired government servants, the Muslim elite was by no means a monolithic group; it had its sub-divisions of Sunnis and Shias, Mughals and Syeds, Rajputs and so on. But in its political orientation, in its loyalty to the British Raj and in its obsession with the spectre of 'Hindu domination', it was a fairly coherent group. Most of its members were not really interested in politics; they were happy enough with the status quo and the patronage of British officials. The political demands of the Indian National Congress, such as the Indianization of the higher services, equitable distribution of financial burdens between India and Britain, reduction in military expenditure, reduction in land revenue, separation of executive and judiciary, did not excite them.

The mindset of the Muslim elite suited the British bureaucracy, which came to look upon the Muslim community—as it did upon the landlords and the princes—as pillars of the British Raj. When the joint effort of Muslim League politicians and the Anglo-Indian lobby in London succeeded in injecting separate electorates into the Minto–Morley reforms in 1909, Lovat Fraser, the editor of the British-owned *The Times of India,* confided to Dunlop-Smith, Private Secretary to the Viceroy: 'Men like the Aga Khan plainly feel that in pressing for large separate treatment for Mohammedans, they are fighting our battle much more than their own. We have far more to lose than the Muslims by an entente between Islam and Hinduism.[1]

The dispute between the modernists and the Islamic radicals predates Pakistan's creation. As he advanced arguments for a separate Muslim state in 1937, Jinnah relied in part on appeal to Islam. Indeed, religious identity provided the basis for his demand. The argument that Jinnah advanced to the British was that the Muslims and the Hindus of the Indian subcontinent constituted two separate nations which could not live together. In 1947 his arguments prevailed and Pakistan was created as a Muslim homeland. But what did that mean? Was it simply a country for Muslims to live in or was it, in fact, a Muslim country?

Many of those who led the Muslim League, including Mohammad Ali Jinnah, never envisaged the creation of a state in which Islam would provide the framework for all political activity. Like most of his followers, Jinnah was a modernist. His educational background drew more from Oxbridge than from Deoband. And his demand for Pakistan was opposed not only by the British Government and the Congress leadership in India but also by many Islamic radical scholars. In pre-partition India, the vast majority of the *ulema* (religious scholars) saw Jinnah as a Western-educated lawyer who had lost his religious moorings. Jinnah viewed most of the *ulema* as ignorant, power hungry and often corrupt theocrats. In 1946, for example, he brushed aside their demand for the imposition of *Sharia* law as laid down in the Quran and *Sunnah*. 'Whose Sharia?' Jinnah asked. And added, 'I don't want to get involved. The moment I enter this field the *Ulema* will take over for they claim to be the experts. I certainly don't propose to hand over the field to the *Ulema*.'[2] Many of Jinnah's speeches before 1937 clearly indicate his progressive attitude to Islam.

So far as the British were concerned, they knew what they were doing, but they needed allies to checkmate the Indian National Congress. Ironically, the most blunt comment on separate electorates is to be found in an official document — the joint report of the Viceroy, Lord Chelmsford, and Secretary of State Edwin Montagu — which formed the basis of the Reforms Act of 1919:

> Division by creeds and classes means the creation of political camps organized against each other, and teaches men to think as partisans and not as citizens; and it is difficult to see how the change from this system to national representation is ever to occur. The British Government is often accused of dividing men in order to govern them. But if it necessarily divides them at the very moment when it professes to start them on the road to governing themselves it will find it difficult to meet the charge of being hypocritical or shortsighted.[3]

This paragraph seems to have been drafted by Edwin Montagu, one of the most liberal and sympathetic of British ministers, who had presided over the India Office in London. It did not represent the policy of the British bureaucracy in India or of the Anglo-Indian lobby in England whose views were succinctly expressed by Secretary of State Birkenhead to the then Viceroy, Lord Reading in 1925: 'The more it is made obvious that their [Hindu and Muslim] antagonisms are profound and immense and affect irreconcilable sections of the population, the more conspicuously is the fact illustrated that we and we alone can play the part of the composers.'[4]

II

The question of safeguards for the Muslim community in the constitutional reforms arose with the incorporation of separate electorates in the electoral system in 1909. The Congress, led by the great Parsi leaders Dadabhai Naoroji and Pherozeshah Mehta, and Gopal Krishna Gokhale, was quick to detect in separate electorates the thin end of the wedge which would ultimately pull the two major communities asunder. But seven years later the Congress reversed its policy under the leadership of B.G. Tilak, who believed that by conceding Muslim demands in toto he was helping to solve the communal problem for good. Jinnah, who was one of the chief architects of the Lucknow Pact in 1916 and presided over the Muslim League session in that year, 'evidently held the same belief, because he frankly acknowledged the spirit in which the Hindu leaders had recognized and met the Muslim communal position'. 'I rejoice to think', he said, 'that a final settlement has at last been reached which sets the seal on Hindu–Muslim co-operation.'[5]

The objective of the Congress was to end foreign rule and to create a united front to fight it. The leaders of the Muslim League, on the other hand, were interested neither in hastening the end of the British Raj nor in embroiling themselves with it; they had more limited and practical concerns: they were concerned with power and patronage in their own provinces. In a letter dated 28 May 1937 to Jinnah, Sir Mohammad Iqbal, the philosopher-poet, described the All India Muslim League as a body of the upper classes of Indian Muslims, not of the masses, whose chief preoccupation was with securing posts for their sons, relatives and friends. Jinnah was not unaware of the character of the feudal and titled gentry with whom and through whom he had to work; he once said they included some 'spineless people, who whatever they may say to me, will consult the [British] Deputy Commissioner about what they should do'.[6]

The idea that in legislatures of self-governing India all Hindu members would vote *en bloc* on political issues was absurd, but the fear of 'Hindu domination' had been firmly planted in the psyche of the Muslim elite since the days of Syed Ahmad Khan. The demands for safeguards continued escalating over the years, until, with Jinnah's 'Fourteen Points' in 1929, they included every possible claim which could have been advanced vis-à-vis the Hindus within the framework of the representative system of government. In 1932 the Communal Award pronounced by Ramsay MacDonald, Prime Minister of England, under pressure from the Government of India, conceded virtually all Muslim demands, but the problem was not solved. The Muslim political elite's obsession with the demographic reality of a three-fourths Hindu majority in India remained. What was needed was a formula in constitutional arithmetic to offset the Hindu majority at the centre in a future constitution for India and to prove 25=75. This formula was conceived by Rahmat Ali, a student at Cambridge, who, in a pamphlet *Now or Never* published in 1933, propounded the 'two-nation theory' and its corollary, the establishment of Pakistan as an independent Muslim state consisting of Muslim-majority provinces in the north-west and north-east.

Most Pakistani historians have attributed Muslim opposition to Indian nationalism from the days of Syed Ahmad Khan to the sentiment of 'Muslim nationalism'. Now, the term 'Muslim nationalism' makes as little sense as 'Christian nationalism' or 'Buddhist nationalism'. Basic to nationalism is its relationship to a specific country or region. Not until the emergence of the concept of Pakistan in the mid-1930s did such a possible relationship emerge, and Muslim separatism in India began to acquire the characteristics of secessionism and nationalism. In the words of S.R. Mehrotra, the eminent historian of the Indian National Congress, it was 'an accident of geography' — the existence of Muslim-majority regions in the north-west and north-east — that brought the idea of Pakistan into the domain of practical politics. If the Muslim population had been evenly distributed throughout the country, it would have been a minority everywhere, which could neither have willed nor been in a position to dominate any region.

By the mid-1930s, the concept of Pakistan was being debated by Muslim politicians. Sir Mohammad Iqbal argued at the Third Round Table Conference (1933) that the Muslims did not want a central government in India because it was bound to be dominated by Hindus. Two years later, the Aga Khan wrote to Sir Fazl-i-Husain that the only safety for Muslims in India lay in working for the achievement of Pakistan.[7] Bimal Prasad has recently argued that Jinnah had been converted to the idea of Pakistan by 1937 but deliberately did not reveal it.[8] He quotes from a letter written by Lord Brabourne, the Governor of Bombay, to the Viceroy, Lord Linlithgow, in June 1937 that Jinnah had told him that he was 'planning to consolidate the Muslim League throughout India; his policy was to preach communalism morning, noon and night and teach [the Muhammadans] generally to stand on their own feet and make themselves independent of the Hindus.'

Jinnah's conversion to the ultimate concept in Muslim separatism was to prove a turning point not only in his own political career, but in the history of India.

III

After the general elections of 1937, there was, as we have seen before, a drastic reversal of Jinnah's policy. He claimed that his nominees would neither join the Congress legislative party nor accept its discipline and the principle of joint responsibility of the cabinet. The Congress leaders thus had reason to fear that if the Muslim League representatives were taken into Congress ministries on such terms, Jinnah would dictate the whole policy of the government through his nominees.

Jinnah's appeal in the name of Islam reached its culmination in the general election of 1945–46. In her book, *Self and Sovereignty,* Ayesha Jalal tells us about meetings in the North-West Frontier Province in which appeals to vote for the Muslim League were made 'in the name of Allah and the Prophet'.[9] The services of *pirs* and heads of religious shrines were requisitioned to urge Muslims in rural areas to vote for the League or face ostracism. Through constant reiteration of the dangers of 'Hindu Raj' and 'Congress tyranny', a fear psychosis was induced in the Muslim masses. This tactic paid rich dividends to the Muslim League. It won all the 30 Muslim seats in the Central Assembly and 439 out of 490 Muslim seats in the Provincial Assemblies. It had fought the election on the issue of Pakistan and won a landslide victory. At last, Jinnah had the mandate he needed for the negotiations for the transfer of power from British to Indian hands, which began with the arrival of the Cabinet Mission in March 1946.

The arrival of the Cabinet Mission brought Jinnah to the negotiating table and compelled him to spell out his terms. In one important respect the political situation was changing. The rift between the Congress and the government which had all along given the Muslim League a favourable bargaining position was closing. The leaders of the League seemed to sense it. From the beginning of 1946, they started harping on dangers of a civil war if their demands were not conceded. In March 1946, Abdur Rab Nishtar, later a League nominee to the Interim Government, declared: 'The real fact is that Mussalmans belong to a martial race and are no believers in non-violent principles of Mr. Gandhi'.[10] Abdul Qaiyum Khan, a League leader of the North-West Frontier Province, pointed out that the people in the tribal areas, 'who were well armed', were for Pakistan. Sir Feroz Khan Noon threatened that if Muslims were placed under 'one central government or Hindu Raj, then the havoc which the Muslims will play will put to shame what Chengiz Khan and Halaku did.'[11]

The triangular negotiations between the British Cabinet Mission, the Congress and the League failed and the Cabinet Mission Plan was stillborn. In July 1946, Viceroy Lord Wavell invited Nehru and Jinnah as leaders of the Congress and the Muslim League respectively to form an Interim Government. Jinnah's conditions were not acceptable to the Viceroy, who then decided to form a government with the Congress alone headed by Nehru. Jinnah was furious. He announced that 16 August 1946 would be observed as the 'Direct Action Day'. 'This day we bid goodbye to constitutional methods'; he told the League Council, 'today we have also forged a pistol and are ready to use it'. On that day communal riots began in Calcutta which took a toll of at least 5,000 lives and more than 10,000 injured. Two months later, communal disturbances broke out in the Muslim-majority district of Noakhali in East Bengal in which local hooligans burnt the property of the Hindus, looted their crops and desecrated their temples. There were also shocking reports of forcible conversions and kidnapping of Hindu women. The communal riots spread like wild fire from Calcutta to East Bengal, from East Bengal to Bihar and from Bihar to West Punjab.

The communal violence, in its scale and intensity in 1946, was in an entirely different category from the local riots on such issues as cow-slaughter and music outside mosques. Gandhi undertook walking tours through the riot-torn areas of Bengal and Bihar. Other Congress leaders condemned the riots and called for stern action against the guilty. Unfortunately, the League leaders reacted with a political rather than a human bias. Even though there was a League ministry in Calcutta, Jinnah blamed the riots on 'Gandhi, the Viceroy and the British'; each communal riot was cited as further endorsement of the two-nation theory and of the inevitability of the partition of India. George Abell, Private Secretary to Lord Wavell, after a meeting with Jinnah's deputy, Nawabzada Liaquat Ali Khan, on 18 November got a 'clear impression that the League could not afford to let communal feeling in the country die down.'[12]

Shaken by the riots, Lord Wavell inducted the Muslim League into the Interim Government, but with results which were just the opposite of what he had hoped for. The Interim Government, instead of becoming more representative and effective, was paralysed by the conflict between the two main political parties. The Viceroy did not have a clue as to what he should do, and proposed a 'breakdown' plan for the evacuation of British military forces from the subcontinent, province by province. Prime Minister Clement Attlee, who had won a decisive majority in the general elections in Britain in 1946, considered Wavell's advice as a counsel of despair and decided to appoint a new Viceroy to devise and implement a scheme for a more orderly termination of British rule.

On 20 February 1947, the British Government issued a momentous statement announcing its definite intention to take necessary steps to effect transfer of power into responsible Indian hands by a date not later than end of June 1948. This statement could well have acted as shock therapy to bring the contending political parties together. But it had just the opposite effect because of a provision in it that if on the appointed date (30 June 1948) there was no single government for the whole of the country, the British Government might transfer power in some areas to 'existing provincial governments or in some such other ways as may seem reasonable'. The Muslim League, which had its ministries only in Bengal and Sind, took this to mean that it had just 15 months to capture provincial governments in the remaining provinces, Punjab, the NWFP and Assam in which it had been defeated in the general election but which it claimed for Pakistan. It launched 'direct action' in the form of demonstrations, which resulted in widespread and serious communal disturbances in West Punjab in March 1947. The response of the Congress Working Committee came in a resolution demanding partition of the Punjab. This was a signal to the Muslim League that it would not be allowed to get away with the Hindu-majority districts of the Punjab and Bengal if it insisted on the secession of Muslim-majority areas in the east and west. After all, the logic which the Muslim League applied to the partition of India could as well justify the partition of these two provinces.

In March 1947 the Muslim League was satisfactorily holding its own, emphatic in its insistence that there had never been one India, that unity was the creation of the British Raj, and that if Hindu rule was forced upon them a civil war more terrible than any in the history of Asia would ensue. To avoid civil war, the League insisted that power be handed over to two separate authorities equally. The onus was firmly placed upon the British Government; it must decide and in so doing must recognize that there must be two Constituent Assemblies, one to draft a constitution for Hindustan and one for Pakistan. It was by this insistence on the transfer of power to two recognized successor states and by his threat to risk all in a civil war rather than accept what he called the Hindu Raj, that Jinnah made any other settlement seem impracticable even to the most bitter opponents of his pretensions.

It was the considered view of N. Mansergh, the Chief Editor of the British official documents under the title *The Transfer of Power 1942-47*, that a civil war 'more terrible than any in the history of Asia would have followed, if power had not been transferred to two successor states.' In any case any other settlement seemed impracticable to the British Government in the summer of 1947.[13]

Even before Lord Mountbatten arrived in India to succeed Wavell at the end of March 1947, the Congress leadership was beginning to reconcile itself to Pakistan as 'a lesser evil'. The choice was narrowing down to partition of the country or a civil war. Nehru and Vallabhbhai Patel had been chastened by their experience in the Interim Government and the growing lawlessness in the country. A *modus vivendi* with the League seemed not remote, but impossible. Parition of India was bad enough, but even worse possibilities had begun to loom before the Congress leaders. The Princely rulers of western and central India, under the inspiration of rulers of some larger states such as the Nawab of Bhopal, were thinking in terms of 'leagues of princes'. It was the intrigue of the ruler of Bastar, a small state in central India, with the Nizam of Hyderabad, and the attitude of the political department of the Government of India to it, which finally convinced Vallabhbhai Patel that it was imperative for the Congress to secure immediate British withdrawal from India even if it meant the acceptance of partition of the country. Nehru arrived at the same conclusion after his frustrating experience in the Interim Government where he noticed 'a mental alliance' between the British officers and the leaders of the League. Thus it was that the partition of India at independence came to be accepted by all the concerned parties, the Congress, the Muslim League and the British, as the way forward.

Chapter 28

Post Partition

Following the achievement of his grand ambition, the creation of Pakistan, Jinnah seemed briefly to revert to the more secular stance he had abandoned a decade earlier. He told Sri Prakasa, the first Indian High Commissioner to Pakistan, that he intended to make Pakistan a secular state and wanted to revert to his old and familiar role of the protagonist of Hindu–Muslim unity.[1]

While inaugurating the first session of the Pakistan Constituent Assembly after being elected its President on 11 August 1947, Jinnah said:

> You are free; you are free to go to your temples, you are free to go to your mosques or to any other place of worship in this State of Pakistan. You may belong to any religion or caste or creed — that has nothing to do with the business of the State .... We are starting with this fundamental principle that we are all citizens and equal citizens of one State .... I think we should keep that in front of us as our ideal and you will find that in course of time Hindus would cease to be Hindus and Muslims would cease to be Muslims, not in the religious sense because that is the personal faith of each individual, but in the political sense .... I shall always be guided by the principles of justice and fair play without any, as is put in political language, prejudice or ill will, in other words, partiality or favouritism.[2]

The British-owned paper, *The Statesman*, interpreted the speech as a plea for a 'secular state'.[3] Sharif al Mujahid, editor of the multi-volume works on Jinnah, described the speech as 'a call for the stability and integration of Pakistan, the healing of wounds, the burying of the bitter memories of the past, the building of trust and confidence in the minorities.'[4] The speech, however, struck so different a note from what Jinnah had been saying for 10 years that Stanley Wolpert, Jinnah's American biographer, wondered whether 'the cyclone of events had so disoriented him that he was arguing the opposition's brief?'[5]

The fact was that by August 1947, Jinnah had travelled far from secularism and modernism which had marked his earlier political life for 30 years. For him, now, post the creation of Pakistan, there was no going back for from the position he had adopted since 1937. This was evident in his address to the Karachi Bar Association on 25 January 1948, the Prophet's birthday. At this address he declared that people were making 'mischief' when they rejected the idea of an Islamic state.[6] 'Some are misled by propaganda', he said. 'Islamic principles today are as applicable to life as they were 1,300 years ago'. He insisted that the constitution of Pakistan would be made 'on the basis of *Sharia*'. A few weeks later, he once again repeated the same theme, expressing the same thoughts and using almost the same words: 'It is my belief that our salvation lies in following the golden rules of conduct set for us by our great law-giver, the Prophet of Islam. Let us lay the foundations of our democracy on the basis of truly Islamic ideals and principles'.[7]

In seeking to base Pakistan's democracy first and foremost upon Islamic ideals and principles, Jinnah seemed to ignore the cultural diversity of Indian Muslims. In March 1948 at a public meeting attended by over three lakh people at Dacca, the capital of East Pakistan, he said:

> ... What we want is not to talk about Bengali, Punjabi, Sindhi, Baluch, Pathan and so on. They are of course units. But I ask you: have you forgotten the lesson that was taught to us thirteen hundred years ago? If I may point out, you are all outsiders here. Who were the original inhabitants of Bengal — not those who are now living. So what is the use of saying 'we are Bengalis, or Sindhis, or Pathans, or Punjabis'. No, we are Muslims.[8]

While Jinnah played the leading role in the creation of Pakistan, he led the country too briefly to impact its post-independence constitution and institutions. This role was to fall to leadership that succeeded him. Within a year of independence in June 1948, Jinnah fell seriously ill. Suffering from tuberculosis and cancer of the lungs, he was moved to Zirat, a hill town about 70 miles from Quetta. On 13 August he was brought down to Quetta. As his illness progressed very quickly shortly after, on 9 September his condition became critical; just two days later, on 11 September, he was taken from Quetta to the Governor General's House in Karachi where he breathed his last later the same day at 10.20 pm. The following day, 12 September, he was buried with full honours at Karachi.

Following Jinnah's death, the arguments between the Islamic radicals and modernists on the framing of the constitution became more intense. As the politicians debated the content of the constitution of Pakistan, the Islam-based parties pressed for a document that would establish Pakistan as a theological state committed to Islam; some of them even asked whether a constitution was necessary. The *Quran* and *Sunnah*, they maintained, laid down all the rules necessary for life and there was no need for mere men to create political institutions that could only distort Allah's word. Throughout the 1950s, the politicians, charged with writing the first Pakistan constitution, grappled with these issues; when they produced the 1956 constitution they came down firmly on the side of the modernists. As a sop to the radicals, the constitution's preamble did include a clause that recognized the sovereignty of Allah over the entire universe. But, read as a whole, the document made it clear that, in practice, the people of Pakistan would be sovereign, as Prime Minister Liaquat Ali Khan had said when proposing the Objectives Resolution that formed the basis of the constitution:

> All authority is a sacred trust, entrusted to us by God for the purpose of being exercised in the service of man, so that it does not become an agency for tyranny or selfishness.

I would, however, point out that this is not a resuscitation of the dead theory of Divine Right of Kings or rulers because in accordance with the spirit of Islam, the Preamble fully recognizes the truth that authority has been delegated to the people ....

This naturally eliminates any danger of the establishment of a theocracy.[9]

Even if the vast majority of Pakistan's first generation of politicians were firmly in the modernist camp, it is significant that they tried to avoid a direct confrontation with the Islamic radicals. Faced with growing challenges from the Baloch, Sindhi, Pukhtoon and Bengali nationalists, even the most secular leaders found it was expedient to appeal to Islam so as to foster a sense of Pakistani unity. In doing so, the politicians established a trend which was to be a feature of Pakistani politics ever since. Pakistani politicians have never wanted to share power with the *ulema* but they have also been reluctant to offend them. Few have wanted an Islamic state, but they have been hesitant to say so with any clarity.[10]

Perhaps there was an inevitability in Pakistan's continuing struggle between modernism and the imperatives of Islamic governance. The dilemmas that succeeding generations of politicians faced were no different from those that Jinnah had faced in the campaign for the creation of Pakistan. He departed from his secular beliefs and played the Islamic card. It worked. But the genie could not easily be bottled after use. The contrary impulses of a more modernist polity and an Islamic one have coexisted uneasily ever since in Pakistan. This is a coexistence that has seen the inexorable rise of Islamic influence over the six decades of Pakistan's existence.

Chapter 29

EPILOGUE

Jinnah began his political career in 1906 under the influence of the senior Congress leadership including Dadabhai Naoroji and Pherozeshah Mehta. He championed joint electorates for elective bodies irrespective of caste and creed. This nationalist orientation was one that he was clearly drawn to and tried to hold on to for many years. However, there was a problem. With the Minto–Morley reforms of 1909 and the introduction of separate electorates, his path to legislative success could only lie through appealing to the Muslim constituency. This conflict between Jinnah's own beliefs and what was required to succeed in the political arena drove a lot of his apparently inconsistent positions over the years to 1937. The fact was that Jinnah's behaviour was governed more by his deep need to be in a position of leadership and power than by a long-term vision centred around his own beliefs.

Having begun his political career in 1906 by championing joint electorates for elective bodies, by 1916 he became an advocate of separate electorates and even persuaded the Indian National Congress to waive its principled objections to them. In the next four years he reached the highest echelons of both the Indian National Congress and the All India Muslim League. However, as ill luck would have it, the Khilafat frenzy and the Gandhian wave in 1920 swept him off the national stage. He fell back on the Muslim League. In 1927 Jinnah once again resumed the role of a bridge-builder between the Congress and the League; he initiated an accord between the two parties which, at the time, seemed to be a breakthrough in the solution of the communal problem in India. Unluckily for him the accord was wrecked by some twists and turns in Indian politics triggered by the appointment of the Simon Commission, the convening of the All-Parties Conference and the debates on the Nehru Report.

Jinnah paid a high price for his initiative in seeking an accord with the Congress in 1927–28. He suffered an angry backlash from his co-religionists and caused the emergence, with the backing of the British bureaucracy, of the All India Muslim Conference as a rival to the Muslim League. Not until 1934 did he come out of the shadows and resume the leadership of the Muslim League. Undeterred by his bitter experience, he returned again to the nationalist position and called for Muslim solidarity and Hindu–Muslim unity in a united front against the British Government. Indeed, he made it his election platform in 1936. To his deep disappointment, he was publicly rebuffed by Nehru who was Congress President at that time. The Muslim League was rejected by an overwhelming majority of the Muslim electorate across the country.

The election debacle confronted Jinnah with an unpleasant truth. His programme of Hindu–Muslim cooperation in order to make a joint front against the British Government had carried no pull with the Muslim electorate. He had failed to foresee that most of the apolitical, pro-British regional leaders dominating Muslim politics in the provinces were not willing to oppose the government. If he wanted their support, he had to offer them something in return. So far he had neither been able to dislodge them nor convert them to his position. Politics is said to be the art of the possible. If he wanted the allegiance of his co-religionists he had to strike the right chord in them.

Jinnah's political predicament in the spring of 1937 led him to play the religious card. So far he had not worn religion on his sleeve. His visit to the Badshahi mosque in Lahore in February 1936 was his first experience of addressing a Friday congregation in a mosque; he had been pleased with it. The Islamic card was to be the route to the revival of his political fortunes after the disastrous election. But this change did involve a reversal of his political stand and a total reorientation of his political credo. Henceforth, the enemy was the Congress and the Hindus, not the British. He shed his life-long hostility to foreign rule and decided to mend fences with the British bureaucracy.

With the declaration of war in 1939, the British were keen to arrive at a long-term understanding which would secure the willing participation of India in the war effort. Jinnah was quick to express his whole-hearted loyalty and readiness to support the British. He urged the government to recognize that the democratic form of government did not suit India and that the constitution under the Act of 1935 needed to be replaced. Jinnah told the Viceroy in reference to the Congress, 'their object ... is nothing less than to destroy both you [British] and us [Muslims]'. He also told Linlithgow that India's attainment of the goal of self-government must be accompanied by the partition of the country to safeguard the interest of Muslims.

By early 1940, Linlithgow's discussions with Gandhi had still not resulted in an understanding with the Congress that would ensure support for the war effort. This is when Linlithgow advised Jinnah not to maintain a purely negative position of opposing Congress proposals, but to formulate the League's own plan for the future. Thus encouraged, the working committee of the Muslim League approved a resolution the same day on the outline of a scheme for the partition of India. Shortly after, at the Lahore session of the Muslim League, Jinnah articulated the demand for Pakistan. He argued that the history of the previous 1,200 years had failed to achieve unity and that the artificial unity of India dated back only to the British conquest.

Jinnah's appeal in the name of Islam reached a crescendo in the general election of 1945–46. Appeals to vote for the Muslim League were made in the name of Allah. Through a constant reiteration of the dangers of 'Hindu Raj' and 'Congress tyranny' a fear psychosis was created in the

Muslim masses. This tactic paid rich dividends to the Muslim League. Its candidates won an overwhelming victory in the Muslim seats. The Muslim League had fought the election on the issue of Pakistan and won a landslide victory. At last, Jinnah had the mandate he needed to negotiate for the creation of Pakistan at the transfer of power from the British. These negotiations began with the arrival of the Cabinet Mission in March 1946.

The triangular negotiations between the British Cabinet Mission, the Congress and the League failed and the Cabinet Mission Plan was stillborn. In July 1946, Viceroy Lord Wavell invited Nehru and Jinnah as leaders of the Congress and the Muslim League respectively to form an Interim Government. Jinnah's conditions were not acceptable to the Viceroy, who then decided to form a government with the Congress alone headed by Nehru. Inflamed at being left out, Jinnah announced that 16 August 1946 would be observed as the 'Direct Action Day'. 'This day we bid goodbye to constitutional methods'; he told the League Council. In saying, 'today we have also forged a pistol and are ready to use it', Jinnah seemed to legitimise violence. On that day communal riots began in Calcutta which took a toll of at least 5,000 lives and more than 10,000 injured. Two months later, communal disturbances broke out in the Muslim-majority district of Noakhali in East Bengal. The communal riots spread like wild fire throughout the country. Each communal riot was cited as further endorsement of the two-nation theory and of the inevitability of the partition of India.

In March 1947 the Muslim League was still holding its position, emphatic in its insistence that there had never been one India, that unity was the creation of the British Raj, and that if Hindu rule was forced upon them a terrible civil war would ensue. By his threat to risk all in a civil war rather than accept what he called the Hindu Raj, Jinnah made any settlement other than partition seem impracticable, even to the most bitter opponents of his pretensions.

In the post-1937 phase of his political career, Jinnah displayed a comfort with whipping up religious frenzy that must have been a surprise even to himself. He seemed not even to be particularly worried about the ensuing communal violence — merely using it as justification for the division of the country at independence. He had travelled a long distance from the nationalist stance that he began his career with and which he tried to hold on to through an understanding with the Congress at various points until 1936. After 1937 there was a different Jinnah in evidence — whipping up Islamic frenzy and ruthless in pursuit of his objective — treating loss of life in riots merely as collateral damage on the road to achieving Pakistan under his leadership.

Jinnah's achievement in the creation of the state of Pakistan was remarkable. The methods by which it was achieved accentuated communal tension and left a bitter legacy between the two successor states to British India. It is a legacy that still haunts India and Pakistan in different and painful ways.

Notes

Chapter 1

1. *Indian Magazine and Review* (London, April 1896), Journal of National Indian Association.
2. M.C. Chagla, *Roses in December: An Autobiography* (Bombay, 1974), p. 53.
3. Ibid., p. 54.
4. Ibid., p. 55.
5. Ibid.

Chapter 2

1. Extracts from B.R. Nanda, *Gandhi: Pan-Islamism, Imperialism and Nationalism in India* (Bombay, 1989) p. 45.
2. Ibid., p. 46.
3. Ibid., p. 54.
4. Ibid., p. 55.
5. Ibid., p. 45.
6. Ibid., p. 47.
7. Ibid., p. 72.
8. Peter Hardy, *The Muslims of British India* (Cambridge, 1972), p. 158.
9. Minto Papers, India Office Library (IOL), London.
10. Government of India, Home Department, Poll. A, February 1916, Files No. 425–28, National Archives of India (NAI), New Delhi.
11. Harcourt Butler Papers, IOL.
12. Nanda, *Gandhi: Pan-Islamism, op.cit.*, p. 77.
13. Ibid., p. 78.
14. Syed Sharifuddin Pirzada (ed.), *The Collected Works of Quaid-E-Azam Mohammad Ali Jinnah, Vol. I (1906–1921)* (Karachi, 1984), pp. 48–49.

Chapter 3

1. Bampfylde Fuller, *Studies of Indian Life and Sentiment* (London, 1910), p. 349.

2. B.R. Nanda, *Gandhi and His Critics* (Delhi, 1985), p. 81.
3. Pirzada, Vol. 1, *op.cit.*, p. 188.
4. Ibid., pp. 188–95.
5. M.C. Chagla, *Roses in December*, *op.cit.*, p. 119.
6. Khwaja Razi Haider, *Ruttie Jinnah: The Story Told and Untold* (Karachi, 2004), pp. 33–34. See Kanji Dwarkadas, *Ruttie Jinnah: The Story of Great Friendship* (Bombay, n.d.), p. 112.
7. Ibid., pp. 60–62. See Hector Bolitho, *Jinnah: Creator of Pakistan* (London, 1954), p. 75.
8. Ibid., p. 73.
9. Ibid., pp. 91–92. See Stanely Wolpert, *Jinnah of Pakistan* (New York, 1984), p. 63.
10. Ibid., p. 139.

Chapter 4

1. Venitia Montagu (ed.), *An Indian Diary by Edwin S. Montagu* (London, 1930), pp. 8–10.
2. Ibid.
3. Matlubal Hasan Saiyid, *A Political Study of Mohammad Ali Jinnah* (Delhi, 1986), p. 213. See also *The Bombay Chronicle*, 12 December 1918.
4. Pirzada, Vol. I, *op.cit.* Text of Jinnah's Interview with the Joint Select Committee on 13 August 1919, pp. 302–62.
5. Chagla, *Roses in December*, *op.cit.*, p. 78.

Chapter 5

1. Quoted in Nanda, *Gandhi: Pan-Islamism*, *op.cit.*, p. 146.
2. Pirzada, Vol. 1, *op.cit.*, p. 124.
3. *Collected Works of Mahatma Gandhi (CWMG)*, Vol. XIII, p. 9.
4. Stanley Wolpert, *Jinnah of Pakistan*, *op.cit.*, p. 38.
5. J.B. Kripalani, in C. Shukla (ed.), *Incidents of Gandhiji's Life* (Bombay, 1949), p. 118.
6. B.R Nanda, *Mahatma Gandhi: A Biography* (Delhi, 1958), p. 130.
7. Ibid., p. 131.
8. *CWMG*, Vol. XIV, p. 127.
9. Quoted in Nanda, *Mahatma Gandhi*, *op.cit.*, pp. 167–68.
10. *CWMG*, Vol. XIV, p. 55.
11. Pirzada, Vol. 1, *op.cit.*, pp. 230–31.
12. *CWMG*, Vol. XIV, p. 476.
13. Ibid., p. 479.

14. Willingdon to Butler, 5 May 1918, Butler Papers.
15. Quoted in Nanda, *Gandhi: Pan Islamism, op.cit.*, p. 164.
16. Ibid., 172.
17. Ibid.
18. *CWMG*, Vol. XV, pp. 31–32.
19. Quoted in Wolpert, *Jinnah of Pakistan, op.cit.*, p. 61.
20. *CWMG*, Vol. XV, p. 87.
21. Chelmsford to Montagu, 20 March 1919, Chelmsford Papers, IOL.
22. Nanda, *Mahatma Gandhi, op.cit.*, p. 174.
23. Ibid., pp. 216–17.
24. Saiyid, *A Political Study, op. cit.*, p. 238.
25. Gandhi's speech at Bombay, 11 April 1919, *CWMG*, Vol. XV, p. 211.

Chapter 6

1. Saiyid, *A Political Study, op.cit.*, p. 239.
2. S.M. 6653, National Gandhi Museum, New Delhi.
3. *CWMG*, Vol. XV, p. 398.
4. Ibid., p. 399.
5. Pirzada, Vol. I, *op.cit.*, p. 370.
6. *CWMG*, Vol. XVI, pp. 360–61.
7. *CWMG*, Vol. XVII, pp. 416–18.
8. B.R. Nanda, *The Making of a Nation: India's Road to Independence* (New Delhi, 1998), p. 141.
9. Pirzada, Vol. I, *op.cit.*, pp. 402–6.
10. Ibid.
11. S.M. Burke and Salim Al-Din Quraishi, *Quid-i-Azam Mohammad Ali Jinnah: His Personality and His Politics* (Karachi, 1997), p. 131.
12. Chelmsford Papers.

Chapter 7

1. Quoted in B.R. Nanda, *The Making of a Nation, op.cit.*, p. 141.
2. Pirzada, Vol. I, *op.cit.*, pp. 409–10.
3. Reading Papers.
4. Ibid.
5. Montagu Papers, IOL.

Notes ❧ 337

6. D.A. Low, 'The Government and the First Non-Cooperation Movement 1920–1922', *Journal of Asian Studies*, XXV, 2, p. 257, quoted in Nanda, *The Making of a Nation*, *op.cit.*, p. 161.
7. M.R. Jayakar, *The Story of My Life*, Vol. I, *1873–1922*. (Bombay, 1958), p. 555.
8. Ibid., p. 567.
9. Purshotamdas Thakurdas to Sivaswami Aiyar, 15 October 1923, Purshotamdas Thakurdas Papers, Nehru Memorial Museum and Library (NMML), New Delhi.

Chapter 8

1. *The Statesman*, 1 December 1923.
2. Reading Papers.
3. Reading to Secretary of State, Lord Olivier, 14 December 1923, Reading Papers.
4. Percival Spear and Margaret, *India Remembered* (Delhi, 1981), p. 14.
5. *Legislative Assembly Debates, 1924*, p. 370.
6. Ibid., p. 407.
7. Ibid., p. 249.
8. Ibid., p. 311.
9. Ibid., p. 333.
10. Ibid., pp. 371–72.
11. A note by Alexander Muddiman, 'General Attitude and Tactics of the Legislative Assembly', MSS Eur. E 238/69, ILO.
12. Frederick Whyte, 'Report of the Indian Legislative Assembly, 1921–1925', MSS, Eur. E 238/69, IOL.
13. Ibid.

Chapter 9

1. *CWMG*, Vol. XXV, p. 305.
2. Ibid., p. 229.
3. Rangaswami Parthasarthy, *A Hundred Years of Hindu* (Madras, 1978), p. 332.

Chapter 10

1. Sharif Al Mujahid (ed.), *Quaid-i-Azam and His Times — A Compendium, Vol. I, 1876–1937* (Karachi, 1990), p. 90.

2. *CWMG*, Vol. XXXIV, p. 207.
3. Mujahid, *Quaid-i-Azam and His Times*, Vol. 1, *op.cit.*, p. 98.
4. Ibid.
5. Halifax Papers, 26 March 1927, ILO.
6. Ibid., 3 April 1927.
7. Mujahid, *Quaid-i-Azam and His Times*, Vol. I, *op.cit.*, p. 95.
8. Ibid.
9. *The Indian Annual Register, 1928*, Vol. I, p. 451.

Chapter 11

1. Debates on Indian Affairs in House of Lords Session 1927, p. 181, quoted in Burke and Quraishi, *Quaid-i-Azam Mohammad Ali Jinnah, op.cit.*, p. 155.
2. *The Indian Annual Register, 1927*, Vol. II, p. 449.
3. Saiyid, *A Political Study op.cit.*, p. 400.
4. Burke and Quraishi, *Quaid-i-Azam Mohammad Ali Jinnah, op.cit.*, p. 156.
5. *Selected Works of Motilal Nehru (SWMN)*, Vol. VI, p. 249.
6. M.C. Chagla, *Roses in December, op.cit.*, pp. 94–95.
7. *SWMN*, Vol. VI, p. 281.
8. Ibid., p. 232.
9. Ibid., p. 227.
10. Ibid., p. 217.
11. Ibid., Vol. V, p. 363.
12. Ibid., p. 385.
13. Ibid., pp. 397–98.
14. *The Proceedings of the All Parties National Convention* (1928–29) reproduced in *SWMN*, Vol. VI, pp. 582, 591.
15. Ibid., p. 585.
16. Ibid., p. 587.
17. *The Indian Annual Register, 1929*, Vol. I, p. 372.
18. David Page, *Prelude to Partition: The Indian Muslims and the Imperial System of Control, 1920–1930* (New Delhi, 1982), p. 191.
19. Burke and Quraishi, *Quaid-i-Azam Mohammad Ali Jinnah op.cit.*, p. 164.
20. Gandhi to Motilal Nehru, 3 March 1928, *CWMG*, Vol. XXXVI, p. 76.
21. Halifax Papers.

Chapter 12

1. *The Statesman*, 13 March 1929.
2. Mushirul Hasan (ed.), *Muslims and the Congress: Select Correspondence of Dr. M.A. Ansari 1912–1935* (Delhi, 1979), p. 20.
3. *SWMN*, Vol. V , pp. 368–69.
4. Quoted in B.R. Nanda, *The Nehrus: Motilal and Jawaharlal* (New Delhi, 2008), p. 305.
5. Ibid., p. 314.
6. Ibid., p. 315.
7. Ibid., p. 316.
8. Ibid., p. 315.
9. Ibid., p. 316.
10. Ibid.
11. Ibid., p. 320.
12. Ibid.
13. Ibid., p. 321.
14. Ibid.
15. Ibid., 324.
16. Ibid.
17. Ibid.
18. Ibid.

Chapter 13

1. Waheed Ahmad (ed.), *Jinnah–Irwin Correspondence, 1927–30* (Lahore, 1969), p. 37.
2. Ibid., p. 36.
3. Halifax Papers.
4. Ibid.
5. *The Times*, London, 13 November 1930.
6. Hailey to Irwin, 14 November 1930, Hailey Papers, IOL.
7. *Indian Round Table Conference Proceedings*, 12 November 1930–19 January 1931 (Cmd 3778), p. 147. See also Pirzada (ed.), *The Collected Works of Quaid-E-Azam Mohammad Ali Jinnah, Vol. III, 1926–31* (Karachi, 1986), pp. 498–568.
8. Ibid.
9. Ibid.

10. Geoffrey de Montmorency to Irwin, 24 February 1929, Halifax Papers..
11. Waheed Ahmad (ed.), *Letters of Mian Fazil-i-Husain* (Lahore 1976), p. 77.
12. Ibid., pp. 109–17.
13. Note dated 18 August 1930 by Fazl-i-Husain in Halifax Papers.
14. Ibid.
15. 25 November 1930, Halifax Papers.
16. Ibid.
17. Azim Husain, *Fazl-i-Husain: A Political Biography* (Bombay 1946), pp. 254–56.
18. Ahmad, *Fazl-i-Husain, op.cit.*, p. 116.
19. Coatman to Irwin, 19 December 1930, Halifax Papers.
20. Ibid.
21. Tej Bahadur Sapru Papers, NMML.
22. Pirzada, Vol. III, *op.cit.*
23. Halifax Papers.

Chapter 14

1. Quoted in B.R. Nanda, *In Search of Gandhi, Essays and Reflections* (New Delhi, 2004), p. 80.
2. Quoted in Nanda, *Mahatma Gandhi, op.cit.*, p. 301.
3. Ibid., pp. 307–8.
4. Mujahid, *Quaid-i-Azam and His Times*, Vol. I, *op.cit.*, pp. 145–46.
5. Fazl-i-Husain Papers, IOL.
6. Ahmad (ed.), *Letters of Mian Fazl-i-Husain, op.cit.*, p. 166.
7. Halifax Papers.
8. V.S. Srinivasa Sastri Papers, NMML.
9. R.J. Moore, *The Crisis of Indian Unity, 1917–1940* (Delhi, 1974), p. 231.
10. Jawaharlal Nehru Papers, NMML.

Chapter 15

1. Mujahid, *Quaid-i-Azam and His Times, op.cit.*, p. 143.
2. Chagla, *Roses in December, op.cit.*, p. 103.
3. S.S. Pirzada (ed.), *Quaid-E-Azam, Jinnah's Correspondence* (Karachi, 1977), p. 23.

4. Mujahid, *Quaid-i-Azam and His Times, op.cit.*, p. 171.
5. Jamil-ud-din Ahmad, *Quaid-i-Azam as Seen by His Contemporaries* (Lahore, 1966), p. 174.

Chapter 16

1. Nanda, *Mahatma Gandhi, op.cit.*, p. 335.
2. Templewood Papers, IOL.
3. Attlee's speech on 4 June 1935, in C.H. Philips (ed.), *The Evolution of India and Pakistan, 1858–1947, Selected Documents* (London 1962), p. 318.
4. Templewood Papers.
5. Home Department, File No. 4-4/32, Poll. K.W. NAI.
6. Ahmad, *Letters of Mian Fazl-i-Husain, op.cit.*, pp. 285–86.

Chapter 17

1. Kanji Dwarkadas, *India's Fight for Freedom, 1913–1947: An Eyewitness Story* (Bombay, 1966), pp. 441–42.
2. Hasan, *Muslims and the Congress, op.cit.*, p. 231.
3. Waheed Ahmad (ed.), *Quaid-i-Azam Mohammad Ali Jinnah: The Nation's Voice — Vol. I, Towards Consolidation: Speeches and Statements, March 1935–March 1940.* (Karachi, 1992), p. 12.
4. K.L. Gauba, *Friends and Foes: An Autobiography* (Delhi, 1974), p. 155.
5. Ibid., p. 99.
6. Ahmad, *Speeches and Statements, Vol. I, op.cit.*, pp. 13–14.
7. Ibid., pp. 25–26.
8. Ibid., pp. 26–27.
9. Ibid., p. 30.
10. Ibid., pp. 37–41.
11. Ibid., p. 43.
12. Ibid., p. 63.
13. Ibid., p. 78.
14. Ibid., pp. 90–93.
15. Ibid., p. 99.
16. *Selected Works of Jawaharlal Nehru (SWJN)*, Vol. VII, p. 181.
17. Ibid., pp. 189–90.
18. Ahmad, *Speeches and Statements*, Vol. I, *op.cit.*, p. 118.
19. Ibid., pp. 37–40.

Chapter 18

1. Waheed Ahmad (ed.), *Quaid-i-Azam Mohammad Ali Jinnah: Speeches, Indian Legislative Assembly, 1935–1947* (Karachi, 1991), p. 139.
2. Bhulabhai Desai Papers, NMML.
3. Ahmad, *Letters of Mian Fazl-i-Husain*, *op.cit.*, pp. 596–98.
4. Ahmad, *Speeches and Statements*, Vol. I, *op.cit.*, p. 37.
5. Ibid., p. 101.
6. Jawaharlal Nehru, *An Autobiography* (Delhi, 1960), p. 68.
7. *SWJN*, Vol. VII, p. 463.
8. Ibid., Vol. VIII, p. 24.
9. Quoted by Sharif Al Mujahid, *Quaid i-Azam and His Times*, Vol. I, *op.cit.*, pp. 298–99.
10. Ahmad, *Speeches, and Statements*, Vol. I, *op.cit.*, p. 106.
11. *The Tribune*, 15 October 1936.
12. Home Department, F. 18/10/36 Poll., NAI.
13. Ahmad, *Speeches and Statements*, Vol. I, *op.cit.*, pp. 104–7.
14. Ibid., p. 108.

Chapter 19

1. Ahmad, *Speeches and Statements*, Vol. I, *op.cit.*, p. 41.
2. Quoted in S.M. Ikram, *Modern Muslim India and the Birth of Pakistan, 1858–1951* (Lahore, 1965), p. 138.
3. Ahmad, *Speeches and Statements*, Vol. I, *op.cit.*, p. 127–28.
4. *SWJN*, Vol. VIII, p. 32.
5. Saleem M.M. Qureshi, *The Politics of Jinnah* (Karachi, 1988), p. 131.
6. S.R. Mehrotra, 'The Congress and the Partition of India', in C.H. Philips and M.D. Wainwright (eds), *The Partition of India: Policies and Perspectives, 1935–1947* (London, 1970), p. 198.
7. *Tribune*, 27 April 1937, quoted by Ahmad, *Speeches and Statements*, Vol. I, *op.cit.*, p.141.
8. *Leader*, 9–10 May 1937, quoted in S.R. Mehrotra, 'The Congress', *op.cit.*, p. 197.
9. Linlithgow Papers, F 125/113, IOL. Also in Bimal Prasad, *Pathway to India's Partition: A Nation within a Nation, 1877–1937*, Vol. II (Delhi, 2000), p. 406.

Chapter 20

1. Ahmad, *Speeches and Statements,* Vol. I, *op.cit.*, p. 176.
2. Ibid., p. 177.
3. ibid., 182
4. Dr Mahmudullah Jung in the *Pioneer,* 7 November 1937.
5. Hailey Papers.
6. Ahmad, *Speeches and Statements,* Vol. I, *op.cit.* p. 190.
7. Ibid., p. 192.
8. Ibid., p. 189.
9. Ibid. p. 185.
10. Ibid., p. 189.
11. Ibid., p. 209.
12. Ibid., p. 221.
13. Ibid., p. 228.
14. *Star of India,* 11 January 1938. See ibid., p. 220.
15. Ibid., p. 261.

Chapter 21

1. Ahmad, *Speeches and Statements,* Vol. I, *op.cit.*, p. 253.
2. Jawaharlal Nehru to Mahadev Desai, 14 March 1938, J.N. Papers, NMML.
3. *SWJN,* Vol. VIII, p. 224.
4. Jinnah to Gandhi, 3 March 1938, *CWMG,* Vol. LXVI, p. 481.
5. Gandhi to Amrit Kaur, 22 May 1938. Ibid., Vol. LXVII, p. 92.
6. Ahmad, *Speeches and Statements,* Vol. I, *op.cit.*, p. 231.
7. Roy's weekly, 16 May 1943, in Purshottamdas Thakurdas Papers, File No. 177/1936–43, NMML.
8. C. Khaliquzzaman, *Pathway to Pakistan* (Lahore, 1961), p. 192.
9. Khalid bin Sayeed, 'Jinnah and His Political Strategy', in Philips and Wainwright, *The Partition of India, op.cit.*, p. 286.
10. Ahmad, *Speeches and Statements,* Vol. I, *op.cit.*, p. 224.
11. The Shareef Committee was appointed by the Working Committee of the Bihar Provincial Muslim League to inquire into some grievances of Muslims in Bihar.
12. Jawaharlal Nehru to Jinnah, 14 December 1939, *SWJN,* Vol. X, p. 401.
13. Home Political F. 4/4/34 – 31/97/32, NAI.

14. Harry Haig to Linlithgow, 23 March 1938, Linlithgow Papers, IOL.
15. Hallet to Linlithgow, 8 May 1939, ibid.
16. Wylie to Linlithgow, 29 December 1938, ibid.
17. Linlithgow Papers.
18. Gandhi to Vallabhbhai Patel, 13 October 1938, *CWMG*, Vol. LXVII, p. 433.
19. Haig to Linlithgow, 23 December 1938. Linlithgow Papers.
20. Home Political, F. 18/8/38, NAI.
21. G.B. Pant to Jawaharlal Nehru, 11 February 1938, J.N. Papers.
22. Report on the political events in Bihar for the first half of April 1939, Fortnightly Reports, 7 May 1939, Home Poll., NAI.
23. Home Political, 18/8/38, NAI.
24. Zetland to Linlithgow, 9 May 1939, Linlithgow Papers.
25. Ibid.
26. Syed Mahmud to Jawaharlal Nehru, 23 March 1940, *SWJN*, Vol. XI, p. 381.

Chapter 22

1. Linlithgow to Zetland, 7 September 1937, Linlithgow Papers.
2. Linlithgow to Zetland, 27 October 1937, ibid.
3. *Harijan*, 1 May 1937.
4. Ibid., 17 July 1937.
5. G.D. Birla, *In The Shadow of the Mahatma* (Bombay, 1953), p. 207.
6. *Harijan,* 4 September 1937.
7. Minutes of the Congress Working Committee Meeting held at Delhi in March 1937. All India Congress Committee Papers, File 42/36, NMML, New Delhi.
8. Jawaharlal Nehru to Krishna Menon, 19 July 1937, J.N. Papers, NMML.
9. Jawaharlal Nehru, *India and the World* (London, 1936), pp. 91–92.
10. Linlithgow to Zetland, 19 March 1937, Linlithgow Papers.
11. Erskine to Linlithgow, 10 March 1937, ibid.
12. Ibid.
13. Zetland to Linlithgow, 12 April and 3 May 1937, ibid.

14. Linlithgow to Governors of the Congress-majority Provinces, 18 May 1937, ibid.
15. Linlithgow's Note of Conversation with Gandhi, 4 August 1937, ibid.
16. Quoted in Nanda, *Mahatma Gandhi, op.cit.*, p. 396.
17. Satyamurti's interview to *The Times of India*, reproduced in *Independent India*, 24 April 1938.
18. *Independent India*, 3 July 1938.
19. C. Rajagopalachari to Erskine, 8 March 1940, C. Rajagopalachari Papers, NMML.
20. Chief Secretary of UP Government to Secretary, Home Department, Government of India, 3 October 1937. Home Political, File No. 32/8/37, NAI.
21. Brabourne to Alexander Hastings, 14 April 1938, Brabourne Papers, IOL.
22. Frances Gunther to Jawaharlal Nehru, 13 February 1938, J.N. Papers, NMML.
23. Brabourne to Zetland, 5 August 1938, Brabourne Papers.
24. Bhullabhai Desai to Agatha Harrison, 19 June 1938, Bhullabhai Desai Papers, NMML.
25. Linlithgow Papers.
26. Jawaharlal Nehru to J.B. Kripalani, 27 July 1938. *SWJN*, Vol. IX, p. 90.
27. Linlithgow to Neville Chamberlain, 11 October 1938, Linlithgow Papers.
28. K.M. Munshi, *Pilgrimage to Freedom, 1902–1950* (Bombay, 1967), pp. 41–42.
29. Linlithgow's note of Interview with Jinnah, 28 February 1939, Linlithgow Papers.
30. Linlithgow to Zetland, 17 April 1939, ibid.
31. Linlithgow to Zetland, 12 April 1939, ibid.
32. Khaliquzzaman, *Pathway to Pakistan, op.cit.*, p. 208.
33. Linlithgow to Zetland, 12 April 1939, Linlithgow Papers.
34. Lumley to Linlithgow, 17 June 1939, ibid.
35. Linlithgow to Zetland, 10 June 1939. ibid.
36. R.S. Cassels' Memorandum dated 20 February 1939 enclosed to the report of the proceedings of a meeting held in the Viceroy's House on 26 February 1939, ibid.
37. Linlithgow to Zetland, 19 May 1939, ibid.

Chapter 23

1. Qureshi, *The Politics of Jinnah, op.cit.,* p. 77.
2. Presented on 1 October 1906 at Simla. Quoted in Nanda, *Gandhi: Pan-Islamism, op.cit.,* pp. 70–71.
3. Ibid., p. 71.
4. Mahomed Ali to G. Cunningham, Private Secretary to the Viceroy [August 1930], Mahomed Ali Papers, NMML.
5. Aga Khan to Fazl-i-Hussain, 13 August 1935, in Ahmad, *Letters of Main Fazl-i-Hussain, op.cit.,* p. 429.
6. Burke and Quraishi, *Quaid-i-Azam Mohammad Ali Jinnah, op.cit.,* pp. 194–95.
7. H.N. Pandit, 'British Inspiration Behind Pakistan Movement', *The Indian Review,* June 1977, pp. 9–11.
8. Ibid.
9. J. Coatman, *Years of Destiny, 1926–1932* (London, 1932), pp. 238–40.
10. Halide Edib, *Inside India* (New Delhi, 2002, first published in UK in 1937), p. 243.
11. Jinnah's speech at a party given by Anjuman-e-Islamia at Simla on 13 August 1938 to the members of the newly-formed Muslim League party in the Central Legislative Assembly, in Ahmad, *Speeches and Statements,* Vol. I, *op.cit.,* p. 268.
12. Jinnah's presidential address to the Sind Muslim League Conference held at Karachi on 8 October 1938, ibid., p. 287.
13. *The Times of India,* 11 October 1938.
14. Ibid.
15. *Eastern Times* (Lahore), 30 December 1938.
16. Jinnah's reply to the address of welcome presented to him by the staff of Aligarh Muslim Univerty, in Ahmad, *Speeches and Statements,* Vol. I, *op.cit.,* p. 615.
17. Ibid., p. 332.
18. *The Indian Express,* 1 July 1968.
19. Khaliquzamman, *Pathway to Pakistan, op.cit.,* pp. 204–5.

Chapter 24

1. Quoted in Burke and Quraishi, *Quaid-i-Azam Mohammad Ali Jinnah, op.cit.,* p. 239.
2. Linlithgow Papers.
3. Ibid.

4. Linlithgow to Zetland, 5 September 1939, ibid.
5. Linlithgow to Zetland, 9 September 1939, ibid.
6. Linlithgow's note of interview with Jinnah on 5 October 1939, ibid.
7. Linlithgow Papers, ibid.
8. Ibid.
9. Raghunandan Saran to Jawaharlal Nehru, 17 October 1939, J.N. Papers, NMML.
10. Jawaharlal Nehru to Jinnah, 18 October 1939, *SWJN,* Vol. X, pp. 359–60.
11. Jamil-ud-din Ahmad (ed.), *Speeches and Writings of Mr. Jinnah,* Vol. II (London, 1964), p. 45.
12. Linlithgow's note of interview with Jawaharlal Nehru on 21 September 1939, Linlithgow Papers.
13. Linlithgow to Zetland, 26 September 1939, Linlithgow Papers.
14. Jawaharlal Nehru to Linlithgow, 6 October 1939, *SWJN* Vol. X, p. 172.
15. Lumley to Linlithgow, 13 February 1940, Linlithgow Papers.
16. R.J. Moore, *Churchill, Cripps and India, 1939–1945* (Oxford, 1979) p. 26.
17. Ibid., p. 28.
18. Linlithgow to Zetland 9 December 1939, Linlithgow Papers.
19. Linlithgow's note of interview with Jinnah, 6 February 1940, Linlithgow Papers.
20. Ibid.

Chapter 25

1. Philips Talbot, *An American Witness to Partition* (New Delhi 2007), p. 14.
2. Ahmad, *Speeches and Statements,* Vol. I, *op.cit.,* pp. 486–95.
3. Ibid.
4. Ibid.
5. *The Hindu,* 27 March 1940.
6. *SWJN,* Vol. XI, p. 17.
7. *The Tribune,* 29 March 1940.
8. *The Hindu,* 4 April 1940.
9. *The Manchester Guardian,* 2 April 1940.
10. *Harijan,* 6 April 1940.
11. Ibid.

12. Linlithgow Papers.
13. Lumley to Linlithgow 30 March 1940, Linlithgow Papers.
14. *The Tribune*, 11 September 1940.
15. *The Hindu*, 17 April 1940.
16. In a letter dated 19 December 1940 to G.D. Birla, Purshotamdas Thakurdas Papers, F. No. 177/1936–43, NMML.
17. Phillips Talbot, *An American Witness, op.cit.,* p. 5.
18. Tahira to Jawaharlal Nehru, J.N. Papers, NMML.
19. *The Hindu*, 11 July 2005.
20. See Moore, *Churchill, Cripps and India, op.cit.,* p. 27–29.
21. Ibid., p. 35.
22. Ibid., p. 36.
23. Burke and Quraishi, *Quaid-i-Azam Mohammad Ali Jinnah, op.cit.,* p. 257.
24. Moore, *Churchill, op.cit.,* pp. 36–37.
25. R.J. Moore, *Endgames of Empire* (Delhi, 1988), p. 85.

Chapter 26

1. Quoted in B.R. Nanda, *Mahatma Gandhi, op.cit.,* p. 445.
2. Ibid.
3. Linlithgow to Amery, 15 May 1941, Linlithgow Papers.
4. Jinnah's presidential address to the All India Muslim League session held at Madras on 14 April 1941, in Waheed Ahmad (ed.), *Quaid-i-Azam Mohammad Ali Jinnah: The Nation's Voice — Vol. II, United we Win: Annotated Speeches and Statements, April 1940–April 1942* (Karachi, 1996), p. 221.
5. Jinnah's Statement to the *News Chronicle* at Bombay on 24 December 1941, ibid., p. 336.
6. See also Francis Williams, *A Prime Minister Remembers: The War and The Post War Memoirs of the Rt Hon. Earl Attlee* (London, 1961), p. 206.
7. Yuvraj Krishan, 'Partition of India: An Anglo-Muslim League Conspiracy', *History Today,* No. 5, 2004.
8. Ibid.
9. Ibid.
10. Roosevelt to Churchill, telegram via Harry Hopkins (personal aide to Roosevelt), 11 April 1942. Quoted in Narendra Singh Sarila, *The Shadow of the Great Game: The Untold Story of India's Partition* (New Delhi, 2005), p. 112.
11. Ibid., pp. 112–13.
12. Ibid., p. 113.

13. Burke and Quraishi, *Quaid-i-Azam Mohammad Ali Jinnah, op.cit.*, p. 263.
14. Ibid., pp. 263–64.
15. Ibid., 264.
16. Nanda, *The Making of a Nation, op.cit.*, p. 288.
17. Telegram dated 21 July 1942 from Linlithgow to G.S. Bajpai, the Agent-General for India in Washington, in Nicholas Mansergh (ed.), *The Transfer of Power, 1942–1947*, Vol. II (London, 1971), p. 423.
18. Waheed Ahmad (ed.), *Quaid-i-Azam Mohammad Ali Jinnah: The Nation's Voice — Vol. III, Unity, Faith and Discipline: Annotated Speeches and Statements, May 1942–October 1944* (Karachi, 1997), p. 74.
19. B.R. Nanda, *Jawaharlal Nehru: Rebel and Statesman* (New Delhi, 1995), p. 147.

Chapter 27

1. Martin Gilbert, *Servant of India* (London, 1966), p. 202.
2. Owen Bennett Jones, *Pakistan: Eye of the Storm* (New Haven and London, 2002), p. 12.
3. Montagu–Chelmsford Report, 1918. See A.C. Banerjee, *Indian Constitutional Documents, 1757–1947, Vol. III, 1917–1935* (Calcutta, 1961), p. 14.
4. Reading Papers.
5. *Mohamed Ali Jinnah — An Ambassador of Unity: His Speeches and Writings 1915–1917* (Madras, 1918), pp. 46–47.
6. Ikram, *Modern Muslim India and the Birth of Pakistan, op.cit.*, pp. 356–57.
7. Aga Khan to Fazl-i-Husain, 13 August 1935, in Ahmad, *Letters of Mian Fazl-i-Husain, op.cit.*, pp. 429.
8. Bimal Prasad, *Pathway to India's Partition: A Nation within a Nation, Vol. II, 1877–1937* (New Delhi, 2000) p. 406.
9. Ayesha Jalal, *Self and Sovereignty* (London, 2000), p. 468.
10. *Dawn*, 26 March 1946.
11. *The Indian Annual Register*, January–June 1946, Vol. I, pp. 196–97.
12. George Abell to Wavell, 18 November 1946, in N. Mansergh (ed.), *The Transfer of Power*, Vol. IX (London, 1980).
13. Diana Mansergh (ed.), *Independent Years. The Selected Indian and Commonwealth Papers of Prof. Nicholas Mansergh* (New Delhi, 1999), pp. 60–61.

Chapter 28

1. Sri Prakasa, *Pakistan: Birth and Early Years* (Delhi, 1965), p. 37.
2. Jamil-ud-din Ahmad, *Speeches and Writings of Mr. Jinnah*, Vol. II, *op.cit.*, pp. 399–405.
3. Editorial in *The Statesman* (Calcutta), reprinted in *Deccan Times*, 12 October, 1947.
4. Sharif Al Mujahid, *Quaid-i-Zaam Jinnah: Studies in Interpretation* (Karachi, 1981), p. 249.
5. Wolpert, *Jinnah of Pakistan*, *op.cit.*, p. 340.
6. Akbar S. Ahmed, *Jinnah, Pakistan and Islamic Identity: The Search for Saladin* (London, 1977), p. 197.
7. Ibid.
8. Jamil-ud-din Ahmad, *Speeches and Writings*, Vol. II, *op.cit.*, p. 488.
9. Ziauddin Ahmad, *Shaheed-E-Milat, Lialquat Ali Khan, Builder of Pakistan* (Karachi, 1990), p. 94.
10. Bennett Jones, *Pakistan*, *op.cit.*, pp. 12–14.

Select Bibliography

Private Papers

India Office Library, London

Brabourne Papers.
Harcourt Butler Papers.
Chelmsford Papers.
Fazl-i-Husain Papers.
Malcolm Hailey Papers.
Halifax (Irwin) Papers.
Harry Haig Papers.
Linlithgow Papers.
Montagu Papers.
Reading Papers.
Templewood (Samual Hoare) Papers.
Zetland Papers.
Alexander Muddiman's Note, 31.3.1925.
Frederick Whyte's Report, 30.3.1925.

R/3/1/109. Lord Wavell's Breakdown Plan.
R/3/1/171–74. Lord Wavell's Breakdown Plan.
IOR/L/PO/10/24. Wavell's Weekly Letters to the Secretary of State for India, January–March 1947.
IOR/L/PO/10/21–4. Private and Secret Weekly Letters between SOS and Viceroy, 1943 to 1947.

Nehru Memorial Museum and Library, New Delhi

All India Congress Committee Papers.
Bhulabhai Desai Papers.
Harcourt Butler Papers (on microfilm).
Chelmsford Papers (on microfilm).

Harry Haig Papers (on microfilm).
Halifax Papers (on microfilm).
Jamiat-ul-Ulema-i-Hind Papers (on microfilm). Minutes and Presidential Addresses, 1925–78.
Linlithgow Papers (on microfilm).
Syed Mahmud Papers.
Muhamad Ali Papers.
Jawaharlal Nehru Papers.
Motilal Nehru Papers.
Oral History Transcripts.
Govind Ballabh Pant Papers (on microfilm).
Purshotamdas Thakurdas Papers.
C. Rajagopalachari Papers.
Tej Bahadur Sapru Papers (on microfilm).
Assorted Diaries of V.S. Srinivasa Sastri.

National Gandhi Museum, New Delhi

M.K. Gandhi Papers.

National Archives of India

Government of India, Home Political Department Files.

Proceedings and Reports

The Legislative Assembly Debates.

All Parties Conference 1928. *Report of the Committee appointed by the Conference to determine the principles of the Constitution for India, together with a summary of the proceedings of the Conference held at Lucknow* (Allahabad).
——— *Supplementary Report of the Committee* (Allahabad).
Proceedings of The All Parties National Convention (1928–29) (Allahabad).

Parliamentary Papers

(Montagu-Chelmsford) Report on the Indian Constitutional Reforms, 1918 (Cmd 9109).
Proceedings of the Indian Round Table Conference, First Session, 12 November 1930–19 January 1931 (Cmd 3778) (London, 1931).
―――― Second Session, 7 September 1931–1 December 1931 (Cmd. 3997) (London, 1932).
―――― Federal Structure Committee and Minorities Committee 1932 (London, 1932), 3 Vols.
―――― Third Session, 17 November–24 December 1932 (Cmd 4238) (London, 1933).

Published Sources (Primary)

Ahmad, Jamil-ud-din (ed.), *Speeches and Writings of Mr. Jinnah*, 7th ed., 2 Vols (Lahore, 1964).
Ahmad, Waheed (ed.), *Letters of Mian Fazl-i-Husain* (Lahore, 1976).
――――, *Quaid-i-Azam Mohammad Ali Jinnah: The Nation's Voice — Towards Consolidation: Speeches and Statements, March 1935–March 1940* (Karachi, 1992).
――――, Vol. II, *United We Win: Annotated Speeches and Statements, April 1940-April 1942* (Karachi, 1996).
――――, Vol. III, *Unity, Faith and Discipline: Annotated Speeches and Statements, May 1942–October 1944* (Karachi, 1997).
――――, *Quaid-i-Azam Mohammad Ali Jinnah: Speeches, Indian Legislative Assembly, 1935–1947* (Karachi, 1991).
――――, *Jinnah-Irwin Correspondence (1927–1930)* (Lahore, 1969).
Banerjee, A.C., *Indian Constitutional Documents 1917–1935*, Vol. III (Calcutta, 1961).
Desai, Mahadev, *The Diaries* (Ahmedabad, 1953).
Gandhi, M.K., *Correspondence with the Government 1942–44* (Ahmedabad, 1945).
――――, *The Collected Works of Mahatma Gandhi*.
Gopal, S. (ed.), *Selected Works of Jawaharlal Nehru*.
Hasan, Mushirul (ed.), *Muslims and the Congress: Select Correspondence of Dr. M.A. Ansari, 1912–1935* (New Delhi, 1979).

Iqbal, Muhammad, *Letters of Iqbal to Jinnah* (Lahore, 1943).
Jayakar, M.R., *The Story of My Life, Vol. I, 1873–1922* (Bombay, 1958).
Jinnah, Mohammad Ali, *An Ambassador of Unity: His Speeches and Writings 1912–1917*, including 'A Pen Portrait' of Jinnah by Sarojini Naidu (Madras, 1918).
———, *Speeches as Governor-General of Pakistan, 1947–1948*, 7th ed. (Lahore, 1976).
Joshi, V.C. (ed.), *Lala Lajpat Rai's Writings and Speeches, Vols I & II* (Delhi, 1966).
Khan, Aga, *The Memoirs of Aga Khan: World Enough and Time* (London, 1954).
Mansergh, Nicholas (editor-in-chief), *Constitutional Relations Between Britain and India: The Transfer of Power, 1942–7*, 12 vols (London, 1970–83).
Mansergh, Diana (ed.), *Independent Years: The Selected Indian and Commonwealth Papers of Prof. Nicholas Mansergh* (New Delhi, 1999).
Mitra, N.N. (ed.), *The Indian Annual Register.*
Mohammad, Shan (ed.), *Writings and Speeches of Sir Syed Ahmad Khan* (Bombay, 1972).
———, *The Indian Muslims: A Documentary Record* (Meerut, 1983).
Montagu, Venetia, (ed.), *An Indian Diary by Edwin S. Montagu* (London, 1930).
Moon, Penderel (ed.,) *Wavell: The Viceroy's Journal* (Delhi, 1977).
Moran, Lord, *Winston Churchill: The Struggle for Survival, 1940–1965*, taken from the diaries of Lord Moran (London, 1966).
Mujahid, Sharif Al, *Quaid-i-Azam Jinnah: Studies in Interpretation* (Karachi, 1981), appendices contain texts of Muslim League resolutions and important speeches of Jinnah.
Philips, C.H. (ed.), *The Evolution of India and Pakistan, 1858–1947: Select Documents* (London, 1970).
Pirzada, Syed Sharifuddin (ed.), *The Foundation of Pakistan, All India Muslim League Documents, Vol. I 1906–1921; Vol. 2, 1924–1947* (Karachi, 1970).
———, *The Collected Works of Quaid-E-Azam Mohammad Ali Jinnah*, 3 vols (Karachi, 1984–1986).
———, *Quaid-E-Azam Jinnah's Correspondence*, 3rd rev. and enl. ed. (Karachi, 1977).

Ravinder Kumar and Hari Dev Sharma (eds), *Selected Works of Motilal Nehru*.
Yusufi, Khurshid Ahmad Khan (ed.), *Speeches, Statements and Messages of the Quaid-E-Azam* (Lahore, 1952).
Zaidi, A.M., and S.G. (eds.), *The Encyclopedia of the Indian National Congress* (New Delhi, 1976–1980).
Zaidi, Z.H. (ed.), *Jinnah Papers: Prelude to Pakistan*, 2 vols (Islamabad, 1993).
Zetland, Second Marquess of, *Essayez: The Memoirs of Lawrence, Second Marquess of Zetland* (London, 1956).

Newspapers

Amrita Bazar Patrika, Calcutta.
Bombay Chronicle, Bombay.
Civil & Military Gazette, Lahore.
Dawn, Delhi (later Karachi).
Eastern Times, Lahore.
Harijan (weekly), Ahmedabad.
Hindu, Madras.
Hindustan Times, Delhi.
Independent, Allahabad.
Independent India (weekly), Bombay.
Indian Express, Delhi.
Leader, Allahabad.
Manchester Guardian, Manchester.
National Herald, Lucknow.
Pioneer, Lucknow.
Statesman, Calcutta.
Times, London.
Times of India, Bombay.
Tribune, Lahore (later Ambala, Chandigarh).
Young India (weekly), Ahmedabad.

Published Sources (Secondary)

Ahmad, Akbar S., *Jinnah, Pakistan and Islamic Identity: The Search for Saladin* (London, 1997).
Ahmad, Jamil-ud-din, *Quaid-i-Azam as Seen by His Contemporaries* (Lahore, 1966).

Ahmad, Ziauddin, *Shaheed-E-Millat Liaquat Ali Khan, Builder of Pakistan* (Karachi, 1990).
Akbar, M.J., *The Shade of Swords: Jihad and the Conflict Between Islam and Christianity* (New Delhi, 2002).
Ambedkar, B.R., *Pakistan or the Partition of India* (Bombay, 1946).
Attlee, Clement R., *As It Happened* (London, 1954).
Azad, Maulana Abul Kalam, *India Wins Freedom* (Hyderabad, 1988).
Aziz, K.K., *A History of the Idea of Pakistan, I & II* (London, 1987).
Baig, M.R.A., *Jinnah* (Patna, 1996).
Beg, Aziz, *Jinnah and His Times: A Biography* (Islamabad, 1986).
Bimal Prasad, *Pathway to India's Partition*, vol. 1: *The Foundations of Muslim Nationalism*; vol. II: *A Nation within a Nation, 1877–1937* (New Delhi, 1999, 2000).
Birla, G.D., *In the Shadow of the Mahatma* (Bombay, 1953).
Bolitho, Hector, *Jinnah: Creator of Pakistan* (London, 1956, first published 1954).
Brecher, Michael, *Nehru: A Political Biography* (London, 1959).
Brown, Judith, *Gandhi's Rise to Power: Indian Politics 1915–1922* (Cambridge, 1977).
Brown, Judith and Francis Robinson (eds), *Oxford History of British Empire, The Twentieth Century* (Oxford, 1998).
Burke, S.M. and Quraishi, Salim Al Din, *The British Raj: An Historical Review* (Karachi, 1994).
———, *Quaid-i-Azam Muhammad Ali Jinnah: His Personality and His Politics* (Karachi, 1997).
Chagla, M.C., *Roses in December: An Autobiography* (Bombay, 1974).
Coatman, J., *Years of Destiny: India, 1926–1932* (London, 1932).
Coupland, R., *Indian Politics, 1936–1942* (Oxford, 1943).
Dani, A.H. (ed.), *Quaid-i-Azam Mohammad Ali Jinnah and Pakistan* (Islamabad, 1981).
Durga Das, *India from Curzon to Nehru and After* (London, 1969).
Dwarkadas, Kanji, *Gandhiji Through My Diary Leaves, 1915–1948* (Bombay, 1963).
———, *Ruttie Jinnah: The Story of a Great Friendship* (Bombay, n.d.).
———, *India's Fight for Freedom, 1913–1947: An Eyewitness Story* (Bombay, 1966).

Edib, Halide, *Inside India* (New Delhi, 2002), with an introduction by M. Hasan.
Fischer, Louis, *The Life of Mahatma Gandhi* (London, 1954).
Fuller, Bampfylde, *Studies of Indian Life and Sentiment* (London, 1910).
Gauba, K.L., *Friends and Foes: An Autobiography* (Delhi, 1974).
Gilbert, Martin, *Servant of India* (London, 1966).
Glendevon, John, *The Viceroy at Bay: Lord Linlithgow in India, 1936–1943* (London, 1971).
Govind Sahai, *42 Rebellion: An Authentic Review of the Great Upheaval of 1942* (Delhi, 1947).
Gunther, John, *Inside Asia* (London, 1939).
Haider, Khwaja Razi, *Ruttie Jinnah: The Story Told and Untold* (Karachi, 2004).
Halifax, Earl of, *Fullness of Days* (London, 1957).
Hardy, Peter, *The Muslims of British India* (Karachi 1973).
Hodson, H.V., *The Great Divide: Britain-India-Pakistan* (London and Karachi, 1969).
———, *Pakistan, Past and Present* (London, 1977).
Husain, Azim, *Sir Fazl-i-Husain: A Political Biography* (Bombay, 1946).
Hutchins, Francis, *Spontaneous Revolution: The Quit India Movement* (Delhi, 1971).
Ikram, S.M., *Modern Muslim India and the Birth of Pakistan 1858–1951* (Lahore, 1965).
Ilahi Bakhsh, *With the Quaid-i-Azam During the Last Days* (Karachi, 1978).
Indian Magazine and Review (London) (April 1896).
Jalal, Ayesha, *The Sole Spokesman, Jinnah, the Muslim League and the Demand for Pakistan* (Cambridge, 1985).
———, *Self and Sovereignty: Individual and Community in South Asian Islam Since 1850* (New York).
Jinnah, Fatima, *My Brother*, (ed. Sharif Al Mujahid) (Karachi, 1987).
Johnson, Allan Campbell, *Mission with Mountbatten* (London, 1951).
Jones, Owen Bennett, *Pakistan Eye of the Storm* (New Delhi, 2002).
Kaura, Uma, *Muslims and Indian Nationalism: The Emergence of the Demand for India's Partition, 1928–1940* (New Delhi, 1977).

Khaliquzzaman, Chaudhry, *Pathway to Pakistan* (Lahore, 1961).
Low, D.A. (ed.), *Soundings in Modern Indian History* (Berkeley 1968).
———, 'The Government and First Non-Cooperation Movement 1920–1922', *Journal of Asian Studies,* XXV, 2.
Lumby, E.W.R., *The Transfer of Power in India, 1945–47* (London, 1954).
Macmillan, Harold, *Winds of Change* (London, 1966).
Majumdar, S.K., *Jinnah and Gandhi* (Calcutta, 1966).
Marquand, David, *Ramsay MacDonald* (London, 1977).
Mehrotra, S.R., *Towards India's Freedom and Partition* (Delhi, 1979).
———, 'The Congress and the Partition of India', in C.H. Phillips and M.D. Wainwright (eds), *The Partition of India: Policies and Perspectives 1935–47* (London, 1970).
Menon, V.P., *The Transfer of Power in India* (Bombay, 1957).
Montagu, Ashley (ed.), *Nature of Human Aggression* (New York, 1976).
Moon, Penderel, *Divide and Quit* (London, 1961).
Moore, R. J., *The Crisis of Indian Unity, 1917–1940* (Delhi, 1974).
———, *Churchill, Cripps and India, 1939–1945* (Oxford, 1979).
———, *Endgames of Empire* (Delhi, 1988).
Mosley, Leonard, *The Last Days of the British Raj* (London, 1961).
Mujeeb, M., *Indian Muslims* (London, 1967).
Mujahid, Sharif Al (ed.), *Quaid-i-Azam and His Times — A Compendium, Vol. I, 1876–1937* (Karachi, 1990).
Munshi, K.M., *Pilgrimage to Freedom, 1902–1950* (Bombay, 1967).
Nanda, B.R., *Mahatma Gandhi : A Biography* (London, 1958).
———, *The Nehrus: Motilal and Jawaharlal* (London, 1962, new edition, New Delhi, 2008).
———, *Gokhale, Indian Moderates and the British Raj* (Delhi, 1977).
———, *Gandhi and His Critics* (New Delhi, 1985).
———, *Gandhi: Pan-Islamism, Imperialism and Nationalism in India* (Bombay, 1989).
———, *Jawaharlal Nehru: Rebel and Statesman* (New Delhi, 1995).
———, *The Making of a Nation: India's Road to Independence* (New Delhi, 1998).
———, *In Search of Gandhi: Essays and Reflections* (New Delhi, 2004).

Nehru, Jawaharlal, *India and the World* (London, 1936).
———, *Discovery of India* (Calcutta, 1946).
———, *The Unity of India* (London, 1948).
———, *An Autobiography*, (Delhi 1960).
Page, David, *Prelude to Partition: The Indian Muslims and the Imperial System of Control, 1920–1930* (New Delhi, 1982).
Pandit, H.N., 'British Inspiration Behind Pakistan Movement', *The Indian Review* (June 1977).
Panigrahi, D.N., *India's Partition: The Story of Imperialism in Retreat* (London, 2004).
Parthasarathy, Rangaswami, *A Hundred Years of Hindu* (Madras, 1978).
'The Partition of India', Special Issue of *Indo-British Review*, vol. 14, no. 2 1988.
Philips, C.H. and Wainwright, M.D. (eds.), *The Partition of India: Policies and Perspectives, 1935–1947* (London, 1970).
Pirzada, Syed Sharifuddin, *Evolution of Pakistan* (Karachi, 1963).
———, *Some Aspects of Quaid-i-Azam's Life* (Islamabad, 1978).
Pyarelal, *Mahatma Gandhi: The Last Phase*, 2 vols (Ahmedabad, 1956–58).
Quaid-i-Azam Number, *Pakistan Journal of History and Culture* vol. XIV, no. 2, July–December 1993 (Islamabad).
Qureshi, Saleem, M.M., *The Politics of Jinnah* (Karachi, 1988).
Rajendra Prasad, *India Divided* (Bombay, 1946).
Rao, B. Shiva, *India's Freedom Movement: Some Notable Figures* (Delhi, 1972).
Reading, Marquess of, *Rufus Issacs, First Marquess of Reading* (London, 1945).
Rizvi, Gowher, *Linlithgow and India: A Study of British Policy and the Political Impasse in India, 1936–43* (London, 1978).
Robinson, Francis, *Separation Among Indian Muslims: The Politics of the United Provinces Muslims, 1860–1923* (Cambridge, 1974).
Saiyid, Matlubal Hasan, *A Political Study of Mohammed Ali Jinnah* (Delhi, 1986).
Sarila, Narendra Singh, *The Shadow of the Great Game: The Untold Story of India's Partition* (New Delhi, 2005).
Sayeed, Khalid bin, *Pakistan, the Formative Phase, 1857–1948* (London, 1968).
———, 'Jinnah and his Political Strategy', in C.H. Phillips and M.D. Wainwright (eds), *The Partition of India: Policies and Perspectives 1935–47* (London, 1970).

Seervai, H.M., *Partition of India : Legend and Reality* (Bombay, 1990).
Shukla, C. (ed.), *Incidents of Gandhiji's Life* (Bombay, 1949).
Smith, W.C., *Modern Islam in India : A Social Analysis* (Lahore, 1969).
Spear, Percival and Margaret, *India Remembered* (Delhi, 1981).
Sri Prakasa, *Pakistan : Birth and Early Years* (Delhi, 1965).
Talbot, Phillips, *An American Witness to Partition* (New Delhi, 2007).
Templewood Viscount (Samuel Hoare), *Nine Troubled Years* (London 1954).
Tinker, H., *Experiment With Freedom: India and Pakistan 1947* (London, 1967).
Tomlinson, B.R., *The Indian National Congress and the Raj, 1929–1947* (London, 1976).
Williams Francis, *A Prime Minister Remembers: The War and Post-War Memoirs of Rt. Hon. Earl Attlee* (London, 1961).
Wolpert, Stanley, *Jinnah of Pakistan* (New York, 1984).
Wrench, John Evelyn, *The Immortal Years* (London, 1954).
Yuvraj Krishan, *Understanding Partition* (Mumbai, 2002).
———, 'The Partition of India: An Anglo-Muslim League Conspiracy', *History Today,* no. 5, 2004.
Zakaria, Rafiq, *The Man Who Divided India: An Insight into Jinnah's Leadership and Its Aftermath* (Mumbai, 2001).

About the Author

Mr B.R. Nanda was born in Rawalpindi (now in Pakistan) in 1917. He graduated from Government College, Lahore, with honours in History in 1937 and two years later, took his Master's degree in History with a First Class and the first position in the University of Punjab. Mr Nanda joined the Indian Railways in 1942 and served as a senior executive in various positions. His book, *Mahatma Gandhi: A Biography* was published in 1958 and has since been reprinted in the UK, the US, and India, and has been translated into French, Spanish, Italian and several Indian languages. His second book, *The Nehrus: Motilal and Jawaharlal* was simultaneously published in 1962 by Allen & Unwin in England and John Day, New York, and translated into several languages.

Mr Nanda's other books include *Gokhale, Gandhi and the Nehrus: Studies in Indian Nationalism* (1974); *Gokhale, the Indian Moderates and the British Raj* (1977); *Gandhi: A Pictorial Biography* (1972); *Jawaharlal Nehru: A Pictorial Biography* (1980); *Gandhi and his Critics* (1985); *Gandhi, Pan-Islamism, Imperialism and Nationalism in India* (1989); *In Gandhi's Footsteps: The Life and Times of Jamnalal Bajaj* (1990); *Jawaharlal Nehru, Rebel & Statesman* (1995); *The Making of a Nation: India's Road to Independence* (1998), *In Search of Gandhi* (2002), *Witness to Partition* (2003), and *Three Statesmen* (2004).

Mr Nanda edited *Nehru and the Modern World* for UNESCO, based on the Nehru Round Table held in New Delhi in 1965. His other edited works include *Socialism in India* (1972); *Indian Foreign Policy: The Nehru Years* (1975); *Science and Technology in India* (1977); *Essays in Modern Indian History* (1980) and *Mahatma Gandhi 125 Years* (1995). He was the Chief Editor of the *Collected Works of Pandit Govind Ballabh Pant,* of which eighteen volumes have been published. He also edited fifteen volumes of the series, *Collected Works of Lala Lajpat Rai.*

In September 1965, Mr Nanda was invited to head the 'Nehru Memorial Museum & Library'. As its Founder-Director for fourteen years, he made it the premier institution for historical research in the country.

Mr Nanda has been a member of the Indian Historical Records Commission, a Trustee of the Jawaharlal Nehru Memorial Fund and the Gandhi Memorial Society, and Chairman of the National Gandhi Museum at Delhi. He was honoured with the National Fellowship of the Indian Council of Social Science Research, New Delhi in 1979 and the Dadabhai Naoroji Memorial Prize in 1981, and was awarded the Padma Vibhushan for his literary work in 2003 by the President of India.

Index

Ahmad, Waheed 260
Aiyar, Ramaswami 74
Aiyar, Sir Sivaswami 82
Al Hilal 26
Ali, Ameer 19, 25
Aligarh school of politics 20
Ali, Mahomed 26, 27, 56, 68, 71, 95, 101, 105, 109, 135, 200, 220, 255, 279
Ali, Maulana Zafar 106, 114, 181
Ali, Rahmat 164, 256, 257, 318
Ali, Shaukat 56, 105, 116, 212, 215
Allahabad Congress 24
All India Congress Committee 11, 29, 68, 70, 79, 100, 102, 207, 246, 273, 292, 303
All India Humanitarian Conference 55
All India Muslim Conference 153–54, 165, 174, 177, 192, 330
All India Muslim League 13, 17, 18, 25, 98; alignment with Indian National Congress 51; annual expenditure of 165, 192; Bombay session 28, 29, 196; boycott of Simon Commission 108, 114; Calcutta session 114, 117; cooperation with Congress in formation of interim government 312; on drafting of Swaraj constitution for India 108; and flag of Islam 217; Lahore session 105, 283, 284, 331; Lucknow session 29, 212, 216, 217, 219, 234, 257; Pakistan resolution 281; Pakistan schemes for territorial adjustment and partition 250; performance in general election in 1937 234; right to speak on behalf of Indian Muslims 310; rival groups 176; for safeguarding Muslim communal individuality 33; scheme for partition of India 276; views on 'Quit India' movement 307
All India Students' Conference 185
All Muslim Parties Conference 122
All-Parties Conference 97, 98, 108, 109, 110, 111, 112, 113, 114, 115, 121, 122, 124, 127, 127, 203, 330
All-Parties National Convention 159, 160
All-party Parliamentary Delegation 312
Anglo-Indian press in India 22
Anglo–Muslim alliance 26, 46, 152
Anti-Non-Cooperation Society 76

Arthur Road jail 169
Attlee, Clement 105, 173, 291, 298, 299, 322
Azad, Abul Kalam 26, 27, 96, 106, 152, 219, 230, 237, 270, 282
Aziz, Abdul 176

Baig, M.R.A. 158
Bajpai, Sir Girja Shankar 287, 288
Balkan Wars 27
Bande Mataram 38, 213, 216, 220, 243, 248, 280
Banerjea, Surendranath 5, 21, 64, 83
Banker, Shankarlal 38, 58, 60
Bar examination 3
Basu, B.N. 38, 74
Bengal Criminal Law (Amendment) Ordinance 89
Bengal, partition of 15, 27, 54, 83, 86, 220
Bengal Regulation III 88
Benn, Wedgwood 129, 131, 133, 137, 138, 142, 143, 145, 149, 154, 167
Besant, Annie 34, 38, 39, 40, 42, 46, 54, 55, 56, 57, 64, 66, 72, 74, 109, 114, 201
Bhave, Acharya Vinoba 295
Bhulabhai Desai–Liaquat Ali Pact 312
Bombay Bar Association 21
Bombay Chronicle 40, 49, 58, 65, 180
Bombay Corporation 11, 12
Bombay Legislative Council 23
Bombay News Chronicle 46
Bombay Presidency Association 11, 12
Bonnerjee, W.C. 15

Bose, Sarat Chandra 230
Bose, Subhas Chandra 4, 111, 127, 129, 132, 219, 221, 230, 269
Brabourne, Lord 210, 243, 244, 247, 248, 250, 319
British India, sovereign states in 260
British Parliament 19, 21, 23, 31, 32, 66, 87, 115, 128, 131, 132, 133, 136, 139, 158, 162, 172, 181, 184, 203, 245, 266
British policy, towards freedom of India 294–95
British Raj 14, 15, 18, 25, 33, 55, 104, 131, 172, 305, 314, 317, 323, 332, 351; Hindu domination on 253; Indian Muslims as natural allies of 26; quit India resolution and 303
Butler, Sir Harcourt 22, 78

Cabinet Mission Plan 321, 332
Calcutta Congress 21, 134
Central Sikh League 108
Chagla, M.C. 9, 10, 35, 46, 105, 114, 117, 163
Chaiwalla, Mohammad Ali 9
Chamberlain, Neville 246, 274, 288, 290
Charter of Fundamental Rights 112
Chauri Chaura 79, 80
Chelmsford, Lord 39, 40, 42, 53, 54, 59, 71, 76, 77, 316
Christian Mission School 2
Churchill, Winston 172, 173, 274, 288, 289, 291, 292, 293, 294, 297, 299, 300, 301, 302, 308

civil disobedience campaign 59, 64, 79, 80, 81, 128, 132, 133, 135, 274; for freedom of India after World War II 290–93; Gandhi's cancellation of 94; under Gandhi's leadership 147, 168, 235; Jinnah's attitude towards individual 289–93; for restoration of Masjid Shahidganj 181
Civil War in America 22
Communal Award 173, 174, 176, 180, 215, 255, 257, 318; attitude of Indian National Congress on 179; British Premier's 194; Hindu Mahasabha opposition to 179; and prospects for Hindu–Muslim unity 178
communal riots 95, 98, 228, 231, 232, 282, 321, 332
Comrade 26
Congress–League Pact 180
Congress–League scheme 30, 32, 43, 50, 51, 101, 122
Congress party *see* Indian National Congress
Congress Socialist Party 187
'Congress tyranny' 225, 320, 331
Coronation Durbar 27
Cotton, Henry 5, 11
Cripps mission 299, 300, 311; and Jinnah 302–3
Cripps, Sir Stafford 206, 224, 297, 299, 300
Curzon, Lord 11, 78

Dandi march 136
Das, C.R. 62, 66, 69, 70, 71, 74, 81, 85
Defence of India Act 58

Defence of India Rules 277
Delhi Manifesto 131, 132
Delhi Muslim Conference 102, 103, 106, 108, 113, 142, 144
Delhi War Conference 53
Desai, Bhulabhai 186, 193, 244, 312
Direct Action Day 321, 332
The Discovery of India (Nehru) 241, 263
Draft Declaration 298
Dutt, R.C. 5, 22
Dwarkadas, Jamnadas 42, 58, 60
Dwarkadas, Kanji 35, 38, 176

East India Association 6
Edib, Halide 257
electoral colleges 18; Morley's scheme of 22
electorates, separate 22, 23, 28, 30, 31, 32, 34, 75, 98, 102, 114, 124, 142, 143, 200; and allocation of seats to various religious minorities 173; Congress opposition to 230; Gandhi protest against grant of 170; incorporation in electoral system 317; *vs.* joint electorates 155; Lord Minto and promise of 17; for Muslims in Minto–Morley reforms 45, 125, 203, 315; opposition for Muslims for having 12; for other depressed classes 155; with proportional representation of Muslims 18; for Shia community 231; Shimla Deputation and incorporation of 19

Englishman 18

Fatwas 259
Fazl-i-Husain, Sir 139, 140, 141, 142, 143, 144, 145, 152, 153, 155, 156, 160, 161, 165, 167, 175, 177, 181, 192, 193, 194, 195, 196, 319
Finance Bill 88, 90, 91
Forward Bloc 305
'Fourteen Points' for constitutional safeguards 124, 125, 142, 144, 160, 186, 224, 257, 318
Fraser, Lovat 19, 315
Free Press Journal 163

Gandhi–Irwin Pact (1931) 150, 152, 153, 168, 274
Gandhi–Jinnah talks 310, 311
Gandhi, M.K. 4, 8, 9, 48, 58, 69, 70; cancellation of civil disobedience campaign 94; Dandi march 136, 147; meetings with Lord Irwin 151; meeting with Jinnah at Bombay 221; non-cooperation programme 80
Gauba, Khalid Latif 181
Gazette of India 263
George, Lloyd 60, 78, 79, 130, 131, 132
George V, King 27, 66
Ghose, Aurobindo 4
Ghuznavi, A.H. 103, 143
'giants of Indian politics' 74
Gokhale, Gopal Krishna 5, 11, 21, 23, 29, 31, 45, 48, 51, 52, 64, 76, 184
Government of India Act 87, 185, 208, 236, 247

Graham, Sir Frederick 2
Grahams Shipping and Trading Company 1, 2, 3
Grand Old Man of India *see* Naoroji, Dadabhai
Gujarat Political Conference 52
Gunther, Frances 223, 243
Gunther, John 223
Gurjar Sabha 49

Hailey, Sir Malcolm 86, 87, 138, 140, 215
Harijan 226, 235, 236, 238, 282
hartal 60, 62, 77
Hasan, Wazir 28, 29, 30, 51, 75, 185, 215
The Hindu 55
Hindu Mahasabha 100, 103, 106, 108, 111, 142, 220; in first Round Table Conference 135; on Hindu–Muslim accord 142; opposition to Communal Award 179
Hindu–Muslim cooperation 28, 32, 33, 204, 330
Hindu–Muslim demand, for self-government 20
Hindu–Muslim Pact 122
Hindu–Muslim riots 261, *see also* communal riots; Muslim–Sikh riots
Hindu–Muslim unity 159, 178; Communal Award and prospects for 180; during post-partition of India 325
Hindu National Congress 20
Hindu Raj 214, 225, 227, 258, 267, 287, 306, 307, 320, 321, 323, 331, 332
Hoare, Sir Samuel 154, 162, 163, 167, 171, 172, 174, 274

Home Rule League 34, 38, 46, 58, 62, 73, 74
Home Rule movement 41, 54, 55, 66, 114, 186, 198
Horniman, B.G. 42, 58
House of Commons 4, 5, 6, 34, 105, 170, 173, 270, 275, 300
House of Lords 18, 108, 137, 251
Hume, A.O. 5, 15
Husain, Dr Zakir 220
Husain, Fazli 126, 154, 194
Husain, Hidayat 176, 177

Imam, Hasan 39, 72, 74
Imperial Legislative Council 11, 23, 24, 30, 39, 46, 58, 59, 60, 62, 67, 82, 84, 203
Independence for India League 127
Independent Party 83, 85, 90, 91, 93, 100, 171, 178, 191
India: American pressure for freedom of 299–300; British policy towards granting freedom to 294–95; demarcation of boundaries with Pakistan 309, 311; proposal for partition of 283
Indian Civil Service 3, 13, 39, 215, 227
Indian Councils Bill 16
Indian freedom movement 121
Indian Muslims: as natural allies of British Raj 26; sympathy for Turkey and Ottoman Caliphate 26
Indian Mussalman Association 13
Indian National Congress 4, 5, 11, 12, 13, 15, 20, 43; alliance with Khilafat organizations 95; attitude on Communal Award 178; boycott of Simon Commission 107, 108; Calcutta session of 12, 23, 127, 159; demands for national independence 309; on drafting of Swaraj constitution for India 108; foreign policy 269; Jinnah's attitude towards 288; Karachi session of 230; position in 1941–42 after Japan joined World War II 296-99
Indian nationalism: Anglo–Muslim plot to thwart 18; Muslim opposition to 318
Indian National Union 97
Indian Opinion 48
Indian Patriotic Association 15
Indian politics, Muslim factor in 199
Indian Rowlatt Act 65
Inside Asia (Gunther) 223
Inside India (Edib) 257
Iqbal, Sir Muhammad 279, 286
Irwin, Lord 122, 136, 142, 147, 148, 149, 150, 151, 161, 167, 171, 255, 274, 290; announcement on dominion status for India 160

Jalal, Ayesha 320
Jallianwala Bagh 61, 105
Jinnah, Fatima 4, 162, 163, 212, 277, 279
Jinnah, Mohammad Ali: achievement in creation of Pakistan 325–28; adoption of role of saviour of Islam

218; attempts for rejection of Nehru Report 120; attitude towards: Congress 288; individual civil disobedience 295–96; birth of 1; boycott of Simon Commission 105, 126, 136; break off with Congress and Indian nationalism 123; celebration of 'Deliverance Day' 269; concept of Muslim separatism 319; condemnation of proposed constitutional scheme 180; constitutional war against Britain 126; cooperation at National Convention 116; Cripps Mission and 302–3; death of 327; demand for: Pakistan 316; separate electorates 316; denouncement of Rowlatt Bills 62; education 1; election to Imperial Legislative Council 23; England visit 2; final settlement of Hindu–Muslim differences 124; and flag of Islam 217; 'Fourteen Points' for constitutional safeguards 124, 125, 186; front against British Government 197; heckling during his speech 71; involvement in nationalist politics 51; isolation and marginalization in Indian politics 161; joining of Sind Madressahtul-Islam in Karachi 2; as a law student in England 11; legal practice at Privy Council 163; letter to Sir Stafford Cripps 206; meeting with: Gandhi at Bombay 221; Lord Linlithgow 263–65; as member of Muslim League 25; negotiations with Congress leaders 224; during outbreak of hostilities in Europe 263 76; pinnacle of happiness 35–37; political career of 19; political moves and state of Muslim politics 248; position in Round Table Conference 161; during post-partition of India 325–28; proposals for Hindu–Muslim accord 104, 124; Quit India movement and 306–8; reaction to Nehru's Presidential Address 189; rebuff at National Convention 121; re-entry into Indian politics 176; registration as advocate of Bombay High Court 8–10; resentment against Gandhi 74; rivalry with Fazl-i-Husain 195–96; role as 'working president' of Muslim League 121, 160, 193; role in Indian politics 25; self-exile 158–66; speeches at Lucknow 216; stand in Second Round Table Conference 154–55; system of self-government on colonial lines 24; territorial solution of Indian problem 260–61; use of Islamic card for revival of his political fortunes 205, 210, 217, 225, 257,

261, 328; views on Hindu–Muslim unity 97; visit to Badshahi mosque 183, 205; war of words with Nehru 199
'Jinnah People's Memorial Hall' 42
Journal of East India Association 6

Kaira no-tax satyagraha 58
Karachi Bar Association 326
Kelkar, N.C. 69
Kesari 21
Khaksars 277, 278
Khaliquzzaman, Choudhary 197, 208, 209, 210, 212, 220, 224, 249, 262
Khan, Aga 12, 16, 18, 19, 25, 29, 120, 122, 135, 140, 142, 143, 144, 145, 152, 153, 155, 156, 160, 161, 177, 193, 194, 195, 254, 255, 256, 308, 319
Khan, Nawab Mehdi Ali 16
Khan, Nawabzada Liaquat Ali 197, 267, 285, 322
Khan, Shafaat Ahmad 140, 142, 143, 144, 153
Khan, Sir Syed Ahmad 13, 16, 20, 313, 314, 318; as 'father-figure' of Pakistan 253
Khaparde, G.S. 69, 72
Khilafat movement 94, 95, 255
Khilafat organizations 79, 96; alliance with Congress party 95
Khoja Shia 20
Khujandi, Maulana Nazir Ahmad 36
Kripalani, J.B. 50, 246

Krishak Praja Party 197, 230, 234, 282

Lal, Dewan Chaman 37, 65, 111, 166
Lamington, Lord 20
League Conference Parliamentary Majlis 177
Lee Commission 88
Lincoln's Inn 3, 4, 8, 48
Linlithgow, Lord 208, 211, 228, 234, 235, 239, 263; federal plan 248; meeting with Gandhi and Jinnah 263; policy towards Muslim League 235; reaction to Pakistan schemes for territorial adjustment 250; views on Vallabhbhai Patel 272
'Little Go' entrance exam 3
Lloyd, Sir George 60, 78, 79, 130, 131
Lucknow Pact 30, 31, 32, 33, 34, 45, 46, 98, 99, 101, 102, 113, 122, 125, 144, 159, 174, 185, 186, 215, 317
Lumley, Sir Roger 232, 247, 250, 283

MacDonald, Ramsay 129, 137, 149, 162, 172, 318
MacPherson, J.M. 8
madrasa 1, 3
Malaviya, Madan Mohan 36, 66, 72, 77, 83, 85, 86, 106, 109, 111, 130, 180
The Manchester Guardian 172, 242, 269, 282
mass contact movement 220, 259

Meerut Conspiracy Case 128
Mehta, Pherozeshah 5, 11, 13, 21, 23, 317, 329
Mill Owners' Association 105
Minorities Pact 155
Minto, Lord 12, 15, 16, 17, 20, 159, 192, 254, 314
Minto–Morley reforms 19, 26, 28, 31, 34, 45, 64, 125, 203, 315, 329
Mohani, Maulana Hasrat 113, 214
Mohsin-ul-Mulk *see* Khan, Nawab Mehdi Ali
Montagu–Chelmsford Reforms 32, 135, 158
Montagu–Chelmsford Scheme 57
Montagu, Edwin 34, 38, 50, 64, 74, 316
Mookerjee, Syama Prasad 185
Moonje, B.S. 69, 72, 135, 142
Morley, John 15, 18, 131
Mountbatten, Lord 323
Muddiman, Sir Alexander 86, 92
Muhammedan community, political importance of 17
Muharrum 18
Muslim communalism 31, 198
'Muslim Gokhale' 38, 47, 107, 159
Muslim League *see* All India Muslim League
Muslim National Guard 218, 279
Muslim nationalism 253, 318
Muslim politics: anti-British sentiments and 28; in India 19, 25, 140; and mass contact movement 259; in post-election scenario in 1937 235

Muslim separatism, in India *see* Muslim nationalism
Muslim–Sikh riots 181, *see also* communal riots; Hindu–Muslim riots
Muslim Waqfs 24

Naidu, Sarojini 34, 37, 42, 54, 58, 60, 102, 126, 131
Naoroji, Dadabhai 4, 5, 12, 13, 15, 23, 29, 317, 329, 352
National Convention 116, 117, 118, 119, 121, 124, 159
National Indian Association 6
National Planning Committee 242
The Nation's Voice (Ahmad) 260
Nehru Committee 115
Nehru, Jawaharlal 4, 66, 96, 102, 127; *The Discovery of India* 241, 263; letter by Frances Gunther 243; socialist rhetoric at Lucknow 189; speeches at annual Congress session at Lucknow 198
Nehru, Motilal 22, 34, 66, 69, 74, 85, 96, 100, 102, 111, 116, 125, 130, 131, 171; letter to Gandhi 126
Nehru Report 117, 330; All-Parties Conference and debates on 203, 330; basic principles of 114; on communal problem in India 112; controversies on 123; issues arising from 119; produced by All-Parties Conference 127, 128; supporters of 120
New India 55
Nishtar, Abdur Rab 320

non-cooperation movement 79, 83, 94, 220, 255
non-violent non-cooperation, doctrine of 76
non-violent rebellion 136
North-West Frontier Province 95, 101, 112, 113, 125, 141, 174, 188, 195, 199, 214, 254, 282, 284, 320, 321
North-West Indian Muslim State 261
Now or Never 256, 318
Nundy, Alfred 6

O'Donnell, C.J. 5
O'Dwyer, Sir Michael 61
Olivant, Sir Charles 8
Olivier, Lord 85

Pakistan: 'father-figure' of 253; formulation of political concept of 253, 313; rise of Islamic influence in 328; schemes for territorial adjustment and partition 250; struggle between modernism and imperatives of Islamic governance 328
Pakistan National Movement 257
'Pakistan resolution' 281, 282, 284
Pal, Bepin Chandra 86, 202
Pant, Govind Ballabh 231, 241
partition of India: proposal for 283; two-nation theory 282
passive resistance *see* satyagraha
Patel, Vallabhbhai 58, 188, 202, 207, 219, 229, 237, 247, 272, 273, 323, 324

Patel, V.J. 58, 70, 72, 86, 90, 130, 131, 132, 133, 134, 148
Pathway to Pakistan (Khaliquzzaman) 249
Peerbhoy, Akbar 9
Petit, Sir Dinshaw 35, 36
Pirpur Committee 226
Prasad, Rajendra 122, 179, 180, 189, 202, 226, 232, 237, 245, 247, 272
Provincial Autonomy (Shah) 237
Provincial Muslim Leagues 116
Provincial Political Conference 50
Public Safety Bill 128–29

Qaiyum, Sir Abdul 103, 282, 320
Quit India movement 302; Congress and Government 303–6; Muslim League Working Committee views on 307
Quran 278, 279, 286, 316, 327
Qureshi, Saleem 206, 253
Qureshi, Shuaib 111

Rafi-ud-din, Maulvi 28
Rahim, Abdur 126
Rai, Lala Lajpat 5, 69, 70, 72, 74, 109, 111, 113
Rajagopalachari, C. 60, 147, 189, 202, 238, 241, 270, 282, 297, 309
Rajaji formula 309, 311
Rangachariar, Dewan Bahadur 87
Reforms Act (1919) 31, 73, 101, 122, 135, 316
Reforms Act (1935) 191, 215, 225

Reforms Bill 19, 31, 63; approval by British Parliament 66
Reforms Schedule 53
Reforms Scheme 16, 18, 30
Retrospect (Simon) 105
Roosevelt, President 299, 300, 301
Round Table Conference 74, 77, 87, 123, 129; first 135–46, 148, 152, 153, 158; Muslim delegation at 173; second 147–57; third 319
Rowlatt Bills 58, 59, 60; denouncement by Jinnah 62; satyagraha against 61
Royal Commission 40, 87, 101, 104, 226
Royal Proclamation, by George V 66, 67, 68

Sabarmati Ashram 58
Saiyaddain, K.G. 220
Salt Laws 136, 147
Salt Satyagraha campaign 169
Sangathan movement 94
Sapru, Tej Bahadur 58, 74, 109, 111, 119, 135, 136, 139
Sastri, Srinivasa 58, 64, 74, 135, 137, 154
satyagraha 55, 57, 79, 150, 236, 294; Kaira 58; pledge 59, 60, 62; against Rowlatt Bills 61
Satyagraha Sabha 59
Self and Sovereignty (Jalal) 320
Sevres, Treaty of 67
Shah, K.T. 237
Shareef Committee 226
Sharia law 316, 326
Shia–Sunni conflict, in Lucknow 231
Shraddhanand, Swami 100
Shuddhi movement 94
Sikh Gurdwara Act 181
Simla Conference 311, 312
Simla Deputation 19
Simon Commission 105, 111, 126, 129, 131, 141, 171, 330; boycott of 106, 107, 108, 114, 126, 136; Indian politics and appointment of 203, 254
Simon, Sir John 105, 115, 131, 289, 299
Sind Madressahtul-Islam 2
Sind Muslim League Provincial Conference 258
Sly, Sir Frank 71
Sobhani, Omar 38
sovereign states, in British India 260
Statesman 125, 285, 325
Studies of Indian Life and Sentiment 26
Subjects Committee 69, 117, 128, 284
Sunnah 316, 327
'swadeshism' 52
Swaraj constitution for India 108
Swaraj Parliament 109
Swaraj Party 81, 83, 84, 85, 88, 89, 90, 91, 97, 101, 171; communal tension of post-Khilafat period 100

Tabligh movement 94
Tanzim movement 94
'Taxes on Income' 90
Tilak, Bal Gangadhar 21, 41
The Times 22, 64, 128
Times of India 12, 18, 19, 23, 41, 240, 247, 285, 315

Tory-bureaucratic-Muslim alliance 154
Tory press in England 22
Trade Disputes Bill 129
The Transfer of Power 1942–47 323
two-nation theory 282, 309, 318, 332

ulema (religious scholars) 259, 316, 328
Unity Conference 95
Universities Validating Bill 11
UP Muslim League Parliamentary Board 209

Versailles, Treaty of 185
Viceregal declaration 132
Vidya Mandirs 229
Vijiaraghavachariar, C. 70

Wardha scheme of education 220, 226
Warner, William Lee 18
Wavell, Lord 302, 308, 312, 321, 322, 332
Webb, Alfred 5
Wedderburn, Sir William 5
Welby Commission 45
Whyte, Sir Frederick 84, 85, 93, 100
Willingdon, Lord 28, 36, 41, 46, 56, 76, 151, 152, 163, 167, 174, 194, 228
Wolpert, Stanley 49, 50, 122, 326

Years of Destiny (Coatman) 256
Young India 95

Zetland, Secretary of State 232, 234, 238, 242, 243, 244, 245, 247, 248, 249, 250, 272, 283, 289, 290, 291

For Product Safety Concerns and Information please contact our EU representative GPSR@taylorandfrancis.com
Taylor & Francis Verlag GmbH, Kaufingerstraße 24, 80331 München, Germany

www.ingramcontent.com/pod-product-compliance
Lightning Source LLC
Chambersburg PA
CBHW072131220426
43664CB00013B/2210